Reading Matters

Narrative in the New Media Ecology

Reading Matters

Edited by Joseph Tabbi & Michael Wutz

Cornell University Press   Ithaca & London

First published 1997 by Cornell University Press.
First printing, Cornell Paperbacks, 1997.

Printed in the United States of America

Library of Congress Cataloging-in-Publication Data

Reading matters : narrative in the new media ecology / Joseph Tabbi and Michael Wutz, editors.
   p. cm.
   Includes index.
   ISBN (invalid) 0-8014-3366-5 (alk. paper).—ISBN 0-8014-8403-0 (pbk. : alk. paper)
   1. Literature, Modern—20th century—History and criticism. 2. Postmodernism (Literature) 3. Literature and technology. 4. Narration (Rhetoric) I. Tabbi, Joseph, 1960–   II. Wutz, Michael.
PN771.R45   1997
809'.923—dc21   97-16216

Cornell University Press strives to utilize environmentally responsible suppliers and materials to the fullest extent possible in the publishing of its books. Such materials include vegetable-based, low-VOC inks and acid-free papers that are also either recycled, totally chlorine-free, or partly composed of nonwood fibers.

Cloth printing   10 9 8 7 6 5 4 3 2 1
Paperback printing 10 9 8 7 6 5 4 3 2 1

FRONTISPIECE: *Das Buch* (The book), 1985, by Anselm Kiefer (Germany, b. 1945). Los Angeles County Museum of Art, Modern and Contemporary Art Council Fund and Louise & Harold Held.

Für Josef und Else Wutz,

and for Thomas B. Rohan,

who would have appreciated it

Contents

Illustrations

Acknowledgments

Books are the efforts of collaboration; they are never produced in an intellectual vacuum, no matter how self-directed and self-sufficient authors believe themselves to be. Besides, stimulation and support can come in many forms; they need not be present in the actual pages of a book, but can be felt on the invisible periphery. With that in mind, we thank Richard Grusin and Joseph McElroy for essays they promised but were unable to write; though the essays never materialized, they gave us the necessary momentum and confidence to get this book under way. Josef Schöpp and Ulfried Reichardt helped to create a working situation suitable to the integration of German media theory and American studies in literature and science by inviting one of us (Joseph Tabbi) to spend a year teaching at the University of Hamburg. We thank our contributors for their fine work and exemplary cooperation, and, above all, their unwavering patience and commitment to this project. We are grateful to readers for Cornell University Press for their perceptive suggestions and recommendations. And finally, I (Michael Wutz) give thanks to Marilee, my wife, and to Christian and Anja, our children, for tutoring me in Life 101. I have been working on this book all their lives. In ways too deep to articulate, they make my work possible.

J.T.
M.W.

Reading Matters

Joseph Tabbi & Michael Wutz

Introduction

A 1985 sculpture by Anselm Kiefer presents to its viewer a vast pair of wings extending out from the open pages of a book. The book, the size of a medieval codex, stands at eye level on a pedestal, immovable, requiring readers to stand stationary before it. The wings span the width of the museum room; they are cast in lead, one of the heaviest of elements, and—if this were not enough to check any suggestion of unfettered flight—they are weighted further on one side by a short plumb line.

Kiefer's image of flight constrained by textual heaviness implies the ponderously slow dissemination of knowledge and desire by the object that we call the book. The artist pays careful attention to the tactile and visual qualities of the open pages, yet the signs written there remain murky, nearly illegible; the texture of the book (itself an image and thus already dematerialized) replaces its textuality. The entire image suggests a phenomenon that is passing. In the so-called late age of print, word processing technologies and instant transmissions of digitized text over global distances have taken the weight out of words on a page. Images are lighter now, unfixed to any one object and morphable in toto at a single keystroke. Readers can access texts and download information from distant sites, and they can bypass all vagaries of interpretation once an author's expert knowledge and ultimately her actual brain waves have been recorded in an ever-expanding magnetic archive. We are now in a position, if the cybernetic fantasies of the past decade are to be believed, to leave the materiality of the book behind.

Predictably, the museum plaque speaks of the myth of Icarus and of humanity's desire to overreach itself in the attempt to transcend its material limits.[1] But other interpretations are possible, in which the myth can be read not as a quest or failed adventure, and not as a flight toward transcendence, but as a steady expansion of possibilities for connection and communication. Such is the realm not of Icarus but of Hermes—the messenger after whom the field of hermeneutics is named—whose winged feet touch both the air and the ground. Or, if these must be an angel's wings, they could belong to the angels in Wim Wenders's film *Wings of Desire,* who exist outside of time but whose desire is to fall *into* the world. The angels give up their panoramic vantage overlooking the Cold War city of Berlin for temporal activity among its inhabitants, for a renewed communication with the people around them. They fall into time, subjecting themselves to the full materiality, and mortality, of human life. The exchange of a spatial overview for temporal experience represents, in Wenders, a fall into *narrative.* What had until this moment in the film been mostly a swarm of voices, talking all together without a human breath of interruption, now separate out; the voices begin to circulate in an embodied space of shapes, colors, and smells, and the angels experience the world as flesh-and-blood subjects.

Kiefer's sculpture suggests a similar embodiment in textuality itself, a continuing resistance in the materials of the printed medium that has become the condition of narrative in the era of digital reproduction (and at the close of the mechanical age). The contributors to this volume share a concern with embodied textuality, and their subjects range over established and yet-to-be recognized narratives of the twentieth century. Drawing on current research into the "materiality" of literature and looking around at new forms of digital and electronic textuality, the contributors to this book seek to identify correspondent narrative forms and to reclaim a tradition of material self-awareness that has been a part of the novel all along. Their hopeful premise is that, as the scene of writing changes, the book will not be left behind—but neither will it be quite the same in its new context. How best to use the book in the new media ecology, and how to write about literary texts without resorting to hermetic modes of "interpretation," are questions that preoccupy even the most text-centered of these contributions.

The problem of "literary texts in a world of information" has been taken up, in the past decade, by William Paulson in *The Noise of Culture,* N. Katherine Hayles in *The Cosmic Web* and *Chaos Bound,* Friedrich Kittler in *Discourse Networks, 1800/1900* and *Grammophon Film Typewriter,* and the various contributors to Hans Ulrich Gumbrecht and K. Ludwig Pfeiffer's collection, *Materialities of Communication.* In these critical works, the technological culture occasions an end-of-history, end-of-the-book rhetoric more complex and less passive than homespun versions by, for example, Frances Fukuyama, Alvin Kernan, and Sven Birkerts; less passive because, although Paulson, Hayles, and Kittler don't primarily "interpret" texts—in fact, they want to move beyond the various forms of hermeneutic practice still privileged in the academy—they come up with new ways of engaging with narrative, and they provide models for intellectual work capable of producing political conclusions that are of use outside English and history departments. Such work is posthistorical not because it chooses to ignore battles that have been fought and often left unresolved in the past; the sense of an ending in this work is reflexive and retrospective, carrying history and the book along with it.

That these writers engage particular narratives at all—rather than Narrative as a category of knowledge—is exceptional in itself. One of the unfortunate effects of the modern information explosion is its redirection of narrative energies and much of the academic reader's time toward works of scholarship rather than literary narratives. At the very moment when narrative is coming to be recognized as the privileged form of cultural knowledge (because stories are still the most efficient and accessible way of organizing vast amounts of information into patterns possessing cognitive value and coherence), narrative theories are in danger of proliferating without the benefit of any material constraints. Despite the ascendancy of "theory" in the humanities, interpretation unfortunately remains the best use we have found for literary narrative. By and large, the literary profession has remained attached to hermeneutic traditions that for over a century have led to the "devaluation of any material surface as secondary in relation to subjective interiority" and as subordinate to exegetical exercise (Gumbrecht, "Farewell to Interpretation," 397).[2] As a result, literary narratives—and the novel in particular—remain underutilized. And literary scholarship has afforded itself little means of shaping the endlessly expanding knowledge base— be it hypertext dreamland or postmodern nightmare—that seems to be the goal of the modern research university.

Modernity and Media Interactions

This introduction is meant to be a historical narrative in its own right, the story of the literary novel's coming of age and its possible future in an era of media multiplicity. Taking our cue from Friedrich

Kittler, we open the narrative late in the nineteenth century, when literature moved away from earlier, primarily print-based "discourse networks." Unlike better-known narratives by Michel Foucault, Kittler's does not conceive of historical change as a series of sudden ruptures, legible and recoverable in print. Rather, the movement into the modern period involves a coming together of many separate developments and a changing relation among various media and the institutions that connect them with people (*Discourse Networks,* 370).[3] If writing has functioned for millennia as humanity's primary serial storage technology, the advent of photography, phonography, and film jeopardized this representational privilege and ultimately "destroyed the alphabetic storage and transmission monopoly, that old-European basis of power" (*Discourse Networks,* 369). Foucault's narrative ends "around 1850," at the very moment when the archive of Western culture ceased to be primarily print-based.[4] Beginning where Foucault left off, our narrative necessarily passes through technologies of auditory and visual inscription—media that, in combination, have seemed better equipped than the isolated medium of print to register the speed and noise of modernity.

The modern narratives treated in Part I, Thomas Mann's *Magic Mountain,* Kafka's stories, and Malcolm Lowry's *Under the Volcano,* all provide evidence of this changing media ecology, when writing and written narrative in general were displaced from their erstwhile centrality and forced to compete with gramophones, kinetoscopes, and their technologically more advanced successors in the marketplace of inscription. In Mann's monumental novel, we can observe narrative vying with X rays and the phonograph for representational rights over the human body; and print's struggle to locate itself in an electric, postprint media environment haunts many of the works under discussion, even when the conflict is energized by the novelist's sense of technological possibilities. But the early modern period offers no clearer site for intermedial boundary conflicts than the typewriter, the machine that—by unlinking the hand, the key, and the imprint of the letter—breaks up the compositional fluidity of handwriting and with it the creative continuity between conception and articulation. In the utopian view of Marshall McLuhan, the typewriter was the portable analogue to the technology of print that "fuses composition and publication," brings the private realm of composition into the public sphere of circulation and consumption, and extends the human body into the space of material production and self-representation (260). Yet this integrative approach (which recurs in contemporary accounts of the "electronic word" as a democratizing instrument of empowerment) contrasts with Kittler's more incisive critique, which sees the typewriter as a machine of displacement and disconnection, invented for use by the blind, perfected by the military (which in the First World War employed the typewriter's rotating platen for use in the repeater rifle), and producing an effect of disembodiment and uniformity that the literary writer was obliged to resist. Indeed, Kafka and Lowry avoided using typewriters during composition and instead cultivated handwriting as a mode of self-authentication and as a form of writerly resistance to the conformities of standardized type (although Kafka the insurance lawyer would often sign professional letters with a typed *K,* as if the objectified typescript allowed him to dissociate himself from impersonal business details [Kittler, *Grammophon Film Typewriter,* 322–30]).[5] Such resistance and willed alienation, forever belated and inevitably trying to return to more "natural" technologies grounded in the human body, proves a defining feature of literary fiction throughout the century.

In reflecting on its diminished representational territory, which can easily come down to the size of the writer's own body, pen, and paper, literary narrative had the paradoxical effect of urging forward the very technologies that were responsible for its own cultural demotion. Walter Benjamin has written that every historical era "shows critical epochs in which a certain art form aspires to effects which could be fully obtained only with a changed technical standard, that is to say, in a new art form." In its development toward an ever-greater realism, literature at the turn of the century created "a demand that could only be satisfied later" ("Work of Art," 237). Pressured by an array of postprint media, print indeed facilitated its own demise; it put itself out of print, as it were, not because it failed but because it succeeded too well in creating in readers a taste for the real that only nonverbal media could satisfy. And it continues to do so. What Geoffrey Winthrop-Young has observed of late nineteenth-century fiction is fully applicable to modern narrative as well: the "effort to describe more, if not everything, in a far more 'life-like,' complex, and detailed way than literature had ever done before was an attempt to incorporate, mimic or co-opt the achievements of competing electric media" ("Undead Networks," 124).

What literature does best—namely, to mediate subjective interiority and the object world that in part constitutes it, and to do so through the detour of language—could be done (and done better) with more "truthful" recording technologies: truthful in that the process of symbolization could be handled directly (not through signs, but through filmic and photographic objects representing only themselves). When Frank Norris observes that the "truth" of the novel exceeds "the meticulous science of the phonograph" or "the incontestable precision of the photograph," because naturalism probes "the unplumbed depth of the human heart" and the "unsearched penetralia of the soul," he claims a literary ground of being inaccessible to the surface inscriptions of competing recording technologies (*Literary Criticism*, 73, 78).[6] In Norris, a modernist retreat into subjectivity, psychology, and the closed space of a private, symbolic universe goes hand in hand with the naturalist desire to explore out into the arena of forces that propel historical events. John Dos Passos's camera-eye passages in *U.S.A.* stand as the classic attempt in American fiction to impart a psychological fluidity to the machine and the media world, to make mechanism the content of the world inside the skin. Working with a suppler prose, Lowry and Mann also sought to bring the mechanical object into the interior spaces of modernist narrative; they engaged the pressure of filmic, photographic, and phonographic accuracy by assembling congeries of facts, figures, and data streams that, in their self-conscious overabundance, were presumed to be uncontainable by these newer media.

That these things were no less containable by the human mind— even the protean mind of a high modernist stylist—is suggested by the hallucinatory realities Lowry and Mann often produced, as well as by a marked narrative inconclusiveness. They had enormous difficulties in bringing *The Magic Mountain* and *Under the Volcano* to a close, and both Mann and Lowry enjoined readers to work through their texts at least twice, and thus to complete a process that would convert the sprawl of a narrative's temporal unfolding into a manageable spatial pattern, something that could provide a contour for its inassimilable mass. This problem of narrative closure is quite common to a certain kind of modern novel that, "in the attempt to contain everything possible, does not manage to take on a form, to create outlines for itself, and so remains incomplete by its very nature" (Calvino, *Six Memos*, 118). We do not find it coincidental that both of the novelists chosen by Italo Calvino to illustrate the difficulty of containing an "enormous mass of material within set limits" were trained in engineering and mathematics: "If we compare . . . [Carlo-Emilio] Gadda, for whom understanding meant allowing himself to become tangled in a network of relationships, and [Robert] Musil, who gives the impression of always understanding everything in the multiplicity of codes and levels of things without ever allowing himself to become involved, we have to record this one fact common to both: their inability to find an ending" (*Six Memos*, 110). The aesthetic of these two engineer-writers, constructive, literally experimental, and remaining close to the moment-by-moment contingencies of material production, allows one to speak of the production of "narrative engines," to invoke Michael Wutz's term for Lowry's engineering of *Under the Volcano*, and an aesthetic that reaches its high-water mark in the narrative designs of Thomas Pynchon, the former engineering student at Cornell University and technical writer for Boeing Aircraft turned undercover author. In engaging the documented reality of the V-2 rocket engineers and their successors in the American space program, Pynchon writes with much the same unstructured sensibility, introducing scientific and technical metaphors with an eye to particular effects and solving unforeseen problems as they arise in the emerging design of the narrative (see Tabbi, *Postmodern Sublime*, 82). As literature and technology now merge in digital and electronic writing systems, the engineering aesthetic promises to become even more pervasive in the culture. Hence Calvino anticipates a veritable *celebration* of endlessness and multiplicity in hypertext theory and looks ahead to a new valuation of incompleteness in chaos theory (which is itself largely a graphic technology that enables one to visualize—and thus work with—complex physical systems that remain recalcitrant to both verbal descriptions and linear, Euclidean, geometries).

Working within this theoretical framework, Jo Alyson Parker, in her contribution, casts the narrative of *Absalom, Absalom!* in the model of "a chaotic, or strange, attractor," a pattern of meaning that converges on the never-stated probability of racial miscegenation at the foundation of the Sutpen empire. Applying the scientific model to Faulkner's text, Parker avoids a traditionalist nostalgia for an "absent center" (without dismissing the reality of slavery and the likelihood of miscegenation). Yet she also resists the opposite tendency of poststructuralist criticism to identify the speculative narratives spun by Quentin, Shreve, and Mr. Compson with an "infinitely proliferating textuality." Instead, she constructs a reading in which "structure emerges out of an apparently chaotic flux." The constraints and contours sought by Calvino, Musil, Gadda, and others thus emerge spontaneously in Faulkner's "play of signification within the bounded area of the strange attractor."

Like other literary revaluations in this volume, Parker's suggests that the novel, in its engagement with nonliterary media and systems, has always had means at its disposal that were less self-defeating than referential realism, less burdensome than modernist encyclopedism, and resistant to a poststructuralist reality in which words and texts refer only to other words and other texts. There has always been something disturbingly impersonal and disembodied in literary attempts to elaborate unbounded narratives within "a multiplicity of codes and levels"—as if literature, like the corporately sponsored technological systems it both resists and wishes to portray, could fulfill its private narrative systems without paying heed to either its own material constraints or the emotional dispositions of those who use the systems (in this case, readers). Faulkner resists disembodiment in part by grounding his narrative in direct human exchanges, picking up and integrating information during the course of many conversations and (especially through Shreve) creating an image of the active reader in the text of the novel. Originating far from Faulkner's U.S. South and its rich oral traditions, *nouveau roman* and Oulipo writers tend to be more text-based in their resistance; for them, the very letters, pages, and physical properties of the book provide the constraints that generate stories, metaphors, and even characters. Two analyses of "materialities of reading" in novels by Alain Robbe-Grillet and Georges Perec fill out the second part of this volume.

The Matter of Letters

An awareness of its own materiality—and a rediscovery of its material basis in print—has always kept literary narrative from extremes of referentiality and disembodiment, and has helped it to sustain its viability in the competitive mediaverse that was already in place at the turn of the century. For once visual and auditory recording technologies had released the alphabet from its burden as a *storage* technology, print could be recuperated as a medium with distinct physical properties, a complex of material signifiers that Jerome McGann has called "the visible language of modernism." Beginning with the artisanal printing revival in late Victorian England, when small hand presses such as Dun Emer and Cuala reintroduced print as a craft-based art form, the physicality of the letter—its material appearance on the space of the page—became a crucial component of meaning constitution, as in the lavish editions issued by William Morris's Kelmscott Press. In their typographical and bibliographical innovations, Morris and his modernist successors cultivated sensibilities that, by inverting the assumption of "print as a vehicle for linguistic meaning," foregrounded "textuality as such, turning words from means to ends-in-themselves" (McGann, *Black Riders,* 74). The

bold, audacious, and oversized letters of *Blast* and the Futurist manifestos—a kind of visual screaming—as well as the typographical play in
Tarr, Ulysses, and a host of high modernist and surrealist narratives,
certainly evolve from this newly emerging self-consciousness about the
matter of letters. Such a material understanding of language replaced
the semiotics of semantics with a semiotics of print and endowed the
word with an aesthetic tangibility and self-conscious heaviness meant to
outlast the ephemerality of light and voice—the fleeting traces recorded
by camera and gramophone.

The Victorian medieval revival and the preoccupation with the craft
of bookmaking have been treated, generally, as nostalgic backward
glances before the eruption of modernism, moments in a short-lived
romantic retreat into England's mythic past (when William Caxton, in
the newly invented medium of print, enshrined the Arthurian legends
that the medieval revival drew upon). By contrast, a media theoretical
view suggests that archaic book designs and self-conscious modernist
texts are the joint reflex of a postprint environment, two forms of material resistance to the pressures of the perceived hostility of a changing
media culture. Instead of the senescence of narrative, print reflexivity
may turn out to be a more forward-looking and reinvigorating response
than either encyclopedic overcompensation or realism (whether the psychological realism of literary modernism or the obsessive accumulation
of details in naturalism).[7] As the systems theoretician Niklas Luhmann
has argued, an enlarged media environment leads not only to "differentiation"—a definition of each medium's alterity from other media—
but also to a productive ecology, a reciprocity between media that ensures the continued presence of older, less advanced storage and communications technologies: "The higher complexity of a new level of
development makes it possible to reinvest the old [in this case, print]
with new meaning, as far as it lets itself be integrated. New technological
achievements do not necessarily mean the forceful negation of older
media, but rather their recombination" (20; our translation).

By calling into question any clear-cut discrimination between media
forms, intermediality as a means of inquiry usefully complicates pro-
gressivist histories, in which every "age" is an "age of" something: iron,
orality, print, information, or (when literary figures are the historian's
raw material) Pound, Eliot, and so on. Kathleen Woodward has revealed
the "ideology of age" that often underlies such histories, and it is com-
forting, this late in the Age of "the Age of," to find interdisciplinary
histories emerging that do not reify time into spatial patterns, each one

unified by the communicative action-at-a-distance that a given technology or set of media provides.[8] Here, for example, are Geoffrey Winthrop-Young and Joseph Donatelli, introducing an issue of the Canadian journal *Mosaic,* focusing on technologies of literary production: "The idea of leaving one communication technology behind in favor of another fails to account for intermediality as the condition of media ecologies over time: the use of speech in cultures with writing, the continuing production of handwritten documents in the 'age of print,' the orality of the telephone and the radio as well as the 'second orality' of television, the simulation of a typewriter by word-processing programs" (xviii). Complicating deterministic and spatializing histories of media, which tend to privilege one technology over another in a simple and polarized binary—McLuhan's favoring of a resurrected orality through television, or the explosion of a superior print-based knowledge in Elisabeth Eisenstein's Renaissance—Winthrop-Young and Donatelli suggest a model of media interaction that takes note of the frequently catalytic interaction and intertwining of media from different historical moments. It is with this model in mind that we turn to the third and fourth sections of our volume, whose chapters demonstrate the stubborn persistence of modernist forms and communications technologies in our postmodernist, hypertextual moment.

Spatial Form in Hypertext and Modern Narrative

It is possible to appreciate the century's changing media ecology, as it makes itself felt in modernist narrative as well as hypertext structures, by referring to the classical coordinates of space and time—specifically, the space of memory and the time of narrative experience, to invoke Michael Joyce's useful distinction. Joyce describes some of the ways our technological age is disposed to spatialize, and thus interiorize, knowledge, so that information is stored and made readily retrievable at a number of specific, redundant locations in a global landscape (somewhat as global long-term memories map onto any number of local neural stimuli in the human brain, when we are reminded of a specific thought, scene, or experience). The present hypertext structure, a complexity without experiential contour, is to be resisted because it is "consumerist at its base," more concerned with negotiable product than process (*Of Two Minds,* 101). In his own work, Joyce would add depth and a material resistance to hypertext as it is defined by Theodor Nelson, a "nonsequential writing with reader-controlled links" between blocks of text

(*Literary Machines*, cited in Joyce, *Of Two Minds*, 113). It is one of Joyce's signature devices to repeat sentences and parts of sentences (such as the two clauses in Nelson's definition) until they lose their primarily referential function, and the words yield something new—a resistance, for example, that was not a part of the original formulation. By creating hypertexts that are "versions of what they are becoming, a structure for what does not yet exist," Joyce would reintroduce time as the material dimension in which we come to know things, and produce a palpable texture within the blocks, as well as an exploratory mapwork of links among them (101). His hypertextual writing thus seeks to move *through* language, as any literary narrative must, creating a sense of time in the reader's experience of the word's materiality.

Joyce's efforts, however, are hardly representative. The dominant hypertext narrative remains "topographic," in Jay David Bolter's phrase, and the capitalist energies driving the electronic structure continue to seek a "frictionless" state (to cite Microsoft CEO Bill Gates.) The majority of hypertext theorists remain, for all their revolutionary rhetoric, wholly within the modernist program of preferring spatial metaphors (especially metaphors of exploration and, given the capitalist regime, of conquest) and an ideology of material transcendence. Hence the current interest in the theory and practice of electronic textuality offers an occasion to reconsider spatial form in modern narrative.

The turn toward the spatial in literary modernism is clearly enmeshed in the growing awareness of the matter of letters at the turn of the century. A material understanding of language and its interaction with graphic images certainly contributed to what W. J. T. Mitchell—beginning with Wittgenstein's meditations on the picture—has identified as the "pictorial turn" in philosophy and the arts (11–12)—a sensibility for space and spatiality that has continued, in its more overtly political manifestations, in such characterizations as Guy Debord's "society of the spectacle," Foucault's notion of surveillance, and Baudrillard's culture of simulations. Such a spatial disposition toward language also reinforces the field concept of modern science that emerged about the same time (Hayles, *Cosmic Web*, 9–28). The turn toward the spatiovisual appears to have been facilitated by the typewriter, whose uniform spacing and linear setting could be counterposed to the more expansive graphic conventions of the page, thus drawing attention both to the page as a space-field and to typewritten letters as aesthetic constructs.[9] As elemental and uniform units of the page design, typewritten letters quickly led to typographic experimentation and, especially in modernist poetry, brought about an understanding of text—more properly, the individual page—as a "laced network of linguistic and bibliographic codes" (McGann, *Textual Condition*, 13).

A chief goal for practitioners of modernist poetry was to exploit, in both manuscript and printed text, the visual power of typography on the canvas of the page, and hence to approach writing, and the production of text more generally, with a spatiovisual sensibility. Ezra Pound, an apprenticed printer and an admirer of William Morris, is only one of many typographic experimenters who, in the balanced arrangement of ideograms, marginal space, and austere typography in the *Cantos,* "imagines the page and the book the way a painter or a book designer would imagine it" (McGann, *Textual Condition*, 141). Pound's interest in typography was shared by Robert Carlton Brown, whose little-known anthology *Readies for Bob Brown's Machine* (1931) McGann revalues as "a work of signal importance," one that will be duly recognized when "the afterhistory of modernism is written" (*Black Riders,* 89). Instead of simply reading a poem, Brown prefers to "merely sit and look at it, take it all in without moving an eye. It gives me more than rhymed poetry. It rhymes in my eyes. Here are Black Riders for me at last galloping across a blank page" (quoted in *Black Riders,* 85). In the first instance Brown's poetry signifies not through the semantic content of words but rather through their material configuration on the page—a poetics of space that is at the center of literary modernism's dialogue with the visual arts, as Wendy Steiner has demonstrated.[10]

Brown's intense interest in typography was shared by many of his contemporaries and reemerges today in Concrete Poetry, and in the "writingdesigns" of both literary and graphic journals, such as *Private Arts 8/9* and *Emigré 36/37.* Typographic experimentation also lends a crucial intermediality to the self-conscious pagework of John Barth in *Letters,* Raymond Federman in *Double or Nothing,* Ronald Sukenick in *Out,* and William Gass in *Willie Master's Lonesome Wife* and *The Tunnel,* works that intertwine the semantic and semiotic aspects of the text and the page. Despite such novelistic achievements, however, the development of a pictorial sensibility in modern narrative has been underrecognized. The lag may be ascribed in part to generic differences between lyric poetry and narrative as they are commonly perceived—the one a configuration of great verbal density and concentration with an affinity for the visual, for the all-over composition of letters in space, the other a "loose baggy monster" whose sentence-by-sentence linearity tends more toward the temporal, the sequencing of words in time. Granted that generic permeability and linguistic heterogeneity largely define what the novel *is*, the necessity of temporal unfolding has limited its ability to accommodate ingenious constellations of letters confined to the single page-field. Wyndham Lewis was the only prominent modernist who actively sought to develop a narrative equivalent to pictorial representation; his intent was to subvert what he regarded as the modernist "time-cult," the fetishization of Bergsonian *durée* across the arts (*Time and Western Man*). Rejecting contemporary techniques of interior monologue and stream of consciousness, Lewis (in his Vorticist phase) presented time as a solely external, nonpsychological phenomenon, and he exteriorized narrative itself by creating sheets of surface decoration and verbal friezes that withhold or interrupt narrative flow in favor of spatialized exposition.

Lewis's techniques, along with the cubist images that inspired them, might be said to anticipate the computer graphic interface, which constructs a rich three-dimensional space through the successive layering of two-dimensional grids. Like Lewis's art, the graphic interface has been generally understood, in the first instance, as visual and spatial. A closer look at the sedimentary overwriting of these grids, however, belies the attempted separation of time and space (just as Lewis's continuous references to a clock in his novel *Tarr*, parodic as they may be, suggest his awareness of the ineluctable groundedness of narrative experience in temporality). A computer graphic is not in itself spatial, at least not in any Cartesian sense. Every location or address in the grid (as in the network of physical addresses on the internet) is in fact equidistant from any other location; what separates one point from another is the processing *time* it takes to link the locations. That many literary commentators continue to regard the electronic image as primarily spatial and immaterial testifies not only to the abstract, unseen, and generally ignored processes that underlie the operation of a microprocessor but to the continuing power of the "pictorial turn," a modernist aesthetic that seeks to convert temporal processes into spatial ones.

One upshot of the pictorial turn has been to help reinforce the great modernist divide between the spatial and the temporal, the abstract visual and the narrative arts (dichotomies supporting that other "great divide" between high and popular art, Andreas Huyssen's way of framing the boundary conflict between literary and mass media). For Lewis's contemporaries, however, the distinctly popular recording technology that was doing the most to condense time and space was film, since it bypassed painting in its ability to enact, not just arrest, time and physical

motion. Erich Auerbach, lamenting the demise of modern narrative coherence into cinematic fragmentation, advised against exploiting "the
structural possibilities of film in the interest of the novel," because "it
is a wrong direction: a [filmic] concentration of space and time . . . can
never be within the reach of the spoken or written word" (*Mimesis*,
546). Auerbach was writing in exile at the close of World War II, a war
that provided the occasion to develop and perfect the same frame-by-
frame analytic technologies that had produced film. As Friedrich Kittler
shows in Chapter 7 (on Thomas Pynchon's *Gravity's Rainbow*), film is
the medium par excellence of "time-axis manipulation," the technology
fully commensurate with the development of supersonic weapons technologies that suspend and reverse causal relations, such as the V-2
rocket, and the deceptive, time-shattering strategies of advanced warfare
generally. (The rocket blast *precedes* the sound of its arrival, a reversal
that stimulates fantasies of running a film backward, a form of *hysteron
proteron,* through which the rubble might reassemble into the intact
building before the explosion.[11])

From Kittler's perspective, the literary-critical resistance to film begins to look like the aftershock of a war that had shattered bourgeois
certainties, and so does the desire (as in the case of Auerbach) to hold
on to a narrative continuity grounded in and capable of giving coherence to individual experience (by defining experience, for example, as
the progression of a central protagonist from a beginning through a
middle toward an end that progressively diminishes possibilities and so
represents that character's fate). At the same historical moment when
Auerbach was declaring film out of bounds for the novel, however, an
American graduate student set himself the task of theorizing the "spatial
form" that the novel had already taken in response to the cinematic
challenge. Yet film, in Joseph Frank's classic account of modernist narrative, is notably absent.

Frank's argument was that the novel could create the illusion of simultaneity within readers by dislocating the chronology of linear narrative—a rearrangement of what the Russian formalists termed the
fabula (occurrences or events in the story) through manipulation of the
sjužet (the form that events take on in written narration). In what Frank
described as "the principle of reflexive reference," modern narrative
challenged its readers to synthesize, in a moment of phenomenological
apprehension, the disparate narrative elements into a distinctly visual
gestalt (*Widening Gyre*, 14).[12] Frank's analogies for this parapictorial perception, however, are uniformly *painterly* in character, as when he re-

lates the paradigm of modernist narrative abstraction, Djuna Barnes's *Nightwood*, to the "work of Braque, the Fauves, or the Cubists" (*Widening Gyre*, 28). The fact that his analogies establish no relation to cinema—the mode of representation that is equally spatial and that flourished in tandem with the modernist novel in the first decades of this century—suggests a critical blind spot, as well as a deeply entrenched academic resistance to seeing literature as one of many information processing technologies vying for position in the field of available representation.[13]

It is, again, within the context of this emerging media ecology that we understand the modern novel's evolution toward spatiality, and toward an interiority that tended to downplay narrative experiences that are felt in our bodies, over time. To be sure, the novel was not the only modern art form that developed toward a greater spatial abstraction and self-consciousness about its own material construction. Painting in the latter half of the nineteenth century had already responded to the realistic modes of black-and-white photography by approximating and sometimes superseding its documentary ethos, as in the minutely detailed and colorful paintings of the Pre-Raphaelites (whose pastoral subject matter was part of the reflex to negate the grime of industrialization through a medieval revival). The French Impressionists reacted to "the encroachments of photography on naturalistic art" by duplicating and refining the blurred images of early photographs, and later, when color photography seemed feasible, by enriching their paintings (of both landscapes and cityscapes) with an unprecedented wealth of pigments and tonal shades, producing colors that "one ought to see" (Scharf, 179). Monet and Renoir, in particular, attempted to realize their artistic ambitions of capturing the fleeting play of light and color by foregrounding *matière*, the physical qualities of their paints and brushstrokes on canvas, which were radically different from the raw materials of daguerreotypes and photography. Their use of large brushes, their thick and dotty application of colors in rapid and "comma-like" strokes (Rewald, 281), and the rough texture of the pigments allowed them to endow light with an ethereal and ephemeral presence distinct from and more immediate than "easy things that come in a flash" (as Monet, late in his career, said in reference to photography [quoted in Rewald, 563]).

By the turn of the century, however, painting was asserting its *otherness* from photography by leaving the plane of immediate referentiality altogether and declaring war on the word. Monet, for all the variegated haziness of his objects, remained interested in representation to the end of his life; yet his younger contemporary Wassily Kandinsky was able to see in his work the "unconscious" beginnings of painterly abstraction, in which the artist's command of the palette made the represented object no longer "an indispensable element of the picture" (quoted in Seitz, 125). The diffusion of light in Impressionist painting also diffused the narrative function of representational art, which in its modernist instantiation would ultimately produce (according to Rosalind Kraus) a "will to silence, [a] hostility to literature, to narrative, to discourse. . . . The barrier . . . between the arts of vision and of language has been almost totally successful in walling the visual arts into a realm of exclusive visuality and defending them against the intrusions of speech" (9).

Threatened by the word's expulsion from the space of painting and cinema, the novel found ways of reasserting its authority and stimulating the reflexive imagination of the reader (so central to the phenomenology of literary spatial form). Witness Kafka's well-known vehemence in declining his publisher's request to illustrate "The Metamorphosis" with an image of its protagonist: "Not that, please not that!" Kafka pleaded. "The Insect itself cannot be depicted. It cannot even be shown from a distance" (quoted in Sarkowski, 71). In essence, Kafka is insisting on the irreducible *literariness* of his writing. His is a whole-cloth investment in the word which Klaus Benesch, in Chapter 3, understands as a nostalgia for a kind of prepictorial presence, an originary "aura" that, according to Walter Benjamin, precedes (and eventually is destroyed by) the mechanical reproduction of the work of art. To have lost the "aura" was also to lose the control that the author imagines he enjoyed at the moment of composition. The sense of this loss and the "precarious status of authorship" generally are further reasons why Kafka characteristically resisted not only the typewriter for literary composition but most forms of publication or reproduction of his handwritten drafts. (Benesch, however, cites evidence that Kafka could also be prodded by visual stimuli, as when a visit to the movie theater ostensibly catalyzed the long-delayed resumption of *Amerika*.)

A certain critical skepticism, then, and a sense of humor are in order when we approach the more powerful expressions of modernist alienation. The hunger artist, for all his tragic stature, may be simply unable to find any food he likes, after all. And as regards Benjamin's conception of the aura, we should always keep in mind the ambiguity of its uses, as Linda Brigham cautions in Chapter 5, on corporeality and media in connection with the *nouveau roman*. For a writer-director such as Robbe-Grillet, who would confront a mass audience with their own isolated inadequacy, attributing excessive value to aura is likely to back-fire. For aura can serve to mystify the act of authorship (and hence actually cooperate in commodity fetishization and the overvaluation of "original" works of art). Worse still, premodern auratic rituals can ree-merge *in* the new media of reproduction, producing in audiences not a sense of their collective power as distinct social and economic classes but (in Robbe-Grillet's aestheticized politics) an immobilization of the viewing body that precedes a mass militaristic mobilization resubordi-nated to a mystified authority.

Ritual takes on still stranger forms in postmodern writing. Don DeLillo's "most photographed barn in America," for example, is "sus-tained," not degraded, by collective processes of reproductive technol-ogy. While regarding the barn, DeLillo's two cultural studies professors feel a kind of "awe" that is "a religious experience in a way" (*White Noise,* 12). When one of them exclaims, "We're here, we're now" (13), he expresses what Jean Baudrillard has called the "ecstasy of commu-nication," in which "all secret spaces and scenes are abolished in a single dimension of information" (131), and reproductive technologies threaten to erase all alterity and metaphorical distance in favor of mass-mediated sameness. One finds on occasion a similar totalizing rhetoric even in Kittler (when he writes of the oncoming digitalization of all media) and, as Brigham points out, in Paul Virilio's potentially nostalgic revaluing of traditional structures of social reproduction—structures irrevocably past.

Not all writers, however, have regarded the media of photography and film with nostalgia, and the late modernist insistence on the irre-ducibly verbal character of literary representation has not always been so defensive. For many novelists and poets, exploration of linguistic reflexivity allowed narrative to build itself back into systems of repre-sentation from which it felt the pinch of exclusion. James Joyce, the cinéaste and would-be founder of the first movie theater in Dublin (Ellmann, 300–311), was always suspicious of having *Ulysses* appear in translation, but he was enthusiastic about the possibility of transmuting his fiction into the medium of film (Ellmann, 561). *Finnegans Wake,* that monument to the dialectic of space and time in the Western literary tradition, conceives of a "soundpicture" that can provide the ideal, tech-nological, fusion of the visual and the verbal (570)—a union of eye and ear, seen image and spoken word, that can "roll away the reel world" (64) in perpetual simultaneity. The very linguistic density of the *Wake,* which is often seen as a farewell to written narrative, reclaims a wholly verbal authority not by rejecting the visual but by transforming the word itself into a spatial form: in Joyce's text(ure), each verbal unit is laden with multiple levels of meaning that make linear reading in a conventional sense well-nigh impossible. Verbal density in this case signifies a return to the pictorial surcharge of each letter and word in modern poetry, a collapse of temporal narrative into the space of word and sound pictures.

We observe along with the drastic decline of literary fiction's cultural currency an equally dramatic intercrossing of the novel's generic and medial boundaries. And this cross-fertilization is seen not only in limit-case novels such as *Finnegans Wake*. Carlos Fuentes, acculturated to a world of television, sees no reason why "the novel should go bankrupt thanks to the visual media," and he is happy to redraw the boundaries of written narrative within a territory dominated by video, television, and film. He asks (echoing Italo Calvino's millennial desire to delimit what is still writable), "What can you say only through the medium of the novel?" One expects something modest to follow, an identification of the novel's verbal niche in the larger mediaverse. Yet Fuentes goes on to say that the very context within which literary fiction is considered marginal "in itself brings the novel back to an elementary position in which it has to become everything to become itself" (in Doezma, 493). From out of tightened constraints on what is writable, Calvino, Georges Perec, and other Oulipo novelists considered by Paul Harris in Chapter 6 end up imagining the *hypernovel*, "the novel that sets out a series of potential novels, that can be configured in any number of ways, that we can traverse in different directions, and that encourages us to continue writing its stories outside the covers of its book-skin."

Such apologies certainly speak well for the continuing vitality of the novel as a genre, even as they provide terms for revaluing a rich and underrecognized strain of late modernist narrative. In Chapter 8, John Johnston reinforces Harris's position when he maintains that the contemporary novel can resituate itself through a new "mediality," the process by which "a literary text inscribes in its own language the effects produced by other media." Of course, the possibility remains strong that most readers, rather than work through the novelistic inscriptions of nonliterary effects, will go to the other media first and remain there. Yet, for now, the novel remains the one medium that allows the historical effects of media differentiation to be remarked. As separate media increasingly merge in cyberspace, human beings can still discover their uniqueness by connecting up with "a complex of heterogeneous spaces" (the polyglot cities and complex interior architectures in William Gibson's *Neuromancer*) and a "temporal multiplicity of times" (in *Vineland*'s "Janus-faced view" of America in the 1980s and 1960s). Through such descriptive details and an irrepressible multiplicity of subliminal events, the "partially connected" medium of print narrative can still offer a means of resistance to a fully incorporated future of media sameness.

The Electronic Future of Literary Fiction; or, Don't Only Connect

It is also conceivable that the novel and its proliferating theories, which have never been so robust (or so commercially viable) since the rise of modernism, are once again helping to dig their own grave by preparing readers' sensibilities and senses for experiences that can be delivered only by other media. Yet the new electronic media, for all their speed of development, have been remarkably slow to deliver new art forms. The hypertext novel, a presumptive *Gesamtkunstwerk* for the electronic age, could easily be undermined by the very literal-mindedness with which its grander ambitions are being realized. It is one thing for a work of imagination to create in readers a sense of infinite narrative possibilities, but quite another to have readers *literally* work out every implication, as Stuart Moulthrop had his students do with the Borges story "The Garden of Forking Paths" ("Reading from the Map," 124–30). The novelist Mary Caponegro, a student of Robert Coover and certainly no literary reactionary, has articulated the literary author's strong case against a medium celebrated for promoting readerly collaborations: such hypertexts call to mind the "exhaustion of having seen too many rental apartments" (25). As an author, Caponegro would maintain control of the privately owned house of nonmimetic fiction: "I want to invite the reader in, and while I want anything but a passive guest inside my page, I want also to be mistress of my own hospitality" (25). Caponegro understands that requiring readers to hold *un*realized literary possibilities in mind is crucial to maintaining narrative drive; and as for hypertext's "promiscuous" interconnectivity and celebrated resistance to closure: "when it's done—excuse my metaphorical bluntness—I want to know I've come" (24).

When one considers the material basis of hypertext connectivity itself, the prospect looks less like freedom from authorial control than the *uncontrolled* expansiveness of a technological system driven by inhuman global markets. In actual systems of communication, the contemporary necessity to "become everything" may prove more "elementary" than Fuentes imagines, especially at a time when technologies of simulation and communication are rapidly subsuming older technologies such as books and long-playing records—and even television and film—into a worldwide web of digitalization. Where there were only technologies, more or less alienating and inhuman but at least different from one another, now there will be one technology. Materially distinct media belong to different conceptual orders and can thus be used to critique one another and correct one another's excesses—even if the critique comes from the "marginal" position that the literary novel has traditionally occupied. The intermedial balance of powers is newly threatened, however, in the age of digital textuality. As we write, fiber-optic cable companies in the United States are negotiating the expansion of services to "the last ten miles," to resisting local markets in the former town and inner city. They have begun to appropriate the airspace made available to them by the Federal Communications Commission, and Internet-related stocks are driving a bullish market daily to record heights, creating a standard of living so high that most Americans can never dream of reaching it. "For the first time in history or for the end of history," writes Kittler, humanity will be able to realize the dream or nightmare of total interconnectivity, when "absolute knowledge can run as an endless loop" ("Gramophone, Film, Typewriter," 101–2).

In Pynchon's *Gravity's Rainbow*, the character Father Rapier gives a sermon that anticipates the totalized oppression of a homogeneous media system: "Once Their systems of connection have reached a certain level, the chances for freedom will be over for good." Jean-François Lyotard, matching Pynchon's crafty Jesuit point by point, argues in *The Inhuman* that in an electronic global hamlet ruled over by "bits" as the elementary "unit of information," "there's no longer any question of free forms given here and now to sensibility and the imagination" (34). The digitalization of sound, image, text, and numerical operations, if left to itself, would produce a global communications system of increasing complexity capable of controlling events without any human interference or regard for human needs (for as long as its material resources lasted).

That Lyotard, Pynchon, and Kittler converge in their thought toward a common image of world domination suggests that, however paranoid their vision, the structure produced by contemporary information technology is precisely the form that future narratives must resist, or, if resistance should prove futile, must help transform by imagining other uses and possibilities for the technology. The vision of these writers is paranoid because it grants a single system the power—no matter how bureaucratically "diverse" in its homogeneity—to enlarge itself indefinitely. An endlessly looping, total knowledge is a goal that can, quite likely, never be achieved, however, because of the material, entropic limitations in technology itself, even in the computer and the Internet, which require vast nonsustainable resources. Put another way, the spatial extension of a technological memory system will always require more time—more machine time and memory—more paper, more and cheaper human labor, more everything than the universe provides.

William Paulson, whose ongoing critique of contemporary information theory informs the last section of this volume, proposes in Chapter 10 a surprising alternative to the "global contemporary system of information stockpiling": namely, the literary canon. For those who regard the canon as part of the problem, not the solution to hegemonic oppression, Paulson's essay will strike an odd note. His revaluation of the canon "in the age of its technological obsolescence," however, bypasses the stale debate between "tenured radicals" and cultural conservatives by exploring the material and "technological subtext to the contemporary undoing of literary canons." It will make little difference, Paulson argues, what scholars include in a revised canon if the entire canon-revising project ends up serving contemporary demands to go on constructing an expanded knowledge base of undifferentiated complexity (the sort of structure that Michael Joyce would describe as an "exploratory" hypertext, as opposed to an as yet unrealized, "constructive" hypertext that emphasizes invention and becoming). If the chapters of this book deal largely with canonical fiction (even as the canon informs such emerging genres as cyberpunk and the "techno-thrillers" analyzed by Piotr Siemion in Chapter 9), our concern is to give shape to, not add to, the "network lengthening" and "ultracommunicativity" that modern information technology is relentlessly producing. With Paulson, we believe that many of the "qualities of printed texts that make them canonizable"—their printedness (as opposed to the erasability of magnetic media), their material existence as aesthetic artefacts that one can go back to (and thus share with others), and their irreducible medial otherness—are "worthy of cultivation as practices of resistance to the hegemony of electronic information processing systems."

Resistance does not mean outright refusal—Sven Birkerts's response at the end of *The Gutenberg Elegies*—which would allow readers to preserve a flawed image of canonical fiction in and as a world elsewhere. Literary practices are not about to stop the rush to wire the globe, but the desire to resist the "inhuman" in contemporary information technology should itself produce not sentimental conceptions of a merely *literary* connectivity (the liberal-humanist syrup of E. M. Forster's "only connect") but a revaluation of the kinds of local, self-reflective, and case-by-case knowledge that one finds in literary narrative. Thus the future of literary fiction is very much caught up in the use we make of its past: the "reading and valuing of old narratives" may yet create (according to Paulson) "spaces of turbulence and even stability" within the larger communication systems, alternatives to their "exclusively cognitive and instrumental marshaling of time and information, [their] program of neutralizing and controlling, rather than experiencing, all possible alterity."

The currently popular conception of literature as a fluid, endlessly enlarging, infinitely connectible hyper*text* seems to us a model that readers and writers would do well to get beyond. Unlike those pioneering literary critics who have proposed a convergence between postmodern theory and hypertext technology, the contributors to this volume seek no theoretical foundation for hypertextual literary practices: they look instead to particular print narratives, works of fiction that, as William S. Wilson argues in the *electronic book review,* are on their own as structures, "without external support." Postmodern novelists especially have been concerned with elaborating self-validating structures that embody all the features currently celebrated in the expanding discourse of hypertext theory. The work of such writers as Pat Cadigan, Robert Coover, Carlos Fuentes, Ursula LeGuin, Thomas Pynchon, and Salman Rushdie (to name only those novelists treated at some length in the last section of this volume) has always entailed "eliminating linear narrative, or weaving several linear narratives into a field without a single center of interest," in Wilson's words. Postmodern novels are self-conscious about their own narrative processes, not because they pretend to a status as autonomous, self-contained worlds, and not because they probe the interior life and adventures of an equally "isolated, self-identical, and autonomous hero." Their self-awareness rather is a way of looking for "reliable and self-validating continuities in existence." These continuities *include* the real in its textual world without being bound by mimetic constraints. For Wilson, the replacement of mimesis with constraints that are freely chosen allows a character to be self-sufficient while "seeking to combine with something beyond the self"; for Lynn Wells (Chapter 11) and Stuart Moulthrop (Chapter 12), such a complex narrative self-sufficiency allows for a political dialogue between authors and readers.

For Wells in particular, the freedom from mimesis produces a greater liberty of representation, in which incommensurable substances and phenomena from both actual and fantastic worlds can combine in a "virtual world" of narrative. The virtual conference that takes place in the mind of a character in Rushdie's *Midnight's Children,* the Theatre of Memory in Fuentes's *Terra Nostra,* LeGuin's nonacquisitive Kesh library, and Pynchon's computer archive where a fourteen-year-old both assembles her mother's story from evidence and imagines it from inside herself—all of these narrative domains produce new kinds of historical information and enact narrative textuality as a *virtual meeting space;* they actualize concepts of intertextuality as characters from various literary texts and historical periods assemble and talk to each other. Unlike their counterparts in current hypertext and virtual reality technologies, which according to Wells offer "responses unmediated by language," these print hypertexts require readers to move *through language,* as one must move through any literary narrative, in order to experience the sensuous unfolding of words and images in a textual equivalent of physical embodiment.

It is too early, of course, to make large claims about the potential for literary interventions in the technosphere. When it comes to actual hypertext fictions, Wells and Paulson sound skeptical, and the best that Stuart Moulthrop, one of hypertext's leading literary practitioners, can venture is a hope for a *"relative* liberty." Embodiment and the notion of material constraints are, moreover, precisely what Moulthrop draws back from. The images that literally infect Moulthrop's prose, the "viral potential of cybernetic language" that refers "not just to HIV but also to cancers, toxicity, and various kinds of environmental stress," represent the troubling side of embodiment, the chilling reaction to a onetime joyous "promiscuity" of hypertext connectivity (whose links might better have been left to our libidinal imaginations). Like many of his colleagues in hypertext theory, Moulthrop tends to conceive of imaginative boundaries negatively; they are not form-giving and story-generating constraints that the novelist freely chooses, but armatures that now ensure a kind of "informational hygiene," a safe zone within the postmodern "war machine."

Clearly, the literary imagination of hypertext connectivity is unlikely to operate independently of the metaphors and gritty realities that the electronic culture itself produces. We have tried to suggest, however, that the novel possesses an extraordinary resourcefulness in the face of a recalcitrant media environment. Evidence that literary narrative may play a direct role in shaping the technological culture is probably too much to ask of our contributors, yet they certainly provide reason to think that technology's energetic reconstruction of relations between authors and readers, text and graphics, virtuality and materiality will help in shaping narratives of the future. What is most promising, perhaps, is that narratives in the new technological environments need not be merely "theoretical" in their deconstruction of these binary oppositions. The current media ecology should at least reveal the novel for what it has always been: a powerful instrument for representing its own media multiplicity, and a discursive practice that can help us to locate ourselves within the changing media environment.

Notes

1. We viewed the Kiefer sculpture, *Das Buch,* at the Los Angeles County Museum of Art in August 1995.

2. For an account of the various shifts in critical-theoretical practice that have begun to complicate the longstanding interpretive paradigms in the humanities, see Gumbrecht's concluding essay in *Materialities of Communication,* "A Farewell to Interpretation" (389–402).

3. Katherine Hayles has a similar conception of historical process, which she calls *seriation,* after a dating technique in archeological anthropology. "In seriation, change is incremental and variegated, overlapping old and new. . . . Consider the automobile: how does one think a car? By starting with an existing artifact, the horse carriage, and imagining that the carriage can move without the horses. Only gradually are the full implications of this shift realized through a progression of artifactual and conceptual changes. Greater speed necessitates windshields; still greater speed, aerodynamic styling. If one looks at two points far enough apart along a time line, the change may appear to be a sharp epistemic break of the kind Foucault described. But lying between those two points are a series of material and conceptual instantiations that constitute the microstructure of change" ("From Self-Organization to Emergence").

4. Kittler reiterates his critique of print-based discourse analysis in "Gramophone, Film, Typewriter," remarking that Foucault's "analyses end immediately before the point in time when other media penetrated the library's stacks. For sound archives or towers of film rolls, discourse analysis becomes inappropriate" (13).

5. Walter Ong has pointed out that handwriting is of course no less a technology than typewriting. Because of the naturalization of handwriting in the Western tradition, however, it is seen not as technological but as "natural" (81–83). This nat-

uralization is, of course, reinforced through the continuity between the hand and handwriting.

6. Zola's naturalism, for example, is for Norris more "than the truthfulness of a camera," because it can go "straight through the clothes and tissues and wrappings of flesh down deep into the red, living heart of things," a kind of scriptive X ray that had (without Norris's knowledge) already become a technological reality (*Literary Criticism*, 71, 75). In what can be described only as an anxiety of technological influence, Norris erases—that is, writes out of existence—the medial competitor to narrative in *McTeague*, the photographer whose vacated apartment is inhabited by Trina and McTeague. He is present only as an absence, the residue of his pungent chemicals leaving a permanent reminder of a contending technology of representation.

7. As McGann's work on a hypertext archive of Dante Gabriel Rossetti suggests, the self-reflexive materialist aspect of Victorian narrative intersects particularly well with electronic and digital textuality, which presents the alphabet, first and foremost, as a scrolling graphic *image*. (See Johnson for an account of McGann's hypertext project.)

8. We are indebted to Jed Rasula for the phrase "the Age of 'the Age of.' "

9. Kittler has observed that the "real innovation" of the typewriter was not increased speed but the organization of the alphabet into "spatially designated and discrete signs" (*Discourse Networks*, 193). Typing replaces the image of a handwritten word with a geometrical figure, usually set off in black against the white background of the empty page.

10. The "intense interest in typography" among many modernists was "aimed at making the relation between poetic synthesis and printed poem more obviously approximate that between pictorial synthesis and physical painting" (Steiner, 40).

11. Kittler notices that the present tense, rather than the potentially totalizing past tense, is dominant in *Gravity's Rainbow*. Kittler himself would go on to write his own foundational book of literary criticism, *Aufschreibesysteme 1800/1900*, in the present tense. Working independently of Kittler, the American critic Steven Weisenburger has read the time sequences in *Gravity's Rainbow* according to the rhetorical trope of *hysteron proteron*.

12. For the evident connections between Frank's notion of "reflexive reference" and the theoretical frameworks of phenomenology, particularly the work of Roman Ingarden and Wolfgang Iser, see Jeffrey Smitten's Introduction to *Spatial Form in Narrative* and Ivo Vidan's essay in the same volume.

13. In part, this critical silence in Frank's essay is related to the philosophical tradition from which "spatial form" emerges, particularly Lessing's *Laokoön* and, more important, Wilhelm Worringer's *Abstraktion und Einfühlung*, which Frank invokes as his critical-theoretical model (*Widening Gyre*, 50–60) and which influenced the high modernist pictorial aesthetic, particularly through the mediation of T. E. Hulme. Hulme's important essay "Modern Art and Its Philosophy" (*Speculations*, 75–109), for example, draws widely on Worringer.

Part I

Modernist Narrating Machines

Geoffrey Winthrop-Young

1 Magic Media Mountain

Technology and the *Umbildungsroman*

Los Angeles, January 30, 1950. Thomas Mann enters a downtown drugstore and buys his first electric razor. Plagued by an endless succession of physical discomforts that makes him even more irritable than usual, he records the event in his diary and on the following two days takes note of his new shaving experience. By the third day sufficient data have been accumulated to allow for a final verdict: "Satisfied with the time-saving acquisition of the electric shaver" (*Tagebücher*, 163). Decades of wet shaving and ritualized excursions to the barbershop are suddenly a thing of the past.

Thomas Mann was seventy-four. Probably the most widely praised author of his day, he had come to nurture a highly productive self-absorption that entailed the belief that almost everything that happened to him had larger symbolic significance and therefore was worthy of literary processing. Unfortunately, electric razors received no such treatment. Other items of modern technology, however, did—and in ways that may surprise those who still think of Mann as too oldfangled, too aloof and *haut bourgeois,* and much too enamored of highbrow literary themes to have anything worthwhile to say about gadgets that come with knobs and dials and have to be plugged in. His writings, so we are told, lack the modern buzz and flair so conspicuously on display in the novels of his technologically more savvy peers Döblin the doctor, Musil

Parts of this essay were first presented at the University of Waterloo, the University of Kentucky, and the Universität Mannheim. I thank Erk Grimm, Jochen Hörisch, and the editors of this volume for support and suggestions.

the engineer, and Kafka the insurance bureaucrat and author of papers on quarries and workplace security. This may be true of some of his texts, but certainly not when it comes to *The Magic Mountain*. This novel is one of the most profound literary texts ever to engage the culture of modern technology. It is nothing less than a prewar *Gravity's Rainbow*, an early postindustrial epic that may have more important things to say about life under electric conditions than about any of the traditional items Mann is famous for—such as love and humanity, art and life, *Bildung* and decline, irony and identity, or whatever else serious German literature is supposed to be about.[1]

The Magic Mountain is a beautifully misshapen novel, a gargantuan textual edifice with the basement of a short story, the mezzanine of a delayed *Bildungsroman,* some of the furnishing of a historical novel, and the bulky roof of an encyclopedic treatise on time, death, and humanity. Its deformity is the result of its genesis; it was begun, put aside, and then resumed, enlarged, and constantly rearranged over a decade of tumultuous politics in which Mann changed almost as much as his surroundings. Much like the human brain, *The Magic Mountain* was at first a fairly simple object; but forced by outside pressures to adapt to new tasks and environments, it evolved layer upon layer, ultimately achieving a stupendous surface complexity without altering its basic makeup. While the tale grew in the telling, not all of its parts grew at the same rate, and some didn't grow at all; as a result, the friction within the novel has been amplified by the impinging critical cacophony ever since its (unexpectedly successful) debut in 1924. But despite the size and diversity of existing scholarship, very few critics appear to have taken seriously what the novel itself takes very seriously indeed: the arrival and impact of new media technologies.[2]

A couple of cursory remarks concerning the history and dynamics of the relationship between literature and other media are in order. We may begin with the obvious reminder that a literary narrative such as *The Magic Mountain* is itself a technology. Briefly put, the relationship between narratives and media technology can be summed up in three points: (1) narrative *is* a media technology; (2) narratives *depend on* media technology; and (3) narratives *deal* with media technology, particularly their own.

Narrative is a technology because it is an operation involving the selection, combination, transmission, and reception of data. It is a pretty sophisticated type of information processing that requires the other end to have received sufficient training in the corresponding techniques of reading, listening, and experiencing. Second, narratives depend on hardware, and whether they appear on paper, screens, or cuneiform tablets, they once again require a certain technical expertise. One of this century's more interesting ideas is that narratives are shaped by their technological format to such a degree that we cannot understand a narrative without first understanding its medial underpinning. This idea is frequently associated with Marshall McLuhan, not because he was the first modern media savant (that was another Canadian, Harold Innis) but because he was the first to (loudly) insist that the *how* of communication—the technology involved in a communication act—is far more relevant than the what—the message or meaning communicated. If there is anything narratologists can learn from him, it is that one and the same narrative appearing under different technological conditions is no longer one and the same.

The third point: from Plato's look back in philosophic anger at the Athenian shift from body-based orality to text-based literacy all the way to William Gibson's uneasy anticipation of the bodiless exultations of cyberspace, writing—that peculiar activity promoted by storage media—has paid special attention to its technological makeup as well as to other, "competing" technologies. These concerns are especially present in times of media change, when societies undergo information revolutions that promote new media technologies and demote others. New technologies, however, are not just simply added to the existing stock like logs stacked up in a shed; media form an ecology in which arrivals and departures change the entire system. Furthermore, our information processing capabilities are not strictly compartmentalized. There is no clear division of data labor with photography focusing exclusively on domain *A,* writing on *B,* movies on *C,* computers on *D,* and so on. Of course a photo of a tree is not the same as a description or a painting of a tree, but all three deal with trees and, more important, the fact that we can photograph trees has influenced the way we describe and paint them. Finally, the ways in which we used to read and write about trees may have contained something that pointed ahead to photography. Painting mimicking photography, writing co-opting phonography, movies imitating or debunking books . . . : these are intermedial boundary conflicts, and of such stuff great art is made.

For media-interested literary scholars the most fertile period runs from about 1850 to 1920, during which the culturally dominant status of writing and typography in the "Gutenberg Galaxy" was challenged by an array of postprint media technologies. Novels of this period are particularly revealing because of their obligation to present something that amounts to a total picture of the world. Stendhal's famous dictum has it that a novel is like a mirror being carried down a country road, reflecting both the sky above and the dirt below; the problem was that soon after Stendhal, gadgets appeared which could reflect and reproduce sky and dirt in a far more reliable and "realistic" fashion than any realist novel. According to Friedrich Kittler in "Gramophone, Film, Typewriter," writing-based techniques of *symbolic* mediation were faced with techniques of recording physical effects.[3] Writing operates by way of symbolic encoding, it squeezes data through the bottleneck of the alphabet, but phonographs and cameras store light and sound waves as retrievable *physical traces* of the real thing.[4] This amounts to a technological differentiation of data streams: visual and acoustic data, hitherto confined to paper, now receive their own, far more appropriate channels in the shape of photography and phonography. Before this demotion of print, readers had been so thoroughly alphabetized (literally imprinted) that their minds became capable of instantly converting printed matter into optical and acoustical images. "Educated people who could skim letters were provided with sights and sounds" without having to vocalize or physically (re)enact what they were reading (Kittler, "Gramophone, Film, Typewriter," 108).[5] In the long run, however, the print-based Gutenberg Galaxy was digging its own grave because it created a growing desire to abandon symbolic mediation in favor of technologies capable of communicating these images in direct, nonsymbolic fashion. Print was its own nemesis. In the words of Walter Benjamin: "One of the foremost tasks of art has always been the creation of a demand which could be fully satisfied only later. The history of every art form shows critical epochs in which a certain art form aspires to effects which could be fully obtained only with a changed technical standard, that is to say, in a new art form" (237).

The Magic Mountain recapitulates the intermedial conflicts at the turn of the century. In order to do so, it depicts a vast panorama of snow, sex, and information—far more than one chapter can handle. I will restrict myself to two technological areas: medical technology and storage technology. Under both headings we will encounter numerous references to death, corpses, and sick bodies with a mind of their own. This is unavoidable not only because the novel takes place in a sanatorium but also because the technological shifts I have in mind had a decisive impact on the cultural construction of the human body. There can be no media history without body history (and vice versa), for as long as we have not completely disembodied ourselves by downloading our consciousness into cyberspace, the "meaning" of bodies—how they are to be evaluated, what their cultural significance is, and where the border is that separates them from their immaterial, more "meaningful" content—will be determined by the technologies that examine, invade, store, and reproduce them. With this in mind, *The Magic Mountain* can be read as an attempt to renegotiate the relationship between body and spirit or meat and meaning under modern technological conditions (Hörisch, 18). The novel sports numerous bodies hovering between life and death; readers will recall that its principal running gag is that young Hans Castorp has not traveled upward into the Alps but downward into Hades to spend seven years among the shades. Scholars have unearthed a myriad of Dantean and other erudite allusions supporting this leitmotif, but it is already contained in the new medical technology Hans's body is subjected to.

Medical Technology: X-Ray Man Meets the Living Dead

Weimar, March 23, 1832. The Grand Duchy of Saxe-Weimar-Eisenach puts on display its most impressive corpse: the earthly remains of the civil servant Johann Wolfgang von Goethe. A former president of the Duke's Council, the deceased had been responsible for road construction, mining, irrigation, the issuing of uniforms, and other technical matters, while also gaining a certain reputation for numerous literary activities. Indeed, so prodigious was his motley output that he came to rely on a string of (in those days: exclusively male) secretaries. Among them was Johann Peter Eckermann, an aspiring young poet who had undertaken a pilgrimage to Weimar to visit his idol only to become hostage to genius. Goethe recognized his acolyte's potential and with a skillful blend of magnanimity and manipulation persuaded Eckermann to stay at his side and record his master's voice rather than develop his own. The result was *Gespräche mit Goethe,* three volumes of oral Goethean profundities later hailed by Nietzsche as one of the few German books worth reading. Indeed, Eckermann appeared to have captured the spirit of Goethe's utterings so faithfully that some readers have difficulty deciding who wrote the book. The second English translation (1850, and still in use) inverted the original title by calling itself *Conversations of Goethe with Eckermann*—which may serve as a first indication of how recording can interfere with authorship. In any case, the one scene Goethe did definitely not write relates how on that bleak day in March the orphaned Eckermann enjoys a last intimate moment with his dead captor and benefactor:

> The morning after Goethe's death, a deep desire seized me to look once again upon his earthly garment. His faithful servant, Frederic, opened for me the chamber in which he was laid out. Stretched upon his back, he reposed as if asleep; profound peace and security reigned in the features of his sublimely noble countenance. The mighty brow seemed yet to harbour thoughts. . . . Frederic drew aside the sheets and I was astonished at the divine magnificence of the limbs. The breast was powerful, broad, and arched; the arms and thighs were full, and softly muscular; the feet were elegant, and of the most perfect shape; nowhere, on the whole body, was there a trace of either fat or of leanness and decay. A perfect man lay in great beauty before me; and the rapture which the sight caused made me forget for a moment that the immortal spirit had left such an abode. I laid my hand on his heart—there was a deep silence—and I turned away to give free vent to my suppressed tears. (572)

Goethe was eighty-two, and we know from his physician's less rapturous report that his death had been preceded by physical decline. Yet in the light of Weimar Classicism's emphasis on clarity, temperance, and spiritual as well as physical health it comes as no surprise that the man known to generations of admirers as "the Olympian" should even as a dead octogenarian possess the body of a Mr. Olympia. Just as he was able to imbue his protocol of Goethe's *obiter dicta* with the master's spirit, Eckermann is able to discern that spirit still shaping its abandoned mortal shell. The materiality of a dead body makes place for an immaterial specter perceived by the mind's eye in exactly the same way as written letters evaporate in favor of imagined messages. The loving gaze, however, concludes with an ad hoc medical examination as touch is employed to remind sight that His Excellency is indeed dead. Not all senses, it seems, function on the same level; for a brief moment—and in violation of the aesthetic principles of the day, which favored the eye over all other organs of perception (cf. Utz)—palpation is more trustworthy than observation when one seeks to determine what is (or is not) inhabiting the body.

Roughly two generations later, in the second chapter of *The Magic Mountain*, the orphaned Hans Castorp is observing his dead grandfather's body. His scrutiny is less refined than Eckermann's, maybe because seven-year-old Hans, having already lost both his parents, has a more somber view of death and its ambiguities: "In one aspect death was holy, a pensive, a spiritual state, possessed of a certain mournful beauty. In another it was quite different. It was precisely the opposite, it was very physical, it was material, it could not possibly be called either holy, or pensive, or beautiful—not even mournful" (27).[6] Death's unseemly materiality is difficult to suppress. For one thing, Grandfather has started to smell. Readers familiar with death and decay on paper may recall the symbol-ridden stench arising from the corpse of Father Zosima in *The Brothers Karamazov*; Hans is reminded of a former classmate who suffered from a certain unpleasant affliction.[7] In addition, Grandfather has come to resemble a wax doll. He is no longer some*body* but some*thing*, a mere shell made of its own substance, neither sad nor beautiful nor mournful—"as things are not *which have to do with the body and only with it*" (27; my emphasis). Unlike Eckermann, Hans cannot overcome the physical obstinacy of a dead body that refuses to be anything but a dead body. Eckermann's gaze had turned Goethe's corpse into an idealized portrait, but Hans, unable to look through a corpse, is forced to separate the body from its lofty representation. Hans already had difficulties appreciating his grandfather's body while it was alive. Grandfather's "pure and genuine form" (25)—so his grandson came to believe—was only marginally present in his everyday physical appearance; the real, "authentic grandfather" resides in an idealized life-size painting hanging above the reception room sofa, an "oldmasterish" portrait depicting Senator Castorp as the embodiment of enlightened Hanseatic sobriety, complete with black coat, silk stockings, and top hat (24). We shall return to this portrait under less solemn conditions.

Dead bodies as well as bodies that act up while still alive are notoriously difficult to handle for any culture that views bodies (like written words) as obedient and inferior material vehicles for superior immaterial contents. Though death appears as the Great Divider that separates body and soul or matter and spirit, the exact location of that rupture and the question whether there really is something beyond the body are subject to constant change. As I mentioned earlier, these changes are closely tied to the introduction of technologies that examine, store, and reproduce the body in new ways, thus influencing its perception and ultimately its cultural construction. The late nineteenth-century shift toward electric recording technologies made it possible to reconstruct bodies in nonsymbolic fashion beyond the systems of words, colors, and sound intervals (Kittler, "Gramophone, Film, Typewriter," 110)—a shift that helps explain these differing corpse viewings. To retrace this development, we have to return to the early nineteenth century.

Sixteen years before Eckermann put his hand on Goethe's imposing chest, the French physician René Laënnec was examining a young woman with a puzzling heart disorder. The diagnostic practices of the day offered three techniques: palpation (pressing, as Eckermann did, the hand on the patient's body), percussion (recently developed by the Viennese physician Leopold Auenbrugger, it consisted of tapping the body with the fingers to produce signs indicating the vitality of the underlying organs), and auscultation (placing one's ear to the patient's chest). As the patient's obesity ruled out both palpation and percussion and her gender made auscultation appear improper, the doctor was forced to improvise. Recalling that sound is augmented when it travels through a solid body, he rolled a sheaf of paper into a tight cylinder, placed one end over the precordial region, and proceeded to listen. Laënnec had invented the stethoscope.

Stanley Joel Reiser—whose *Medicine and the Reign of Technology* tells much the same story as *The Magic Mountain*—has compared the effect of the stethoscope on physicians with that of printing on Western culture:

> Print and the reproducible book had created a new private world for man. He could isolate himself with the book and ponder its messages. . . . Similarly, [mediate] auscultation helped to create the objective physician, who could move away from involvement with the patient's experiences and sensations, to a more detached relation, less with the patient but more with the sounds from within the body. Undistracted by the motives and beliefs of the patient, the auscultator could make a diagnosis from sounds that he alone heard emanating from body organs, sounds that he believed to be objective, bias-free representations of the disease process. (38)

For a long time it was not unusual for doctors to base their diagnoses on information contained in letters written by patients they had never met, let alone examined. But with the shift from verbal to more manual techniques, physicians demoted the patient's own story as less trustworthy. They developed a systematic way of questioning to avoid useless talk and elicit "objective" information in support of the increasingly important physical examination.[8] *The Magic Mountain* recapitulates this development: after the head doctor, the "extraordinarily gifted auscultator" (133) Hofrat Behrens, concludes his examination of Hans (a short overview followed by a long session of percussion and mediate auscultation), he fires off a couple of short questions and then, without listening further, proceeds to give a surprisingly exact description of Hans's symptoms and related behavioral traits (180). Mann, the great modern bard of infirmity, was intimately familiar with diagnostic procedures and recognized their weakness: if we limit ourselves to the physical symptoms, Behrens's diagnosis is "correct," but it turns out to be useless—which may not have been the case had he listened to Hans's story and discovered the psychosomatic anamnesis.

As serendipitous as Laënnec's invention of the stethoscope was, the stage had been set for its arrival. In the course of the eighteenth century medical discourse had gradually accepted the evidence provided by anatomists linking diseases to anatomical lesions. Patients who happened still to be alive would profit from this knowledge, however, only if physicians devised tools that would enable them to examine internal body parts, something that up until then had been possible only in autopsies. The stethoscope was just such a tool. There is a Kittlerian twist to this development: just as photography and phonography implemented the optical and acoustical data flows hitherto confined to print, nineteenth-century medical tools were the technological realization of the eighteenth-century tradition of "imaging the unseen" inside the body[9]— which, of course, had relied to a large degree on knowledge gained from disposable corpses. In the words of a doctor, it was now possible to "anatomise by [mediate] auscultation . . . , while the patient is yet alive" (quoted in Reiser, 30). This notion continues throughout the evolution of nineteenth-century medical technology, culminating in Wilhelm Röntgen's serendipitous discovery. X rays—which Behrens referred to with great precision as *Lichtanatomie*—turn living beings into skeletons, thus giving the final touch to a development that had refined ways in which physicians could autopsy the living patient. The X ray scene in *The Magic Mountain* (214-19) captures the awe, amusement, and "stirrings of uneasy doubt" (218) triggered by the first X ray photos, while also playing on the theme that this apparatus turns patients into living dead. Peering at (or into) his cousin Joachim, Hans is reminded of a woman "who had been endowed or afflicted with a heavy gift . . . : namely, that the skeletons of persons about to die would appear before her. Thus now Hans Castorp was privileged to behold the good Joachim" (218). At this point Joachim has 300 pages of life left while Hans has seven years to go. Passing his own hand through the rays, Hans also catches a glimpse of his own future:

> And Hans Castorp saw, precisely what he must have expected, but what is hardly permitted man to see, and what he never thought it would be vouchsafed him to see: he looked into his own grave. The process of decay was forestalled by the powers of the light-ray, the flesh in which he walked disintegrated, annihilated, dissolved in vacant mist, and there within was the finely turned skeleton of his own hand. ... (218)

According to one of McLuhan's canonical insights, the introduction of each new media technology affects the sense ratio. Print, so the story goes, privileged sight over sound, while phonographs and radios retrieved acoustic space. While Auenbrugger's percussion technique had temporarily privileged touch, Laënnec's invention had boosted sound, yet he named it stethoscope—as if to underscore the widely held belief that for the purposes of objective medical diagnosis light is a more trustworthy channel than sound. The medical journal *Lancet* referred to photography as the "Art of Truth"; and the invention of the carbon-filament lamp facilitated the manufacture of a wide variety of visual scopes, each specially constructed to light a different orifice through which physicians could enter to explore the human body (Reiser, 56). As one doctor put it: "There is an old and trite saying that 'seeing is believing'; and, in a realistic age like the present, it might almost be said that not seeing is not believing" (quoted in Reiser, 56). The apotheosis of light as the most trustworthy channel of information was the X ray, as Hans Castorp's reaction to the sight of the very center of his cousin's physical interior demonstrates:

> "I am looking at your heart," he [Hans] said in a suppressed voice.
> "Go ahead," answered Joachim again; probably he smiled politely up there in the darkness. But the Hofrat told him to be quiet and not betray any sensibility [*Empfindsamkeit*]. Behrens studied the spots and the lines, the black festoon in the intercostal space; while Hans Castorp gazed without wearying at Joachim's graveyard shape and bony tenement, this lean *memento mori*, this scaffolding for mortal flesh to hang on. "Yes, yes! I see! I see!" he said, several times over. "My God, I see!" (218)

If the cardinal message of *The Magic Mountain* is that "man shall let death have no sovereignty over his thoughts" (497), Hans will have to stop gazing at X rays as if they were depictions of medieval death dances. When high-energy electromagnetic radiation makes the none too solid flesh melt away to reveal the heart to be nothing but a "pulsating shadow," the time for poetic "sensibility" is indeed over. New media that explore and store the body without paying the slightest attention to any resident immaterial spirit have only one message: a body is a body is a body. Even Goethe's Olympian leftovers, if propped up behind an X ray screen, would be nothing but skull and bones.

Finally, there remains a noteworthy detail. Reiser argues that recent developments in telecommunications may change the organization of medical practice back to a more decentralized state (196). The shift away from the nineteenth-century demand that doctor and patient be in close physical proximity started as early as 1880, when physicians began to use the telephone and the telegraph for diagnostic purposes. Thomas Mann himself benefited from this development. While visiting his wife in a sanatorium in Davos in 1912, he fell ill with a bronchial cold. The head doctor examined him, promptly discovered a moist spot in his lung, and advised him to join his wife for six months or so. Unlike gullible Hans, Mann phoned home and got hold of his doctor, who told him to dismiss the diagnosis. He returned to Munich to write *The Magic Mountain*; Hans remained in Davos to experience it. And to make sure that he stays up there, the novel all but banishes the telephone. It appears, like a last beacon of hope, right in the beginning—it is one of the very first things Hans sees upon entering the sanatorium (10)—but from then on all contact with the "flat land" will be restricted to telegrams and (frequently typed) letters. The one communication technology that would have enabled Hans to stay in close contact with "those down there" (and thus might have facilitated an escape) disappears from his otherwise technologically advanced surroundings.

Storage Technology: Books for the Record

Munich, February 10, 1920. Returning from a two-week trip to the Starnberger See, Thomas Mann records a momentous event that will have a lasting impact on his life: "The highlight of the visit: [a] superlative Gramophone, which I put to continuous use. . . . The *Tannhäuser* Overture. *La Bohème*. The finale of *Aïda* (an Italian Liebestod). Caruso,

Orphée, descendant aux Enfers, dédaigne sa lyre et lui préfère le **Lioretgraph**.

"Descending into hell, Orpheus discards his lyre in favor of the Lioretgraph": an advertisement for Lioret phonographs. From Peter Copeland, *Sound Recordings* (London: British Library, 1991). By permission of The British Library. ML 1055 C74 56 1991.

Battistini, Madame Melba, Titta Ruffo, etc. A new theme for *The Magic Mountain*, a rich find both for its intellectual possibilities and its narrative value" (*Diaries*, 84). A rich find indeed. Thus begins one of the few great love affairs in Mann's life: his ongoing relationship with mechanical sound reproduction. Soon the Mann family acquired its own gramophone and settled into decades of listening to records (an aural ritual boosted by the arrival of the radio, which finally allowed Mann to get to know one of the few American artists he truly appreciated: Jack Benny). The "narrative value" of the gramophone is exploited toward the end of *The Magic Mountain*, but before Hans can undergo what must rank as the greatest phonographic experience in literature, he has to rid himself of old media allegiances.

Concluding a voyage Valerie Greenberg has very aptly compared to the launching of an astronaut into space (60), Hans arrives in Davos with a book titled *Ocean Steamships.* "Earlier in the journey he had studied . . . off and on, but now it lay neglected, and the breath of the panting engine, steaming in, defiled its cover with particles of soot" (3). The symbolism is obvious: the book's neglectful treatment points toward the reluctance with which Hans is studying to become a naval engineer; and owing to his innate laziness and the seductions of his new abode, his career plans will soon be as forgotten as the reading material he brought along. The fate of *Ocean Steamships,* a volume more mentioned than read, prefigures the fate of all books on *The Magic Mountain.* Though the narrator assures us that "no little reading was done" up there, it is mainly restricted to "new-comers and 'short-timers' " whose "beginners' awkwardness" (272) has delayed their discovery of more entertaining and sophisticated means of killing time. When the resident liberal humanist Settembrini—who repeatedly praises print as one of the outstanding achievements in the service of humanity—unsuccessfully proposes to his fellow patients that they give Behrens "a newly projected encyclopedic work called *The Sociology of Suffering*" (270) for Christmas, the choice of this most Gutenbergian of print objects which arranges information in a strictly linear fashion is supported only by a book dealer. Instead, Behrens receives a chaise longue, upon which he "stretched out full length . . . closed his eyes, and began to snore like a saw-mill" (290). Physical comfort overrides intellectual nourishment: this shift from books to bodies is one of the novel's more obvious running gags. For example, one print product that does elicit the attention of all patients, even the old hands, is titled *The Art of Seduction,* a very literal translation of a French "exposition of the philosophy of sensual passion" (272). Books that elevate physical pleasure are, it seems, exempt from the prevailing bibliophobia. Hans goes a step further: his reading experience described in the subchapter "Research" shows that any reading material, no matter how dry, can be turned into a sexual primer.

To investigate his feelings for his fellow patient Clawdia Chauchat— or, to be more precise: to study why her body has certain effects on his—Hans consults a trilingual plethora of expensive volumes on anatomy, physiology, and biology. Mann scholarship has yet to pinpoint which books the master raided; some of the science is outdated, yet there are passages about the "form-preserving instability" of life balancing itself on the edge of decay and renewal (274–78) which sound as if Mann had read an advance copy of Ilya Prigogine and Isabelle Stengers's *Order out of Chaos*. For us, however, what Hans reads about life as the "fever of matter" is less important than how he reads it:

> The books lay piled upon the table, one lay in the matting next to his chair; that which he had latest read rested upon Hans Castorp's stomach and oppressed his breath; yet no order went from the cortex to the muscles in charge to take it away. He had read down the page, his chin had sunk upon his chest, over his innocent blue eyes the lids had fallen. He beheld the image of life in flower, its structure, its flesh-borne loveliness. She had lifted her hands from behind her head, she opened her arms. . . . Something warm and tender clasped him around the neck; melted with desire and awe, he laid his hands upon the flesh of the upper arms, where the fine-grained skin over the triceps came to his sense so heavenly cool; and upon his lips he felt the moist clinging of her kiss. (286)

On this day Hans reads no further; in fact, he stops reading altogether. This is the last *Bildungserlebnis* of German literature; it depicts nothing less than the undoing of the long-term physical-training programs that had been indispensable for the establishment of the highly alphabetized discourse networks of the Gutenberg Galaxy. In a world dominated by the written word, the body is no longer permitted to be a medium for experiencing texts. The bodies of those who write and of those who read must be eliminated, because a text can turn into a trusted provider of messages only after the human body is screened out of the consciousness of communication and no longer acts as a principal vehicle for the constitution of meaning (Gumbrecht, 215). In the most comprehensive study to date of the German reading culture of the Enlightenment, Erich Schöne has retraced the gradual exclusion of the body from the reading process. Readers who had earlier been standing or reclining were taught to sit; books that had been either resting on readers' laps or grasped between their hands now lay on the table; the hands moved away and the only "physical" contact remaining was eye contact. Mouths were prevented from voicing words as silent reading (subvocalization) was enforced, and a whole pamphlet industry evolved to prevent unstable readers (especially women and young men) from reading anything that might excite their bodies. The suppression and immobilization of the reader's body and the trained neglect of the material qualities of the book resulted in a cognitive gain; it became easier for readers to read more and faster and instantaneously convert black signs on white paper into instructive messages. Hans, however, regresses into a reclining position, the book regains its physical qualities by squashing his chest, and the reading process interacts less with his intellect than with his libido.

Once he abandons books, his life becomes a picaresque journey through alternative media experiences in search of a technology capable of storing desired bodies. Clawdia, though she does on one occasion lend Hans an all too phallic pencil, is too lazy to write (353), but she does leave him a wallet-sized X ray of her chest—a stored physical effect of her body far superior and closer to her body than any symbolic mediation. (This conceit is, incidentally, less original than it sounds; exchanging personal X ray memorabilia was quite common after Röntgen's discovery [Reiser, 60].) Apart from this shift from print to photography, the novel also addresses the intermedial conflicts involving photography and painting. Hans learns that Behrens is an amateur painter who has made a portrait of Clawdia. He manages to get himself invited to Behrens's home, where he unabashedly unhooks the painting and starts carrying it around. The physical movement of the painting from Behrens's living room to the cabinet sofa parallels the movement of the portrait of old Senator Castorp that once hung in the house of Hans's parents but now resides above the sofa in his reception room (24). The two portraits represent different epochs, the one before and the one after the intrusion of modern technology into painting. As I mentioned earlier, the senator appears as an idealized representative of a certain time and age, with all the accoutrements befitting his social position. In marked contrast to this "capital painting by an artist of some note" (25), Behrens has produced a "rather botched performance . . . only distantly related to its original" (257). Yet, much to Hans's satisfaction, the doctor has admirably captured Clawdia's skin:

> The roughness of the canvas texture, showing through the paint, had been dexterously employed to suggest the unevenness of the skin. . . . It was as though a scarcely perceptible shiver of sensibility beneath the eye of the beholder were passing over this nude flesh, as though one might see the perspiration, the invisible vapour which the life beneath threw off; as though, were one to press one's lips upon this surface, one might perceive, not the smell of the paint and fixative, but the odour of the human body. (258)

What books can only conjure up by way of typographically induced hallucination, paintings may represent in a far more direct way—particularly if the artist has been educated by the technologically enhanced medical gaze. To use the canvas texture to approximate the "plasticity of the female form" (261), otherwise known as fat, and even conjure up the olfactory properties of the original, is to simulate physical effects in ways closer to modern technology than to any "oldmasterish style" (25) that aspires to capture the platonic form of dead senators.

The inability of old media to provide or explain new experiences recurs in the subchapter "Fullness of Harmony" (635–53), which explores Hans's passionate affair with the sanatorium's gramophone. Once again, the introduction of a new technology is linked to the debunking of what came before. "This is not just a machine," Behrens announces,

> "it's a Stradivarius, a Guarneri; with a resonance, a vibration—*dernier raffinemang*, Polyhymnia patent, look here in the inside of the lid. German make, you know, we do them far and away better than anybody else. The truly musical, in a modern, mechanical form, the German soul up to date. And here's the libretto," he said, and gestured with his head toward a little case on the wall, filled with broad-backed albums. (637)

The original uses *Literatur* instead of *Libretto*; and it merely requires a lowering of the voice at the end of the sentence to turn *Da haben Sie die Literatur!* into a dismissal of literature. There is nothing ambiguous, however, about Hans's reaction; he clearly recognizes something new on a grand scale: "Hold on! This is an epoch! This thing was sent to me!" and filled with "surest foreknowledge of a new passion, a new enchantment, a new burden of love" (639), he assumes the role of high priest of mechanical sound reproduction (Hörisch 21).

The musical allusions of "Fullness of Harmony" have been analyzed so many times that there is no need to peruse the links between Hans's favorite records and events in the novel once again (for a detailed analysis, see Symington). Various critics have pointed out that Hans's truly inspired listening takes place when he is alone. In fact, he is interrupted only once by Behrens—and as if to underscore how important sound-reproducing technologies are at this moment, the narrator points out that the doctor's "stethoscope [was] showing in his pocket" (641). This new solitary aural confinement marks a clear break with earlier recitals, during which Hans tended to be disturbed by the sight of Clawdia, the sound of other patients, or the taste of beer and tobacco. As he listens alone at night in the salon, recorded music becomes as illuminating an experience as the X ray—not an astonishing epiphany, for the novel presents both as technologies that manage to isolate a specific data flow (thereby isolating the corresponding sense organ) and to communicate a more intimate knowledge of death.

It is very revealing that the most famous icon of the recording industry next to Mick Jagger's tongue is Francis Barraud's painting *His Master's Voice*. Printed on millions of covers and labels, it depicts a fox terrier called Nipper staring down the brass horn of an Eldrige Johnson Improved Gramophone. Nipper—who is (need we say it?) listening to a dead man's voice[10]—appears slightly befuddled because he is hearing something he cannot see. Barraud's rendition of the dog's puzzled gaze is somewhat reminiscent of Laënnec's significant misnomer "stethoscope," for in both cases seeing is stressed in connection with a technology that addresses the ear. We tend to forget that phonography, with its literally unheard-of possibility of storing sound, introduced us to what R. Murray Shafer calls "schizophonia": the split between an original sound and its electroacoustical transmission or reproduction (370). We have internalized phonography's ability to replace an audiovisual event with a primarily audio one so well that we no longer "miss" seeing anything, but in the early days the listeners' scopic drive, suddenly deprived of its object, often focused in a Nipper-like way on the sound apparatus (Laing, 7-9). There is an echo of this tendency in the long, slightly fetishistic description of Hans's gramophone, in which the narrator mobilizes his considerable stylistic resources to impress upon the reader that this is truly the "latest triumph of art" (636). Later, descriptions of the object make way for descriptions of the music itself and its visual associations, a shift that parallels historical developments as people became more used to the new technology and developed mental techniques of converting acoustic into visual data.

The descriptions of the "sarcophagus of music" (653) are laced with death, and once again the running gag echoes ideas and fantasies spawned by the technology in question. When Edison suggested that phonographs be used to record voices for posterity, he introduced a theme that rapidly captured the public imagination and culminated in such phonographic fantasies as Jules Verne's *Castle in the Carpathians* and Villiers de l'Isle-Adam's *Tomorrow's Eve*: to store sound was to overcome time, history, and even mortality because a moment in time could be saved and moved into the future. Times past were no longer "lost," they could be stored and retrieved at any given moment and with them all the people who had passed away. The records Hans listens to not only recapture the characters and constellations of his alpine sojourn, they manage quite literally to retrieve his dead cousin Joachim. During a séance a song from Gounod's *Faust* makes Joachim, anach-ronistically dressed in a World War I uniform, return as a ghost from a future he never experienced (679–81). Within the narrative framework of *The Magic Mountain,* the purpose of "Fullness of Harmony" is to build on the revelation Hans had during his walk in the snowstorm: that death should have no dominion over his thoughts. But this does not mean that death is to be banished from his mind altogether; on the contrary, it is necessary always to be mindful of death and realize that it remains an indispensable part of life and that so much of what we identify with life will betray its nature and turn toward death.

This knowledge is imparted to Hans by a recording of Schubert's famous *Volkslied* "Der Lindenbaum." Given the thanatolatry of German romanticism, the connection is pretty obvious and far less of a "vile detraction" (652) than the narrator, in a gratuitous gesture of self-condemnation, proposes. What interests us is a final comment that points out a certain potential behind Schubert's phonographic revival:

> Ah, what power had this soul-enchantment! We were all its sons, and could achieve mighty things on earth, in so far as we served it. One need have no more genius, only much more talent, than the author of the "Lindenbaum," to be such an artist of soul-enchantment as should give to the song a giant volume by which it should subjugate the world. Kingdoms might be founded upon it, earthly, all-too-earthly kingdoms, solid, "progressive," not at all nostalgic—in which the song degenerated to a piece of gramophone music played by elec-tricity. (653)

This passage can easily accommodate numerous interpretations. One way of reading it is to follow the veiled reference to the "soul-enchantment" engineered by the media magician Richard Wagner,[11] who (despite the fact that we are dealing with a Thomas Mann novel) is only marginally present in Hans Castorp's top ten list of classical hits. The reference becomes clearer if we recall that the passage, indeed the entire conclusion of "Fullness of Harmony," was reproduced verbatim in a short speech Mann gave in 1924 in honor of Nietzsche's eightieth birthday. Nietzsche, it is said, had a passionate love for music, above all Wagner's, and since passion is love that doubts its object, it became Nietzsche's destiny to overcome his love for this romantic temptation by way of a "heroic" self-conquest. This story may have little to do with Nietzsche (a Thomas Mann essay is, unfailingly, about Thomas Mann, not about the personnel announced in the title), but it has a lot do with Hans, for it is precisely this awareness of "self-conquest" that Polyhymnia—the gramophone, not the muse—shares with him at the peak of his phonographically induced romantic rapture, a self-conquest that might enable him to speak "the new word of love and the future that whispered in his heart" (653). Of course he never speaks the word, whatever it may be; the last words we hear from his lips are from "Der Lindenbaum": "Its waving branches whispered / A message in my ear. . . ." (715). A fitting epitaph. The story of Hans Castorp is the story of a mind besieged by messages it cannot convert into action or experience; the only thing left to do is to replay them.

And here a more sinister reading of the "Lindenbaum" passage emerges. The reference to the new technological possibilities of retrieving a collective past—to repeat Mann's disparaging account: the *Volkslied* "degenerated to a piece of gramophone music played by electricity"—is reminiscent of McLuhan's more euphoric celebration of the retrieval of old tribal structures by electric media. Bypassing and effectively annihilating long periods of history, the updated past "in modern, mechanical form" is always in danger of being short-circuited with an aggressive future in order to serve "all-too-earthly" kingdoms. In Mann's novels, particularly in *Doctor Faustus,* this (technologically enforced) union of the very old with the very new spells fascism. Mann knew that *his* time, the era of bourgeois decorum and deliberation with its associated networks of print-bound literacy, had come to an end, and he began to see himself as the last great bourgeois author, a noble and sophisticated fossil as anachronistic as a sanatorium existence in the Swiss Alps. This self-dramatization made it all the easier for him both to acknowledge and to distance himself from technocultural trends that were acclaimed in the works of Ernst Jünger and other reactionary modernists and that bolstered the "not at all nostalgic" forces of National Socialism.[12]

Modern technology's aggressive potential is displayed at the end when the reader catches a last glimpse of Hans on the battlefields of World War I. A glimpse, no more: faced with soldiers ripped apart by the "product[s] of a perverted science, laden with death" (715), the tale refuses to linger; an overconfident narrator, who at the outset had boasted that "only the exhaustive can be truly interesting" (x), is reduced to a despairing "Away! No more!" The conclusion of *The Magic Mountain* illustrates the inability of Gutenbergian literacy to process the shocks and sensations that pound bodies in a world of modern technology. This or that story may emerge from the carnage, but—as Benjamin wrote in his beautiful and profoundly sad essay "The Storyteller"—the realities of modern war and its affiliated societies transcend old communicative capacities:

> With the [First] World War a process began to become apparent which has not halted since then. Was it not noticeable at the end of the war that men returned from the battlefield grown silent—not richer, but poorer in communicable experience? . . . And there was nothing remarkable about that. For never has experience been contradicted more thoroughly than strategic experience by tactical warfare, economic experience by inflation, bodily experience by mechanical warfare, moral experience by those in power. A generation that had gone to school on a horse-drawn streetcar now stood under the open sky in a countryside in which nothing remained unchanged but the clouds, and beneath these clouds, in a field of force and destructive torrents and explosions, was the tiny, fragile human body. (84)

Conclusions: Streetcar Sparks; or, Technology and the *Umbildungsroman*

The philosopher Theodor Adorno once faced the difficult task of praising Thomas Mann without recycling the clichés that had come to dominate the academic industry before Mann was (somewhat) debunked in the late sixties. Adorno rose to the occasion by commending the way in which the master had captured sparks flying off a Munich streetcar in *Doctor Faustus*. Mann dismissed the compliment—*so etwas können wir* (roughly: come on, I can do *that*)—as if offended by the idea that he of all Nobel laureates should be singled out for such mundane details (Adorno, *Noten zur Literatur*, 20).

Adorno had a point. Mann is celebrated as an author of ideas, a writer whose texts rely heavily on the aesthetic and philosophic stockpiles of the last two centuries. While he was neither a very "deep" nor an "original" thinker (and never claimed to be), he was a master of ironic intellectual pastiche and rearrangement. On the one hand, he treated ideas like things: he reified them, reduced them to their bare essentials, sometimes even turned them into mere gestures, and then—as in the discussions between Settembrini and Naphta in *The Magic Mountain*—proceeded to play elaborate games with a restricted body of themes, positions, and concepts that he recycled in novel after novel.

On the other hand, he treated many things and gadgets like ideas, particularly those that had just recently arrived. Like Kafka, he gave them a life of their own, a "story" that was closely linked to the fears and hopes they evoked and the changes they provoked before they became familiar enough to be, in effect, invisible. Technologies, after all, are like discursive practices; that is, most powerful when least noticed. If you want to know how a telephone works, call your local phone company; if you want to know what a telephone is and what resistance it had to overcome before turning into an inconspicuous appliance, read Kafka's *Castle* or Benjamin's recollection of the first telephones in *A Berlin Childhood*. To return to Adorno's example: while it may not take much to describe streetcars, it takes a lot to describe a world in which streetcars make sense; and it takes genius to depict faithfully how streetcars are changing the people who use them. This is what *The Magic Mountain* does with X rays, gramophones, and other gadgets: Mann conceptualizes new media technologies by showing how they work, which fantasies they fulfill, what they will lead to, and how they are changing our bodies and minds—and all the while depicting them with a living (as opposed to deadly) accuracy few writers can match.

What makes *The Magic Mountain* such a remarkable piece of literature for media theorists, then, is that it establishes a link between the reeducation of taste, smell, sound, and sight and the arrival of new technologies: it is less of an *éducation sentimental*—and therefore less of a *Bildungsroman*—than an *éducation des sens*. This re-formation or *Umbildung* of the senses occurs against the background of differentiations in information processing in the course of which visual and acoustic data leave the printed page and acquire their own technologies. In the novel anatomically correct paintings, kaleidoscopes, cinematographic cylinders, X rays, movies, and a mania for amateur photography, "flashlights and colour photography after Lumière" (627) stand for the liberation of visual data from their paper prison, while the phonographic ecstasy of "Fullness of Harmony" celebrates the arrival of sound recording. Under these circumstances, the old concept of the *Bildungsroman*—if it ever was more than an obstinate figment of scholarly imagination—must come to an end; for *Bildung*, programmed by the Goethean algorithm to result in the unfolding of a personality core, was tied to a harmonious mixture of worldly experience with education derived from reading the proper books. *The Magic Mountain* does not fit the bill, not only because it demotes the cultural role of books. It is simply not a "formation novel," which features the ups and downs of youthful development and climaxes in some kind of mature self-awareness and integration of self into society; it is rather, in the words of the author's son, "a delicately carved puppet-theatre for the display of intellectual and historical possibilities, a stage on which everything is discussed and nothing decided" (Golo Mann, 371).[13] In short, *The Magic Mountain* is the first epic of modern information. If such novels as *Dracula* depict the full-scale mobilization of postprint technologies in order to fight dangerous bodies from abroad,[14] *The Magic Mountain* announces that the campaign has ended in total victory: books are demoted, information is circulated by more effective technologies, and those technologies now dominate, invade, and will eventually replace bodies.

And yet, you say, *The Magic Mountain* is a book and meant to be read. Sure, but Mann himself wasn't all that happy about it. He wondered whether "filming *The Magic Mountain* . . . might have produced a wonderful spectacle, a fantastic cyclopædia [sic], with a hundred digressions into all points of the compass" ("On the Film," 266), thereby suggesting that alternative media formats might make the complex narrative more accessible. Readers who wanted to approximate this nonlinear experience were told to read the novel twice, because "only so can one really penetrate and enjoy its musical association of ideas" and "read the symbolic and allusive formulas both forwards and backwards" (*Magic Mountain*, 725). This will sound familiar to hypertext experts. I do not want to present *The Magic Mountain* as yet another harbinger of hyperfiction, but I do believe that the novel's informational overload, which Mann tried to amend by redirecting much of what was slotted for *The Magic Mountain* into the book-long essay *Reflections of a Nonpolitical Man*, is pointing toward the mid-century crisis in information processing technologies, which resulted in the development of technologies capable of organizing information in easily accessible nonsequential fashion.

The Magic Mountain demands a reader who experiences the novel much as Hans experiences his alpine sojourn. Life, so Hans learned before he stopped reading, is temporary self-organization on the edge of lifeless matter; likewise, his elevated story, located on the edge of equally lifeless regions, tells us that we are able to experience our existence and provide it with some kind of temporary order only if we employ media capable of recording and organizing data extracted from the indifferent white noise surrounding us. There is more than a passing resemblance between Thomas Mann's Castorp and William Gibson's

Case: both are medianauts intent on relishing up-to-date media experiences. Both demonstrate that who we are is defined by what we can experience; that what we can experience depends, in turn, on our media (including our body); and that literary representations of what our experiences have made of us will therefore have to be mindful of changing technological standards. Should we say that both are, therefore, science fiction? In any case, both authors do not necessarily agree with the protagonist's media-addicted behavior. Thomas Mann, the quintessential nineteenth-century latecomer peering into our world, was not the first to write about these things, but he was so good at it because he was (like Plato, St. Paul, Cervantes, Victor Hugo, Villiers de l'Isle-Adam, Stoker, Rilke, Gibson, Neal Stephenson, and other media authors) at heart a conservative—someone who takes the future seriously enough to worry and fantasize about it. Meanwhile, back in Weimar in 1825, Germany's greatest conservative had, of course, seen it all coming:

> Everything, my dear friend, is now ultra, everything is inexorably transcending both in thought and deed. . . . Young people are excited much too early and are swept away by the rush of times; all the world praises and strives for wealth and speed; the educated avail themselves of trains, express mail, steamers and all possible facilities of communication to outdo and over-educate themselves, thus never rising above mediocrity. . . . Let us remain steadfast and loyal to the way of thinking we grew up with, and together with a few others we shall be the last of an epoch the like of which we shall not see again for a long time. (*Goethes Briefe*, 4: 146–47)

Notes

1. One of the occasions on which Mann demonstrated that he wasn't so far removed from technology is a remarkable interview published in the *Vossische Zeitung* on January 9, 1929. He discusses the influence of the gramophone on art, speculates on the potential of film to replace the novel as the truly narrative medium, throws in a reference to Heisenberg, and points out how the automobile enables authors to witness changes in nature (Hansen and Heine, *Frage und Antwort*, 142–45).

2. The exception I am most indebted to is Jochen Hörisch, " 'Die deutsche Seele up to date': Sakramente der Medientechnik auf dem *Zauberberg*." An earlier paper by Winfried Kudzus, "Understanding Media: Zur Kritik dualistischer Humanität im *Zauberberg*," does not quite live up to its promising title.

3. The essay "Gramophone, Film, Typewriter" is a translation of the introductory chapter of *Grammophon Film Typewriter*, which in turn is a long technical

addendum to the second part of Kittler's magnum opus, *Aufschreibesysteme 1800/1900*, translated as *Discourse Networks, 1800/1900.*

4. Times have changed. Living in an era of simulation—the digitized creation of hyperreal copies for which there is no original—we have progressed beyond this obsolete naive distinction between symbolic and real representation. Now that morphed images have learned to lie better than printed pages ever could, it is almost conceivable that once again "text will emerge as a primary indicator of trustworthiness" (Saffo, 48).

5. Kittler describes the comprehensive training programs responsible for this naturalization of the alphabet in the first part of *Discourse Networks.*

6. All page references to Mann's novel follow the Lowe-Porter translation. The (in)adequacy of this translation has been a touchy issue ever since Mann's initial misgivings (see Berlin). I have decided to stick to it and point out shortcomings only when necessary.

7. The odor of death pervades Mann's work. It is especially apparent in *Buddenbrooks:* the more decadent and run-down the family members, the longer they take to die and the more it stinks (cf. Rindisbacher, 198–201).

8. See Reiser, p. 32. This is a type of preprocessing information that, according to James Beniger, the nineteenth century introduced on a broad scale. Readers familiar with Foucault's *Birth of the Clinic* will notice how close Reiser comes to Foucault (importance of autopsies, doctor-patient distancing, new nosological classifications, importance of nineteenth-century medical technology). *The Magic Mountain* has yet to be fully analyzed in light of Foucault's work on the medical gaze and the belief that life can be understood only by way of death.

9. For a beautiful analysis see Stafford.

10. Barraud had inherited Nipper from his deceased brother, and the story goes that the dog used to sit in front of his new master's phonograph listening to recordings of his old master's voice. Barraud captured the scene but later turned the phonograph into a gramophone to increase the market value of the painting (Gelatt, 107).

11. It has become a commonplace in German media discourse analysis to present Wagner as an artist who pioneered the shift away from symbolic mediation by launching a multimedia attack on the nerves of his captive audience, a strategy Norbert Bolz refers to as "Pink Floyd in Bayreuth." See also Kittler, "World-Breath," 215–35.

12. The term "reactionary modernists" was coined by Jeffrey Herf. His *Reactionary Modernism* remains one of the best studies of the reactionary appropriation of technology during the Weimar Republic and the Third Reich.

13. Hans Wysling, the Nestor of Thomas Mann scholarship, has categorically stated that the concept of the *Bildungsroman* cannot be applied to *The Magic Mountain:* "The story lacks the basic characteristics of the genre: the hero is no personality, he behaves in a passive, reflective way; the goal toward which he is striving is known neither to him nor to the author. Castorp never grows up . . ." (420).

14. See Kittler, "Dracula's Legacy," and my essay "Undead Networks."

Michael Wutz

2 Archaic Mechanics, Anarchic Meaning

Malcolm Lowry and the Technology of Narrative

"The typewriter," writes Martin Heidegger, "tears writing from the essential realm of the hand, i.e., the realm of the word. The word itself turns into something 'typed' " (81). As if sharing Heidegger's resistance to the technologization of the word, Malcolm Lowry avoided using a typewriter to compose his fiction drafts. At the same time he conceived of himself as an engineer of fiction, and of his writerly practice as a narrative technology. This form of textual engineering, which is evident in the component-part assembly of his texts and in his use of machine models, has its origin in a modernist aesthetic of design and is particularly visible in his masterpiece, *Under the Volcano*—a novel whose machine design Lowry envisioned as an assembly of one of the oldest human technologies, which he appropriated from numerous cultural traditions: an aggregate of interlocking wheels. The assemblage of this *narrative engine* in the manner of a collage also puts Lowry in the proximity of postmodernism's play with intertextuality and signification, as does the resultant textual apparatus, which affords virtually anarchic semiosis. If, however, *Under the Volcano* operates as what Gilles Deleuze has called a "literary machine," as a text that draws attention to the

The archival research for this chapter was made possible by generous grants from the International Council of Canadian Studies and Weber State University's Research and Professional Growth Committee. I also appreciate the help of George S. Brandak, Curator of Special Collections at the University of British Columbia, Patrick A. McCarthy, and Frederick Asals; their expert knowledge helped me to navigate the maelstrom of the Malcolm Lowry archive.

process of meaning making and to its condition as a commodity available for readerly consumption, the novel's postmodern ethos is counterbalanced by an archaic mechanical design that codifies, on the level of form, Lowry's ambivalence toward technology.

The schism between romantic artificer and narrative engineer, between the hand-based production of script and aesthetic formal design, is already suggested by the topographical coordinates of Malcolm Lowry's life and work, which generally unfold along the fault line of Nature and Culture. As is well known, Lowry progressively removed himself from the cultural centers of Europe and America to a wooden shack on the Pacific waterfront in British Columbia, in part because of what he called "the sthenic confusion of technological advance" (*Hear Us O Lord*, 180). Eridanus, the prelapsarian sanctuary his post-*Volcano* alter egos inhabit, is indeed endangered by the onrush of civilization, as when, in a propitious moment in *October Ferry to Gabriola*, Ethan Llewelyn envisions progress as technological apocalypse, when the forces of progress will have "totally ruined most of the beauty of the country with industry, and thoroughly loused up the watersheds and the rainfall, and the last old sourdough [will have] traded in his gold sifting pan for a Geiger counter and staked out the last uranium claim" (202).

But while this passage, in the fashion of his romantic predecessors, ostensibly rewrites Genesis as a dialectic between the natural and the technological—the presence and absence of prelapsarian perfection—suggesting the Fall of the global pastoral community into an industrial wasteland and, indeed, associating machines with diabolic machinations, Lowry's oeuvre also complicates this binary. While technology can doubtless be destructive to the natural, Lowry describes it as an appropriate and aesthetic fixture of the modern world. In his project statement to *Hear Us O Lord from Heaven Thy Dwelling Place*, Lowry suggested that, even though the protagonists should, through their life at Eridanus, experience intimations of a lost Paradise, the story "has no 'back to nature' or Rousseau-like message: there is no '*back*' permanently to anywhere, the aim is harmony, so that the view is not to be sentimentalised."[1] Appropriately, while concerned with environmental pollution, the narrator of "The Forest Path to the Spring" finds the oil floating on the water—remnants of a refinery across the bay—"oddly pretty" (236). The brilliance of the sunrise, they come to realize, "isn't pure nature. It's the smoke from those wretched factories" across the bay (235). And in what may be the most poignant moment of industrial pastoralism in all of Lowry's work, he transvaluates the nature-culture dichotomy in favor of the latter, as he contemplates the beauty of the night sky from his wooden shack:

> It was not the moonlight or even the inlet that gave the scene its new, unique beauty, but precisely the oil refinery itself, or more precisely still, the industrial counterpoint, the flickering red pyre of the burning oil waste. Now over the water . . . came the slow warning bell of a freight train chiming on the rail over Port Boden as for a continual vespers, now closer, now receding, . . . but always as if some country sound heard long ago that might have inspired a Wordsworth or Coleridge to describe church bells borne over the fields to some wandering lovers at evening. But whereas the moonlight washed the color out of everything, replacing it by luminousness, providing illumination without color, the flaming burning vermilion oil waste below the moon . . . made the most extraordinary lurid color, enormously real. (*Hear Us O Lord*, 193–94)

By inverting the romantic aesthetic of natural beauty, Lowry in effect suggests the fluid renegotiation, if not the deconstruction, of the opposition of the natural and the technological. In the age of massive resource management and energetic consumption—that is, in a world of consumer culture—"nature" and "technology" have become unstable categories that interpenetrate and mutually implicate one another, even if they are not necessarily interchangeable. Rather than succumb to an unreflective nostalgia for a pretechnological utopia, a Garden without Machine, Lowry in this passage harbors "a nostalgia conscious of itself, a lucid and remorseless dissatisfaction with the present on the grounds of some remembered [imaginary] plenitude" (Jameson, *Marxism and Form*, 82). He advocates a kind of technological *Realpolitik* that mediates between nature and machine without (as in Don DeLillo's sunsets in *White Noise*) fully naturalizing the machine and mechanizing nature. Certainly, throughout *Under the Volcano* especially, Lowry reminds the reader continuously of the ultimately colonial history of the industrialized world, such as Geoffrey's mysterious involvement as a submarine commander during World War I, the Spanish Civil War, and the technological specter of World War II—Geoffrey's vision of "the inconceivable pandemonium of a million tanks" and "the blazing of ten million burning bodies" (375). Such references become a kind of ground music announcing the apocalyptic potential of the machine, while reiterating the political dimension of Lowry's work. The harmonizing tendencies between nature and culture in Lowry's fiction, however, the breakdown of the romantic binary in favor of a fluid interimplication, are more representative of his position toward technology. As he comments in *October Ferry* on their life at the edge of the wilderness, "Back to nature, yet not all the way. Rousseau with a battery radio, Thoreau with a baby Austin" (154).

The Engineer, the Hand, and the Machine

As is generally acknowledged, Lowry was a self-styled possessed artist with an ailing soul who subscribed to the romantic mystifications surrounding the creative process. Writing, in that sense, was fundamentally a matter of inspiration, of a divine afflatus engendering creative activity—a kind of transcendental agency exercised, in Lowry's case, by an infernal demon. Feverish creative outbursts mixed with long creative dry spells suggesting the *agon* and absence of inspiration; unfinished fragments evoking a hieratic celebration of the fragment; an obsessive fear of plagiarism betraying the concern with genius and original creation; and the heavy use of mescal to facilitate artistic activity (Lowry's version of laudanum)—these are the elements of Lowry's romantic self-definition.

Less often acknowledged is Lowry's second artistic self-conception as an engineer of fiction. While Sherrill Grace has demonstrated that Lowry's notion of engineering derives partly from Ortega's theory of self-fabrication in *Toward a Philosophy of History*,[2] Lowry's interest in the nexus of engineering and form is complemented by his recognition of the engineer as an icon of modern ingenuity and the maker of aesthetic design. Witness the following genealogy of engineering: The protagonist of the short story "June the 30th, 1934" was "training to be an engineer at Bradford Tech" before the war (*Psalms and Songs*, 42); Sir Thomas in the story draft "Noblesse Oblige" had been "in the Engineers" during the war, "so that he was an extremely handy man" (UBC SC, 16–6:3); Ethan Llewelyn in *October Ferry* was originally conceived as "an electrical engineer, a child of machinery and the modern age" (*UBC SC,* 12–13:23); the great-great grandfather of the writer in "Elephant and Colosseum" was "not only a poet but a successful inventor and engineer," and the first to propose a scheme for the Panama Canal (*Hear Us O Lord*, 151); and Sigbjørn in "Through the Panama," continuing the lineage, is "hereditarily disposed in favor of canals," because an "ancestor of [his] also had a plan for the Panama Canal that was favorably received." Sigbjørn, in fact, suggests that building a canal is "the first piece of engineering a child does figure out," only to correlate, shortly afterward, the engineering of water with the engineering of words: "the Panama Canal . . . is a work of genius—I would say, like a work of child's genius—something like a novel—in fact just such a novel as I . . . might have written myself" (*Hear Us O Lord*, 58–61).

Lowry, indeed, developed an aesthetic of engineering, a sensibility for the gear-and-girder design of modern technology. In *October Ferry*, Lowry's doppelgänger, Ethan (who is "no enemy per se of the machine: quite the contrary," as Lowry suggested in an early draft [UBC SC, 12–13: 24]), begins to study a series of books on "modern architecture" and discovers himself "to be an admirer of Le Corbusier, Frank Lloyd Wright, and in general agreement with the socio-architectural tenets of Lewis Mumford" (166). These designers and cultural critics, of course, largely formulated the early twentieth-century aesthetic of the machine that encouraged the formal and functional interdependence of structure and machine designs. "The clean surfaces, the hard lines, the calibrated perfection"—this is how Lewis Mumford described the essential components of this sensibility "that the machine has made possible" (*Sticks and Stones*, 178). Ethan remembers Mies van der Rohe's famous dictum, "Less is more" ("Which meant having the greatest effect with the least means," Lowry adds in an early draft [UBC SC, 16–14:207]), and he comes to revision the oil refinery across the bay in precisely such minimalist and functionalist terms. Early in the novel, Ethan deciphers the structure as a portent of infernal doom, when the burned-out S of the SHELL sign looms as HELL, before his emergent engineering sensibilities allow him (and Jacqueline both) to appreciate it "as an entity aesthetically pleasing," whose "cylindrical aluminum retorts and slim chimneys like organ pipes" (158) suggest the engineered blend and proportioned balance of a "well-behaved Meccano structure" (166, 159).

Thus, combined with Ortega's theory of self-construction, modern engineering provided Lowry with a complementary model for his narrative practice—for seeing himself as a technologist of narrative and for using machines as structuring devices in his fiction. The efficient engineering of functionalist machine design, in particular, valorized his belief in the necessity of structure and elegance, and in the structural reciprocity of form and function: the modernist reformulation of the Aristotelian balance between form and content. As well, the clarity of form and minimal structure of engineering restrained Lowry's impulse toward excess, a theoretically infinite proliferation of signs and an uncontrollable encyclopedism that threatened to turn his texts into loose baggy monsters. Engineering, in that sense, afforded him a model of discipline and formal restraint that held in check his drive toward "churriguer-esque" overloading, toward narrative surplus and superfluity (*Sursum Corda!*, 502), while the idea of the romantic craftsman—the erratic man-uscript worker laboring in suffering seclusion—upheld and legitimized the impulsive element of art in his mind. The presence of this dual definition of authorship, the interimplication between "old-fashioned" writing and "contemporary" engineering, is another symptom of the ideological rift traversing Lowry's mental topography.

This schism, the difficulty of writing in a consumer culture, is also visible in the disparity between Lowry's writing practices and the pres-sures of the market, asking (as his publishers did after the publication of the *Volcano*) for the measured production of publishable script. Lowry's prodigious output—the multiple drafts of each of his novels and novel fragments, his prolix correspondence, and his impulse toward incessant note taking—suggests the industriousness of a machine and is easily legible as a response to a publication environment in search of commodifiable text. Yet Lowry's very definitions of authorship deny such regularized production. Just as the writer-qua-craftsman suggests a casual pacing without an eye toward market demands, the engineer, as Lowry understood the profession of engineering, suggests formal el-egance and unique design, not the machine processing of text. (In that sense, the trope of engineering may be a kind of metaphorical compro-mise, since Lowry, for the moment, appears to ignore the engineer's other associations, the exploitation and despoliation of the nature that was so dear to his environmentalist's heart.) As models of writing, both (romantic) craftsmanship and (modern) engineering elevate the creative process and distance writing from the commodifications of the machine age. Similarly, and more important, Lowry did not as a general rule avail himself of the typewriter, the technology that could have enabled the speedy generation of script and the machine that, in theory, "fuses composition and publication, causing an entirely new attitude toward the written and printed word" (McLuhan, 260). Instead, Lowry *com-posed* (both his fictions and most of his letters) in longhand and then, customarily, hired a female typist or, after his second marriage, had Margerie generate a typescript from his holographs (Day, 250, 270).[3] Why did Lowry resist using a machine for the generation of text?

Lowry's resistance to the typewriter is intimately connected to his double conception of the writer as romantic craftsman and romanticized engineer, a conception based on the assumption that both are original creators and "extremely handy" men, the craftsman no less than the engineer. In Lowry's writerly romanticism, the hand—without any mediation beyond quill, pen, or pencil—functions as the central organ of artistic execution, the corporeal transfer point between divine inspiration and human expression. "True art," therefore, is the result of ingenious and unmediated creative activity, whereas "false art" is the product of mechanical intervention, which cheapens both the writing process and the result of that process: the degeneration of art into artefact—into commodity.

In the context of Lowry's infernal productivity, Patrick McCarthy has argued that "Lowry seems precariously poised between romantic and modern concepts of art and reality, a situation that undoubtedly contributed to his anxiety over the nature of his work and made it even more difficult to complete his projects" (210). When Wilderness, suffering from writer's block, begins to admire writers who "turned out their work as easily as if it came out of some celestial sausage machine," and when he yearns to read an undisguised account of a writer's struggle, for "to learn something of the mechanics of his kind of creation, was not that to learn something of the mechanism of destiny?" (*Dark as the Grave*, 12), he crystallizes these conflicting impulses in Lowry's thinking. The repeated (semi)ironic association of writing with mechanical, assembly-line production suggests its status as a commercial trade, as a full-time profession in the age of text-qua-commodity. A writer's success is determined primarily by the steady flow of his productions, his "mechanism of destiny." On the other hand, conceiving of writerly art in such a regularized and unmanual fashion demystifies the essential mystery of creative activity and depreciates the craft of writing.

Equally important, the protocols of standardization and regularization built into the typewriter, as well as the manual dislocations of typing itself, would have militated against Lowry's hand-based definition of art as well. As Friedrich Kittler has demonstrated, the typewriter is a machine fundamentally conceived as a prosthetic device that enables writing when the physiological linkage between eye, hand, and pen—as in the case of blindness—is suspended. Unlike a pen or pencil, a typewriter "creates in the proper position on a paper a complete letter, which not only is untouched by the writer's hand but is also located in a place entirely apart from where the hands work" (Angelo Beyerlen, quoted in Kittler, *Discourse Networks*, 195). For Lowry, this ruptured act of typing, the unlinking of hand and key and the imprint of the letter—and the separation of the body from writing, generally—disrupted the creative continuity between conception and articulation, and along with it authentic *self*-expression, since it compromised Lowry's philosophical belief in the hand as fundamentally human.[4]

Lowry defines virtually all major characters in his fiction in manual terms. Dana Hilliot's "bleeding hands enveloped in cloths" suggest, in juvenile dramatic pose, the stigmata of crucifixion (92); Laruelle's "refined nervous fingers on which he was aware he wore too many rings" reveal his anxious vanity (6). He also saw the hands as the elementary human instrument of artistic expression, and hence self-definition. As a young guitarist, for example, Hugh in *Under the Volcano* is concerned that "the worst possible thing that could befall me seemed some hand injury," suggesting that any incapacitation that prevented him from playing the guitar would deprive him not only of his income but also of his sense of personhood (178). Bill Plantagenet in "Lunar Caustic" ascribes his failure as a pianist to his "small hands," which do not allow him to stretch over an octave (*Psalms and Songs*, 266). And the subtext of *Volcano*'s cinematic leitmotif, *Las Manos de Orlac*, tells of a pianist who, after having lost his hands through a technological mishap—a railway accident—has the hands of a murderer grafted onto him and is fit no longer to express himself artistically but only to commit murder. It is no coincidence that the Chief of Municipality does have "both his trigger finger and his right thumb . . . missing," and eventually collaborates in the murder of Geoffrey (357). Lowry clearly presents the hand as a marker of humanness and *self*-expression—of artistic execution—or, as in the case of a mutilated or "false" hand, as the opposite: a marker of animality or inhumanness. Heidegger observed that "the hand is, together with the word, the essential distinction of man. . . . Man does not 'have' hands, but the hand holds the essence of man, because the word as the essential realm of the hand is the ground of the essence of man" (80). Lowry, who felt a basic congeniality to the philosopher (*Selected Letters,* 210), would have agreed.

Lowry foregrounds this nexus of hand and word and human self, of manual motion and inscription, particularly in Geoffrey Firmin's handwriting. When Laruelle discovers Geoffrey's famous letter fluttering out of Geoffrey's book of Elizabethan plays, he is at first unsure as to the identity of its author. Once he sees "the marginless writing in pencil" on both sides, however, "there was no mistaking . . . the hand, half crabbed, half generous, and wholly drunken, of the Consul himself, the Greek e's, flying buttresses of d's, the t's like lonely wayside crosses save where they crucified an entire word, the words themselves slanting steeply downhill, though the individual characters seemed as if resisting the descent, braced, climbing the other way" (35). Laruelle here recognizes in the idiosyncrasy of Geoffrey's "hand" a window to his soul. He sees Geoffrey's identity encoded in his penmanship; it is transparent in his script. For Laruelle, indeed, as for Lowry, Geoffrey's epistolary characters become, in effect, a shorthand for his character; his tragic stature is literally inscribed in the morphology of his lettering.

That Lowry was, however, disturbed precisely by the erasure of individualized—and hence individuating—lettering, by the erasure of scriptive difference through the standardized type of a keyboard, is evident. Responding to Christopher Isherwood's handwritten letter praising his and Margerie's film script of F. Scott Fitzgerald's *Tender Is the Night*, Lowry observes that "I began to write this letter originally, returning the compliment (which I appreciate) in my own handwriting, such as it is . . . taking advantage of this to write outside"; but after their cats had spilled coconut oil and beer on the letter and it had blown into the sea, he continues, "I gave in, temporarily, to the machine age," resigning himself to type the letter (*Letters*, 208). While other writers of "the machine age," such as Stephen Crane or Stefan George, labored to stylize their handwriting until it became a virtual typeface (Fried, 145–47, Kittler, *Discourse Networks*, 259–64), Lowry saw his "hand" as an anachronistic alternative to the conformity of printed script. In his handwriting, "such as it is" (meaning: an almost undecipherable manuscript, as any Lowry scholar can confirm), he recognized a countermechanical form of expression that undermined the regularity of print. He cultivated precisely what typewriting was designed to erase: manual illegibility. Indeed, Lowry, no less than Geoffrey in *Under the Volcano*, "worked outside, longhand, as he liked to do," while Margerie "sat typing at the desk by the window—for she would learn to type, and transcribe all his manuscripts from the slanting e's and odd t's into neat clean pages" (271). (Furthermore, the implied division between handwriting/outside and typewriting/inside suggests the greater "naturalness" of writing by hand [271].)[5]

Similarly, when Lowry congratulates David Markson on the acceptance of a piece of writing in the *Saturday Evening Post*, he admonishes him "not to lose your style," not to be rewritten by a "magazine noted for 'typing' its authors," and then recommends the cultivation of one's "own self-editorship," so as not to get "caught in a 'type' " occasioned by "the amount of conformity" within the New York magazine industry (UBC SC, 3–10). Though he was not directly concerned with the typewriter *an sich,* Lowry's self-conscious linkage of style and "type" here again hints at his belief in the impossibility of locating the self in a keyboard-generated script; "type" is understood as the absence of an authentic style, as the equidistant spacing between uniform signs that is incompatible with individual self-expression. It is no coincidence that Lowry fetishized a quill-like eagle feather as writing instrument to sign important documents (Day, 293), just as it is no coincidence that Geoffrey has consistently refused to engage Quauhnahuac's "little public scribe," whom both he and Yvonne observe "crashing away on a giant typewriter," to answer some of her letters (53). Since Geoffrey's person-hood is vested in his expressive handwriting, any typed (and dictated) script would "naturally" efface his writerly individuality and represent an unauthentic self to Yvonne. Whereas in longhand the hand *is* the executive organ in the writerly fluidity between mind, pen, and paper, in typing it is reduced to a transfer point of instantaneous physiological impulses and is completely severed from the production of the letter on the page, and hence from the self-qua-letter. In the words of Heidegger, whose logocentrism Lowry would certainly endorse: "Mechanical writing . . . conceals the handwriting and thereby the character. The typewriter makes everyone look the same" (81).

As it turns out, the value of Geoffrey's very life amounts to no more than "a mere misprint in a communiqué" (5). It is through a telegram, a machine-produced and ruptured script, that Geoffrey at the end must die. When the Unión Militar fish Hugh's telegram out of Geoffrey's jacket pocket, they see only cryptic, unpunctuated phrases without semantic cohesion: " . . . *mexpress propetition see tee emma mexworkers confederation proexpulsion exmexixo* . . . " (94). Not being able to decipher the print, and over Geoffrey's protestations that his name is Blackstone, they misconstrue the telegram as "a disguise" that leads quickly to Geoffrey's death (370). This is Lowry's most resonant concluding gesture about the metaphysics of scriptive presence. The telegram functions as an extended—that is, truncated—metaphor for the incapacity of machine-generated text for full communication—whether of information or of personal essence—that, in Lowry's logocentric view, handwriting affords.[6]

Added to the commercial penumbra of typing and the self-falsification of typed script, the linearity of machine-produced text fettered Lowry's fundamentally spatial sensibility as well. Scholars of the orality-literacy debate have observed that, while "chirographic control of space tends to be ornamental, ornate," "typographic control typically impresses more by its tidiness and inevitability: the lines perfectly regular, all justified on the right side, everything coming out even visually, and without the aid of guidelines" (Ong, 122). Such an orderly and linear directness, however, was anathema to Lowry; his mode of composition required, almost at a stroke, the expanse of the whole manuscript page. Whereas in typing the sheet is immovably pressed against the platen to ensure linear script, the blank page and the pen afforded Lowry a compositional fluidity roughly analogous to that of a drawing board. His holographs are notably produced on unlined paper in unleveled handwriting and are replete with asterisks, inserts, and marginal additions that suggest the interweaving of textual fragments into a spatial bricolage that composing on a typewriter would not have allowed him to do. To Yvonne, for example, Geoffrey's poem draft on the back of a menu appears in "handwriting at its most chaotic," as a "wavering and collapsed design, and so crossed out and scrawled over and stained, defaced, and surrounded with scratchy drawings—of a club, a wheel, even a long black box like a coffin—as to be almost undecipherable" (330). In Lowry's pictorial logic, the center and the margin become interchangeable sites of composition that merge into a dialogic field of meaning. Unlike the orderly, segmented sheet of typing, Lowry's page is a space of drafting, a zone of delineation with an almost painterly sense of order: a word picture. As he himself put it (anticipating Ong's comment on chirographic control), the "Blank Page . . . exists but to be decorated" (UBC SC, 3:4).[7]

Thus Lowry was resistant to the technology of typing, even as he relied on typists to translate his turbulent manuscripts into orderly—that is, "professional"—type. He felt that the removal of the hand from the script and thus from the writing subject negated the possibility of manual self-authentication and that the linearity of typing compromised the spatial sensibility so crucial to his hand-based artistic practice. These objections and contradictions are encoded in the first name of his protagonist, Wilderness: Sigbjørn. Lowry was "infatuated with the line through the O" (*Letters*, 327), not only because the letter paradigmatically exemplifies his romantic, essentialized conception of character that is inscribable in a character: for Sigbjørn—a Norwegian surname meaning "Self-bear"—is both baring and bearing the self and has "a considerable emotive value in print that it lacks without the ø" (UBC SC, 3: 5, letter to A. Porter). Lowry was enthralled with this letter also because it hints centrally at his pictorial imagination, because (as double symbol for the wheel and the lowercase zero in European typography) it can

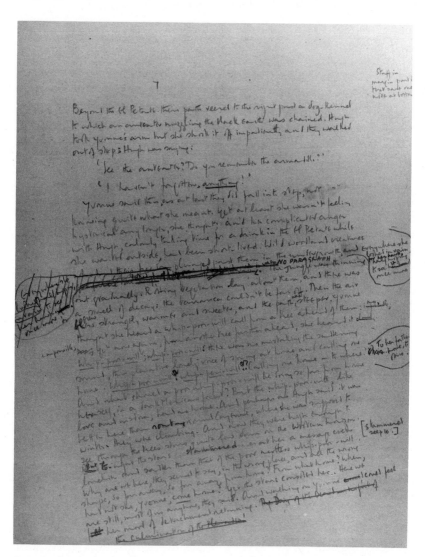

A page of a draft of Malcolm Lowry's *Under the Volcano*. The Malcolm Lowry Archive, Special Collections, University of British Columbia, box 31, folder 10.

represent everything and nothing, and, most important, because the letter suggests his desire to transcend the limitations of typing and printing technology: for when he notes that he had "no such letter on his typewriter" and, in a letter to his publisher, that "it would be understandable if your printer would resent this ø. . . . I shall understand it if your printer should say, 'To ø with Lowry's ø,'" he mischievously suggests that his manual lettering escapes the standardized signs of the keyboard (UBC SC, 3:5, letters to A. Porter and P. Hudson).

Narrative Technology: The Myth and the Machine

What is characteristic of the whole sweep of Lowry's mythopoetics is the constant recourse to technological models as structuring devices or narrative engines, what Lowry was fond of calling "design-governing postures" (*Sursum Corda!*, 321), and Lowry's setting up of a dialectic between that formal modeling and its investment with mythological content. To balance his real fascination with the aesthetic of technology with his equally real reservations toward technology, he endows his machine models with a mythological flush. By tempering their contemporaneity with a gloss of ancientness, he suggests a kind of derealization, a muting of technology's controversial historicity, and hence its ideological liberation for purposes of literary form.

Under the Volcano is engineered around the wheel, one of the most ancient, and hence archetypal, human machines in Lowry's symbolic world. Lowry was explicit about the "very form of the book [which] is to be considered like that of a wheel, with 12 spokes," a wheel he identifies with the Ferris wheel in the square of Quauhnahuac (*Sursum Corda!*, 507, 511).[8] Just as Geoffrey comes to see the Ferris wheel as an aesthetically appealing design of component parts—as "an enormously magnified child's structure of girders and angle brackets, nuts and bolts, in Meccano" (218)—so Lowry assembled *Under the Volcano* from a series of prefabricated chapters into a narrative *Gesamtkunstwerk*. The twelve chapters should be considered as "twelve blocks," since each "is a unity in itself," forming self-contained segments within the narrative architecture (*Sursum Corda!*, 505-6). While the text is given a kind of superstructural cohesion through a twelve-hour period, the Mexican locale, and the texture of the novel's allusive coordinates, Lowry emphasizes the integrity of each chapter through shifting points of view and the absence of connective transitions. *Under the Volcano* was "designed, counterdesigned, and interwelded" (*Sursum Corda!*, 527); it is like the "new kind of pipe" invented by Yvonne's father, "insanely complicated, that . . . none but [he himself] knew how to put . . . together again" (259). The pipe was assembled from a series of components and not perfected until after the Armistice; Lowry's "insanely complicated" novel was assembled from a series of chapter modules at the end of World War II; both emerged after numerous revisions on a master plan known only to their respective creators. The engineer of the pipe, who in Hawaii attempted to "harness the volcano behind their estate to run a hemp machine" (258), has engineered a smoking mechanism playfully reminiscent of a miniature volcano.

This "static" design of *Under the Volcano* Lowry reproduces in the engineering of the text's "internal" dynamic, the montage of its elementary conceptual units: an aggregate of wheels in simultaneous motion. Lowry appears to have drawn for this design from various heuristic models of ancient mythology and scientific traditions. Scholars have already acknowledged that J. W. Dunne's concept of serial time and the Kabbalah inform Lowry's understanding of the universe (New, 11; Ackerly & Clipper, 237). Lowry adopted Dunne's notion of layered enclosure (in the manner of a "Chinese box") as his privileged vision of the universe and, it appears, as one of the models of his text-machine: the novel as a series of integrated wheels. Analogously, Lowry intimates an additional origin of his machine design when he has Geoffrey invoke Ezekiel's vision of the Divine Chariot, "The wheels within wheels this is" (174)—the pivotal revelation of the Kabbalah's *Merkabah* tradition, which describes Genesis as a "Mechanism of Creation" (Blumenthal, 13–51).

In a way similar to Dunne's model of seriality, the Aztecs as well envisioned time and space as "concrete multiplicities" that were integrated into one another "like so many hollow wooden Russian dolls." In their view, this chronotopic intricacy was sanctioned by divine intervention, as was the individual's birth into any one of these space-time loci. Hence they believed that each human being was, by predestination, inserted into a divine order, "the grasp of the omnipotent machine" (Soustelle, 112). This additional mythological influence is all the more likely, given Lowry's suggestion that Geoffrey can be read as a political allegory of Mexico and that he believes himself to be at the mercy of just such a universal machine, the Máquina Infernal.

Superimposed on Aztec mythology, Newton's idea of a "world machine" also seems to have provided Lowry with a model for his novel-machine. Lowry acknowledges Newton's achievement in the marginal gloss of "To the Panama," and in *Under the Volcano* he endows Yvonne, a onetime astronomy major, with dreams "of becoming the 'Madame de Curie' of astronomy," with the knowledge to explain the Newtonian universe to Geoffrey (as Margerie did, in fact, to Malcolm). In *Principia Mathematica*, Newton proposed his well-known galactic machine, in which the "primary planets are revolved about the sun in circles concentric with the sun" (543). And Yvonne, similarly, envisions galaxies as a "sublime celestial machinery," with "the earth itself turning on its axis and revolving around the sun, the sun revolving around the luminous wheel of the galaxy, the countless unmeasured jewelled wheels of countless unmeasured galaxies, turning . . . into infinity" (322).

Thus Lowry's conception of *Under the Volcano* is informed by machine models from various epistemes of human history that merge into a synchronically existent aesthetic coherence and that make the novel an archeology of "world machines": a virtual *paideia* of machine models amalgamated into a kind of archetypal machine. In Ezekiel's "wheels within wheels," especially, Lowry appears to have recognized an Urengine of sorts, whose simplicity was generalized enough to subsume all the other machine models he crammed into his text and a model that allowed him to codify, on the level of form, his fundamental ambivalence toward technology: for when he models his novel-machine on the primordial or scriptural mechanics of the Aztecs and Ezekiel, instead of on contemporary machine design, he suggests again his distance from modern civilization, while yet ratifying the aesthetic of machine design as such. This dialectic toward modern technology makes visible what Fredric Jameson has called "the ideology of form," the political content of narrative reflected in its deep structural design (*Political Unconscious,* 99). In a sense, this content of form *is* the design of *Under the Volcano.* The schismic bar of Sigbjørn that, Cainlike, marks the halves of Sigbjørn's dual sensibilities registers in the split of the novel's form: archaic mechanics, but mechanics nevertheless.

Such machine models begin to emerge in late nineteenth-century European and American fiction as, for example, the steam engines in Dickens, the multiple machines in Zola (*Brooks,* 43–47), or the miniature machine designs in Stephen Crane (*Seltzer,* 113–18). Their inclusion marks the cultural absorption of the machine—its naturalization—for purposes of narrative meditation, and hence indicates the reawakening self-consciousness of fiction and its compositional strategies.

Begun as a metaphor in *Principia,* a model of intelligibility to encode the benevolent causalities of divine design, the notion of a "world machine" functioning with the precision of clockwork was transformed into a "metaphysics of mechanism" that dominated much of the eighteenth and nineteenth centuries (Turbayne, 5). Geoffrey's belief in such a metaphysics is evident primarily in his political passivity and historical fatalism, his assumption that "there's a sort of determinism about the fate of nations" (309). His own fate appears to be similarly determined

by the inexorable logic of his philosophical convictions. Just as the Máquina Infernal spins as one wheel within the wheels of the plaza, and
as such operates as the pivot within Lowry's narrative engine, so Geoffrey, wheeling Ixion-like inside the Infernal Wheel, integrates himself
into a negative, mechanical universe. At the end of the day, once he has
been deprived of his wristwatch—his portable model of the Newtonian
world machine—the effect of what (in his mind) the infernal gods have
orchestrated systematically concludes the narrative: his death.

Yet Lowry's machine model also raises the possibility of construing
Geoffrey's death in terms of not (only) necessitous causation but of
contingency, the coincidental result of multiplying disparate effects. This
model has its origins in Hume's skepticism and the emergent philosophy
of science in the nineteenth century, before leading turn-of-the-century
scientists (such as Karl Pearson in England, Henri Poincaré in France,
and Ernst Mach in Austria) variously qualified the Newtonian paradigm
by advocating a notion of probability distinct from traceable cause and
effect. Witness the following passage from "Ghostkeeper":

> The minute an artist begins to try and shape his materials . . . some
> sort of magic lever is thrown into gear, setting some celestial machinery
> in motion producing events or coincidences that show him that this
> shaping of his is absurd, that nothing is static or can be pinned down,
> that everything is evolving or developing into other meanings, or can-
> cellation of meanings quite beyond his comprehension. There is some-
> thing mechanical about this process, symbolized by the watch: on the
> other hand the human mind . . . which has a will of its own, becomes
> automatically at such moments in touch as it were with the control
> tower of this machinery. (*Psalms and Songs*, 223)

Lowry here suggests, following Romantic tradition, that complete and
conscious control during the creative process is impossible, but that, at
the same time, the artist's unconscious appears to enter into a deep level
of rapport with the changing raw material of art, enabling the imposi-
tion of structure and order anyway, in however preconscious a way.
Recalling Ortega's premise that a writer "becomes an engineer for the
sake of giving [life] form" (223), Lowry affirms engineering as a traditional activity of systematized and ordered shaping, yet this shaping can
accommodate that which is ostensibly nonsystemic and unpredictable:
the engineering of chaos and coincidence. The unforeseeable and coincidental—that which defies system or order—are as integral to that
system as prediction and causation. Accident, contingency, disorder, in-

determinism, and unpredictability fall under the metaphoric orbit of Lowry's machine as much as their systemic absences.

This second epistemology becomes visible in the synchronization of *Under the Volcano*'s final two chapters, when Lowry engineers the convergence of a series of seemingly disparate narrative strands. The virtual simultaneity of the two chapters, and of the coincidental death of Geoffrey and Yvonne, suggest the plotted coordination of the narrative machine. Yvonne, who has haphazardly returned to Quauhnuahuac just that morning, dies under the hoofs of the horse released by Geoffrey as she overhears the fatal shots fired at him; and Geoffrey, through Hugh's cryptic telegram and the membership card in his jacket and his own incriminating pronouncements, becomes the victim of a case of mistaken identity in a politically volatile country. As plot complications thicken and causalities ramify into a diffusive spray of effects, the reader loses sight of those primary, secondary, and tertiary nodes of causation that "determine" the narrative outcomes and contingencies.

Against a background of ticking clocks and "an abysmal mechanic force out of control," a little girl turns "a succession of cartwheels" (347), a level of interlocking alignment that is complicated through images of widening concentric circles: a menu that features "a design like a small wheel round the inside of which was written 'Lotería Nacional Para La Beneficiencia Pública,' making another circular frame"; the beam of Hugh's electric torch that projects a "luminous target, gliding before them, in sweeping concentric ellipticities"; and Yvonne's concluding re-vision of the cars at the fair as "constellations, in the hub of which, like a great cold eye, burned Polaris, and round and round in here they went" (329–35). These multiple concentricities, moving from a miniature wheel to the wheels of galaxies, not only suggest the reopening of the novel's aperture from the microcosmic to the cosmic (and thus balance the novel's topographic satellite image of the opening before zooming in on human destinies); their oscillating radii also delineate the maelstrom of causalities that is only partly accessible to human observation. Determinism, order, and their respective absences, "two distinct forms of destiny [that] each fractionally assumed the other's field" (*October Ferry*, 213), are both engineered into *Under the Volcano*'s narrative engine. Appropriately, Lowry asks his publisher, "Could Thomas Hardy"—that other English romantic (pre)modernist who negotiates the dialectic of causality and contingency—"do as much?" (*Sursum Corda!*, 523).

The Narrative Engine as Difference Engine

As an instrument of production in a classically Marxist sense, the machine is an ideal figure to suggest the "product" manufactured during the reading process—interpretation—and Lowry once remarked that "the wheels within wheels within wheels" keep evolving "newer, yet more wonderful and more meaningless meanings" (*Psalms and Songs*, 227). Such hermeneutic proliferation is fully commensurate with a text stuffed with machines and money, billboards and travel guides, menus and price lists—those exemplary icons of a commodity culture that advertise not the novel's autonomy as a modern objet d'art existing in aesthetic suspension but its condition as a postmodern artefact available for consumption. Thus commodified, *Under the Volcano* operates as an exemplary difference engine, as a *perpetuum mobile* of signification that foregrounds the readers'participation in the production of narrative, in effect making them engineers of meaning themselves.

Gilles Deleuze has, indeed, argued that high modernist and post-modern texts operate as a "literary machine," since "the work of art is a form of production" and as such "does not raise the problem of meaning, but rather of use." What is put to use is the reader's inter-pretive faculties, since each textual sign "according to its nature awakens one [interpretive] faculty or another, but never all together, impels it to the limits of the voluntary and disjunct exercise by which it produces meaning." In Deleuze's model, a text is always "essentially productive—productive of certain truths" (a term synonymous, for Deleuze, with "'interpreting,' 'deciphering,' and 'translating'"), but since readers' imagination is always only partially activated by the provocative nature of the sign, they always only produce partial, nontotalizing interpreta-tions (129–30). The "literary machine" thus enables the making of a product by empowering the reading subject as actual producer to effect a closure of the textual signs; that is, to determine their meaning.

Under the Volcano is such a "literary machine." The production of meaning in Lowry's text, just as in Deleuze's model, depends on the interaction between text and reader, between the spectrum of interpre-tations made possible by the text and the reader's signifying practices. Lowry once remarked that *Under the Volcano* was "written on numerous planes with provision made, it was my fond hope, for almost every kind of reader," suggesting that upon each navigation through the textual topography, and each time in a different register, (ideal) readers can assimilate textual signs into a momentarily coherent interpretation (*Sur-*

sum Corda!, 506). During each reading loop, readers engage not only their idiosyncratic structure of knowledge, their own "text" or *déjà lu,* to speak with Barthes, but also the experience of prior readings of the novel, in turn enlarging "the already read." Each new reading generates, in theory, increasing semantic stratification and is delimited by *Under the Volcano's* horizons of finality (the interplay of what I like to call the novel's grammar of syntax and grammar of allusion). On the one hand, Lowry's involuted and seemingly never-ending syntax suggests a deferral of closure, a kind of semantic suspension that is reinforced by Lowry's rhetoric of rupture. Sentences trailing off into dots, truncated pieces of writing and fragments ending in hyphens form a recurrent part of Lowry's syntactic practice and represent, in their elliptic blankness, the text's semantic lacunae, what Wolfgang Iser has called its "gaps" or "elements of indeterminacy" (*Act of Reading,* 165–78). Complementing this void of signification, however, is the novel's surplus of signification, the *combinatoire* of mythic and esoteric allusions from which readers are asked to fill the textual blanks, only to experience the text's interpretive inexhaustibility, a plenitude that is as infinite and indeterminate as the causalities of its plot. *Under the Volcano* is indeed "a semiotician's dream, or perhaps nightmare," partly because the novel's polyphonic textuality cannot be "activated or apprehended simultaneously" (Asals, 105–7).

What sets *Under the Volcano* apart from most other polysemous texts is Lowry's formal self-consciousness about machine-like meaning making. He achieves the novel's circular design through the chronological dislocation of Chapter I, which—seen through the eyes of Laruelle and taking place precisely one year after the main events—functions as a kind of advance epilogue and which, after a reading of the novel proper, has to be reread so that its cryptic references may be integrated into a "complete" interpretation. Similarly, Lowry effects a circular reading process through the Ferris wheel at the end of Chapter I, which operates "in an obvious movie sense as the wheel of time whirling backwards until we have reached the year before and Chapter II" (*Sursum Corda!,* 511) . The reader who has already returned to Chapter I is thus retransported into the narrative through the Ferris wheel, which mediates between advance retrospective and delayed story and which, after a second reading of Chapters II through XII, makes possible—or better, enforces—a cycle of reading that knows no end, a kind of vicious circle without escape. Even for the reader, it appears, Lowry playfully engineered *Under the Volcano* to be an infernal machine, a conspiracy against the agent whose imagination is required for its coming into being.

More important, Lowry provides a literalization of Deleuze's "literary machine" through the apparatus in the center of his novel-machine, the Máquina Infernal. The Máquina operates as a mechanism of meaning making whose centrifugal acceleration suggests infinite trajectories of reading: an anarchy of meaning. When the Consul, during his infernal ride, believes he has lost the passport he appears not to have brought along, the absence of this text opens a zone of identifications, and hence a zone of interpretations, that extends from No-man to Everyman and thus allows the writer and reader to affix multiple identities to the legally nameless protagonist. During his rotations, Geoffrey indeed assumes the identity of Prometheus, "that poor fool who was bringing light to the world." He is also transformed into Jesus Christ when he sees an inverted—that is, negated—announcement of the coming of the Antichrist ("999") the moment he is crucified on the Machine itself, only to be legible simultaneously as the Antichrist: while Geoffrey (who has just quoted from Ezekiel) in effect sits on the Divine Chariot, the "wheels within wheels" of the infernal machine convert his seat into an Infernal Chariot. Exceeding these immediate correspondences, Geoffrey here also represents the death figure of the tarot cards when he hangs "upside down at the top," and a Don Quixote gobbled up by a windmill (now that he has escaped the supervision of his Sancho Panza, Laruelle), and numerous other identities such as Sisyphus and Ixion, which surround him with various haloes of associations. Each loop in the hermeneutic engine puts a new spin on Geoffrey's identity, allows the loss of his diplomatic—that is, interpretive—immunity to be reinvested with meaning (221–23).

Thus *Under the Volcano*'s explicitly dialogic relationship between text and reading suggests the self-consciously provisional and interactive quality of much of postmodern fiction—what one could call a hermeneutics of instability. The writing on the wall of Señor Bustamente's movie theater, "the hieroglyphic of the times," projects the fundamental undecipherability, and hence multiplicity, of a contemporary world of surfaces, mirrors, and reflections (25). Further, through the infernal machine, Lowry also suggests a meaning-making process akin to the postmodern notion of intertextuality. It is only fitting that a machine that declares itself to be a simulacrum of other literary models and whose constitution from other machine models make it into a veritable pastiche of engines produces a character as an intertextual composite. While

Under the Volcano may not, as one critic has argued, perform the post-modern twist "against interpretation, denying either its possibility or its legitimacy" (Spariosu, 61), the novel's texture suggests that interpretive allegorical frameworks characteristic of much of "high" modernism are becoming destabilized. Certainly, the novel's stylistic and allusive over-loading is in danger of collapsing under its own weight. But Lowry's experimental play with meaning, the writing of a novel in which allusion and cross-reference, depth and surface ("sub"text and "hyper"text) have become the dominating principles of composition, ushers us into a carnival of reading that is quintessentially postmodern in character. *Under the Volcano,* in that sense, engages a Derridean grammatology of citation, a heteroglossia in which linguistic signs reverberate with, and indeed draw from, their prior significations.

This threshold postmodernism, as I like to call it, is also evident in Lowry's engagement with technology. While his writings suggest an incipient critique of corporate capitalism, the agent behind the technological exploitation of Canada's natural resources, he also advocates a measured "conquering of wilderness" as part of the human "process of self-determination" (*Hear Us O Lord,* 205). As well, his enthusiasm for modern engineering and his design of narrative engines signify the modernist preoccupation with form and an appreciation for the aesthetic of technology, while his presentation of the Machine as a technologized figuration of the Fall reveals a fundamentally romantic ethos at odds with the modernist aesthetic. Indeed, Lowry's conflicting definition as narrative engineer and romantic craftsman, his resistance to a mechanized mode of textual production in an age of commodified print, the patina of myth gilding his modern machines, as well as the archaic design of *Under the Volcano*'s formal machine model, all indicate a vast ideological rift, a personal *barranca* between allegiance and resistance to the Machine, and a schizophrenia again encoded in the ø of his protagonist, Sigbjørn. The letter centrally illustrates the double consciousness of Lowry's involvement with technology, the multiple negotiations between "Wilderness" and Civilization, between the Garden and the Machine—what Sigbjørn himself describes as "a conservationist divided against himself" (*Hear Us O Lord,* 95). It suggests a mind torn between an originary desire to return to a prelapsarian, detechnologized world and the realization that technology is a central constituent of the (post)modern condition. For Lowry, as for the romantic tradition from which he emerges, the wedding of technology and nature, of the machine and writing, was indeed a marriage of Heaven and Hell.

Notes

1. The Lowry Archive, Special Collections at the University of British Columbia, Box 12, folder 13, p. 3 (Lowry's emphasis). Further references to the archive appear as UBC SC in the text, followed by box, folder, and page number, if possible.

2. In *Hear Us O Lord,* Lowry suggests that "everybody on this earth is a writer, [in] the sense in which Ortega . . . means it. Ortega has it that man's life is like a fiction that he makes up as he goes along. He becomes an engineer and converts it into reality" (271; see also *Psalms and Songs* 223).

3. The gender issues visible in this manual-technological division of labor are beyond the scope of this chapter. I would like to note, however, that throughout his career, as Gordon Bowker's biography has shown, Lowry hired female typists, apparently feeling so intimidated by the prospect of having to type himself at one point that he agreed to pay one typist (and lover), Carol Phillips, 25% of the future royalties of *Under the Volcano* (Bowker 260), before eventually marrying Margerie Bonner, a "Hollywood secretary" and former silent movie actress with ambitions of becoming a writer (263). What is important here—leaving aside questions of possible chauvinism and Lowry's proverbial clumsiness—is that the typewriter, especially in the case of Malcolm and Margerie, became a kind of mediating device of the creative process. With Lowry drafting in longhand and Margerie typing and adding her own suggestions during the various stages of revision, they engaged in a kind of compositional collaboration that in effect problematizes the notion of self-contained "authorship" ("author" was the occupation both claimed on their marriage license [Bowker, 305]). Work on *Under the Volcano,* in Bowker's words, became a kind of "communal thing," eventually—as Margerie resumed her own writing—developing into "a pattern of companionate authorship and parallel writing" (292; see also Day, 270–71). The deindividuation of typed script, therefore, could be seen as the corresponding mode of a form of textual production that makes individual contributions difficult to identify. The Lowrys are no doubt a necessary addition to Kittler's beginning "register" of "literary typewriting couples of this century" (*Grammophon Film Typewriter,* 311–29). In his words, "text processing today is the business of couples that write together, rather than sleep together" (310; my translation). The Lowrys did not have children (Margerie had had a hysterectomy) but they engendered a brainchild that, in true romantic fashion, assures their literary immortality. In more senses than one, it appears, love may have been mediated by the typewriter.

4. Day explains that Lowry's obsession with hands stems largely from the reputedly small, ugly, and clumsy hands that were "a source of shame and frustration . . . all his life" (90). Day also suggests that the repeated accusation of being a masturbator (evident in *Ultramarine* and Lowry's Haiti notebook [UBC SC, 7:9]) could also be an "important causative factor in [Lowry's] continuing preoccupation with the *hands* of his various protagonists" (130). Within the framework of deconstruction, it would be interesting to investigate the suggestive relays between writing—understood as an infinite chain of supplementation—and masturbation, what Derrida calls ' "That Dangerous Supplement' " (*Of Grammatology,* esp. 141–63).

5. The proto-Marxist attitude behind this hand-machine division and the re-

sistance to the mechanization of the body more generally are reminiscent of the left-wing politics of the Pylon poets, of whom Isherwood was a member, together with W. H. Auden and Stephen Spender, among others. To the bureaucratic structures of capitalist modernity—which they understood as the enabling condition of fascism and individual alienation—they juxtaposed the self-conscious politicalism of their art and actions (and the typewriter, not surprisingly, became an easy symbol of bureaucratic control and "official" textual processing). Moving among intellectual circles in Cambridge in the late twenties and early thirties, Lowry was well aware of the Pylon group. Like his mentor, Conrad Aiken, he was heavily influenced by the "Complex Boys," the "adolescent audens spenders with all their pretty little dexterities, their negative safety, their indoor marxmanship" (Aiken in Bowker, 281; see also Spender, esp. xxv–xxvii). Yet "whereas writers like Orwell, Spender and Auden set out to find the alternative society through organized political action, Lowry embarked on a lonely and seemingly undirected search for an alternative identity in and through literature" (Bowker, xvii). Indeed, while Hugh in *Under the Volcano* may well have been partly modeled on Auden or Spender, for both participated on the Republican side during the Spanish Civil War, the "professional indoor Marxman" (8) is the only one of his Cambridge circle who didn't, instead allaying his guilt by helping to smuggle a shipload of dynamite to the Spanish Loyalist forces.

6. In an early draft of *Volcano*, Lowry identifies his protagonist (then still named "William Ames") with a passport. A marginal note reads "telegram," thus suggesting that Lowry saw the potential for further miscommunication through the telegram's ruptured textuality (UBC SC, 27–5:396, D-draft).

7. Even in "Through the Panama," where Lowry breaks open the scriptive cohesion of the printed page to establish a fluid dialogue between margin, marginal gloss, and "actual" text, he achieves "an amalgam of fragments and typographical dynamics" that sabotages the structured rationality of print (Grace, "Strange Assembly," 192).

8. Scholars have frequently drawn attention to the centrality of the wheel in Lowry's oeuvre. Sherrill Grace, for example, has observed that "the narrative strategy of *Under the Volcano* is best approached through the symbol of the circle or wheel which whirls on forever in the same place" (*Voyage*, 43).

Klaus Benesch

3 Writing Machines

Technology and the Failures of Representation in the Works of Franz Kafka

Writing at a time of tremendous technological and cultural change, Franz Kafka, as a number of critics have noted, was obsessed with the machine and its repercussions on early twentieth-century public and private life.[1] Even at a cursory glance, Kafka's highly fragmented texts abound with allusions to (electro)mechanical "gadgets" such as the typewriter, the telephone, the Parlograph (a forerunner of today's Dictaphone), the phonograph, the camera, and various other icons of modern technology. Moreover, in articulating the ongoing mechanization of both the professional (as epitomized in Kafka's notion of the "office") and the private spheres, Kafka effectively exposed the differentiation and self-alienation of the subject under conditions of modernity.

Kafka's interest in technology was informed primarily by biographical factors. First, there is the purely textual, almost masochistic liaison with Felice Bauer, his would-be fiancée and typist at the Carl Lindström AG, then one of Europe's leading phonograph and record manufacturers. Second, his position as secretary and lawyer at an accident insurance company for industrial workers demanded at least rudimentary expertise in technical matters pertaining to accident prevention and safety regulations (a demand Kafka tried to meet by signing up to audit Professor Mikolaschka's lectures on "mechanical technology" at the Technische Universität Prag [see Bauer-Wabnegg, 347]). And third, Kafka conceived his failing struggle to embark on a career as professional writer, as his diaries and letters readily demonstrate, in terms of a conflict between (hand)writing and dictating, between the genuine, quasi-religious format of the personal manuscript and the ever-proliferating texts of the typewriter, the Parlograph, and the copying machine (the notorious markers of the *office* world).

By the same token, Kafka's attitude toward the new technologies of writing and communication seems to have been ambiguous and shifting. On the one hand, his anxiety about the newly invented *Sprech- und Schreibmaschinen,* to borrow a term from Wolf Kittler, informs much of his earlier fiction, especially his unfinished novel *Amerika,* and "In the Penal Colony," a highly complex novella that explores in gruesome detail the relays of body, machine, and text. On the other hand, Kafka was also aware of the claustrophobic limitations imposed on the original—that is, "literary"—writer. Thus in his short story "The Metamorphosis" he dramatizes the conflicting realms of public and private space by having its protagonist, the young salesman Gregor Samsa, transmogrify into a giant beetle. Incarcerated in his mutilated body (a metaphor of the creative but also distancing power of art), Gregor finally pines away through isolation and disregard. Having been caught between competing modes of representation—his privately written, literary manuscripts (most of which the author had explicitly excluded from publication) and the mechanically reproduced texts of his office—Kafka was well qualified to give voice to the ambivalent status of the modern artist.

The Authorial Body and the Letter That Kills

Kafka's diaries, in which he commented extensively on the painful genesis of his literary works, bespeak a neoromantic notion of authorship and authenticity. For the professional producer of countless business letters, statistical evaluations, and legal documents, all of them dictated into either the typewriter or Parlograph, the act of writing *literature* still possessed a mystic or, in the words of Walter Benjamin, "auratic" dimension. In his now classic essay "The Work of Art in the Age of Mechanical Reproduction," Benjamin describes Western Art as being on the verge of a fundamental shift from originality to repetition, from the unique and authentic work of art to the mass-produced, dissimulating works of the machine. "Around 1900 technical reproduction had attained a level that permitted it to affect all transmitted works of art and to subject the impact of works of art to profound changes; moreover, technical reproduction conquered a place of its own among the artistic processes" (219). One of the key terms of the essay is "aura," the ritual function of art, its ongoing negotiation between distance and presence, between authenticity and artificiality. According to Benjamin, aura occurs only in the original and unique work of art, and for this reason "it does not permit of reproduction nor replica" (223).

Although Benjamin focuses mainly on painting, photography, and film, his argument applies to written texts as well. Here, too, technological progress and the concomitant proliferation of potential forums for amateur writers (newspapers, professional and special-interest magazines, dime novels, serials, etc.) increasingly began to blur the distinction between author and reader, between the "real" and the "sham" writer. In the age of mechanical reproduction, as Benjamin explained in more than one essay, "at any moment the reader is ready to turn into a writer" (232). Because of the ongoing differentiation of work process, the majority of workers are turned into "experts" (if only in a very circumscribed and specialized area), which is also to say that they are turned into potential authors: "As expert, . . . even if only in some minor respect, the reader gains access to authorship" (232). By thus relating the oft-quoted death of the (literary) author to the burgeoning means of reproduction (Benjaminean authors simply suffer from their increasing numbers), Benjamin, as early as 1934, presaged a phenomenon that was to become one of the basic concerns of poststructuralist theory. Moreover, inasmuch as he attributes the disappearance of authorship solely to technological progress, Benjamin touched upon a recurring theme of Western cultural discourse; that is, an essentialist, technophobic anxiety about the loss of authorial control, a fear that resurfaced with each invention of new modes of writing and communication.

Kafka seems to have been keenly aware of this development. In his diaries, his private letters, and some of his earlier narratives he took issue not only with the profane and "illiterate" setting of the office (the primary locus of the dilettante) but also with the new writing technologies that accompany it. In a revealing entry in his diary of October 3, 1911, he tells of an instance that makes apparent the precarious status of authorship in an age of mechanical reproduction. The passage bears being quoted at length:

> While dictating a rather long report to the district Chief of Police, toward the end, where a climax was intended, I got stuck and could do nothing but look at K., the typist, who in her usual way, became

especially lively, moved her chair about, coughed, tapped on the table and so called the attention of the whole room to my misfortune. The sought-for idea now has the additional value that it will make her be quiet, and the more valuable it becomes the more difficult it becomes to find it. Finally I have the word "stigmatization" and the appropriate sentence, but still hold it all in my mouth with disgust and a sense of shame as though it were raw meat, cut out of me (such effort has it cost me). Finally I say it, but retain the great fear that everything within me is ready for a poetic work and such a work would be a heavenly enlightenment and a real coming-alive for me, while here in the office, because of so wretched an official document, I must rob a body capable of such happiness of a piece of its flesh. (*Diaries*, 76–77)

Contrary to authoring an official document, Kafka seems to imply here, poetic writing is rather unmediated and natural, a gushing forth of textual bits and pieces that symbolically contain and represent the creative subject. As Wolf Kittler has argued, this entry instances a basic dilemma of Kafka's earlier works ("Schreibmaschinen, Sprechmaschinen," 85). On the one hand, it registers the mutilating effects of highly organized work forms: body and text are irreversibly separated by the typewriter/ typist. (Kafka, as we shall see, repeatedly conflates the tool and the user into a sort of animated writing machine.) And on the other hand, the professional administrator at the government-sponsored Arbeiter-Unfall-Versicherungs-Anstalt dreams up a fairyland of creative writing, a utopian space where the exigencies of rationalization and technology are presumed to be suspended. If we follow Kittler's reading, this was Kafka's principal and most fatal illusion. To write, be it poetically or officially, always is to kill (when the writing is mechanically reproduced), always to bury the subject *in* and *by* what is written; hence Kafka seems to be entangled not so much in a conflict between body and machine as in the paradoxical signification of writing as such. This view, however, needs to be amended.

The modern understanding of literary work, as many critics have noted, dates back to the Enlightenment and its notion of man (or rather, *le citoyen*) as an individual, a distinct, rational human monad, incorporated into the social body by free will and consent. Similar to the rising bourgeois, the modern artist refuses to accept transcendent standards (established mainly by way of tradition), repudiates all judgment outside his own universe of production, transforms him- or herself from an imitator or *homo faber* into a performer of "authentic," original acts.

The Letter That Kills: collage by Oliver Veder

In doing so, as Martha Woodmansee puts it, "from a (mere) vehicle of preordained truth—truth as ordained either by universal human agreement or by some higher agency—the *writer* becomes an *author*" (429). By the same token, "true" art (as opposed first to mere craftsmanship and later to mass production, popular taste, and kitsch) was increasingly considered an antidote to the *Uneigentlichkeit*, the differentiation and self-alienation, of modern life. "From the mid–eighteenth century to the very recent past," writes Jochen Schulte-Sasse, "art has . . . been posited as a utopian space within modernity" (93). In his illuminating essay "The Prestige of the Artist under Conditions of Modernity," Sasse describes the ambiguous role that art played as a sanctuary for the endangered autonomy of the modern self. "As a functionally differentiated space," he explains, "art under modern conditions is at once structurally equivalent to other differentiated activities and burdened with the primary function of sublating differentiation in a reconciliatory manner" (87). In other words, while trying to exist wholly by the laws of its own being, modern art simultaneously attempts to provide symbiotic imaginary experiences.

It is precisely this notion of art as an imaginary counterspace that Kafka appeals to in many of his literary as well as autobiographical texts. For Kafka, writing certainly is not a marker of the subject's killing and burial. On the contrary, as the following commentary on his short story "The Judgement" suggests, he envisions artistic production as a life-giving activity, a putting forth of his other, his *true* self: "While I read the proofs of *The Judgement*, I'll write down all the relationships which have become clear to me in the story as far as I now remember them. This is necessary because the story came out of me like *a real birth*, covered with filth and slime, and only I have the hand that can reach to the body itself and the strength of desire to do so" (*Diaries*, 278; my emphasis). True, in the story it is indeed the letter—in both of its meanings, oral verdict and mailed document—that kills. Yet, as Kafka's commentary reveals, the father's death sentence for his fictional son (which, significantly, is to be executed by drowning) will only prepare the way for his rebirth as author, as originator of a written text. As I have mentioned, our modern concept of authorship is deeply rooted in the nineteeenth-century Romantic understanding of creative genius. Though pertaining to works of art in general, this Romantic idea of the original genius most rigorously held sway in the realm of writing. Only consider the *terminus technicus* for the one who writes, the *auctor* or, in its modern variant, the *author*. It is indeed striking how the cultural ascription of the (obviously male) capacity to beget, to "father," a text coincides with the very beginning of prose writing itself. In one of the earliest discourses on the effects of literacy, Plato's *Phaedrus*, writing is described as an act of sowing "immortal" seed. And according to Edward Said, an author is "a person who originates or gives existence to something, a begetter, father, or ancestor, a person also who sets forth written statements." If we follow Said's analysis, *auctoritas* or authorship literally signifies invention and production, the power of "an individual to initiate, institute, establish." Hence the product of this power, the written text, always is something new; that is, again in the words of Said, an "increase over what had been there previously" (48–49). As feminist critics have convincingly argued, it was by way of highlighting this gendered, paternal conception—which had already been associated with the process of writing for centuries—that the modern view of the writer as originator and proprietor of his text was established.

There is, however, also an alternative mode to constructing an all-male image of writerly work. If the forces of reproduction were essentially female (as Thomas Laqueur's anatomist discourse of gender and sex in the nineteenth century has suggested), how then could authorship, the putting forth of literary texts, prevail as a domain of exclusively male activity? To circumvent the irritating paternalism that accompanies authorship, various nineteenth-century writers had recourse to a refined if queerly androgynous model. "As naturally as the oak bears an acorn, and the vine bears a gourd, man bears a poem" (91). Written at the dawn of American industrialism, these lines by Henry David Thoreau (like Kafka, a rigorously technophobic writer) convey an organic conception of authorship, a vision of literary work based on sexual, procreative processes. Yet the adoption of the female reproductive role had its pitfalls, too.

Because of their reproductive capacities, women were cast as bound up with the realm of matter and practical reason. (It is certainly not by coincidence that the textile looms at Lowell, Massachusetts, the first large-scale production site in America, were operated exclusively by women.) It is thus only by replacing female reproductive power with an alternative practice, at once generative and spiritual, that Romantic authors were able to reconcile the forces of organic and artistic production. Insofar as he represents nature's procreative principle on a more refined and consummate level, the artist simultaneously incorporates and transcends the feminine. While negotiating the antagonistic powers of generation for his artistic purposes, the man of art reaches for a subtler, ethereal form of paternity. However frail and transient his imaginative child may be, as carrier and conduit for an original idea it takes on a quality more real than reality itself. "When the artist rose high enough to achieve the beautiful," as we learn in the concluding paragraph of Hawthorne's story "The Artist of the Beautiful," "the symbol by which he made it perceptible to mortal senses became of little value in his eyes while his spirit possessed itself in the enjoyment of the Reality" (475). In construing writing as a form of maternal labor, Kafka shares this Romantic notion of art as a natural, cogenerative activity. Whenever Kafka the secretary privately buries himself in writing, he does so only in order to restore Kafka the poet (that is, his second, literary self).[2] As he said in a letter to Felice Bauer in 1913, "I am awake only among my imaginary characters" (*I Am a Memory*, 81). Rather than from the deadening effects of writing as representation, Kafka's principal conflict thus seems to result from an anachronistic representation of writing, a concept of authorship completely out of synch with the ongoing mechanization of the word in modern society.

A Passion for Machinery

During the latter half of the nineteenth century, artistic production became a contested issue with social as well as aesthetic repercussions. The artist struggling to develop a sense of professional identity was both accorded a position as inventor and originator and challenged the moment this privilege was bestowed. As a result of the ongoing differentiation under "conditions of modernity," the *fine* and the so-called *useful* arts—a telling ideological term for the gamut of manufacturing and mechanical trades—increasingly were set against each other.[3] Its self-righteous claim to sublimity notwithstanding, the former were considered as just another specialized sector of modern society and were thus continuously forced to compete with a highly effective culture of mechanical invention and production. Given the ubiquitous technological progressivism of the era, the ambitious artist had to face up to a threefold dilemma: First, how should one respond to the utilitarian stance of modern society; should one dismiss or embrace (as Filippo Tomasso Marinetti and the Futurists, for example, did) the rapid modernization and mechanical ingenuity? Second, how could one represent one's writing as work, as a measurable, substantial figure comparable to (and competitive with) the productive power of the ever-increasing industrial workforce? And third, how could one vindicate a claim to artistic authenticity at a time when new means of mechanical reproduction were already threatening to substitute the sham, the duplicated/duplicating work of the machine, for the original work of art? Many of Kafka's literary texts engage these questions in terms of a failure of representation. They describe the implacable onrush of modern technology as the nemesis of authorship, the undoing of the "existential," physical relation or connectedness between body and text. Two of his earlier works, the unfinished novel *Amerika* and his disconcerting, mysterious novella "In the Penal Colony," are especially noteworthy in this context.

"I have always had a passion for machinery... and I would have become an engineer in time, that's certain, if I hadn't had to go to America" (*Amerika*, 6).[4] These lines by the novel's young picaresque hero, Karl Rossmann, set the register for the various discourses on technology that are found throughout *Amerika*. The stoker, to whom Karl's words are addressed here, is only the first of a number of characters directly associated with machinery: the obscure, unemployed mechanics Robinson and Delamarche, the telegraphists at Uncle Jacob's office, the young stenographer and typist Therese Berchtold, and the numerous lift boys and operators at the Hotel Occidental. Moreover, in his first novel Kafka has invented an American cityscape blistering with mechanical gadgets, steel structures, and automobiles. Although many of his representations of American technology are wildly inaccurate, they nevertheless create a convincing fictional world where mechanization has taken command. This is how Karl describes the view from the balcony of his uncle's mansion, apparently located in downtown Manhattan:

> From morning to evening and far into the dreaming night that street was the channel for a constant stream of traffic which, seen from above, looked like an inextricable confusion, forever newly improvised, of foreshortened human figures and the roofs of all kinds of vehicles, sending into the upper air another confusion, more riotous and complicated, of noises, dust and smells, all of it enveloped and penetrated by a flood of light which the multitudinous objects in the street scattered, carried off and again busily brought back, with an effect as palpable to the dazzled eye as if a glass roof stretched over the street were being violently smashed into fragments at every moment. (39)

It is not surprising that Kafka, in the heyday of Fordism, would comment on the ubiquity of the automobile and its increasing influence on metropolitan life. More remarkable is that he obsessively conjoins the various icons of modern technology with aspects of writing and representation. As one can easily see, the passage culminates in a metaphor of warped vision ("foreshortened human figures") and unstable reflection: "the multitudinous objects" appear to the dazzled eye "as if a glass roof over the street were being violently smashed into fragments at every moment." Given the chaotic, ever newly improvised confusion of the technological cityscape, Kafka seems to imply, there is no point of reference, no straightforward representation outside the maelstrom of its divergent forces. For the uninitiated observer, as Karl self-consciously remarks, this powerful spectacle of signifiers gone astray may eventually lead to "sheer ruination." In order thus to protect the newcomer from the hazards of an epistemological breakdown, "the solitary indulgence of idly gazing at the busy life of New York" has to be avoided by all means.

Among the numerous mechanical gadgets that had already begun to change dramatically the life of turn-of-the-century Europeans and Americans alike, none was to excel the new technologies of communication and visual representation. The daguerreotype (and the later, more "accurate" forms of photography) "erased the difference between the original and the reproduction" and were thus calling "into question some of the fundamental values of cultural entitlement" (Orvell, 37). What had formerly been the privilege of artistic genius, the probing and metaphoric representation of the real, was increasingly associated with the photographic eye; that is, a mechanical—and therefore "objective"— means of reproduction. Sometimes, as an advertisement for a *Portfolio of the Chicago World's Fair* in 1894 claimed, the photograph was even considered more "real" than the thing itself: "In some respects this splendid portfolio is better and more to be desired than an actual visit to the Exposition, for through the magic agency of photography the scenes are transferred in marvelous beauty and *permanent* form to the printed pages" (quoted in Orvell, 75; my emphasis).

With the dawn of photography, however, writing not only ceased to be the predominant means of storing data. The ever-increasing distribution of photographic images also helped to shape what Jean Baudrillard calls the hyperreal world of simulacra and simulations: in the age of technologically recorded sense data, the real enters into competition with the nonreal; put differently, the imaginary loses its representational value and thereby turns into pure simulacrum. With the proliferation of sights and sounds in acoustic and visual media, "the real of speaking," as Friedrich Kittler has observed, "took place in the gramophone; the imaginary produced in speaking or writing belonged to film" (*Discourse Networks*, 246).

In *Amerika*, visual representations not merely are foregrounded as part of the plot, they figure as an instance in the composition of the novel itself. On September 25, 1912, Kafka noted in his diary: "This evening tore myself away from my writing. Movies in the National Theater. Miss O., whom a clergyman once pursued. She came home soaked in cold sweat. Danzig. Life of Körner. The horses. The white horse. The smoke of powder. 'Lützows wilde Jagd' " (278). This entry, as Max Brod explained, is followed by the final version of "The Stoker," the first chapter of *Amerika*. It is thus possible to assume that Kafka's renewed interest in the novel—as well as his final revision of its opening chapter—was inspired by his visit to the movie theater.[5]

But photography is equally highlighted as a narrative and structural device in the novel. Among the few private things that the young immigrant desperately tries to safeguard is a photograph of his parents. Karl, who has been expelled from his Prague home after allegedly impregnating a servant (a charge that in itself is due to a gross misrepresentation of the facts), muses extensively on the representational qualities of the picture. Again, the entire scene deserves to be quoted:

> Then he took up a photograph of his parents, in which his small father stood very erect behind his mother, who sat in an easy-chair slightly sunk into herself. One of his father's hands lay on the back of the chair, the other, which was clenched to a fist, rested on a picture-book lying open on a fragile table beside him. . . . [He] tried to catch his father's eyes from various angles. But his father refused to *come to life*, no matter how much his expression was modified by shifting the candle into different positions; nor did his thick, horizontal moustache look in the least *real*; it was not a good photograph. His mother, however, had come out better; her mouth was twisted as if she had been hurt and were forcing herself to smile. It seemed to Karl that anyone who saw the photograph must be so forcibly struck with this that he would begin immediately to think it an exaggerated, not to say foolish, *interpretation*. How could a photograph convey with such complete certainty the secret feelings of the person shown in it? (103–4; my emphases)

The passage hinges on the very question that is central to all forms of visual and pictorial reproductions: How far can a picture be said to be true to life, to come out as a true representation of the real? Kafka's comment on this issue is clear-cut but treacherous. Although Karl tries to catch his father's eyes from various angles, his father's picture stubbornly refuses to come to life, to become real. Its elusive quality seems to exemplify a striking feature of photography at large: the tendency of the photograph to "defamiliarize" the familiar, to make strange and deform even the most banal objects of everyday life. Their apparent visual similarities notwithstanding, model and portrait, object and photographic reproduction, will always be dissociated by the eye of the camera, the disruptive click of the mechanical shutter. It is disturbing, however, that Kafka at first attributes this flaw not to photography as a mode of representation but to the way in which this particular picture was taken: it is simply not a good photograph. Unlike his father, his mother had come out much better. In fact, she is mirrored so true to life that Karl ponders how a photograph could "convey with such complete certainty the secret feelings of the person shown in it." Kafka's answer to this rhetorical question directly leads us from the realm of visuality to the techniques of writing and poetic imagination: The picture triggers an interpretive, poetic act. Vis-à-vis the visual explicitness of the photograph, storytelling—for that is what is involved here—may very well be "an exaggerated, not to say foolish, interpretation." Yet, as Kafka observed in an interview with Gustav Janouch, if "we photograph things in order to drive them out of our mind," it is only our imagination that can bring them back to life (quoted in Leblans, 52). The barrenness of pictorial representations, to venture a pun on Edward Young's famous phrase, draws forth the creative pen of an original writer who enlivens the picture. ("The pen of an original writer," says Young, "out of a barren waste calls a blooming spring" [319].)

When we read on, it becomes clear that in the above passage it is actually *writing* that is at stake, not the representational qualities of photography per se. Taking a second look at the photograph of his mother, Karl "noticed his mother's *hand,* which dropped from the *arm* of the chair in the foreground, near enough to kiss. He wondered if it might not be better to *write* to his parents, as both of them (and his father very strictly on leaving him at Hamburg) had enjoined him" (104; my emphases). It is therefore simply by gazing at the corporeal image of the hand that the act of writing or, more precisely, of writing letters as an alternative mode of representation is evoked. (Sure enough, it is again the *female* body by which this metaphorical twist is enacted.) As technology takes command of the writing process, however, this conflation of body and text—a core concept of Kafka's aesthetic—becomes increasingly problematic. Under the impact of new forms of transmission and communication, the writer turns into a cyborg, into an animated writing machine. As Karl's description of the telegraphist at his uncle's office makes plain, the movement of the hand, rather than being guided by the authorial brain, is now induced by electric impulses:

> In the glaring electric light Karl saw an operator, quite oblivious to any sound from the door, his head bound in a steel band which pressed the receivers against his ears. His right arm was lying on a little table as if it were strangely heavy and only the fingers holding the pencil kept twitching with inhuman regularity and speed. In the words which he spoke into the mouthpiece he was very sparing and often one noticed that though he had some objections to raise or wished to obtain more exact information, the next phrase that he heard compelled him to lower his eyes and go on writing before he could carry out his intention. (47–48)

Via the steel band pressing the receiver to his brain, the telegrapher's body is continuously tuned to the rhythm, the "inhuman regularity" of the machine. He is muted by the sheer quantity of incoming messages, and his hand becomes a fleshly extension of the apparatus, a tool for "downloading" the system's encoded signals.

It is indeed striking how the violence attached to this encroachment of the body by the machine reflects Kafka's own painful experience with office technology, especially dictating machines. Based on Edison's discovery of the principle of voice recording, the Parlograph—a recording machine produced by the Carl Lindström AG—used a wax cylinder to record and transcribe the spoken word. According to *The Encyclopedia Americana*, the method required three working units: first, the dictating or recording unit used by the person giving dictation; second, the transcribing unit, which allows the recorded material to be played back, so that it may be transcribed into typewritten form; and third, the so-called shaving unit, a device for shaving off the layers of wax that contain the recording ("Business Machines and Equipment," 74e). In a letter to his fiancée, who had sent him advertisements for the Lindström Parlograph, Kafka betrays his apprehension of this new medium: "He who dictates is master, but faced with a Parlograph he is degraded and becomes a factory worker whose brain has to serve a whirring machine. Think how a long chain of thoughts is forced out of the poor, naturally slow-working brain!" (*I Am a Memory*, 71). This remark on the factory worker ties in with an early diary entry that articulates his conservative, technophobic views in an equally telling vein:

> Yesterday in the factory. The girls, in their unbearable dirty and untidy clothes, their hair disheveled as though they had just got up, the expressions on their faces *fixed* by the incessant noise of the transmission belts and by the individual machines, automatic ones, of course, but unpredictably breaking down, *they aren't people,* you don't greet them when you bump into them, if you can call them over to do something, they do it but return to their machine at once, with a nod of the head you show them what to do, they stand there in petticoats, they are at the mercy of the pettiest power and haven't enough calm understanding to recognize this power and placate it by a glance, a bow. (*Diaries,* February 5, 1912, 23; my emphasis).

This is certainly not the Whitmanesque stance of the poet hailing the modern age and its corollary, rapid technological progress. Rather, Kafka chimes in with the antimodernist discourse of humans becoming machines.

Kafka's view of the new technologies of writing and transmission is marked by his paradoxical concept of the body-text relation. He conceives of writing as a bodily experience. That is, the written text, as Malcolm Pasley writes, closely "relates to the physical act of writing and even to the small calamities that can occur during the writing process" (203). As Pasley has shown, the genesis of Kafka's manuscripts is closely linked to the material circumstances of his writing: Kafka's preference for the fountain pen, the reduced format of the notorious miniature notebooks he used, and even the tiny room on the Alchimistengasse where many of his earlier pieces originated. "Wherever Kafka mentions a writing instrument in his texts, one can be fairly sure that his own instrument has occupied him in some way shortly beforehand" (202). In his analysis of Kafka's manuscripts, Pasley comes up with the following description of the author's writing method: First, Kafka preferred spontaneity, "the greatest abbreviation of the passage from an idea to its written form"; second, fluidity, the ongoing, uninterrupted movement of the fountain pen; and third, the stress on the open, unprejudiced quality of "writing that doesn't know where it is going and lets itself be carried along by the developing story" (209). It is obvious that Kafka's idiosyncratic writing methods were directly affected by modern technology. "Whereas handwriting is subject to the eye," as Friedrich Kittler argues, "a sense that works across distance, the typewriter uses a blind, tactile power" (*Discourse Networks*, 195). Moreover, automatic writing exhibits a tendency toward acceleration. With dictation always racing ahead of the pen, it denies the generation of meaning through—as in traditional handwriting—the slow inscription of sensible data on the page. By way of its continuous mechanization, the word, as contemporary writers complained, "is gradually losing credit." The ability to transfer the process of inscription to a nonsensible apparatus, which then writes with superhuman precision, had thus a tremendous impact on the discourse network of 1900. In Kafka's pretechnological worldview, the hand still represents the pen represents the text represents the man; in the real world of the turn of the twentieth century, however, body and text always represent only the machine.

Among his literary works none addresses this failure of representation under conditions of modernity as uncompromisingly as the ominous novella "In the Penal Colony." As Kafka has repeatedly remarked, there is an ontological, almost uncanny relation between *Amerika* and "In the Penal Colony." He had written the latter story during the first half of a two-week vacation, and had finished at least one chapter of the former during the second half. But correspondences do not end here. As we have already seen in his longer narrative, Kafka articulates his anxiety about technology in terms of humans becoming a machine; "In the Penal Colony" he even goes one step further. Not only does the machine assume significance as *the* central narrative event, the story also encapsulates the disconcerting vision of the body as palimpsest; that is, its painful but illegible inscription by a writing apparatus.

In Kafka's most infamous fictional machine, writing and representation meet with unprecedented clarity. Though this exotic, awe-inspiring apparatus was designed as a *machine à tuer,* an instrument for execution, its most prominent feature is its capacity to write on flesh, to inscribe on the prisoner's body "whatever commandment [he] has disobeyed" (144). As the officer in charge of the machine explains, there is no trial, no formal hearing before the actual execution: "If I had first called the man before me and interrogated him, things would have got into a confused tangle. He would have told lies, and had I exposed these lies he would have backed them up with more lies, and so on and so forth. As it is I've got him and I won't let him go" (146). Hence, it is only at the moment of his punishment that the prisoner becomes aware of both his alleged crime and the sentence that has been passed on him. "There would be no point in telling him," the officer smugly remarks, "he'll learn it on his body."

Shortly after the completion of "In the Penal Colony," Kafka wrote a compelling parable that was among the few pieces to be published during his lifetime. The story, ambiguously titled "Before the Law," dramatizes the impossibility of gaining access to the law; that is, of objectifying a general truth in individual terms.[6] He who inquires about the law behind the law, Kafka tells us, will ultimately pine away in waiting for the opening of a door that has stood wide open all along. The meaning of the law, therefore, is essentially deferred; it materializes only at the moment one stops questioning it. This somber vision of an abstract power that always falls short of its individual representation equally inspires Kafka's treatment of the law and its mechanical enforcement in "In the Penal Colony." Here, however, the babble of possible interpretations seems to make way for the fiction of its literal transcription: the letter(s) of the law become instrumental in the process of carrying out the very sentence they stipulate. Or, to put it differently, by way of mechanically reproducing the verdict on the victim's body (a procedure that slowly kills him), law, judgment, and actual punishment fall into one.

That Kafka articulated the merging of different levels of the law in terms of a writing machine is by no means accidental. Even though critics dispute the roots and historical sources of this infernal apparatus, it is quite plausible that Kafka, a lawyer, should probe the gains and losses of mechanical reproduction for legal purposes. As Wolf Kittler observes, Kafka's interest in the interfaces of writing, jurisdiction, and machinery may well have been instigated by the use of Parlographs in the courtroom as a means of turning *statements* into *facts*. According to Kafka's academic teacher Hans Gross, the search for legal evidence equates the scientific search for causality. Gross and his colleagues were looking for ways to circumvent the trapdoors of interpretation (i.e., to prove the defendant's guilt by rhetorically deconstructing his statement) and thus to subject all accessible data to scientific analysis. By way of phonographic reproductions and typescripts, forensic psychology at the turn of the twentieth century wanted to exclude "faulty" representations due to the unreliability of aural-oral discourse.[7] Indeed, the apparent similarities between the mechanisms of early recording machines (such as the phonograph) and the writing apparatus of "In the Penal Colony" are remarkable.

"You see," said the officer, "there are two kinds of needles arranged in multiple patterns. Each long needle has a short one beside it. The long needle does the writing, and the short needle sprays a jet of water to wash away the blood and keep the inscription clear. Blood and water together are then conducted here through small runnels into this main runnel and down a waste pipe into the pit." (147)

Through its use of needles and its sophisticated drainage system, Kafka's penalizing apparatus clearly recalls the reproductive technology of the phonograph (which deciphered a coded diagram needle-imprinted on a wax cylinder). In the story, the recording device is designed to allow for the shortest possible distance between the law and its various representations. Fed with the commander's instructions, the machine directly reproduces the trespassing act on the body of the perpetrator, and in doing so supplies him, at least in the exalted terms of the executioner, with a wondrous form of *enlightenment*. Here, too, a lengthy "reproduction" of the original text seems appropriate:

> The Harrow is beginning to write; when it finishes the first draft of the inscription on the man's back, the layer of cotton wool begins to roll and slowly turns the body over, to give the Harrow fresh space for writing. Meanwhile the raw part that has been written on lies on the cotton wool, which is specially prepared to staunch the bleeding and so makes all ready for a new deepening of the script. . . . The first six hours the condemned man stays alive almost as before, he suffers only pain. . . . But how quiet he grows at just about the sixth hour! Enlightenment comes to the most dull-witted. It begins around the eyes. From there it radiates. A moment that might tempt one to get under the Harrow oneself. Nothing more happens than that the man begins to understand the inscription, he purses his mouth as if he were listening. You [the explorer] have seen how difficult it is to decipher the script with one's eyes; but our man deciphers it with his wounds. To be sure, that is a hard task; he needs six hours to accomplish it. By that time the Harrow has pierced him quite through and casts him into the pit, where he pitches down upon the blood and water and the cotton wool. Then the judgement has been fulfilled, and we, the soldier and I, bury him. (149–50)

Yet in the end, the meticulously envisioned conflation of body and text only produces the horrors of machinery run amok. The Harrow is not writing, the Bed is not turning, and even "the last action failed to fulfill itself, the body did not drop off the long needles, streaming with blood it went on hanging over the pit without falling into it" (165). The machine, if we follow Kafka's allegorical tale, represents only its own failure, a cogwheeled nightmare of sheer (but indifferent) power. Moreover, where there should have been the inspired gaze of enlightenment, "no sign was visible of the promised redemption" (166). The officer, who has finally given in to the temptation of getting under the Harrow himself, searches his textualized body in vain for what he believes his former victims must have experienced: the sensation of something more real than just the brutal reality of the machine.

"The Nature Theater of Oklahoma": America as a Technological World Elsewhere

It is significant that Kafka, who never left the confines of Central Europe, located (at least) two of his probings of the body-machine-text complex in the New World: his first novel, *Amerika,* and "In the Penal Colony," which allegedly is set in New Caledonia.[8] In both cases Kafka seems to have been intrigued by the utopian, ahistorical quality already ascribed to this part of the world for centuries. Not only was America traditionally a powerful signifier of new beginnings and uninhibited progress; at the end of the nineteenth century it also became the archetypical locus of technological innovation and machine culture. Although Kafka thoroughly noticed Edison's visit to Prague in 1911, his interest in the state of American technology was rather vague and imaginative.[9] Informed by its mythopoeic quality, Kafka seems to have used America merely as a foil for his biographically coded, technophobic fictions.

Kafka's texts repeatedly question the status of the body in modern technological society. In so doing they not only foreshadow the present-day concerns about the vanishing point of the real—an anxiety, shared by conservatives and liberals alike, which almost always boils down to the fear of a fraying body, losing its gendered/biological contours in cyberpunk fiction. (Just think of the impending extension of the body into—purely informational—cyberspace or, even more irritating, Baudrillard's denial of the "body in pain" when he claims that the war in the Persian Gulf never took place outside the computer screens of the Pentagon!) Moreover, like many of his American contemporaries, Kafka foregrounds the failures of artistic representation in an age of machinery. As Mark Seltzer has argued, American naturalism is centered on "the redrawing of the uncertain and shifting line between the natural and the technological in machine culture and also the ways in which such shifts in the traffic between the natural and the technological make for the vicissitudes of agency and of individual and collective and national identity in that culture" (4). The coupling of mechanical and natural processes that is a prominent feature of naturalist writing is seen as well in many of Kafka's texts. In Frank Norris's *Octopus*, Presley—the poet figure in the novel—bravely hangs on to a preindustrial notion of organic nature. One of the central scenes takes place in a blooming churchyard, an enchanted counterspace reminiscent of many a Romantic story. Kafka's *Amerika* ends in a similar vein. Its last chapter, "The Nature Theatre of Oklahoma," once more evokes the dated myth of the American frontier as an antidote to the differentiation and self-alienation of modern life. As he rode on a crowded train through the American West, Karl tells us, "everything . . . faded into comparative insignificance before the grandeur of the scene outside" (297). It is certainly not without irony that, even for the ailing German author from cosmopolitan Prague, the sheer vastness of the American territory could still function as a site for redemption and reconciliation, a utopian natural space where the demands of mechanization seemed, for the time being, suspended.

Notes

1. The most informative criticism on Kafka's attitude toward machinery is Wolf Kittler's "Schreibmaschinen, Sprechmaschinen." On Kafka and mechanical reproduction, see also a special issue of the *Journal of the Kafka Society of America* 1, no.2 (June–December 1988).

2. Nietzsche, whom Kafka read extensively, interprets writing in a similar vein. "It was not for nothing that I buried my forty-fourth year today," he writes in *Ecce Homo*. "I had the right to bury it; whatever was life in it has been saved, is immortal. The first book of the *Revaluation of All Values*, the *Songs of Zarathustra*, the *Twilight of the Idols*, my attempt to philosophize with a hammer—all presents of this year, indeed of its last quarter." A few pages later, Nietzsche again comments on his shifting identity, on this doubling into a public and fictional self: "This *dual* series of experiences, this access to apparently separate worlds, is repeated in my nature in every respect: I am a *Doppelgänger*, I have a 'second' face in addition to the first. *And* perhaps also a third" (221, 225).

3. "Through the mid–nineteenth century," as John Kasson points out, "the very word 'arts' encompassed skilled crafts generally, including invention, though increasing use of the qualifying adjective *fine* or *useful* signified a growing sense of division" (146).

4. All quotations from *Amerika* are from the Schocken edition. Kafka's manuscript, as Max Brod noted, originally bears no title. At various times Kafka referred to it as his "American novel," but he also called it "The Stoker" (after the title of

the first chapter) as well as, according to more recent scholarship, "Der Verschollene" ("The Man Who Disappeared"). Today the authoritative German edition is
Der Verschollene, ed. Jost Schilleweit, Frankfurt: Fischer, 1983. The English translation
of the novel retains Brod's original choice, *Amerika.*

5. On the role of the cinema in Kafka's works see Augustin and Jayne.

6. Written in the winter of 1914, "Before the Law" was first published in the
almanac *Vom jüngsten Tag* (1916). It is also incorporated in the ninth chapter of
The Trial. For an extended philosophical discussion of the parable, see Derrida,
Préjugés.

7. For a discussion of Gross and his so-called *Aussagenpsychologie,* see Wolf Kittler, "Schreibmaschinen, Sprechmaschinen," 129–40.

8. Some critics even argue that his two other novels, *The Trial* and *The Castle,*
are also set in America (for example, Loose, 7).

9. On Kafka's relation to Edison, see Urzidil.

Part II

Materialities of Reading

Jo Alyson Parker

4 Strange Attractors in
Absalom, Absalom!

We live in an age of what we might call metaconsciousness, saturated with cultural artifacts (both low and high) that reflexively comment on their own generative processes. Although self-conscious narrative is nothing new (as the texts of Shakespeare, Fielding, and Sterne vibrantly demonstrate), in the last few decades our fictional texts have become increasingly "meta-," even the lowly comic strip and the mass-audience action film drawing upon this destabilizing gesture. The infinite regress seemingly implicit in metanarrative goes hand in hand with a poststructuralist critical perspective that argues for the infinite deferral of meaning inherent in all discourse, and metanarratives of earlier eras can be (and have been) assessed in light of postmodern critical methodology.

The argument can be made that metanarratives simply bring to the fore what is implicit in all narratives—their inherent inability to be about anything other than themselves. They are representations of representations, "ripples in water" without an originary pebble, echoes without an originary sound (*Absalom, Absalom!*, 261). By making such an argument, however, we risk divorcing narrative from the sociohistorical context out of which it arises and ignoring not a fixed or fixable truth of the text but its bounded potential of meaning. As Ian MacKenzie has pointed out, narratives "*are* always *by* somebody and *about* something," and narratological operations "cannot adequately deal with the thematic interest that generally inspires our acts of responding to narratives." Here I put forward a heuristic framework for modeling narrative dynamics that brings together metanarrative structure and theme, while avoiding both claims of a text's radical indeterminacy and claims of its ultimate meaning. By looking closely at William Faulkner's metanarrative *Absalom, Absalom!* through the lens of dynamical systems theory (popularly, if not precisely, known as chaos theory), I propose to show the value of modeling narrative meaning along these lines.

Dynamical systems theory is changing the way we conceptualize so-called chaotic structures in the natural world. Whereas chaos was once regarded as "poor in order," it has come to be seen as "rich in information," as Katherine Hayles points out (*Chaos Bound*, 6). The nonlinear and the random are regarded no longer as aberrant but as prevalent, and physical behaviors once disregarded and dismissed are now seen as legitimate areas of inquiry. Perhaps the most far-reaching insights that chaos theory offers us are the following: that deterministic systems can generate random behavior when small uncertainties are amplified as the system develops through time, that order itself comes out of chaos, and that models of such chaotic systems demonstrate the entanglement of system and systematizer in generating meaning, a feedback loop thus running between the subjective observer and the object under observation. The implications of chaos theory are beginning to make themselves felt throughout our cultural landscape. Work by Hayles, Thomas Weissert, and Alexander Argyros, among others, has demonstrated its applications within the realms of literary studies and semiotics, and has remarked upon both its affinities with poststructuralist thinking and its divergences from it.[1] Although Hayles and Weissert argue for, respectively, an isomorphic and an isotropic connection between the methods of Derridean deconstruction and modern dynamics, each points out that, rather than repudiating order, as deconstruction seems to do, chaos theory puts forward new possibilities for it. Argyros draws upon the tenets of chaos theory to mount a sustained attack against the valorization of randomness and relativity that he regards as common to poststructuralist thought. Chaos theory may, in fact, bridge the gap between notions of an indefinite play of meaning and that of a fixed or fixable truth. Arguing for the prevailing nonlinearity of narrative, Argyros suggests that "narrative exists in the economy between Platonic fixity and Foucauldian relativity"—the very sort of determinate indeterminism that chaos theory allows us to see (319).

Poised on the brink of our postmodern era, *Absalom, Absalom!* invites, even demands, that we focus on the narrating process. A discourse about discourse, essentially all talk and no action, the novel lends itself to a poststructuralist narratological analysis—and reveals its limitations.

Peter Brooks, for instance, puts forth what is perhaps one of the most cogent explorations of the way the text signifies its own textuality. Brooks subsumes Sutpen's story to the plot of its narration, suggesting even, it seems, that there may be no there there:

> A further, more radical implication might be that the implied occurrences or events of the story (in the sense of fabula) are merely a byproduct of the needs of plot, indeed of plotting, of the rhetoric of the sjužet: that one need no longer worry about the "double logic" of narrative since event is merely a necessary illusion that enables the interpretive narrative discourse to go further.... This in turn might imply that the ultimate subject of any narrative is its narrating, that narrative inevitably reveals itself to be a Moebius strip where we unwittingly end up on the plane from which we began.... Narrative plots may be no more—but of course also no less—than a variety of syntax which allows the verbal game—the dialogue, really—to go on. (305)

Although he touches on the issue of miscegenation, Brooks is more concerned with its semiotic implications than with its representational ones, arguing that it signifies a " 'wild,' uncontrollable metonymy" (308). Brooks's concentration on the text's palindromic structure and the reader's "assumption of complete responsibility for the narrative" ultimately makes a case for a "centerless" narrative (304).

Stimulating as Brooks's study is, it effectually divorces the narrative from any connection with the "historical" circumstance of miscegenation that led to the fall of the house of Sutpen. Poststructuralist narratology does little to illuminate Faulkner's thematic indictment of slavery. The downplaying of theme in critical evaluations of *Absalom, Absalom!* tends to deny the importance of the slavery issue, much as Thomas Sutpen denies his own issue in the person of the mixed-race Charles Bon. By employing a dynamical systems model, however, we may find a means to connect the text's multiperspectival, looping narrative structure—seemingly circling round a hollow center—with the theme of the South's denial of the black blood on which it is built. Radically nonlinear, Faulkner's text provides a fruitful area for exploring the way a meaning structure emerges out of an apparently chaotic flux. Thomas Sutpen's story itself demonstrates the so-called butterfly effect common to chaotic structures—that is, the nonlinear development of small causes into great effects.[2] The absent center of Brooks's reading can more appropriately be characterized as a chaotic, or strange, attractor. Whereas applying a poststructuralist methodology to *Absalom, Absalom!* leads us into the hall-of-mirrors view that there is nothing but infinitely proliferating textuality, chaos theory enables the infinite play of signification within the bounded arena of the strange attractor.

Thomas Sutpen and Classical Determinism

Classical, or Newtonian, science is predicated upon deterministic thinking—its ability to relate cause and effect so that accurate predictions can be made about the natural world. The logical extension of such thinking is Laplace's demon, an imaginary entity "capable at any given instant of observing the position and velocity of each mass that forms part of the universe and inferring its evolution, both toward the past and toward the future" (Prigogine & Stengers, *Order Out of Chaos*, 75). Essentially, we end up with the notion of a completely predictable universe, its human components as subject to deterministic laws as anything else in the system. As James Crutchfield and his colleagues point out, "the literal application of Laplace's dictum to human behavior led to the philosophical conclusion that human behavior was completely predetermined: free will did not exist" (47–48). Chaos theory, however, shoots holes in the notion that all can be predicted in the macroscopic natural world and, by extension, in human behavior. Systems may be deterministic, but we may not be able to predict their future states.

With his portrait of Thomas Sutpen—a "demon" in his own right, according to Miss Rosa Coldfield—Faulkner explores the consequences of deterministic thinking as it applies to human behavior. Sutpen's entire adult career is based upon fulfilling his design. As Quentin puts it, Sutpen regards himself as a sort of baker, who need only mix the right ingredients together to achieve the desired result: "it was that innocence again, that innocence which believed that the ingredients of morality were like the ingredients of pie or cake and once you had measured them and balanced them and mixed them and put them into the oven it was all finished and nothing but pie or cake could come out" (263). Certainly, following a recipe, even with a few slight variations, leads to pie or cake—over and over and over again; the equations describe a stable system. But, as Faulkner indicates, human behavior is not stable.

By conceiving his design as a classically deterministic system, Sutpen brings about his own undoing. The implementation of his design exemplifies the butterfly effect in that little causes bring about big results. The undelivered and clearly inconsequential message ("*so he cant even know that Pap sent him any message and so whether he got it or not cant even matter, not even to Pap"* [237]) and the barring of the front door, a no doubt regular and unremarkable occurrence in Pettibone's household, lead to the dirt-poor Sutpen's wresting a plantation out of the land and setting up his progeny, briefly and fatally, as aristocrats of the Old South.

Caught up in deterministic thinking, Sutpen cannot account for the unpredictable, although he himself represents an unpredictable element at the local level within the global stability of the Southern caste system. In one of the few passages in Sutpen's own words (if we can so designate an account that comes through the intervening "consciousnesses" of General Compson, Mr. Compson, and Quentin), Sutpen puzzles over the failure of his meticulously planned design: "You see I had a design in my mind. Whether it was a good or bad design is beside the point; the question is, Where did I make the mistake in it, what did I do or misdo in it, whom or what injure by it *to the extent which this would indicate.* I had a design" (263; my emphasis). What leads to the destruction of the design is the random element that causes the system trajectory to diverge from its predicted course—in this case, the fact of Eulalia Bon's black blood, an amount apparently so negligible as to allow her to pass herself off as half Spanish. A paradoxical situation occurs here; Sutpen knows that this negligible amount cannot be encompassed in the design of the patrilineal South (implicit acknowledgment that deterministic thinking can maintain its sway only by suppressing perturbations), yet he thinks that the denial of this small perturbation in his own past will have no consequences. The metaphor Quentin uses when he discusses Sutpen's account of his first wife reinforces our sense of unpredictable, destabilizing forces at work: "He also told Grandfather, dropped into the telling as you might flick the joker out of a pack of fresh cards without being able to remember later whether you had removed the joker or not, that the old man's wife had been a Spaniard" (252). The "Spanish" blood is the joker in the pack—that wild card whose presence may disrupt the most winning system. By countenancing it, Sutpen would "see [his] design complete itself quite normally and naturally and successfully to the public eye," yet he would regard its culmination as "a mockery and betrayal of that little boy who approached that door fifty years ago and was turned away" (274). Admitting miscegenation and incest within the family structure works against Sutpen's fixed idea of a flawless dynasty.

Sutpen clings to his design, his deterministic thinking, in the face of recurring destabilizing perturbations. Throughout his career, it is the seemingly small things that lead to the catastrophe at Sutpen's Hundred: Charles Bon's black blood (half that of Eulalia); "that flash, that instant of indisputable recognition" (319) he withholds from Bon; a few spur-of-the moment words to Rosa Coldfield; the casual repudiation of Milly Jones. A thinking that cannot account for random elements and non-linear effects is doomed to failure. Significantly, Sutpen's desire to become a wealthy plantation owner "with dressed-up niggers," who can "lie in a hammock all afternoon with his shoes off" (229), only replicates an already-existing social design, one that is itself, as I have suggested, predicated upon (patri)linear thinking. In effect, by clinging to that design, Sutpen undermines the very reason for its inception. Sutpen initially plans not only to be the wealthy plantation owner, but to change the terms by which such a man exerts his power:

> He would take that boy in where he would never again need to stand on the outside of a white door and knock at it: and not at all for mere shelter but so that that boy, that whatever nameless stranger, could shut that door himself forever behind him on all that he had ever known, and look ahead along the still undivulged light rays in which his descendants who might not even hear his (the boy's) name, waited to be born without even having to know that they had once been riven free from brutehood just as his own (Sutpen's) children were—. (261)

But, by thinking deterministically, Sutpen cannot concurrently replicate the preexistent social design and rework the pattern. It is the nameless stranger/his firstborn son whom he turns away from the "white door," whom he sends, in Bon's words, "a message like you send a command by a nigger servant to a beggar or a tramp to clear out" (341). The pattern is, or course, reworked, but in a manner Sutpen had not intended, and what he replicates are the evils he had hoped to change.

Lest we not get the point about the flaws of classical determinism, Faulkner underscores it with his portrait of the conniving lawyer, whose balance sheet, as has often been remarked, parodies Sutpen's design. He attempts to equate mathematically what he can actually gain from Sutpen, even figuring the possible incest threat into the accounting: "*Incest threat: Credible Yes* and the hand going back before it put down the period, lining out the *Credible*, writing in *Certain*, underlining it" (310). Here the moral consequences of deterministic thinking come into play—

acquisitiveness, the urge to dominate and control. But, like Sutpen, the lawyer cannot account for the unpredictable:

> He was never worried about what Bon would do when he found out; he had probably a long time ago paid Bon that compliment of thinking that even if he was too dull or too indolent to suspect or find out about his father himself, he wasn't fool enough not to be able to take advantage of it once somebody showed him the proper move; maybe if the thought had ever occurred to him that because of love or honor or anything else under Heaven or jurisprudence either, Bon would not, would refuse to, he (the lawyer) would even have furnished proof that he no longer breathed. . . . (309)

Interestingly, the nonlinear effects that the lawyer cannot account for are linked with moral virtues; deterministic thinking thus appears not only incapable of correctly assessing the world but even morally deficient. To treat human beings as predictable components in a well-oiled machine is to reduce their humanity.

Sutpen's story, detailing the consequences of his design, is, of course, set in the framework of Faulkner's own design, one that necessarily involves a certain amount of deterministic thinking. It hardly took the destabilizing assumptions of poststructuralist linguistics to make us aware that a writer's determinations, or more aptly intentions, cannot be realized. Even so, texts exist that attempt, however futilely, to control our responses. *Absalom, Absalom!*, by contrast, intentionally plays against its own intentionality. With its multiperspectival, nonlinear structure, it resists overdetermination, or at least relishes the unpredictable response. In an oft-quoted response to an interviewer's question about the "truth" of the novel, Faulkner himself said: "The truth, I would like to think, comes out, that when the reader has read all these thirteen ways of looking at the blackbird, the reader has his own fourteenth image of that blackbird which I would like to think is the truth" (Gwinn & Blotner, 274). The text thus presents itself so as to encourage, in Roland Barthes's terms, a "writerly" as opposed to a "readerly" reading, encompassing within its own structure an acknowledgment of the ongoing interpretive process that undermines a predictable truth about the meaning of the text (4–6). Yet out of the plurality of meanings mobilized by its writerly nature emerges the structure of the strange attractor, bounding the text's plural in a zone of meaning.

The Attractor Structure of *Absalom, Absalom!*

I have heretofore spoken of the black blood as if it were a given. But it is not a given at all, at least not within the narrative proper (a particularly suspect designation in regard to this text). The only place where Bon's black blood is presented as a "certainty" is in the Chronology affixed to the end of the text. Indeed, the Chronology and Genealogy serve as supplements (in the most saturated sense) to the narrative proper, for they not only restate the information that is given there but also provide information that appears to be unavailable to the internal narrators. Nowhere in the narrative does an internal narrator present a narratee with the "fact" of Bon's black blood—not at any of the temporal sites at which someone might be expected to do so. Whether such a scene might be supposed to have taken place is beside the point. What we actually get is an italicized passage in which Quentin and Shreve have so fully engaged themselves in Henry and Bon's story that they seemingly become the very characters of whom they speak. Here Thomas Sutpen tells Henry that after Bon's birth he "*found out that his mother was part negro*" (355). But what are we to make of a "fact" brought forward during some apparently intuitive leap by Quentin and Shreve into the lives of their now-dead counterparts? Too, as we discover in an earlier passage, the italics signify "the long silence of not-people, in notlanguage" (9), a nullification within discourse of discourse itself. The narrative thus elides any authoritative presentation of information. As Gerald Langford demonstrates in his comparison of the manuscript version with the public book, the elision appears to have been a deliberate move on Faulkner's part. In the manuscript version Mr. Compson actually knows about Bon's black blood, and this knowledge is a given in his conversations with Quentin, the linear sequence of transmission thus made clear (Thomas Sutpen to General Compson, General Compson to Mr. Compson, Mr. Compson to Quentin, and Quentin to Shreve).[3] By refusing to provide an explanation for Quentin's acquisition of this crucial piece of knowledge, Faulkner draws attention to its uncertain origin.

In fact, the text consistently emphasizes the indeterminable origins of the "facts" of Sutpen's life. Sutpen's own beginnings cannot be fixed. According to what might be called a communal myth, Sutpen arrives in Jefferson "*out of nowhere* and without warning" (9). As Rosa Coldfield tells her tale, Quentin imagines he can see Sutpen and his slaves "drag house and formal gardens violently out of the soundless Nothing and clap them down like cards upon a table beneath the up-palm immobile and pontific, creating the Sutpen's Hundred, the *Be Sutpen's Hundred* like the oldentime *Be Light*" (8–9). In the beginning, in the void, Sutpen, like God proclaiming "Fiat lux," always already is. Attempting to explain himself to General Compson, he cannot account for his presence in the Virginia Tidewater: "So he knew neither where he had come from nor where he was nor why. He was just there . . ." (227).

To the internal or, more precisely, intradiegetic narrators, Sutpen presents an impenetrable enigma.[4] They know him mainly through various texts—carvings on headstones, entries in family Bibles, letters, tales passed down through several generations. Each narrative reworking of Sutpen's story is predicated on a previous reworking, even Rosa Coldfield and General Compson (those who actually knew the man himself) depend on others' stories (Ellen's, Sutpen's) to come up with their version of his life. Sutpen's own story is told only through a layering of several intervening voices, when Quentin tells Shreve a story that he heard from Mr. Compson, who heard it from General Compson, who heard it from Sutpen himself. The narrators often describe him in terms of an absence or a lack. He is the "nothusband" for whom (perhaps) Miss Rosa has worn black for forty-three years, *"a walking shadow"* who *"was not articulated in this world"* (171). In his attempt to explain the peculiar relationship between Miss Rosa and Sutpen, Mr. Compson provides a suggestive metaphor. He considers that Sutpen's face must have seemed to her "like the mask in Greek tragedy, interchangeable not only from scene to scene, but from actor to actor and behind which the events and occasions took place without chronology or sequence" (62). The passage serves as a self-reflexive comment on Faulkner's technique, emphasizing Sutpen's lack of ontological fixity.

Like Sutpen, Charles Bon is described as lacking origin and corporeality. He suddenly impinges upon the town consciousness, "a personage who in the remote Mississippi of that time must have appeared almost phoenix-like, fullsprung from no childhood, born of no woman and impervious to time and, vanished, leaving no bones or dust anywhere . . ." (74). He is a nullity, "shadowy: a myth, a phantom, something which they engendered and created whole themselves; some effluvium of Sutpen blood and character, as though as a man he did not exist at all" (104). Rosa falls in love with Bon's picture, not requiring *"even a skull behind it"* (147), but she never sees the actual man, even when he lies dead in Judith's room. When she helps to carry his coffin down the stairs, she tries *"to take the full weight of the coffin"* to prove to herself that he had indeed existed, but she cannot tell; she is left feeling that they *"had buried nothing"* beneath *"that mound vanishing slowly back into the earth"* (158).

As I have earlier pointed out, the temptation is to make of this motif of absence and lack exactly that—a gaping hole at the center of the text around which the various narrative explanations endlessly circle. But we do better to envision Faulkner's structure in terms of a strange attractor, that multidimensional emplotment of a certain class of nonlinear systems. There *are* real "facts"—an actual "history"—around which the narrative explanations twine, but they are unreachable in themselves. Nevertheless, the trajectories of the narratives fall onto an attractor that is generated by those unreachable facts.

Attractors, as Crutchfield and his colleagues succinctly define them, are "what the behavior of a system settles down to, or is attracted to" (50). A pendulum, for example, will eventually come to rest on a fixed point, and a frictionless pendulum will stay in a periodic orbit. The orbit does not depict the actual path of the pendulum; it is the representation of the dynamical system's evolution. This representation is plotted along the Cartesian coordinates of what is called state space, wherein each point represents one possible, unique configuration of the system. If the orbit of the dynamical system assumes a repeating pattern in state space, then we say it has reached the attractor. Dynamical systems that exhibit classical deterministic behavior (such as the pendulum) obtain exactly repeating cycles—that is, we can vary the initial conditions (starting the pendulum swinging in a different way each time, for instance), but it will always fall onto the same attractor.

Chaotic systems, by contrast, are not completely predictable, and when we represent their evolution in state space, we often end up with a strange attractor.[5] The behavior of a dripping faucet is chaotic, as Robert Shaw's landmark study demonstrated: a sudden change in mass that occurs when a drop detaches from the string of water gives way to nonlinear behavior (and, as we know, a great deal of annoyance if we happen to be in the vicinity of that faucet). Certainly, the behavior of the drops is deterministic; laws of classical physics guarantee that they *will* fall and that their mass and rate of speed in falling will lie within certain boundaries. But we cannot solve the equations that would enable accurate predictions of when, where, and how the drops will fall. When we map the system's behavior in state space, however, we find that the orbit hovers around certain coordinates—a basin of attraction—al-

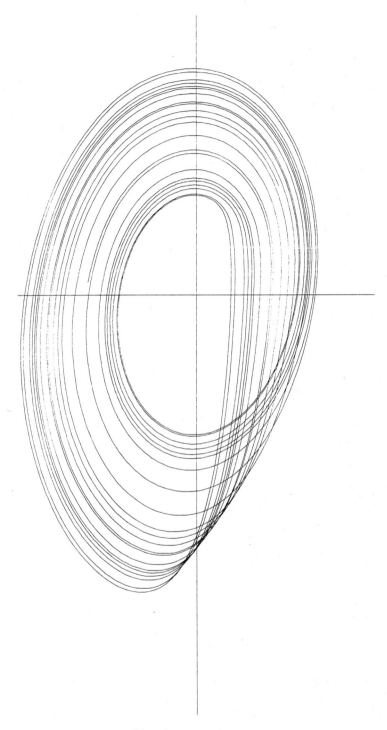

Strange attractor, generated by Thomas Weissert.

though precise prediction of the system's state at any particular time is impossible.

A computer simulation of this behavior gives us access to the three variables of the drops' position, velocity, and mass over an indefinite period of time, and thus enables us to see, in Shaw's words, "the geometry of the 'attractor' describing the motion of the fluid system" (17). As the figure indicates, trajectories at times diverge and at times almost converge but never repeat themselves exactly—hence the strangeness of the attractor. As Crutchfield and his colleagues point out, "in a typical chaotic transformation recurrence is exceedingly rare, occurring perhaps only once in the lifetime of the universe" (46). State space might fill up completely with orbits, the attractor (the ultimate fate of the system) might reveal itself—had we but world enough and time. In a chaotic system, there is, in fact, an actual attracting point (or points, depending on the system). However, unlike the stable fixed point upon which the pendulum eventually comes to rest, the attracting point in a chaotic system has become unstable. It concurrently attracts and repels the system trajectory, ensuring that the trajectory will never actually pass through it but come closer only to veer away. In a computer simulation, the system is always in the process of becoming—determinate in its spatiotemporal patterning, indeterminate in regard to the precise nature of its future state.

What is the significance of the strange attractor to the narrative structure of *Absalom, Absalom!*? In the text, Sutpen's story ostensibly is puzzled over by four intradiegetic narrators—Rosa Coldfield, Mr. Compson, Quentin Compson, and Shreve McCannon—whose narratives are themselves presided over by the extradiegetic narrator, seemingly there to locate us in place and time and provide stage directions as the characters engage in their incessant discourse. I say ostensibly because no clear-cut boundaries exist between the narratives of Quentin and Shreve, and the intra-intradiegetic narratives are embedded within the main internal narratives—Sutpen's story to General Compson, General Compson's story to Mr. Compson, Bon's letter to Judith, and so forth. Too, the boundary between extradiegetic and intradiegetic narratives is itself fuzzy, Sutpen's story at times coming from the extradiegetic narrator yet tenuously focalized through an internal narrator. We often cannot know where one voice ends and another begins. The overall structure seems to fit John Casti's description of a strange attractor—"one big tangled mess" (29).

It is out of this tangled mess, however, that the plot of the text emerges, just as the attractor pattern emerges as the system's evolving behavior is plotted in state space. We can compare each of the stories that is told about Sutpen to a trajectory upon the strange attractor.[6] In effect, each of the intradiegetic narrators might be considered as beginning from a different set of "initial conditions." In regard to time, proximity, and connection to the principal players in the events at Sutpen's Hundred, each narrator is either nearer or further away. Rosa Coldfield is, of course, seemingly closest in all respects: she actually knew all of the principal players except Bon, and she actually lived for a time at Sutpen's Hundred. Shreve McCannon is furthest away: he was born after all the players except Henry and Rosa had died; he hears of the events at second, third, and fourth hand; he has never even been to the South, let alone to the cursed parcel of land where Sutpen's tragedy played itself out.

Beginning from these sets of initial conditions, the extradiegetic and intradiegetic narratives trace trajectories through the state space of the text. As Sutpen's story is (re)iterated, we begin to see that these trajectories fall onto an attractor. All of the trajectories are attracted to, but never pass directly through, what seems to be the crucial event—the revelation of Bon's black blood. We might consider that event as the unstable attracting point, concurrently attracting and repulsing each narrative trajectory. Henry's shooting of Bon, the apparent fatal consequence of this revelation, is another unstable attracting point, for it is another event about which we have no definitive knowledge. The episode is presented as an imaginative re-creation by Quentin, interrupting an otherwise seamless narrative by Mr. Compson that elides the actual encounter. In effect, each narrative trajectory lies on the attractor that constitutes the plot of *Absalom, Absalom!*.

Because each narrator begins from a different set of initial conditions, the story he or she tells falls onto the attractor at a different point. The further away from the time of the events the narratives occur, the more those narratives have concurrently incorporated the information of preceding iterations but also replaced it with new information. In fact, initial conditions are themselves lost; we have no precise way of knowing how any of the narratives got the way they are—which "rag-tag and bob-ends of old tales and talking" (303) went into the reconstructions of the various narrators. The behavior of the trajectories is analogous to what happens when we map a chaotic system. At times, trajectories almost converge; at times they diverge widely. At times, trajectories come close to the attracting point; at times they veer away. Some trajectories visit certain regions more frequently, such as Rosa Coldfield's rehashing of Sutpen's insulting behavior. (Interestingly, the insult itself is never actually stated.) Each reiteration fills in more information but diverges from what has come before so that the narrative never exactly traces its own footsteps.

In chaotic systems, once we start from a set of initial conditions, we have no way of knowing when (and hence where) the trajectory will come close to the attracting point or veer away from it. If we regard the (veiled) revelation of Bon's black blood as the absent event that all the trajectories attempt to reach, the joint narrative trajectory of Quentin and Shreve comes closest to this unstable attracting point. The temptation has been to view their joint narrative as most accurately explaining what happened at Sutpen's Hundred. Certainly, it makes fall into place pieces of the puzzle that have previously not seemed to fit: Sutpen's repudiation of Bon, Henry's shooting of Bon, Judith's "adoption" of Charles Etienne, Charles Etienne's Sutpen-like "furious and indomitable desperation" (202). The temptation, too, has been to view their narrative as most accurately explaining what happened because it has the benefit of preceding iterations of Sutpen's story upon which to draw. But should we do so? No and yes.

To a certain extent, the text deliberately works against our regarding the joint narrative as some sort of Sherlockian solution pieced together once all the evidence has been gathered. As I have discussed earlier, the actual transmission of the vital piece of information never occurs between any narrator and narratee. Too, the logic that holds the joint narrative together is put on an equal footing with other sorts of what we might call narrative "glue," the story that Quentin and Shreve tell having no more basis in fact than the stories told by the other narrators: "the two of them, whether they knew it or not, in the cold room, (it was quite cold now) dedicated to that best of ratiocination which after all was a good deal like Sutpen's morality and Miss Coldfield's demonizing . . ." (280). Again and again, the text calls attention to the fact that the joint narrative is a reconstruction of other reconstructions, themselves based on suspect knowledge. The temporal and geographical distancing of the narrating instance—Harvard, 1910—from the actual events further reinforces the problematic nature of the knowledge to which Quentin and Shreve lay claim.

This distancing receives additional emphasis with Shreve's assumption of the role of sole narrator. Shreve's narration is not simply a retelling in a distinctive style of something Quentin told him previously.

Certainly, Shreve *has* garnered information about the South from Quentin. Yet Shreve tells Quentin things that Quentin does not already know. Significantly, he alternates between surmise and assertion, not knowing and knowing. He does not attempt to guess what goes on in the mind of Judith Sutpen: "And the girl, the sister, the virgin—Jesus, who to know what she saw that afternoon when they rode up the drive . . . " (320). But he does know Charles Bon's innermost thoughts. He asserts that it was Henry, not Bon, who was wounded at Shiloh, flatly contradicting Mr. Compson's opposing information and actually calling any other narrator's access to truth into question: "Because your old man was wrong here, too! He said it was Bon who was wounded, but it wasn't. Because who told him? Who told Sutpen, or your grandfather either, which of them it was who was hit?" (344). Yet the very doubt Shreve casts on the other narrator's lack of direct knowledge necessarily rebounds on him. We are explicitly told that Shreve invents his "facts": "four of them . . . sat in that drawing room of baroque and fusty magnificence which Shreve had invented and which was probably true enough . . ." (335). And when he takes over the narrative from Quentin, he demands, "Let me play a while now" (280). Clearly, it is not knowledge per se that gives Shreve's narrative an explanatory power greater than that of the other narratives.

At the same time, however, we are told that Shreve's invention is "probably true enough." Thus Shreve's lack of direct knowledge is complemented by insights that enable the pieces of the puzzle to fall into place. His accession to such insight makes sense in light of the dynamical systems model that I have been employing. The joint narrative does not result from some sort of piecing together of partial information from other iterations of Sutpen's story. Shreve's insights instead come from an intuitive leap—a leap, in fact, onto the attractor structure that can be discerned through the previous iterations. Shreve's leap is analogous to that made by the dynamicist who watches as a trajectory evolves in state space and discerns the emergent pattern. As Hayles explains, the dynamicist does not simply initiate the simulation and leave it at that, but interacts with it:

> She watches as the screen display generated by the recursion evolves into constantly changing, often unexpected patterns. As the display continues, she adjusts the parameters to achieve different effects. With her own responses in a feedback loop with the computer, she develops an intuitive feeling for how the display and parameters interact. . . .

And she is subliminally aware that her interaction with the display could be thought of as one complex system (the behavior described by a set of nonlinear differential equations) interfaced with another (the human neural system) through the medium of the computer. (*Chaos and Order,* 6)

Chaos theory takes into account the feedback loop between the modeler and the model, foregrounding the way in which the emerging pattern of the attractor is not simply observed but influenced by the dynamicist. Just so does *Absalom, Absalom!* take into account the way in which the reader of Sutpen's story influences the narrative and is influenced by it, functioning as both narratee and narrator. Shreve performs as a writerly reader of the other narratives through his intuitive leap onto the attractor upon which their narrative trajectories fall. But this process is more than simply a conventional reader-response approach of filling in gaps; Shreve's iteration simultaneously adds to the pattern and changes it. Although the original information is irrecoverable, what remains is, in Weissert's terms, "a residual meaning sustained by the purely internal relations of the ... signification system" ("Dynamical Discourse Theory," 125). And these internal relations are not static but dynamic, entangled in a feedback loop with Shreve.

Our own insights as to the truth about Sutpen (always approximate, never fully revealed) emerge from the ensemble of narrative iterations that make up the novel. We do not privilege that final narrative trajectory jointly put forward by Quentin and Shreve, but instead take into account all the previous trajectories, discerning and influencing the attractor upon which they fall. We might even say that this emergent ensemble is the fourteenth image of the blackbird of which Faulkner speaks. To some extent, we, as well as Shreve, leap onto the attractor, our commentary on the text constituting yet another trajectory that (presumably) adds to the pattern and changes it. Shreve thus serves within the text to model the reading experience that the text invites us to have. He is both the model reader and the model for the reader.

As I have discussed, the attractor structure of *Absalom, Absalom!* arises from a suppressed piece of information in the text—the repudiation of the black other by the white master. Structure and theme are thus integrally entangled, the attractor serving as a means for reinforcing the theme of the novel. The truth that the Canadian Shreve approximates is one that the southern narrators cannot directly acknowledge— hence the fact that the narrator furthest from the events comes closest to their meaning. It is a truth that concurrently attracts and repulses because actually to arrive at it undermines the (patri)linear master narrative of the rise of the "civilized" South. Sutpen must deny his own issue in order to preserve the purity of his design.

But that so-called purity was never there to begin with. Sutpen's dynastic ambitions, like those of his fellow southerners, can be achieved only at the expense of black blood. Slave labor enables him to wrest his mansion out of the "soundless Nothing" and supply it with the accoutrements of southern gentility. Sutpen's wife and daughter, like other southern wives and daughters, can keep their feet warm during a carriage ride on a winter's day only because there is "an extra nigger on the box with the coachman to stop every few miles and build a fire and re-heat the bricks on which Ellen's and Judith's feet rested" (103). The plantation belles' virginity is preserved because of the rape of their black sisters, as Mr. Compson points out:

> The other sex is separated into three sharp divisions, separated (two of them) by a chasm which could be crossed but one time and in but one direction—ladies, women, females—the virgins whom gentlemen someday married, the courtesans to whom they went while on sabbaticals to the cities, the slave girls and women upon whom that first caste rested and to whom in certain cases it doubtless owed the very fact of its virginity. (109)

The myth of southern gentility can be preserved only because the fact of southern brutality is suppressed.

Through the Sutpen story, the text demonstrates the fractal property of similarity across scale, consistent with a dynamical systems model. In a dynamical system, what we often find are similar structural features at both the local and global levels. The local event of Sutpen's denial of Bon is replicated globally in the southerners' denial that the black Other they exploit and brutalize is, in fact, kindred: "all boy flesh that walked and breathed stemming from that one ambiguous eluded dark father-head and so brothered perennial and ubiquitous everywhere under the sun" (299). Sutpen's progeny, with their legacy of fratricide and potential miscegenation/incest, enact locally the curse that slavery brought to the South, the war, as Mr. Compson claims, springing from "a family fatality" (118).[7]

The risk we run when we resort to a model is that we may end up applying it to any and all texts, regardless of the sociohistorical circumstances from which they arise. After all, strange attractors are not a feature of all dynamical systems, not even of all chaotic systems, but only of a particular type of chaotic system. The model is thus useful for discussing a particular kind of text—one such as *Absalom, Absalom!*. We must ask ourselves, what are the epistemic implications of an attractor structure? Faulkner was himself not privy to dynamical systems theory, although it could be argued that, like many visionary writers, he was capable of articulating the incipient elements in the cultural matrix. What we can certainly argue, however, is that the attractor structure of *Absalom, Absalom!* indicates his dissatisfaction with the over-determination of linear narrative and its (spurious) claims for revealed knowledge. Faulkner's gift lies in his ability not only to apprehend the dynamics of narrative, with its resistance to totalizing perspectives, but also to foreground this dynamics so as to encourage our active engage-ment in the process. Perhaps more important, however, the attractor structure brings to the fore the very difficulty of the historical problem that Faulkner's text deals with—the terrible consequences of slavery. As a southern writer, Faulkner had to address that issue, but he was im-mersed in a culture that itself could not come to terms with it. When Faulkner shows his characters' difficulty with getting at the truth about Sutpen, he may be mirroring his own difficulty as a writer concurrently drawn to and repulsed by the tragic story he tells. Quentin Compson's ambivalent final words about the South may reflect his own feelings: *"I dont hate it! I dont hate it!"* (378).

That we can even speak in terms of a strange attractor in regard to Faulkner's text comes from our particular cultural circumstances. Through computer technology, dynamicists can perform the iterations of equations from which the dynamic pattern of the strange attractor arises. Granted, such iterations can be done without the aid of the com-puter, but the process would be so time-consuming as to make it un-feasible. Computer technology enables simulation and, consequently, allows us to apprehend the indeterminate determinism common to cer-tain chaotic dynamical systems, such as a dripping faucet or, in this case, a narrative.

Although I want to avoid putting forth the strange attractor model as a global theory about textual dynamics, it nevertheless can prompt us to think about narrative in new ways. It may provide a way of en-hancing notions of spatiality in narrative, wherein the structure is re-garded "as a spatial configuration rather than as a temporal continuum," in Joseph Frank's terms ("Spatial Form," 225). The strange attractor is simultaneously spatial configuration *and* temporal continuum—a spatialization of a temporal process, if you will. Through a fixed (potential) pattern with infinite depth, the system configuration continuously evolves. As well, to return to an earlier point, the strange attractor model also provides a means for getting beyond the infinite regress of the poststructuralist theoretical perspective. Narrative, ultimately, is not simply discourse about discourse, driven by lack; neither does it drive toward a fixed meaning or truth that would stop discourse. The image of "the original ripple space" that frames this chapter may serve as the most fitting analogy of the workings of Faulkner's narrative and narrative in general. When we throw a pebble into a pond, it becomes as inaccessible as the attracting point in a chaotic system. All we can see is the pattern made by its ripples, a continuously evolving configuration. But, as Faulkner envisions, "that pebble's watery echo" moves across the water "at the original ripple-space"—testimony to the irrecoverable attracting point that determines the pattern in the first place.

What the attractor model also gives us is a way of assessing our own critical procedures. When we evaluate a text, we get on the attractor, our own narrative trajectory approaching an unstable truth and then veering away from it. If we had infinite time, so that we could turn (state) space into a Borgesian library filled with commentary, a truth might emerge—about Sutpen, this text, texts in general. As it is, we can only make our way along the attractor, knowing that we will never arrive at the attractor point and that our own trajectory is just one segment in the ever-evolving whole.

Notes

1. See, in particular, Hayles's chapters "Chaos and Poststructuralism" (175–208), "The Politics of Chaos: Local Knowledge versus Global Theory" (209–35), and "Conclusion: Chaos and Culture: Postmodernism(s) and the Denaturing of Experience" (265–95). See also Weissert, "Dynamical Discourse Theory"; Argyros; and Harris, "Fractual Faulkner." For a useful compilation of chaos theory applications to literary studies, see Hayles's *Chaos and Order.*

2. More technically, the "butterfly effect" constitutes a sensitive dependence on initial conditions and an exponential separation of orbit pairs. The term comes from the notion, popular in chaos dynamics, that the seemingly negligible flapping of a butterfly's wings could have a major effect on distant weather patterns.

3. Critics often attempt to provide a rational explanation for Quentin's and Shreve's apparently sudden accession of knowledge by arguing that Henry Sutpen

told Quentin of Bon's black blood during the visit that Quentin made to Sutpen's Hundred. (See, for example, Millgate, 164, and Cleanth Brooks, *William Faulkner,* 424–33, and "Narrative Structure," 301–28.) But even if the revelation could be assumed to have occurred at this time, Faulkner elides the actual scene.

4. Genette's distinction between extradiegetic and intradiegetic narratives (228–29) is especially useful in a text so complexly layered as *Absalom, Absalom!*

5. Although strange attractors are the manifestations of deterministic chaos in dissipative systems, they are not possible in conservative systems, which can also exhibit deterministic chaos.

6. Although Weissert does not extend his discussion to a particular text, he makes the comparison between a dynamical system and narrative dynamics: "As a working hypothesis, I make the analogy between a text considered as a complex trajectory space of narrative and signification, generated by an author's conscious and unconscious model of cultural relations, and the phase space of a dynamical system, generated from the dynamicist's model of the relations among the degrees of freedom of the referent physical system" ("Dynamical Discourse Theory," 124).

7. Harris's essay "Fractal Faulkner" provides an extended analysis of self-similarity in *Go Down, Moses.*

Linda Brigham

5 Cinema and the Paralysis of Perception

Robbe-Grillet, Condillac, Virilio

As the result of a global electronic network, getting and spending hurtle near light speed, too fast for the merchants themselves, but caught and weighed in their nets of software. Further down the food chain—no longer the nanosecond events of commercial exchange, but the comparatively slow macroevents of the terrorist's bomb blast, the executive veto—political analysis proceeds in sound bites, autonomized blips, infinitesimals of public exchange. Finally, slower than all, the arts ponder media; media, after all, are the stuff of art. Objects as rhizomatically tangled as hypertext—objects unhousable by any "real" space—rotate gently in the space of contemplation, a space the critic still articulates in words.

In what sense, in the age of the speed of light, is this "space" an illusion? Echoing Marshall McLuhan's medium-as-message pronouncements upon relatively early developments in the "information age," Paul Virilio would claim it masks what he insists lies ubiquitous though unthematized in new modes of exchange that now achieve global domination: the reorganization of relations between environment and organism on a vast, perhaps catastrophic scale. In short, perception itself, the empirical foundation of all opinion, now lies entirely within the purview of electronic media.

But can electronic media manufacture the percept in toto? To do so would be no small feat. Much of contemporary research both by scientists, such as Humberto Maturana and Gerald Edelman, and by psychologists and philosophers—Francisco Varela, Gilles Deleuze, and Félix Guattari, for example—present the percept as a complex, not a mon-

119

olithic sensory given. Brian Massumi, following up the results of clinical experimentation and the work of Deleuze, writes that "affect," often considered the most "raw" component of perception, defies the mind/body dichotomy. "The body," he explains, "doesn't just absorb pulses or discrete stimulations; it infolds contexts, it infolds volitions and cognitions that are nothing if not situated" (92–93). Controlling perception, then, is a matter of neither training the mind nor training the body; even more important, artificial media cannot simply displace an embodied history with a virtual one. Elements of a perception-to-be compete for becoming, and only a portion of those elements are "new" stimuli.

Virilio's fear of media-driven apocalypse recalls the fifties paranoia typified in such movies as *Invasion of the Body Snatchers,* where gradually, imperceptibly at first, real human beings are replaced by duplicates: hollow, alien simulations. The reference to film, especially fifties film, is no accident; the filmic medium is the jump-off point for much of contemporary media theory, such as Virilio's own. The scene of cinema colludes with such fears: as Virilio himself has pointed out, moviegoers, immobilized into rows and columns of clinically individuated yet identical seats, are the patients par excellence. The theater audience is the passive object of manipulation through the lights and sound of a hidden technical apparatus. Yet this audience is a myth; although it may be true, in Guattari's words, that subjectivity today "remains under the massive control of apparatuses of power and knowledge" (35), my purpose is to explore limitations to that control. I first turn to the eighteenth century, the work of the philosopher Condillac, for a critique of the notion of "simple" perception. Subsequently, I will locate a parody of media's "power" over perception in Alain Robbe-Grillet's fifties novel *Jealousy,* where the struggle for unequivocal interpretation emerges as a veiled repetition of the struggle between media, in this case between film and prose.

Etienne Bonnot, abbé de Condillac, a prerevolutionary French Ideologue, provides an elegant argument for the necessary complexity of perception: without an intermedial mix of experiences, no subject could emerge from psychotic solipsism. In the *Treatise on Sensations* (1754) his purpose is to explicate "which are the ideas we owe to each sense, and how, when they are reunited, they give us all the knowledge necessary for our survival" (158). Condillac describes with excruciating detail a *Gedankenexperiment* in support of the fundamental Lockean notion that all ideas proceed from sensation, but in the process demonstrates that sensation cannot, in this context, be simple. Simple sensation is an inadequate basis for objective judgment; for ideas to have any value concerning the world beyond the self, sentience requires not only the senses but also the movement of the body, a very intimately attached body.

Condillac's *Treatise* imaginatively traces the experience of a hypothetical statue as it acquires one by one the senses of smell, hearing, taste, sight, and finally touch-cum-locomotion. Only with the last is it possible for the statue to become aware of anything beyond itself; without movement, it exists in a necessary solipsism, enclosed within the serial modifications of its being. The statue experiences smells as differential waves of odor, sight as a confused manifold of light and color. Touch alone, without movement, remains a wash of tactility, painful or pleasurable. But with motion, a coordination of these differential sensations can occur. Correlations between position and experience become possible when patterns of voluntary action accompany changes in sensations. Most important among these sensations are those that distinguish between the statue's own body and other bodies; touching itself, it has two sources of sensation, the hand and the surface it touches; touching another object activates only a single receptor. The comparison reveals a programmatic distinction between self and other. Resistance makes perception "work," both in the sense of function and in the sense of labor.[1]

Condillac's demonstration literally organ-izes experience into coherence—perhaps even into narrative. To map this perception-based organization distinctively, Condillac enacts a disorganization, a decomposition of the sensorium, a dismantling of the machinery of subjectivity. But his decomposition is analytical and critical; it has the character of art, not action. It provides a kind of regression analysis; it does not provide a technique for inducing mass passivity. When cinema appeared on the artistic scene in opposition to the dominant novel, it raised the same questions, offered the same opportunity for a kind of regression analysis to the semioticians who at first rather gingerly probed its adequacy for narrative. It appeared to be simple. As an alternative to language as a narrative medium, film provided theorists the opportunity to examine the elements necessary for an intelligibility that traditionally consisted of an integration of the senses, erupting finally into noetic transcendence as a "sign"—paradigmatically, a verbal sign. The film retreats from the purely intellectual domain of language into the domain of the percept; it regresses from a realm that requires a form of competence for access to one where the price of admission seems free, and might offer a subversion of the bondage inherent in linguistic and cultural competence, an undercutting "objectivity."

Early film theorists such as Roman Jakobson celebrated this "regression" of cinema as a welcome revolution against the logophilia of nineteenth-century realism. "In art it was the cinema that disclosed clearly and emphatically to countless viewers that language is merely one of the possible sign systems," he writes in the ground-breaking essay "What Is Poetry?" F. W. Galan, a historian of the Prague School movement in semiotics, observes that the basis for the cinematic subversion of the "verbal sign" lies in its medium: rather than representing objects by means of signs, as other arts do, cinema represents by means of the objects themselves (94). Film has a causal "trace" relationship, rather than a symbolic, representative relationship, with what it portrays, and this shift to a more primordial relation to objects disrupts narrative. This priority suggested possibilities for a defense against linguistic impurity, a protection against the distortions inherent in the derivative quality of language, inherent in the artificiality that is synonymous with culture. The objects confront the camera and demand that the cinematographer create a meaning, a language, and a narrative sequence, out of entirely new elements. Before convention naturalized film into a narrative medium, film analysis suggested that sequential mimesis and narrative not only are separable; they constitute polarities. The object's direct presence destroys its sign function. Furthermore, because it operates in real time, film might, in contrast to the reader-paced consumption of the spatial medium of written texts, reorganize the perception of time. Jan Mukarovsky, in his discussion of the cinematic shot as the basic unit of film, observed that, unlike the novelist, the cinematographer, by accelerating or slowing the movement of the film, can control directly and mechanically a viewer's sense of time. Film creates artificial "real" time and uncovers time as a function of attention by displacing it with the attention of a camera—in Virilio's phrase, the "cinematic motor" (*Aesthetics of Disappearance*, 15). Yet to do so it requires an immobile viewer, a viewer who will not touch. Thus "decomposed," in the sense of Condillac's statue, film might facilitate a reconstitution of habits of perception.

For Jakobson and Mukarovsky, film offered a perfect laboratory for the investigation of artistic *Entfremdung*. Such "estrangement" had an important, if conflicted, political role to play in the context of the rise of totalitarianism because of its potential to loosen the logocentric grip of ideology. At the same time, though, the technological displacement of the traditional artist by a cyborgian cinematographer, and the consequent mechanization and synchronization of an audience's sense of space-time, made film appealing to the fascist Filippo Tommaso Marinetti as well as to the critics of the nation-state. Walter Benjamin's famous essay on art in the age of mechanical reproduction treats just this issue. With characteristic complexity and ambiguity, Benjamin cautiously celebrates film's destruction of artistic "aura"—the work of art's historical uniqueness, its elevation to a realm beyond the everyday world of the masses. The destruction of aura has egalitarian value: "To pry an object from its shell," writes Benjamin, "to destroy its aura, is the mark of a perception whose 'sense of the universal equality of things' has increased to such a degree that it extracts it even from a unique object by means of reproduction" (233). Authenticity, with its correlate, authority, no longer matters, and with the passage of these traits, Benjamin also sees the separation of art from cult value, from ritual.

Despite its dangers, for Benjamin the mechanization of artistic production epitomized by film is its proletarian value, valuable precisely because the artist has disappeared. The audience views a product emptied of technique by virtue of the fact that its production is so laden with technology, the medium of alienation. The actor, like any common worker, has no contact with the audience, only with the machine. Illusionism is achieved off-site by feats of engineering, behind the scenes where the film is cut, spliced, accelerated, or slowed. "Thus, for contemporary man the representation of reality by the film is incomparably more significant than that of the painter, since it offers, precisely because of the thoroughgoing permeation of reality with mechanical equipment, an aspect of reality which is free of all equipment. And that is what one is entitled to ask from a work of art" (234). Subjection to flickering light and sound might be less dangerous than subjection to a more personified and individuated authority, the authority of genius. Benjamin's audience, although undergoing the filmic illusion, is not utterly subject to it; the appeal of film is a function of the social conditions that contextualize it. Further, this mechanization of the product and its concealment effect a unification of audience experience, a collectivization that Benjamin relates to a "progressive" response, a response that on some level constitutes an awareness of class, an ordinariness that conceals and subjugates "mastery."

As the century progressed, Hollywood stormed the formalist laboratory and the movies lost their strangeness. Artists dispersed into stars, cinematographers, directors, producers—but mostly stars. Such a medium lowered writing to the team-player status of the screenplay. But the shadow of fascism featured another narrative intertwined with the commercial triumph of mechanical reproduction. Fascist censorship presented what may have been the least important threat to creative liberty. Instead, the failure of art under totalitarianism seemed to lie in the artist's failure to control the message of art, or more precisely, in the failure of the artist to exclude art from a domain of messages already appropriated by the same mass culture in which Benjamin placed his idiosyncratic hope. As a case in point, Hannah Arendt describes the Nazi German public's reaction to Bertolt Brecht's *Three-Penny Opera*:

> The theme song in the play, "*Erst kommt das Fressen, dann kommt die Moral*" [Food first, morality after], was greeted with frantic applause by exactly everybody, though for different reasons. The mob applauded because it took the statement literally; the bourgeoisie applauded because it had been fooled by its own hypocrisy for so long that it had grown tired of the tension and found deep wisdom in the expression of the banality of which it lived; the elite applauded because the unveiling of hypocrisy was such superior and wonderful fun. The effect of the work was exactly the opposite of what Brecht had sought by it. (33)

Brecht, failing to manage audience response, lost the battle between social criticism and the dominant culture. One of the chief reasons he lost is the complexity of the audience's perception, its lack of unity; in Arendt's analysis, its class divisions. Objects appear differently to different groups; the ideologies that constitute class also provide protocols for appropriating the work of art, and so maintaining the status quo on all levels, foremost on the level of class—class unaware of itself as such.

In this account, then, far from posing an early form of virtual reality, film, for better or worse, could not escape the history of its own viewers. The work of the artist was posed against history, an exercise in body snatching: such was the mission of Robbe-Grillet's *nouveau roman*. Yet the exercise was a parody; *nouveau roman,* as exemplified in *Jealousy,* is in Lacanian terms a "working through fantasy" wherein the object of desire, control, a holdover from earlier notions of artistic "genius," reveals itself only as unattainable.

Like a disgruntled Pygmalion, Robbe-Grillet deploys an immobilizing prose, riveting attention to objects in order to prevent the philandering interpretive protocols of culture. Not only is this rigor a hedge against fascist misuse, it also ostensibly retaliates against the culture's disenfranchisement of the artist, the artist's effective marginalization by an intensely normative bourgeoisie. Robbe-Grillet ridicules what he calls the nineteenth-century notion of the artist as a "kind of unconscious monster, irresponsible and fate-ridden, even slightly stupid, who emits 'messages' which only the reader may decipher" (*For a New Novel*, 11). He depicts the writer's battle with reception as a battle against constantly fossilizing forms, forms fixing the artwork in the freeze frame of the familiar, rendering it hospitable to the expectations of the critics and the public; the endurance of such forms generates hostility to—or worse, blind appropriation of—innovations and innovators. Hence the creator of the "new novel," who seeks

> forms capable of expressing (or of creating) new relations between man and the world, to all those who have determined to invent the novel, in other words, to invent man. Such writers know that the systematic repetition of the forms of the past is not only absurd and futile, but that it can even become harmful: by blinding us to our real situation in the world today, it keeps us, ultimately, from constructing the world and man of tomorrow. (9)

It is of central importance that the primary constituent of the new novel, like that of film, is the object. In "A Future for the Novel," Robbe-Grillet writes, "No longer will objects be merely the vague reflection of the hero's vague soul" (*For a New Novel*, 21). He continues:

> In this future of the novel, gestures and objects will be *there* before being *something;* and they will still be there afterwards, hard, unalterable, eternally present, mocking their own "meaning," that meaning which vainly tries to reduce them to the role of precarious tools, of a temporary and shameful fabric woven exclusively—and deliberately— by the superior human truth expressed in it, only to cast out this awkward auxiliary into immediate oblivion and darkness. (21)

The freeing of the object is a synecdoche for the liberatory premises of the avant-garde. But Robbe-Grillet's manifesto also fosters a paradox: the artist's freedom to control constitutes his own fantasized escape from the culture industry. His manifesto is a symptom, and in *Jealousy* Robbe-Grillet's characters demonstrate the Möbius strip–like connection between material barriers to interpretation and the interpretive impulse for symbolic imbrication that constitute the symptom in Lacan's sense. In symptoms, extending from the embodied and ultimately untranslatable nature of perception, subjects escape even the most rigid discipline imposed by the regimentation of society, and by the work of art. And like the old, new technologies of perception cannot neutralize interpretation, but perhaps only intensify it, politicizing all the more powerfully both history and desire—and this is due to the very materiality of the medium. *Jealousy,* a "filmic novel," the site of competition between novel and film, exposes the recalcitrant materiality of both, and with that, the vanity of the artist as well as the hermeneutically inclined reader/viewer. Meanwhile, the "man of tomorrow" of Robbe-Grillet's manifesto arrives; corporations replace the lone genius. (For a lucid discussion of the misleading classification of Robbe-Grillet as a *chosiste,* or "object-ist," see Ramsay, 7-10.)

Jealousy parodies the artist's struggle against waning potency by bringing about a clash between word and image, an aggression that extends to its audience. It squeezes the reader between media. Its first requirement for the reader, like the cinematic viewer, is position. The cinema viewer must face the screen from a stable location to occupy the site of the camera, yet written text, unable to rely upon the instinctive attraction of the eye to light in a dark room, must coerce the reader into position by a barrage of noise, by the textual cacophony that ensues unless the reader occupies the right point of view. The narrative, like the camera positioned as the eye of the voyeur, elides the narrator, yet the punishing inertness of objective description without the narrator forces the reader to insert him. *Jealousy*'s viewpoint is that of a keenly analytical jealous husband, whose observations of objects gradually produce "evidence" for an obsession that grows concurrently with his "depth" of observation, with the accrual of significant visual data: evidence that his wife is cheating on him. But whether his passage from indifference to suspicion to obsession represents any gain in positive knowledge of the world remains in irremediable doubt—in fact, the success of the husband in decoding his wife's behavior by seeing and the success of the reader in decoding the artistic text by reading become steadily more indistinguishable.

From the start, the husband's mental processes intermingle with the reader's, although it is not until later that we, like the husband, become aware of this similitude. We find in the novel suggestive details that imply the husband's position: more place settings, more chairs than the number of characters who appear. But this is not simply a narrative device; the fact that the "narrator" does not mention himself drifts into focus as a personality trait for the nimble interpreter; as a scientific observer, the husband considers the scene under subjective removal. His very analytic rigor sets up the novel as a "tale" of the disillusion of objectivity. Such a disillusion must take place in the reader as well for the tale to become a narrative; to experience plot, the reader must to some degree follow in the footsteps of the narrator. At the same time, the tale that emerges in consequence of "correct" reading undercuts every one of the steps taken to achieve it. Both the reader and the narrator operate under the pressure of psychological need in an affectively deprived world, yet the cleverness of neither the husband nor the reader can generate certainty. Objects only seem to yield to narrative exigency through the simple fact of their repetitive selection, their reception of close attention; yet what these processes reveal remains hopelessly "subjective," in Condillac's terms, solipsistic.

Throughout, *Jealousy*'s medial hybridity generates dissonance. The operation of point of view within the novel is a clash of novel and film. The medium is verbal, but the content is filmic. Without conventional verbal cues, the reader simply "sees" out of the husband's cinematographic eye. The effect is jarring, ill proportioned: *Jealousy* opens with a tedious paragraph explaining the location of a line of shadow produced by the roof of the plantation house, a great waste of prose for one filmic shot. It is true that form follows function: the angles of the house, painstakingly specified, generate the angles by means of which the plantation manager surveys the rows of banana trees that support his living. A strict attention to point of view disciplines the natural jungle growth into a regulatable cash crop. Yet why not simply make a movie? Bruce Morrisette reports that *Jealousy*'s novelistic form excited ridicule upon its publication: "Robbe-Grillet was called a competitor with the cadastre or record book of county property lines, because of his minute, geometric descriptions, some of which (like the notorious 'counting the banana trees' passage in *Jealousy*) were read over the radio, for laughs" (2). Yet, keeping Benjamin's enthusiasm for film in mind, it would be a mistake to simply dismiss this laughter. The filmic novel is ridiculous, a holdover from the nineteenth-century colonial domination of print over other media. But even more important, this joke at the expense of prose conceals an irony: in ridiculing print, it also parodies filmic surveillance; as print struggled vainly against film, so the tyranny of the eye basic to the filmic mode struggles impotently for the interiorities of viewers, much as the European struggled impotently in the jungle, the man impotently against the woman. The narrator cannot "read" his wife by means of a camera.

In the opening of the novel, A., the narrator's wife, is described as a kind of homeostatic cipher, a woman without preferences: "... she never suffered from the heat, she had known much worse climates than this—in Africa, for instance—and had always felt fine there. Besides, she doesn't feel the cold either. Wherever she is, she keeps quite comfortable" (39). The narrator attributes similar absence of qualities to the expression in her voice:

> She says "hello" in the playful tone of someone who has slept well and awakened in a good mood; or of someone who prefers not to show what she is thinking about—if anything—and always flashes the same smile on principle; the same smile which can be interpreted as derision just as well as affection, or the total absence of any feeling whatever. (55)

A. is uninterpretable because all meanings are possible; all meanings are possible, the narrator tells us, because of the ubiquitous nature of A.'s desires, her lack of preferences—or so she appears. But there is another factor: an intrinsic "depth" is imputed to A. An accurate description of A. falls short of the necessary "grammar" of her motives, particularly since an invisible interior opens the possibility of active deception on her part.

Repeating the medial struggle within the "filmic novel," a struggle on the level of form, competition brings the impossible-real object of desire to light on the level of plot: the narrator may have a rival interpreter, one whom A. herself has given the key to her reception: perhaps Franck, the narrator's neighbor, whose wife never appears on account of illness. The narrator must locate the key he fears Franck may already possess, a means to unlock his own imprisoned sensibilities: "A. is humming a dance tune whose words remain unintelligible. But perhaps Franck understands them, if he already knows them, from having heard them often, perhaps with her" (49). Yet each "clue" to the liaison becomes incorporated only into the narrator's inert fantasy, however plausible that fantasy might be. The narrator does not become an actor in a real world, but remains a cinematographer, cutting and splicing phenomenal images. The variety of angles and foci of the narrator's snapshot-memory yields to him what the most subtle features of a crime scene yield to Sherlock Holmes. But instead of advertising the brilliance of the narrator's powers of observation and reason, the analytic acquisition of information reveals only his failure, an a priori failure due to the limitations of sensibility.

There seems no way out. Even so, the narrator does change: he becomes, for a brief moment, something other than an interpreter, or a decoder. He encounters the ultimate material sign, in Lacanian terms: a "sublime object." This object is a centipede, wriggling and phallic, the "memory" of which recurs up to the point of the novel's climax. The centipede exposes the narrator's uncontrollable tendentiousness; not only are his perceptions insufficient for conclusion, they are distorted by an erupting material (and thus uninterpretable) sign, a sign that works as a thing, and not as a sign; a hybrid of sign and thing. The first mention of the centipede occurs a few pages into the novel, consisting only of a subordinate clause: "She had just moved her head back and was looking straight ahead of her down the table, toward the base wall where a blackish spot marks the place where a centipede was squashed last week, at the beginning of the month, perhaps the month before, or later" (47). A.'s attention to the spot perhaps, perhaps the violence of the event itself, accounts for the increasing detail of the narrator's recollection. He takes note of the stain a second time, on this occasion dwelling on the details of the mark at length (62). On the third mention, however, his attention shifts from the stain to the memory of the centipede itself. Here he elaborates on the invertebrate's appearance, an appearance which identifies it as a certain genus (*Scutigera*), unworthy of A.'s response: "it is far from being one of the most venomous" (65). After this remark, though, the narrator describes Franck looking at A., then rising and squashing the centipede. Once again, the narrator's recollection hovers around an instance of communication between his wife and his neighbor, while his own assessment of the centipede, a mere feature within his database of knowledge, remained impotent, not answering to A.'s unverifiable but presumed desire, a desire for violent action. He recalls the squashing subsequently from various angles, emphasizing various details, with varying degrees of dramatic intensity, until, finally, recollection triggers the fantasy of A. and Franck making love in the hotel, and dying for it in a car crash (110–12). The existence of the crash is belied by subsequent appearances of A. and Franck; the clear falsehood of this element in the narrator's "story" brings all "facts" into doubt. At this point too, the centipede disappears from the novel; it has done its work.

The centipede incident, unlike the other repeatedly scrutinized details of the novel, does not "inform" the narrator about activities between A. and Franck, nor does it comment on the nature and limitations of codes. It lies in an associative nexus, charged yet inarticulate; its effect is automatic. As a sublime object, its subjection to interpretation—as literary symbol or filmic image—only obscures, in Slavoj Žižek's words on the *Titanic*, "the terrifying impact of its presence" (68). It has that impact because it collects within itself the extremity of thinghood, uncontainable within signifying systems; it gives the lie to all interpretation. It reveals the uncontainable, untranscendant, unanalyzable complex of the percept.

With the final centipede-driven fantasy of the wreck, moreover, the reader encounters the paradox of the artist's "illusion," facilitated by the unquiet union of film and novel. So the reader parts ways not only with the narrator through whom she has been gazing, but with the artist as well: the reflexive message of the narrative undercuts the narrative itself.

Not surprisingly, then, the "picture" of reading comes under the husband's camera-eye at the end. Early in *Jealousy*, with stereotypical critical pedantry, the husband complains that his wife and his neighbor lack sophistication; A. and Franck, discussing a novel, treat the aesthetic object as a matter of fact, true or false, accurate or inaccurate; they uncritically identify with the characters and their circumstances. Yet by the end of *Jealousy*, the narrator's final confused and projection-laden account of the novel indicates that he too has completely lost sight of its formal nature and transformed it by his own experience, but the product is quite different than the unsophisticated interpretations of A. and Franck:

> The main character of the book is a customs official. This character is not an official but a high-ranking employee of an old commercial company. This company's business is going badly, rapidly turning shady. This company's business is going extremely well. The chief character—one learns—is dishonest. He is honest, he is trying to reestablish a situation compromised by his predecessor, who died in an automobile accident. But he had no predecessor, for the company was only recently formed; and it was not an accident. Besides, it happens to be a ship (a big white ship) and not a car at all. (137)

The narrator has given way, like A. and Franck, to treating the novel as a matter of fact, but with a complete absence of any form—even self-consistency. His interpretation suggests that the eruption of a hybrid material signifier in a scientifically restrained observer destroys not only objectivity but identity. The narrator, strapped into his voyeuristic chair, collapses under the weight of the unknowable into an impossible compromise of observation and desire. The dependency on simple surveillance confirms the narrator's solipsistic isolation, but cannot eliminate his suspicion that this isolation is his condition only; the others exist intersubjectively. For over and against this destruction of narrative is the conspiratorial reading of A. and Franck, whose synchronization of their interiors results in the possibility of a univocal exchange of messages—for them. Yet this suggestion itself is only the product of the narrator's gloriously failed attempt to read his own inadequate perceptions. They too might be mere constructs of desire, hallucinatory projections of other selves—an ambivalent consolation: if the narrator is an isolated cuckold, at least somewhere, someone out there is getting it.

If jealousy, sexual and medial, provides the force behind desire for artistic control, Paul Virilio expands the scope of this force beyond sexual desire to more sweeping, egocentric urges to control the fundamentals of space and time. From the dawn of cartography to the latest innovations in virtual reality, technology adjusts the interface between subject and environment, placing more and more of the physical world either within the grasp of the technologist or outside the pale of human contemplation. Twentieth-century culture has seen a rapid acceleration of such adjustments, with violent results. The advent of aerial surveillance, for example, and the reduction of three-dimensional topographical space to a two-dimensional image transformed the range and velocity of military destruction, and they also enabled a military reduction of populous cities to graphic targets. But Virilio's apocalyptic view of technology arises not simply from the increased prosthetic span of perception but from the possibility of its mass synchronization. Rationality itself constitutes the dominant example of such totalizing technology, with its definition of the project of modern science and its restriction of science to certain coordinable techniques. "The rational study of the real is just like the movies," writes Virilio in *The Aesthetics of Disappearance*; "the tabula rasa is only a trick whose purpose is to deny the particular absence of any active value." Cinema, refashioning time as well as space, illuminating a "false day," constitutes Virilio's touchstone for a whole range of media innovations.

Yet these movies' sinister simulacra are belied by Robbe-Grillet's art. Its violence, often some form of sadoerotic violence against women, bursts forth from the confinement of the mere datum, the "simple" percept, with destroying power, dramatizing the wrenching ambivalence over the existence and value of other subjects, of the interpretive drive in the face of its own impossibility. If other subjects—"depth"—exist (and their appearance through barriers, windows, and jalousies only underscores doubt), they present both the ultimate object of desire and its inevitable frustration. Intersubjectivity and solipsism present both seductive appeals and tormenting limitations. Other minds—in the form of collaboration, of multimedial dispersion—threaten betrayal, humiliation, even castration. Solipsism, the alternative, traps the subject in an infantile world of self-validating games. So as the perceiver struggles to mature, to achieve the objective, the result is a passion that finds the Other only to annihilate it, to achieve a momentary respite from uncertainty in action, if only to return once again to the spectatorship of the voyeur.

Virilio, as a media theorist, recasts like Robbe-Grillet the question of what apparatus is necessary to determine that something is "out there" into a question of what mechanisms determine the form of phenomena. But unlike Robbe-Grillet, Virilio's depiction of the perceiver's enclosure, her subjection to a deceptively simplified percept, takes its own staged regression seriously; "fact"—intermedial resistance—becomes impossibly reformulated into the unresisting synchronization of alienated bodies. Virilio's reflections imply a disembodied percept, as a media effect, and in modern times that effect results from an apathetic technology that elides the body as one's own. While Robbe-Grillet presents an ambivalence about control because of its necessary failure, its belatedness, its sour grapes, Virilio does not: technology, as the source for coordinating perception, *is* control, and the reality we want to experience is precisely what is nonfactic. Conversely, the absence of control is Virilio's operational definition of the Real; reality consists of the perceiver's subjection to a spatiotemporal dimension beyond the self. The Real is what someone else controls, operating like Descartes's evil genie, or like the artist with perfect authority. Its effect thus corresponds to a kind of lack, an absence Virilio compares to the Hebraic term *Shemama,* a desert of "laws, ideology, order" (*Aesthetics of Disappearance,* 31). *Shemama* is a societal set of protocols for the regulation of the percept, a discipline that substitutes itself for what are literally the internal disciplines of the heart: the pulse of blood, the alternation of flows in arteries and veins, all of which undergird the homeostatic flickering of neurons.

But Virilio's counterpoint to culture's desert of *Shemama* is not "real" nature, not the "objective," so much as a privatization of control; the individual replacement of the mass audience's cinematic motor with a lens of one's own. He begins *The Aesthetics of Disappearance* with a description of picnoleptic children, children who suffer brief lapses of awareness of the world around them while fully wakeful; they lose segments of time. Their world has an idiosyncratic temporality that only as they mature becomes integrated into the law of temporal continuity that governs the world at large: "There is a tendency to patch up sequences, readjusting their contours to make equivalents out of what the picnoleptic has seen and what he has not been able to see, what he remembers and what, evidently, he cannot remember and it is necessary to invent, to recreate, in order to lend verisimilitude to his discursus" (10). An analogous departure from the master motor of culture exists in descriptions of women's mentality in the early part of the century: Virilio cites accounts of "Hysterical women" who possess "transitory and vivid feelings, mobile and brilliant imaginations and, with it all, the inability to control, through reason and judgment, these feelings and imaginations" (11).

Women and children, precisely because they lack power, provide a critical standpoint with respect to the dominant culture; they lift the naturalizing veil concealing rationality's true nature as a cultural strategy for mass synchronization and deployment—attributes that best serve the purposes of a military state. Women's "power" consists in the alternative to the rational, in the seductive appeal of a countertechnology that full participation in the dominant culture destroys and devalues. Like Robbe-Grillet's artists, Virilio's women and children have the capacity to awaken their spectators from mundane illusions of control—fantasies enabled by the anaesthetic of convention and the naturalized but artificial rhythms of narrativity—to the real contingency of all control, the contingency of every aspect of the object. Such knowledge can, in turn, transform *Shemama*, the wasteland of the totalized city-state, into *Midbar*, an alternate term for absence signifying "a field of uncertainty and effort," a field of creative experimentation. For here the object is merely a percept; unlike Robbe-Grillet's object, it has no enduring capacity to mock illusion.

Unlike Robbe-Grillet's artists, though, Virilio's women and children by definition write no manifestos, make no attempt to divert power to themselves. Their struggle as an alternative political potential, illuminable in a latent memory as it flashes up in a moment of danger in Benjamin's essay, is completely elided in Virilio's historiography; by definition, they remain invisible. This absence of "real" political potential is due to Virilio's thoroughgoing monism; in the final analysis, Virilio's women and children, like objects themselves, do not exist as an opposition to technological hegemony at all, but only constitute phases of it. And in the case of women, that phase is past. Their claims on the dominant culture have been sacrificed by their assimilation. In obtaining equal rights and a slice of the technological mastery necessary to participate in the dominant culture, women, for Virilio, only accelerate the reconfiguration of control speeding the contemporary world to an asocial apocalypse.

Virilio's conception of the relation of technology to the percept is a linear one; his account of history is a monistic version of faculty psychology that ignores the implications of Condillac's statue, which remains decisively deprived without an active body. Virilio's somewhat nostalgic version of an opposition to totalizing technologies, consisting in the natural, heterosexual, and procreative basis for societal bonding, contrasts contemporary mediatized networks in terms of only one dimension: speed. Speed, the source of all military advantage, determines the success of each technological advance, and just as the cinematic motor displaces the sidereal day with the flickering lights of the filmic image, the general motor of electronic advance displaces all traditional space—the city, the road from here to there, the national geographical collective—with a nodal "space"—not space at all—that consists only of electronic receptors, networks, and conduits. Yet Virilio's speeding subject is, in the most important sense, immobilized, as alienated from the moving body as from the cinema screen; this is movement without impact. Speed, ultimately defining everything, is actually a flight from the differential inputs that Condillac's statue needs to become a self, to determine otherness.

Robbe-Grillet's immobilization of the subject in order to torment it, to parody its struggles in the cybernetic age, at least illustrates failures of both intersubjectivity and solipsism, together with their respective symptoms, word and image. The displacement of language by lies, or by signals, dramatizes the relation of technological imprisonment to a loss of the real as a "real" loss. For Virilio, though, this loss is a desirable rejection; the elimination of the Real has always been the supreme wish providing the trajectory of technology from its most primitive beginnings, a trajectory whose contemporary narrative is the story of "the famous Big Bang,"

> the explosion of causality that, according to physicists, was supposed to end tomorrow in a gigantic implosion of finality, a theoretical or meta-theoretical construction capable of saving the matter of the absence of sense, of preserving the creation of a creator, a secret desire for autonomy and for universal automation uniting all contemporary

apocalyptic trends, this revelation of the precariousness of the human will, this face of hopelessness that is perfectly matched to the degree of ambition among the sciences, this deception into which the idea of nature from the Enlightenment blurs into—and finally becomes confused with—the idea of the real, left over from the century of the speed of light. (*Lost Dimension*, 140–41)

If Robbe-Grillet's jealousy of art and his retaliatory imprisonment of the audience responds to fascist appropriations of art, Virilio extends this jealousy beyond the work of art to reality itself. The older fifties-style conspiracy theory that suspects an integrated intersubjective community of exclusion gives way to the suspect exclusiveness of technologies of coordination: the electronic net, decentralized but lightning-fast. Certainly both perspectives acknowledge real horrors, the first garishly illuminated by the Holocaust, the second by the more insidious but pervasive forms of genocide radiating outward from the economic exigencies of corporate transnationalism. Yet Virilio's de facto declaration of the death of sublime objectivity in the wake of the cybernetic signal makes Eros the minion of Thanatos, while it logically follows from Condillac that subject formation requires their equal struggle. Moreover, for much of the earth, the ascendance of a technofascism is only the exchange of one form of tyranny for another. For the masses who have barely managed subsistence, for all those whose ethnicity, gender, and sexuality have guaranteed only self-renunciation and sacrifice on behalf of powers that, however obscure the source, strike out with unmitigable violence, for these the problem of liberation is not new and needs no hermeneutic to uncover. To return to Benjamin's reflections, "history" is a history of victors, and presents a monologic illusion of progress that technology and its history simulate—but the power granted by that simulation cannot erase the multiplicity of subjectivities that persist, despite their erasure from many generations of two-dimensional screens.

Notes

1. Lest Condillac's statue analogy be dismissed as just a quaint but cumbersome eighteenth-century curiosity, I point out more "sophisticated" expositions of the same issue: Henri Poincaré makes Condillac's point concerning the necessity of motility to the sensorium's organization of space in an 1895 essay, "L'Espace et la géometrie," and more recently, Heinz von Foerster extends Poincaré's notion to present "intersubjectivity" as the convergence of perceptual perspectives achieved through a recursive analysis and correction of error.

Paul A. Harris

6 Exploring Technographies

Chaos Diagrams and Oulipian Writing

as Virtual Signs

In the complex historical line of relations between literature and technology, we seem to be coiled in an interestingly self-reflexive moment where the form of literature, always dependent on the encoding systems used to write it down, is being itself changed by technological innovations. As writers and scholars begin to integrate hypertext novels, interactive fiction, and new writing media into their sense of the literary, we find a different sense emerging of such basic notions as authorship, textuality, and the reading process. And as the computer becomes the primary scene of graphic practices across the human and natural sciences, its various uses change the way other modes of writing are carried out. It is widely assumed, for instance, that the burgeoning study of chaotic systems would never have occurred without the advent of computers, because the computer's calculating and graphic capabilities are necessary to represent the mathematical models being used.[1] Thus, as Brian Rotman observes, "the computer, a technoscientific product of mathematical thought, impinges on and begins to determine the 'internal' growth of mathematics itself" (*Ad Infinitum,* 150). Chaos theorists now use the seemingly oxymoronic phrase "experimental mathematics" to describe the graphic study of nonlinear models intractable to analysis (Campbell et al., 1985).

Precisely because the computer screen is the scene of writing across so many fields, it also seems to have the potential to act as a zone of exchange among disparate disciplinary discourses. All kinds of images and equipment already encourage us to mix modes of inscription; we already imagine our screens as a kind of virtual landscape, in which we can digitize words, numbers, images, and models, and circulate them all as configurations of pixels floating on a screen. Naturally, great store is set by the possibility of a new cross-disciplinary production of knowledge. For instance, Richard Lanham proclaims that as visual arts and music are digitized and thereby rendered in "desubstantialized" form, "digitization gives [the arts] a new common ground, a quasi-mathematical equivalency that recalls the great Platonic dream for the unity of all knowledge" (11).

Accompanying such celebrations of the computerized epistemological unity, however, we often find an underlying drive to let the medium subsume the message. Most often, the excitement over the technological tool seems to displace our focus from what it is used to produce.[2] But even if we recognize that the medium subsumes the message, we tend to frame this issue along semantic lines ("message" as denotative content). However, when we imagine the digitization of pictures, numbers, and words into a common medium, we also reduce the syntactic dimension of different sign systems to their medium—we cease thinking of signs as constitutive components of communication, with their own textures and nuances.

For this reason, I propose to follow a semiotic analysis that compares two very different technographic practices: the applied mathematics behind the graphic representations of chaotic systems (which I will call chaos diagrams) and the writings by members of Oulipo, the Paris-based "workshop for potential literature" cofounded by Raymond Queneau and François Le Lionnais in 1960. Oulipo consists of about twenty-five members who conduct experiments with literary form and syntax, writing texts that adhere to self-imposed constraints or rules. Oulipo has gained more attention in the United States with the publication of *A Void*, the translation of Georges Perec's *La Disparition* (1969), a novel written without an *e!* In following an extended parallel analysis of chaos diagrams and Oulipian writing, I suggest that we need not simply accept the dichotomy maintained between mathematical and linguistic signs. Rather than seek to reduce one to the other, however, to show a "quasi-mathematical equivalency" between them, I develop categories within which we may fruitfully compare their respective modes of signification.

My choice of these semiotic practices naturally reflects larger motivations. With respect to chaos diagrams, I seek to show how mathematical inscriptions are susceptible to semiotic treatment. I single out chaos diagrams for analysis because they have brought applied mathematics back into the popular eye in a remarkable way. These computer-generated graphics may be seen as a turn away from a Platonic sense of mathematics—mathematics as the manipulation of numerals that represent pure numbers. We may instead perceive them as material signs, for as Rotman asserts, the computer-generated graphics of chaos "are nothing less than a new mode of mathematical writing" (*Ad Infinitum*, 150). Rotman offers a semiotic taxonomy that helps clarify this claim: he divides writing between alphabetic and numeric inscriptions, and then divides mathematical writing into ideograms (symbols for numbers and operations) and diagrams ("Thinking Dia-Grams," 16). Once seen in this way, fractals and chaos models amount to "previously undrawable kinds of diagrams." And their rendering in graphic images draws attention to their materiality *as* signs. Rotman points out that, whereas ideograms inscribe purely abstract propositions about ideal entities within a fixed sign system, diagrams "are inseparable from perception"; they "call attention to the materiality of all signs and to the corporeality of those who manipulate them in a way that ideograms . . . do not" ("Thinking Dia-Grams," 21–22).

If chaos diagrams may show how computer-generated mathematical forms are in fact a type of writing, Oulipian writing conversely may remind us that electronic textuality only realizes or concretizes certain ways of perceiving or relating to language. Thus as hypertext and interactive fiction ostensibly change our relation to graphic practices, we may cast a retrospective eye over literary experiments and find that a technographic sensibility has informed them all along. If the computer screen as scene of writing transforms textual production into the manipulation of pixels on a screen, we can see how for Oulipians this pixel-shifting sensibility is already inscribed in the very premises of writing.[3] Simultaneously, as many members of Oulipo were computer scientists or trained in mathematical graph theory, they began integrating the computer into their literary experimentations long before the practice began to be theorized by literary critics (see Motte). Broadly speaking, if chaos diagrams show how numerical calculations can materialize as mathematical writing, Oulipian writing shows how mathematical formalisms can be used as the basis for generating literary texts. Raymond Queneau centered the workshop on *potential* literature because the literary is "less a question of literature strictly speaking than of supplying forms for the good use one can make of literature. We call potential literature the search for new forms and structures which may be used by writers in any way they see fit" (in Motte, xi). According to Jacques Roubaud, the Oulipian writer treats "language as if [it] could be mathematized." Roubaud, also a professor of mathematics, proposes that "writing under Oulipian constraint is the equivalent of the drafting of a mathematical text which may be formalized according to the axiomatic method" (in Motte, 15).[4]

A Semiotics of the Virtual

Both chaos diagrams and Oulipian writing, we could say, persist in a virtual space in which signs are manipulated directly, and new forms are invented through combinatoric play. Both chaos diagrams and Oulipian texts entail a sort of experimental research in their respective media, an "exploration of virtualities" (Benabou, 42). The virtual space that marks chaos diagrams and Oulipian writing as virtual signs is delineated by a kind of syntactic boundary constructed around the play of signs; in both cases, the researcher sets up initial parameters or constraints, and then seeks out the unexpected result or configuration.

Chaos theorists use the computer as a tool for conducting experimental mathematics in order to analyze the dynamics of nonlinear systems; simulations enable them to study the evolution of nonintegrable dynamical models. Simulations and the chaos diagrams they generate persist in a virtual realm complexly nestled between theory and experiment. The digital computer's calculating powers enable simulation to act, on the one hand, as "an experiment into an unknown area of mathematical structure, using a physical apparatus" (Weissert, "Fermi-Pasta-Ulam Problem," 161). On the other hand, the simulation is also read as a source of information about physical reality, an act that truncates a series of layers that stand between the graphic representation and the physical phenomenon (see Weissert, "Fermi-Pasta-Ulam Problem," 158–210, for details). The initial values, parameters, and constraints of the simulation mark a sort of selection boundary; after that, it is a matter of running the simulation and following the evolution of its trajectory in a multidimensional mathematical space. Thus the production of chaos diagrams represents a research into forms as they evolve in virtual space.

Even though Oulipian writers are not bound to a technological medium, we may develop a similar picture of them. The notion of literature as a *potential* domain delineates it as a zone of inscription in which one intervenes in calculated ways. The larger object of Oulipo's investigation is always language—language understood as a complex system whose components may be combined in a variety of ways. The combinatorics of Oulipian investigations are dictated by the choice of constraints. Constraints thus draw a sort of syntactic boundary that marks the text; as Marcel Benabou puts it, constraint is "a commodious way of passing from language to writing" (41). Just as the chaos scientist generates forms from specified parameters, the Oulipian writer generates texts within self-imposed constraints. Constraints enable the writer to conduct a sort of experimental research into language because they open up language to new possibilities—the constraint "forces the system out of its routine functioning, thereby compelling it to reveal its hidden resources" (Benabou 41).

The most magisterial exploration of the possibilities of language through the use of constraints is probably Georges Perec's *Life, a User's Manual.* Each chapter describes a room in an apartment building; the order of chapters is decided by "la polygraphie du cavalier"—using a knight's move on a 10 × 10 chessboard to touch each square once; each chapter contains a component from each of forty-two lists; these components are in turn selected from bi-Latin squares, whose paired coordinates are matched to the chapter's coordinates on the chessboard-text-map.[5] The intricate inscriptions that define the virtual space of the text precede the finished work, but may themselves be thought of as a genre of literary diagram. Looking through the *Cahiers des charges de "La Vie, mode d'emploi,"* one is struck by the diagrammatic layout of its contents, the combination of mathematical constructions and linguistic lists that form the machinery for generating what Perec called his "universe of lists." In general, Oulipian texts have a marked propensity to generate diagrams, whether within the text, as paratexts, as pretexts, or in critical exegetical texts.[6]

Such diagrams become an integral tool for critics writing on Oulipian texts, because part of the skill of these writers is to efface the traces of the formal principles from which the texts are constructed. On one level, the writer thus both adheres to and overcomes the constraints—hiding them is a game that wins the writer a kind of victory over the reader. On another level, though, it is an Oulipian stipulation that the formal constraints of a text must be played out in a metafictional game: Roubaud postulated that "a text written according to a constraint must speak of this constraint," and "a text written according to a mathematizable constraint must contain the consequences of the mathematical theory it illustrates" (in Motte, 12). In *La Disparition/A Void,* the absence of the *e* is alluded to throughout the novel—for instance, lists of twenty-six objects or people appear, only to have the fifth member missing. Part of Perec's ingenuity in writing *Life, a User's Manual* was to allude slyly to the text's exhaustive formal rules all the time, while yet writing a book whose surface betrays none of the immense constraint under which it was produced. The protagonist, Bartlebooth, imposes on himself a project that clearly allegorizes Oulipian constraint: he spends ten years learning to paint, then takes twenty years to paint five hundred seascapes that are turned into jigsaw puzzles, and is then to complete all the puzzles in another twenty years. The novel's preamble on jigsaw puzzling is a thinly veiled meditation on the relation between the reader and the text; it thus enjoins the reader to engage in the game of puzzling out the textual constraints.

The Oulipian text that speaks of its own constraint in this way is thus different from a chaos diagram, which has no self-referential dimension. The self-referential dynamics of the Oulipian text creates an interestingly strange loop between the semantic and syntactic dimensions, for the text is constantly crossing the very syntactical boundary (the constraints) within which its signs are played out; yet at the same time, the self-conscious game that violates the syntactic boundary also folds the semantic dimension back into the syntactic—as the characters and plot that emerge allude back to the constraints. As readers, we do not seek the "meaning" of the text in the usual sense; for as Sydney Levy explains, "the chimera of the Oulipian message is that information and message are one and the same. We move thus to the tickling of a second level of abstraction: the different forms of a single message are, in themselves, the message" ("Oulipian Messages," 160).

Virtual Reading

The chimerical effect of the Oulipian text locates the reader within an unfolding game played out according to the textual constraints. The textual constraints of a book like *Life, a User's Manual* form a sort of network within which a reader moves about; we are invited to recombine components and constraints in new ways, thus literally playing out the text, realizing its virtual form in different ways. This notion of the reading process merges toward the picture drawn by theorists of electronic writing, who, playing up the digital medium of signification, envision the writing or reading subject as dispersed across "a de-centered (or centerless) network of codes that, on another level, also serves as a node within another centerless network" (Landow, 73). But this view in essence disembodies the reading subject, for we read not only with our minds but in our bodies; no matter the textual medium, reading is an embodied process.

Following Rotman's semiotic model, we may rather think of the reader of virtual signs in terms of a curious kind of split—a split between an embodied person reading and an imagined, potential reader who could in principle be injected into a cyber-semiotic space, and would go on pursuing infinite counting or infinite permutations. Rotman's semiotics encompasses several aspects of the inscription process: in analyzing mathematics, he divides what we call "the mathematician" into three agencies. The Person is a historical, self-conscious being who writes "the underlying story organizing the proof steps" of a mathematical theorem in "metacode." Metacode designates the source and domain of signs that provide a context in which the formal mathematical Code can function. The Subject writes in this strictly mathematical Code, showing the deductive chain of steps in the proof. The Agent is an imaginary figment of the Subject, a mental being that the discourse projects as the one who executes the steps demanded by the proof. In *Ad Infinitum*, Rotman shows how formalizations of infinity in mathematics depend upon this disembodied Agent, a noiseless, immortal entity (not unlike Maxwell's Demon) left to do the infinite counting and calculating involved in problems of infinity. Rotman has compared this model of how mathematics is conducted to how we interact with virtual reality technology. The Person corresponds to a "real-I," who manipulates a "virtual-I" (the proxy-Agent); and these two are mediated by a "goggled-I," the Subject, who is logged or jacked into cyberspace. In both mathematics and virtual reality, we propel an imago around in a virtual space, and both demand interaction in an embodied sense— virtual realists enact journeys in a reality and mathematicians actively manipulate signs. Mathematics has become "the creation of pixel arrangements on a computer screen," and thus resembles Artifical Life worlds and virtual realities ("Thinking Dia-Grams," 31–33).

These aspects of Rotman's semiotics are especially relevant for Oulipian texts, because the latter enjoin the reader to enter into the space of what is explicitly a virtual text. The role of the reader in Oulipian texts is that of a "player" as much as a "reader" in a traditional literary sense. Rather than invite the reader to interpret a work, the ludic dimension of Oulipian texts makes the reader actually intervene in and almost coproduce a text. The idea of a potential literature entails texts that are like seeds for generating different particularized versions of the text. Raymond Queneau's *Cente Mille Millards de poèmes* contains a set of 10 possible lines for each line in a sonnet, allowing for 10^{14} possible sonnets. Queneau calculated that "if one read a sonnet per minute, eight hours a day, two hundred days a year, it would take more than a million centuries to finish the text" (Motte, 3). Jacques Bens, Claude Berge, and Paul Braffort call such works "recursive texts," because they contain a kind of generative algorithm or set of "generative rules that invite the reader to pursue the production to infinity" (109). It is this mathematical (as opposed to purely literary) formalism that sets Oulipian texts apart from other postmodern novels that engage the reader in a playful, ironic, self-conscious exchange.[7] We may translate Oulipian texts and readers into Rotman's semiotic model as follows: The flesh-and-blood individual who holds the book corresponds to the Person, while the reader as one immersed in the rules of the textual game is the Subject. The potential reader who would pursue all possible readings is the Agent. The Oulipian reader becomes in effect one who executes a program in which a "virtual-I" zips around in textual cyberspace. (Thus it is apt that Jean-Jacques Thomas titled his analysis of Oulipo "README.DOC.")

The Instability of Description

Precisely because of the chimerical quality of the Oulipian message, the textual game changes our gaze, our very way of looking at the written signs. Part of the Oulipian game is that we wonder about the text's formal secret—what constraints have shaped its surface. Thus we look more and more closely at the signs themselves, seeking to discern the syntactical principles underlying their organization. And as we do so, the actual nature and function of the signs becomes less and less certain. As constraints jar language from conventional or habitual usages, words begin to appear somewhat strange; I find that reading a text such as *La Disparition/A Void*, one where the strain of the constraint is so great that the writer must make all kinds of effort to accommodate it, the language becomes distinctly other, unsettlingly estranged. Words begin to look mispelled, sentence rhythms become irregular; and rather than being able simply to skip along, pass off these effects as temporary, I look more and more closely at the words and sentences; of course, the uncanniness of the prose only grows more intense as a result. The way in which microscopic scrutiny of the Oulipian sign yields a certain instability has a certain counterpart in chaos diagrams: the closer we zoom in on chaos diagrams, the less certain the larger picture they draw; the smaller the scale at which we use these diagrams to predict physical behavior, the less certain we can be about our predictions.

We could say that one distinguishing feature of virtual signs is that we not only lose a simple referential relation between signifier and signified, but the signifiers seem to draw us into them in such a way that they collapse in on themselves. Even as virtual signs seemingly describe a world outside themselves, they become almost opaque, and our gaze rather takes in the *texture* of the signs themselves. But at this moment the semantic once again rises from the breakdown of the syntactic, for as soon as we look at signs "themselves," the signs form an object—the signifier has become a signified of some new kind. As Rotman points out, this is a process played out again and again in mathematical discourse: problems of one type or within one mathematical discourse generate solutions that then define a new domain of study. Put more generally, the combining of signifiers takes part in the creation of what it subsequently comes to name and refer to as a signified.[8]

With his very first words in *Life, a User's Manual,* Perec notifies the reader that the sense of his book is concerned with our visual encounter with its signs—the novel's epigraph is "Look with all your eyes, look." The phrase is taken from Jules Verne's *Michel Strogoff,* at a moment when the main character is about to be blinded. The epigraph thus evokes Bartlebooth's eventual blindness brought on by completing Winckler's puzzles and indirectly warns the reader of the perils of scrutinizing the text as closely as it demands. Anna Botta observes that in the text as a whole Perec's written signs become caught up in a relation of *mise-en-abîme* to visual ones: Valène's painting will narrate stories, while Perec's text describes his painting (154).

Despite the dangers, Perec does get us to "look with all our eyes," first, simply by imposing a tremendous amount of description on us. The texture of Perec's novel is dominated by a clutter of things, a density of descriptive detail and endless enumerations. The pace of storytelling— and Perec tells many fabulous stories in the novel—is disrupted by the slow neutrality of bland declarative sentences that meticulously describe photos, texts, or rooms. Objects are given in outline, the faces of characters are seldom described, and space is filled with frames and traces of things that await a reader to give them embodiment.

In part, this insistently neutral mode of description, this cataloguing procedure, stems from Perec's obligation to his lists—he is assembling and copying down predesignated components. But lists exceed any sort of transparent function in Perec's economy of writing. *Life, a User's Manual* takes shape in a "universe of lists," as the editors of the *Cahiers des charges* put it; like diagrams, the lists instantiate a material textual space within or from which the work unfolds, they mark a physical schema that traces the formal outlines of the book. And as Roubaud has pointed out, Perec developed a veritable "poetics of lists" throughout his writing ("Notes," 202). The role of lists in Perec's writing is brought home when one examines all of the pre-texts that surround his novels—for instance, the draft pages of *La Disparition* are interspersed with lists of words without an *e*, lists made by association (places, cigarette brands, types of objects), lists literally surrounded by an outpouring of *e*'s in the borders of the pages, a calligraphic showering that attests to the weight of the constraint.[9]

In *Life, a User's Manual*, Perec points to the fact that much of the text is just copying lists by telling several stories involving forgeries and copies. But the very extreme degree to which Perec pursues this descriptive mode gives the objects a vertiginous quality; we linger over them like Bartlebooth at the puzzle board, where he finds that "the main problem was to stay neutral, objective, and above all flexible," because the puzzle pieces take on a life of their own, "as if the pieces were being polarised, or vectorised, or were solidifying into a perceptual model" (333). Thus once the pieces become illusions of other things through a sort of trompe-l'oeil, they can be fitted into their proper places only when they are "reversed, revolved, decentred, desymbolised: in a word, de-*formed*" (334). Behind Perec's seemingly mechanical economy of description lurks what Claude Burgelin calls Perec's fascination with "the strange alchemy that produces something new from the identical" (211; my translation). The precise outlines of things and people in Perec's system of signs begin to waver; their sharp cuts lose their rigidity and become flexible, rubbery.

The mathematical signs and diagrams of chaos theory used in processes of simulation contain a certain inherent instability as well. Simulation in this context may be defined as "the entire process of numerically integrating a set of differential equations on a computer and displaying graphically for analysis the sequential solution states as an ordered set of points in a phase space portrait" (Weissert, "Fermi-Pasta-Ulam Problem," 19). In other words, chaos diagrams emerge as the computer plots a series of points that are solutions to a set of differential equations. The inherent slippages in this process come about, first of all, because the computer operates in discrete states, called time-steps. In chaotic regions of the phase portrait, small differences make a big difference; even as the computer plots what look like continuous trajectories, the space "between" time-steps allows for divergences from the "actual" system. Thus from the necessary approximation entailed by digitizing a continuous time evolution into discrete steps emerges a difference between a "true solution" and "simulated solution" to the equations (Weissert, "Fermi-Pasta-Ulam Problem," 20).

We could say that, by definition, the sensitive dependence on initial conditions that defines deterministic chaos inscribes a degree of imprecision in the model, because the ever-present imprecision of specifying conditions has a large impact on the resultant evolution of the system. While attractors in systems usually mark a predictable repetition or stability, strange attractors undermine this stability because trajectories from initial conditions that are extremely close together will diverge very quickly. As Ilya Prigogine and Isabelle Stengers point out in *Entre le temps et l'éternité*, the entire scheme of causality changes here, because what may seem like the same causes give rise to very different effects. What we find, then, is that in a sense the quantitative limits on precision inherent in chaos diagrams inscribes "the strange alchemy that produces something new from the identical" that Perec creates from language. Prigogine and Stengers observe that the risk of "all description, all definition," is that "words like numbers have a finite precision. All description, verbal or numerical, defines a situation not in so far as it were identical to itself, but in so far as it belongs to a class of situations completely compatible with the same words or the same numbers" (76; my translation). On a strange attractor, because of sensitive dependence on initial conditions, "numbers define not a point but a small region of the space, as restricted as the sequence of decimals is long" (77; my translation).

If we now step back and look at chaos diagrams from a metaphorical or general perspective, we see this quantitative imprecision replicated by the qualitative texture of strange attractors—they do not occupy space like sharply delineated objects, but form a sinuous, intricate mesh. Looking at cross sections of strange attractors, or viewing them across different self-similar scales, we experience something of the vertigo of Bartlebooth poring over Winckler's puzzles. And both strange attractors and Perec's verbal surface induce us to see them in a way that Bernard Magne, describing Perec's book, calls a "redoubling of our gaze": "Neither the stories alone, nor the constraints alone, but their incessant interweaving in all senses" (31, "Puzzle de 100 pièces"; my translation).

The Heterogeneity of Time

The tangled skein or "incessant interweaving" of chaos diagrams provides a powerful, visual metaphor for a sense of time that we find across a number of contemporary theoretical writings. The impact that electronic media and inscriptions have had on this sense of time is difficult to measure but certainly significant. Clearly, we have lost an image of time as stretching out across long, horizontal trajectories, an image predominant in nineteenth-century evolutionary and historical models. Instead, we experience time across a huge range of scales, from atomic clocks that measure time in incredibly precise increments to the movement of galaxies toward some cosmological "great attractor." As a result, we may conceive of time as a tangle of these different scales; it is as if, just as we always inhabit several types of space simultaneously, we are always moving in several dimensions or modes of temporality.

The information technologies that we regularly use contribute to a compression of time. One of the first practical applications of fractals was in digital imaging: fractal techniques enable the image to be compressed into much smaller strings of information. More generally, cultural critics diagnose the temporal dynamics of electronic writing, its sheer speed, in terms commensurate with chaos diagrams: Mark Poster claims that "computer writing, instantaneously available over the globe, inserts itself into a non-linear temporality that unsettles the relation to the writing subject" (128). In analyzing the logic of temporality in electronic networks, Vivian Sobchak argues that "temporality is dispersed and finds resolution as part of a recursive, if chaotic, structure of coincidence. . . . Temporality is constituted paradoxically as a *homogeneous* experience of *discontinuity* in which . . . time seems to turn back on itself recursively in a structure of equivalence and reversibility" (26).

The sense of time Sobchak describes in general conceptual terms can be extrapolated from some of the technical properties of strange attractors. The complex mathematical object is a compressed image of time, in that it represents the evolution of a system. And, as Sobchak argues, the computer screen does seem to homogenize the texture of time and render it in discrete form. However, time figured in chaos diagrams is not reversible, because the sensitive dependence on initial conditions affects the outcome of trajectories no matter which way they are plotted—if we plot a trajectory from an initial point, simply reversing the process does not, in chaotic regions, simply lead us back to the point.

We also should remember, however, that even though we may interpret chaos diagrams as time-maps by discussing the patterns of trajectories, this way of thinking is still based on a linear conception of time—that is, seeing the twists in trajectories as bending the line of time. But in chaos diagrams, "time" becomes a function of the behavior of a system as a whole—time is figured less as unfolding along trajectories than as the shifting shape of attractors. As Hayles explains, "the system no longer is conceived as masses of points moving along a predictable path, but is seen as the evolution of the internal structural principles that describe the propagation of its self-similar symmetries" (*Chaos Bound*, 218). Rather than a time-measure that corresponds to an individual history or the motion of an object, we have what must be called simply a system-time. The age of system-time can be measured only in topological terms: Prigogine and Stengers calculate a system's time evolution by its "internal time," which they define as a function of the number of foldings of its topology (185).

Within this multidimensional system-time, if one imagines time only in terms of what happens to single trajectories, then one can sense time only as an impossibly tangled weave. When a strange attractor is examined at the micro level, the divergence of nearly identical initial conditions produces different histories of a system; this exponential rate of divergence is called the "characteristic time" (Ruelle, 74). Prigogine and Stengers term this "a scale of time," which defines a "temporal horizon." "Like a real horizon," they write, "the temporal horizon of chaotic systems marks the difference between what we can 'see' and what is beyond—the evolution that we can describe not in terms of individual behavior, but only in terms of erratic behavior common to all systems characterized by chaotic attractors" (*Entre le temps et l'éternité*, 77–78; my translation). Our predicting grasp or controlling hold on time is simply lost, as our temporal horizon shrinks.

Perec's novel is analogous to the way chaos diagrams inscribe time in that, while it unfolds several individual story lines that meander around throughout history and across the globe, the book as a whole is constructed according to structural principles. The form of the book, in other words, develops in what one could call a sort of system time. In abstract terms, we may imagine the unfolding narrative as a trajectory through Perec's constraint space—each chapter, as it incorporates elements from each of the lists, is like a forty-two-dimensional strange attractor through the building space. And as we pass from chapter to chapter, we keep folding the topology of the attractor, so that the time evolution of the system is not predictable. We could say, using Sydney Levy's words, that each chapter along the narrative trajectory, "each arrangement, each configuration of the pieces . . . constructs a new reality, a new order, that disrupts that of the preceding arrangement and will itself be destroyed by the following move" (*Play of the Text*, 9).

The overall result in Perec's text is a peculiar mixture of temporalities. On a large scale, we move about in time to an unusual extent, while on the micro scale, the meticulous mode of description harbors heterogeneous temporalities. Jean Bessière concisely expresses the way in which Perec's descriptive techniques generate a particular ensemble of temporalities: "By the effect of visibility, the narrative demolishes its own system and constructs a topology and follows a nonchronological time. The description constitutes the only object, decomposed, multiple in itself. It becomes a sort of screen where there passes, without any distance, the past and the future, the inside and the outside. Time and space . . . become specific to the work: that which organizes the optical scenes" (7; my translation). This insight provides an important stipulation about literary system time: while we may be wary in political terms of systematizing time, the system time proper to a literary work is produced from within the text. It exfoliates, as it were, from the internal dynamics of the form, rather than being some preexisting, homogeneous medium in which the text unfolds. Simultaneously, time is compressed and flattened, rendered into a shifting graphic form.

A New Realism?

In the wake of Baudrillard and other critics who envision the world collapsing into a hyperreality of pure simulation, theorists have been quick to equate the onset of digital technologies with a loss of reality as we think of it in common-sense terms. And after we have seen time recede into strange attractors and the world of the text radiate out into innumerable potential configurations, it would seem curious to speak now of "realism." Indeed, virtual signs seem closer to "constructivism" than "realism." But as simulations affect the philosophy of science, we witness a curious convergence between realism and constructivism.[10] While traditional scientific realism claims that theories and equations correspond to actual physical entities, in the work of leading realist philosophers of science such as Richard Boyd and Richard Miller we see a shift toward a limited idea of correspondence and a locally defined theory of how theories refer to reality.

In these respects, realism resembles what Hayles calls "constrained Constructivism." Hayles argues that scientific theories are always human constructs, that "we are always already in the theater of representation." However, she also recognizes a local, context-sensitive form of truth testing: "Within the range of representations available at a given time, we can ask, 'Is this representation consistent with the aspects of reality under interrogation?' " ("Constrained Constructivism," 81). Hayles's formulation captures quite concretely the way realism enters into simulations and models in chaos theory. Alain Boutot points out that chaos diagrams are constructed only as locally valid descriptions of physical reality—objects are modelled with what Mandelbrot calls the "effective physical dimension." Boutot explains that "the effective dimension of a concrete object is not its actual dimension, but that of the geometrical figure that best represents it at the scale of observation under consideration" (98–99; my translation).[11]

We should be wary of simply proclaiming that now science is self-conscious of its own descriptions, as if scientists put into practice what theorists like to read into chaos theory. But the virtual, taken in its general sense as the domain of computer graphic practices, has a nebulous but decided and increasing impact on our basic sense of reality. Even if chaos theorists are not stirred by the inherent instabilities of description, some contemporary philosophers think of the real as an unstable field. In Clement Rosset's work, the real is, like an Oulipian text, not concerned with a hidden semantic dimension, a deeper meaning that the real contains. Rosset thus speaks of the radical "insignificance of the real."

While the combinatoric play of Oulipian texts seems to preclude any concept of a reality outside their own parameters, we may discover this idea of an insignificant real inscribed in them.[12] The self-contained formal conception of *Life, a User's Manual*—its lists, puzzles, and stories—marks an emphatically antimimetic approach to the novel. However, we could also think of Perec's text as a form of second-order mimesis: a self-reflexive text mimetic only of itself on one level, but on another level one that creates a distinctive texture of the real. Rather than representing a preexisting reality, Perec instantiates the real as a dynamic field; the texture of the real exfoliates from the play of textual signifiers. The combinatoric possibilities inscribed in the text open up a virtual dimension that recapitulates the combinatoric fabric of the world. This natural philosophy is Epicurean; Calvino reminds us that for Lucretius letters were atoms, so that new alphabetic permutations model the physical processes of reality. And just as Serres (1982) discovers in Lucretius's *De rerum natura* a poetics that simultaneously designates a physics (and vice versa), so the combinatoric machinery of *Life, a User's Manual*, its very ontonlogy as it were, contains a constructive principle, a mode of worldmaking. Oulipian literature, even as it plays its own intricate games, thus is mimetic of the combinatoric nature of reality. Jacques Bens argues that "if one begins to reflect that *potentiality*, more than a technique of composition, is a certain means of conceiving literature, one would perhaps admit that it opens onto a perfectly authentic modern realism. For reality never shows more than a part of itself, authorizing a thousand interpretations, significations, and solutions, all equally probable" (72).

As we enter into an age of writing that will without doubt become increasingly digitized, the stakes for the way we process and understand virtual signs increase, and it is crucial not to forget the embodied individual in the midst of the proliferation of potential combinatorics of signs. The Oulipian game seems on one level to deny time, as one may play with the text ad infinitum. It is crucially telling, however, that the novels by Perec and Roubaud are built on death—Roubaud's work is one of mourning his dead wife, Alix, while Perec's novel all occurs at the moment of Bartlebooth's death. Bartlebooth dies holding a piece shaped like a *W*, but the blank space in the puzzle forms an *X*—the *W* evoking Perec's allegorical novel about fascism. Here we see how the semiotic game embodies the thematic thrust of the text: the self-enclosing moment of the book, the end where it disappears into an unfillable blankness, simultaneously exfoliates onto several levels of meaning. Furthermore, Perec's novel stages its own death at the structural level: the razing of the apartment building is described, Bartlebooth's painting-puzzles are erased, and the Epilogue ends with a report of Valène's canvas of the building, which is blank. In *The Great Fire of London*, Roubaud interprets Perec's use of the *W* and *X* images as a "metaphor of Oulipo . . . a recognition of the failure . . . of the planned constraint, of the impossibility of its completion" (255-56). He reads the *W* as a visual palindrome of *M*, the *M* in Perec's last chapter being Meander, the city painted on the puzzle Bartlebooth is completing; Meander, of course, is the river that resists completion or arrival at its destination.

What we find, then, is just how much the "meaning" of chaos theory and fractals depends upon the inflection we give them. Speaking of the "synthesis of time" that is represented in chaos diagrams, Edmond Couchot points to their implicit denial of mortality and finitude: "The time of synthesis is, like the image of synthesis, a virtuality, a quasi-infinite reservoir of instants, of durations, of simultaneities, of chains or bifurcations of causes and effects, not simply reversible, or readable in reverse, but completely redefinable and reiterable: a *potential* time" (120; my translation). Yet we may trace this potential time back to a material sign and an embodied writer. Brian Rotman writes, "In my understanding of infinity, fractals are not representations of an ideal—infinitistic—situation in the complex plane or wherever, but pictures on the screen, the physical objects produced as a result of real calculations. As such, they don't go on producing new patterns forever, but like any series of physical objects get cruder, lose integrity, and eventually disappear" (personal communication). To James Gleick's proclamation that "in the mind's eye, fractals are a way of seeing infinity" (98), we could respond that fractals disappear from the eye of perception. Even in relation to a virtual semiotic reality, our last words may be: Ashes to ashes, Cantor dust to Cantor dust.

Notes

1. One predominant reason to support this thesis is that the mathematical tools necessary for chaos theory have been in place since the late nineteenth and early twentieth centuries. For other accounts of why chaos theory has taken so long to "materialize," see Ruelle, 49–50, and Kellert, 199–58.

2. Richard Grusin calls this phenomenon "mistaking . . . the physical manifestations [electronic technologies] for the linguistic or discursive text" (475). On an anecdotal level, when I saw the computer graphic artist David Em present his work, for 45 minutes members of the audience asked him questions that centered exclusively on the computers and printers he used; not one person asked him about his work or the relation of the art to the technology.

3. Here I share William Paulson's sense that "computers and information technology are more important to literature as conceptual models and shapers of intellectual and social context than as concrete devices with immediate applications in the production, storage, and manipulation of texts" ("Computers, Minds, and Texts," 299). (It is no accident that Paulson's assertion follows directly on the heels of a discussion of Oulipo.)

4. Roubaud's novel *The Great Fire of London* takes its structural model from treatises by Bourbaki, the elite group of mathematicians who sought to render mathematics in its purest axiomatic form. Roubaud's text unfolds in an intricate series

of axioms, assertions, and derivations, and then concludes with sections of inter-polations and bifurcations. Moreover, Roubaud apparently conceives of *The Great Fire of London* as one of six novels that, when completed, will form a single mathematical structure.

5. I give a more detailed exposition of Perec's constraints in "The Invention of Forms."

6. For instance, the edition of the *Cahiers Georges Perec* that explicates the formal underpinnings of Perec's heterogrammatic poetry (poems written under several intricate constraints on what letters are used, in what order, etc.) contains innumerable diagrams, revealing the rules by which these poems were written and showing how the frequency of letters is distributed (Ribière). Beyond the intricacies of constraints on letters, the formal elegance of a text such as Italo Calvino's *Invisible Cities* incites critics to chart its structural principles. Laura Marello displays the inverted symmetry and regenerative rotation of the novel's mathematical structure in a sequence of diagrams that take up more space than her exposition; words are less needed (or effective) in explicating such principles. And in "Diagramming Calvino's Architecture," Michael J. Palmore uses a figure to demonstrate the series of two-dimensional formal relationships one may construct among the cities and then renders the architecture of the cities in both ideograms and diagrams.

7. Of course, several postmodern novels play games similar to those played by Oulipian writers. Calvino wrote *If on a Winter Night a Traveler* before joining Oulipo; it is as if his membership only confirmed a prior literary identity. But to reiterate, the use of constraints as a syntactical boundary sharpens this propensity, giving it a rigor and precision for which literary experimenters usually find no need.

8. For instance, first there is a diagram of a right triangle with sides 1; then the solution, the square root of 2, generates a new problem, that of irrational numbers. Or first the equation $X^2 + 1 = 0$, then the imaginary number i is created to satisfy the equation.

9. I am grateful to Hans Hartje, secretary of the Association Perec, housed at the Bibliothèque Arsenale, for the opportunity to examine Perec's original manuscripts.

10. For a different spin on the question of realism and science, see Porush's discussion of Bachelard and science that is aligned along the lines of rationalism, the irrational, and realism ("Hacking the Brainstem").

11. However, Boutot extrapolates philosophical consequences rather freely from the realism of chaos diagrams. Fascinated by the mixture of microscopic description and macroscopic simulation in chaos theory, Boutot proclaims that it is "a science that enables us to understand reality, not simply to act on it," and envisions chaos as plunging science into "the ethereal region . . . to regain the soul, that is to say, the humus of the world of life, the ultimate source of sense" (13–14; my translation). Boutot's statement, even as it envisions a new philosophical turn in science, depends on a traditional, rather stable definition of the real as something whose "ground" or essence can be discovered, and the scientist as one who grasps the previously secret formative principles of nature.

12. I discuss the relations between Rosset and Perec in "The Invention of Forms."

Part III

Postmodernisms
The Novel in the Era of Media Multiplicity

Friedrich Kittler

7 Media and Drugs in
Pynchon's Second World War

Translated from the German by Michael Wutz

and Geoffrey Winthrop-Young

In the fall of 1983, the German press agency issued the following report: The leader of the Christian Social Union (CSU) and Prime Minister of Bavaria, Strauss, claims to be in possession of "fairly concrete information" that the GDR has for years been reconstructing subterranean facilities from the Third Reich for the deployment of atomic weapons. During an international symposium of the Hanns Seidel Foundation, Strauss observed that some of these "natural fortresses" are located 300 to 400 meters underground, making them safe against nuclear attack. (*Frankfurter Allgemeine Zeitung*, November 3, 1983, p. 12)

What the press agency failed to note was that these "natural fortresses," especially those in the vicinity of Nordhausen in the Harz Mountains, had once before housed and even mass-produced rockets. Which is why the Soviet SS 20s in their bunkers or the Pershings on the autobahns describe only an arc, the rainbow of an eccentric homecoming.[1]

War

Gravity's rainbow, the arc of gravity, is the trajectory of the V-2 rockets that—launched from bases in Holland or Lower Saxony against such metropolitan areas as London and Antwerp—flew over the

German-Allied fronts during the last six months of the war,[2] from September 8, 1944, until March 27, 1945. *Gravity's Rainbow* is also Thomas Pynchon's attempt to read the signs of the times as a novel, for these signs—notwithstanding all postwar fantasies[3]—were written by the Second World War: as the "mother" of those technologies that have engendered us, as well as a postmodernity that "threatens the idea of cause and effect itself."

The V-2, which Wernher von Braun and Army Proving Ground (Heeresversuchsanstalt) Peenemünde developed from a technician's toy to a serial *Wunderwaffe* and which, in Pynchon's most abysmal projection (and in keeping with Braun's blueprints), anticipated at war's end manned flight into space, was the first liquid-fuel rocket in the history of warfare. That is why it is at the center of a novel that reads the signs of our times. The parallel development of American arms, on the other hand, emerges at the most remote horizon of the novel or theater of war in Hiroshima and Nagasaki (559, 588, 627). The only thing you have to do is replace the conventional warhead of the V-2—a ton of amatol (111, 363) to be detonated, according to Hitler's personal suggestion,[5] before impact—with uranium or plutonium to arrive at the state of things in the last decades of the twentieth century. For while the Army High Command, according to a secret memo of October 15, 1942, planned to use "atomic decay and chain reaction only as a possible form of rocket-propulsion" (Ruland, 268), Fermi and Neumann had already begun work on an appropriate payload that (as progress has since shown) was far too precious for their own *Enola Gay* (685) and other bombers.

German-American friendship understood as the transfer of technology is hence Pynchon's subject. What began at the beach of Peenemünde and developed into assembly-line production in the bunkers of Nordhausen (built by I.G. Farben and taken over by the Reich)[6]—the manufacturing site, by the way, of the first jet fighters (354)—continues in Huntsville (651) and Baikonur (823). The sum total of all innovations produced by the Second World War—from the reel-to-reel (609), color film, and VHF to radar (452), UHF (378), and computers—results in a postwar period whose simple secret is the marketing of *Wunderwaffen* and whose future is predictable.

Certainly, even during the Second World War people still believed that they were dying for their fatherlands. But Pynchon, the erstwhile engineer at Boeing, precisely observes that "the enterprise [of] systematic death" (88) "serves as spectacle, as diversion from the real movements of the War" (122). "The real crises," after all, "were crises of allocation and priority, not among firms—it was only staged to look that way—but among the different Technologies, Plastics, Electronics, Aircraft," and so forth. (607).

But if the war was literally a theater of war and its body count a simulacrum that concealed the competition of diverse technologies for their own or our future, everything takes place as if in the media that, from the drama to the computer, only process information. Competition among and priority disputes between technologies have always amounted to competition over information about them. As a melancholic figure in the novel well connected to industrial espionage circles puts it: only "before the first war," when "drugs" and "sex" were still of interest, was life "simple." But since 1939, "the world's gone insane," because "information [has] come to be the only real medium of exchange," and even industrial espionage is about to switch from agents or human beings to "information machines" (300).[7]

Under conditions of total semiotechnology, what remains is the question of the media that implement it. And if, as in one of Pynchon's formulas, "personal density is directly proportional to temporal bandwidth" (593), media theorists do well to remind themselves of the martial history of the subjects of their own investigation. What may appear as narrativity, and hence entertainment, in the media possibly only obscures semiotechnological efficiencies. Media such as literature and film and records are all in a state of war—which is precisely why *Gravity's Rainbow* combines them in such a systematic way.

Literature

In those prehistoric times when drugs and sex were still of interest, war may have been a soldier's song, a story told orally. But ever since conscription demanded that "everybody had to be in the field," there were, as Goethe was quick to realize, no more listeners for tales: all are involved now.[8] Therefore, the wars of liberation that from 1806 to 1815 made the people of Central Europe into underlings of nation-states, into people's armies, needed a new medium as well. That medium was literature as writing and command. The new—that is, absolute—enemy[9] first had to be named and its destruction ordered—which is precisely what was done by plays such as Heinrich von Kleist's *Hermannsschlacht*, that monument to war propaganda.

As is widely known, such poetic fortune is only short lived. When the field monuments disappeared during the material battles of World War I, literature was forced to descend into the trenches (as Paul Fussell's brilliant study of English texts illustrates). An absolute enmity that was taken over by machines was no longer in need of stories, justifications, and plans. In the absence of inconceivable orders and invisible enemies, literature was left to present battle as inner experience, as Ernst Jünger's title (*Der Kampf als inneres Erlebnis*) so accurately puts it. And that was simply film. At the boundary of the medium of the book, where explosions negate all verbal expression, appeared its technological replacement.[10] Whenever Lieutenant Jünger encountered the real behind morning fog and barbed wire, instead of composing expressionist studies of individual experience, he always hallucinated the enemy as a cinematic doppelgänger.[11] For that reason alone, novels that captured life in the trenches, as the work of Erich Maria Remarque demonstrates, cried out for cinematic treatment.

But when the enterprise of systematic death and the simulation of relations between enemies and friends only serves as a pretext for the competition between various technologies that are themselves based not on adventure and narration but on blueprints, statistics, and intelligence operations, life in the trenches becomes obsolete. In order to secure the traces of the Second, technological World War, *Gravity's Rainbow* employs from the very beginning different narrative techniques.

Instead of a war with its inner experience, we witness a stochastic distribution of figures and locales, of front lines and discourses, of Allied and German sites. Only the coincidence of two coincidental distributions brings about the focusing of the hero and the action. The Poisson equation, whose distribution corresponds to the impact pattern of the V-2s, happens to coincide point by point with the private statistic of an American lieutenant named Slothrop with which he aims to keep track of his coincidental erotic encounters. And just as the rockets, because of their supersonic speed, reverse cause and effect and audible threat and visible explosion (26),[12] Slothrop's erections are an index (in the double sense of Peirce and all prophets) that mark the next hit. The V-2s follow the erections, just as their sounds follows their impact. In other words: Slothrop's love or "imagination has a bomblike structure," too (Kamper). This is reason enough for Allied intelligence services to use the lieutenant as a guinea pig, in the most technical sense of the term. He infiltrates the collapsing Reich in order to gather information on that last, unique, and mythic rocket which transports his German doppelgänger, Gottfried, into space or death.

However, Slothrop escapes the "operational paranoia" (28) of those secret services in the same measure that he is possessed by it. The medium of this transfer is writing. The lieutenant comes from a line of Puritan paper manufacturers; that is, people who convert America's "diminishing green reaches . . . acres at a clip into paper—toilet paper, banknote stock, newsprint—a medium or ground for shit money, and the Word" (31). This symbolic, to speak with Lacan, reclaims him as he studies the V-2 documents he has obtained. Reading and paranoia coincide with each other. All the findings Slothrop learns to decode in Fortress Europe point to the fact that the military-industrial complex has always risen above war fronts—that it has programmed the conditioned sexual reflexes of American GIs just as it did the innovations of German rocket technicians. From his dossiers, which for a while have controlled what passes for a so-called experience or life story, Slothrop can infer that, even as an infant—through the historically correct link between I.G. Farben and Rockefeller's Standard Oil[13]—he was the guinea pig of the same Professor Jamf whose work on synthetic polymers will also make possible manned flight into space. After the fact, as always, it becomes apparent that the detective and his doppelgänger in the V-2 cockpit are one and the same; and also that the coincidence of two iconic patterns, those of the real-historical map of the points of impact and those of the novel's erotic map of London, is anything but a coincidence. Upon a thorough study of documents, coincidences always betray conspiracy.

The sole premise of this sinister conclusion, however, is not the immanence of fiction, as readers might assume, given their conditioned obliviousness. Rather, it is the historical exactness of what the text itself calls "data retrieval" (678). Step by step, Slothrop's intratextual paranoia repeats a critical-paranoid method that the novelist might have learned from Dali. Even if writer and protagonist encounter documents after the fact, such reverse temporal sequence does not make them fictional. As a textual example of so-called postmodernity, Gravity's Rainbow has been acknowledged a hundred times, but literary scholarship has yet to acknowledge the scope and precision of its integrated research. The text builds almost exclusively upon documentary sources in a manner akin to historical novels of the type of Salammbô or Antonius,[14] to which it adds, for the first time, schematics and differential equations, corporate contracts, and organizational graphs (easily missed by literary scholars).

Gravity's Rainbow is the data retrieval from a world war whose secret documents have become accessible in proportion to the way their contents are implemented in the real world and are thus no longer in need of so-called secretiveness. For that reason alone, paranoia—which, according to Freud and Morris, is only a confusion of words and things, of designates and denotates, like all psychoses[15]—is recognition itself. When the symbolic of signs, numbers and letters exercises control over so-called realities, the securing of traces becomes the first obligation of the paranoid.

Consequently, the critical-paranoid method of the novel infects its readers. They turn from consumers of a narrative into hackers of a system. For Slothrop, despite his Puritan predilection for the word (241), does not decode all the war secrets encoded in the novel. He is not in a position to decipher that the fictional U.S. major Marvy, who is responsible for the transfer of V-2 technology to the United States, is merely a cryptogram for the historically correct name Staver;[16] or that Pointsman, the chief behaviorist of British intelligence in the novel, is given his name only so that he can coincide with his German namesake and counterpart in a multinational conspiracy: the engineer Weichensteller, who in Peenemünde was one of the "reentry people" responsible for, of all things, the reentry of the V-2s into British airspace (529).

In *Gravity's Rainbow*, fictional names and narrative structures conceal a level of information that is, moreover, a relay that connects to other, no less paranoid novels (see 684) and hence, for the most practical reasons in the world, had better not be told. In this respect, the novel is fully in synch with its time. When technologies assume domination over science and aesthetics, the only thing that counts is information. After all, some of the origins of semiotics itself derive from the behaviorist semiotechnologies Pynchon analyzes as strategies of war.

Even after the analysis and recombination of both distributed and secret data, however, two problems remain: the closure and self-application of the system. It is not only because Slothrop's data retrieval takes place in 1945, years before the release of crucial intelligence archives, that he dances on "a ground of terror, contradiction, absurdity." For once, it is child's play for the military-industrial complex to bring in "programmers by the truckload . . . and make sure all the information fed out was harmless" (678)—as harmless, for example, as a narrative novel. Second, Tyrone Slothrop's paranoid insight, which he believed solely to be his own desire (252), turns out in reality to have always been, to echo Lacan, the desire of the other or lab chief. Extending the work of his historical predecessors Watson and Baby Albert, Jamf had the "elegant"—that is, "binary"—idea to condition in Baby Slothrop not such nonquantifiable data as fear but the simple and unambiguous fact of an erection as a conditioned reflex (97). Consequently, what surfaces in Slothrop's dreams is "a very old dictionary of technical German," which translates "JAMF," the proper name of his lab chief, with the English index "I" (334; see also 726).

In other words, but still Pynchon's, the I is only "a branch office in each of our brains, his cover known as the Ego, and their mission in this world is Bad Shit" (831; see 332). End of quote, which could just as well come from Foucault and which is the end of all paranoia; for nothing remains of the involuntary private detective who has finally cracked the alibi (the other) of his own ego. Under conditions of total remote control, the narrativity of the protagonist dissipates. In an endless series of disguises and metamorphoses, Lieutenant Slothrop loses his uniform, his proper name, and his literacy; he dissolves into episodes, comic strips, myths, and, finally, record covers (866). Thus, and only thus, does he escape the trap that the medium of writing—itself only a part of the military-industrial complex—sets up for its readers. For if there is paranoia, understood as an ominous reading of one cohesive and narratable conspiracy (820), then "there is still also anti-paranoia, where nothing is connected to anything else" (506).

And while the historical genre of the novel was defined by the fact that the ramifications of its Markoff chains diminished in direct proportion to the path traveled by the hero, eventually resulting in a structure or solution, *Gravity's Rainbow*'s anti-paranoia, conversely, produces an increase in information and hence (following Claude Shannon) an increase in entropy. In a progressive merging of figures, organizations, and front lines the novel repeats precisely the second law of thermodynamics. The law of increasing entropy ascribes direction to time and can clarify—following the wonderful example of Eddington—whether films, in real time, run forward or backward.[17]

Film

In this technical and temporal sense, *Gravity's Rainbow* is a film, not because the novel could be made into a movie, as in the case of Remarque's, or that it could project invisible enemies, as in the case of Jünger's, but because it juxtaposes its own progressive decomposition to the negentropy of the military-industrial complex. The present tense alone, which Pynchon sustains throughout in contrast to the classic past tense of the novel, ensures a narrative surface that suppresses linear intersections of cause and effect. "Each [V-2] hit is independent of all the others. Bombs are not dogs. No link. No memory. No conditioning." Hence, it is not a question of "which places would be safest to go into." Thanks to such training, there is "a whole *generation*" whose "postwar [existence is] nothing but 'events,' newly created one moment to the next" (64–65).

Only the "Monte Carlo Fallacy" (64) can assume that a bomb hit, a film image, a narrative event n are governed by the series 1 through n-1, as if they had a memory. Certainly, to the chief behaviorist in the text the bombfire over London signals that "the reality is not reversible." Things could come to an end only if "rockets dismantle, [and] the entire film runs backward: faired skin back to sheet steel back to pigs to white incandescence to ore, to Earth" (163). But as nobody less than Walther Rathenau, the inventor of German war economies, and hence of Soviet five-year plans, explains in his capacity as an invoked spirit, the "talk about cause and effect is secular history, and secular history is a diversionary tactic" (195), or rather "a conspiracy" (192). Secular history, as is commonly known, existed in the medium of the book; technological media, on the other hand, allow (above and beyond the diversionary tactic of their entertainment effect) for the variation of precisely those parameters, which they alone are capable of recording, including that of physical time. Just as the impact of the rocket exchanges the sequence of explosion and noise, so the many fictitious movies in *Gravity's Rainbow* operate with the trick that, in the jargon of electronic engineering of the real, goes by the wonderful name of time-axis manipulation.

The last work of Gerhardt von Göll, who in the novel stands for his historical colleagues Pabst, Lang, and Lubitsch (131), is called "*New Dope*" and demonstrates "24 hours a day" how that kind of dope renders you incapable of "ever telling anybody what it's like, or worse, where to get any.... It is the dope that finds *you*, apparently. Part of a reverse world whose agents run around with guns which are like vacuum cleaners operating in the direction of life—pull the trigger and bullets are sucked back out of the recently dead into the barrel ... to the accompaniment of a backwards gunshot" (869–70). Such cinematic tricks, however, are not confined to the imaginary of hallucinations and film. The novel also describes the British bombing of a V-2 launch site as a retransformation that changes "vehicles ... back to the hollow design envelopes of their earliest specs" (652), and hence intimates the gloomiest of its paranoid recognitions; namely, that Germany's industrial parks—following the ruin theory of its chief architect, Albert Speer[18]—

were built with the anticipation of their eventual destruction by the Royal Air Force. Only then can they fulfill their function as postwar ruins in the multinational conspiracy (606–7).

Von Göll's first work, a false documentary in the best Allied black propaganda fashion, performs similar reversals of time, albeit in a less programmed way.[19] British soldiers made up as Hereros pose as one of Major General Kammler's motorized rocket batteries. The finished film is damaged and given an antiquated appearance—enriched by the white noise that defines technological media as well as their background (108–9)—in order to disseminate, as a pseudo document from a counterfeit V-2 firing site, German rumors about blacks in the Waffen-SS (131). That is what von Göll calls, "with the profound humility that only a German movie director can summon," his "mission"; namely, "to sow ... seeds of reality" (451; see also 320). And in truth: in 1929, Lang's film *Die Frau im Mond* sowed the Countdown (878) and the future V-2 more generally.[20]

But the spiral does not end with the reversal of cause and effect and of programming and documenting. In the case of von Göll, what comes to light late in the novel is that the Waffen-SS Hereros were not the effect but the magical cause of their propagandistic simulation. Since they already exist, von Göll's forgery ought to run backward, just as countdowns do. And once again, what surfaces is the puzzling question as to the relationship between program and narrativity in the media.

Paul Virilio's *War and Cinema* attempts to document that the relationship between world wars and film technologies is one not simply of simultaneity but of strict solidarity. War strategies that depend militarily, technologically, and propagandistically on speed and information cannot do without the speed-up, dilation, and reversal of time; that is, without time-axis manipulation. What would be impossible in the medium of writing or literature—notwithstanding Ilse Aichinger's *Spiegelgeschichte*—has been a staple of film since its beginnings, which (among other things) in turn originated with the revolver.[21] Of course, literature had the capacity to manipulate those times that simulate education or struggles as an inner experience. But to work with physical time itself, into which education and mortal combat are embedded, technological media become necessary. Rocket technology needs film technology, and vice versa. The fact that the V-2 homed in on its targets in London in the first place, despite the incredulity of the newly created technical division of the British secret service,[22] can be attributed to an ingenious innovation: its measured parameter was not its traveled distance, as with armies, or speed, as with the more recent tanks; it was its acceleration, which was accessible only to the rocket itself in the shape of information, and which, through simple and double integrals, made it possible to determine speed and distance, respectively (350). A pendulum, followed by two serial RC circuits—that's how simply Virilio's dromology can be constructed or (as in the case of the British experts) overlooked.

According to Pynchon, there exists a "strange connection between the German mind and the rapid flashing of successive stills . . . since Leibniz, in the process of inventing calculus, used the same approach to break up the trajectories of cannonballs through the air" (474; see also 660–61). The technological medium that implements motion as calculus, however, is film. All cinematic illusions of continually moving pictures, beginning with Marey's photographic gun, have been simple integrals, just like the speed of the V-2—dependent variables of a time-axis manipulation, which is the only thing that counts as you optimize weapons of destruction.[23] Similar to this predecessor of film technology of 1885, the Ascania high-performance cameras of 1941 were developed not for the imagination of moviegoers but for purposes of slow-motion studies of the V-2 trajectory (474). Which, of course, does not mean that these techniques should not be extended "past images on film, to human lives" (474).

One of the many tales whose entropy is *Gravity's Rainbow* questions narrativity through technology itself. It concerns an engineer of Peenemünde who is fooled by the trick of time-axis manipulation. The simulacrum in this feature film or life is his twelve-year old daughter, whose conception, by the way, is due to the semiotechnology of film. It is one of von Göll's late expressionist rape scenes—its climax cut in the released version, but played through to the bitter end in both the studio and Joseph Goebbels's private archive—that impregnated not only the film star but numerous wives and girlfriends of returning moviegoers. Under conditions of advanced technology, children are only the doppelgängers of their doppelgänger on the screen: cannon fodder in the case of boys, pinups in the case of girls.

Thirteen years later. The film-engendered cannon fodder wage a blitzkrieg, pinups are in demand. The rocket engineer—Pynchon figure that he is—has long forgotten his daughter and her appearance. Since 1939, however, she has appeared to him during each summer furlough: as an extra bonus courtesy of Army Proving Ground Peenemünde. Only after his pinup daughter has seduced him does it become clear that she has been constituted, year after year, from a doppelgänger without original. Since 1939, the concentration camp Dora in the vicinity of Nordhausen simply began to give leave to its inmates, at first a twelve-year-old, then a thirteen-year old, and so on, until the end of the war. In the words of Pynchon: "The only continuity has been her name ... and [her father's] love—love something like the persistence of vision, for They have used it to create for him the moving image of a daughter, flashing him only these summertime frames of her, leaving it to him to build the illusion of a single child" (492). Hence moviegoers as such are the victims of a semiotechnology that projects coherence onto a world of snapshots and flashbulbs. Feature films began, in Germany at any rate, with doppelgängers who filmed and propagated moviemaking itself,[24] and culminate for Pynchon, as for Virilio,[25] in the countless Japanese who were, through the bomb, reduced to "a fine-vapor deposit of fat-cracklings wrinkled into the fused rubble" of their city, Hiroshima (685).

The exposure time? Sixty-seven nanoseconds, or blitzkrieg in the literal sense of the word.

However, a war that coincides with representation becomes unrepresentable. In the figure of Slothrop's German antipode, *Gravity's Rainbow* clusters all impossibilities of representing technological warfare. On the one hand, there is a GI who is led on to the V-2 through coincidences and orders; on the other hand, a boss who directs not only the production and launching of the *Wunderwaffe* but also, with the help of lifelike film tricks, the sexuality of his engineers. The representation of the head of Peenemünde would be a reissue of the war-film cliché of the ugly German. The fact that Pynchon bypasses that cliché in order to dramatize the puzzling relationship between fact and fiction has, at this point, dumbfounded his interpreters. And that is the greatness of the novel.

Historically, the HA Peenemünde was under the command of General Walter Dornberger of the Army Ordnance Office (Heereswaffenamt), who in 1932, then a major and aide to Professor Becker, had discovered the young Wernher von Braun. And so the administrative staff of Kummersdorf remained in Peenemünde until the planned, proliferating entropies of the Hitler state (497) transformed the SS into a state within the state. In 1944, after the Army Ordnance Office had done its technological duty and the Wehrmacht had lapsed into agony, the command over Peenemünde, Nordhausen, and an assigned special-purpose army corps[26] (the only one in the history of the German army) fell to Chief Group Leader (Obergruppenführer) Dr. Kammler of the

Chief Office of Economy and Administration of the SS (Wirtschafts-Verwaltungshauptamt).[27] Born in 1901, Hans Kammler shares with Thomas Pynchon, born in 1937, the rare quality of having destroyed all his photographs.[28] In precisely such an unrepresentable way is he present in the novel.

Pynchon's fictitious head of rocket technology erases all of his own markings because he is not a figure but the product of a double exposure. Beginning in 1932, the head of rocket technology is called Major Weissmann; he is a Wehrmacht officer and (like Dornberger) "a brand-new military type, part salesman, part scientist" (467). All the way down to his conversations with subordinate officers, who camouflage wartime economic pressure with scientific interest (485), Pynchon's Weissmann follows his one source: the involuntary candidness of Dornberger's memoir.[29] Consequently, the name Dornberger does not surface in this most precise of all novels, as if fact and fiction were the two sides of a sheet of paper.

Later in Peenemünde, however, the same Weissmann carries without justification the title "group leader" (488), before finally, in 1944, even exchanging his own name for the SS code name Blicero, a paraphrase of death (375). As Blicero, Weissmann adopts all the formalities of the German generals' staff; he turns into a roaring animal, chasing leftover rocket batteries over the bombed-out autobahns of the Reich. Dornberger, Braun, and their appalled ghostwriters report nothing less about Kammler and his need to decide the outcome of the war all by himself, as if all the entropies of the Hitler state had been made flesh.[30]

The merging of Dornberger and Kammler, Weissmann and Blicero, Army and SS, order and entropy is the eccentric center of the novel, the site of its unrepresentability. Whether Blicero is dead or alive remains an open question (see 777), as in the case of the real Kammler for many years after the war.[31] His deeds and deliriums exist only as the narratives of the narratives of witnesses who were under the influence of the drug Oneirine (540, 780). Oneirine, naturally once again synthesized by the fictitious Professor Laszlo Jamf (405), has, however, "the property of time-modulation" that was "first to be discovered by investigators" (453; see also 819–20). That's why Blicero, this double exposure of 1932 and 1944, of Dornberger and Kammler, can come into being in the first place. That's why his madness can launch a manned flight into space amidst the rubble of the Reich, which will become historical reality only twenty years later. And that's why, finally, Pynchon's Second World War can end with the intercontinental missiles of the next war, for Blicero's manned V-2, launched in Lower Saxony, touches down on the last page of the novel in the Hollywood of 1973, the year of the novel's publication. Its off-ground detonator is calibrated to respond precisely to the movie theater in which Pynchon and his readers are sitting. We "old fans, who've always been at the movies," are finally reached by a film "we have not learned to see," but which we have been dreaming of ever since the days of Muybridge and Marey: the melding of film and war (887).

Oneirine has additional, less sensational qualities. In contrast to the dreamlike quality of *Cannabis indica* (see 404), the hallucinations produced by Oneirine "show a definitive narrative continuity, as clearly as, say, the average *Reader's Digest* article." In other words, they are "so ordinary, so conventional," so American (819). That is Pynchon's contribution to the topic of narrativity in the media, and his explanation as to why each medium, including the novel itself, is a drug, and vice versa.

According to Stresemann, people "pray not only for their daily bread, but also for their daily illusion" (529). And industrial concerns, such as the real I.G. Farben and Jamf's fictitious Psychochemie AG (291), do everything to answer "the basic problem . . . of getting other people to die for you" in a positive—that is, psychopharmaceutical—way, now that theological and historico-philosophical illusions are no longer viable alternatives (817). As early as 1904, "the American Food and Drug people took the cocaine out of Coca-Cola, which gave us an alcoholic and death-oriented generation of Yanks ideally equipped to fight WW II" (527). What remains—following the words of the Oneirine-connoîsseur von Göll—is to hope for the eventual melding of film and war. Slothrop, who observes that "this ain't the fuckin' *movies* now," may be rightly concerned for awhile that people are getting killed, even though "they weren't supposed to"—that wasn't part of the script. Von Göll knows better. According to the director, we are "not yet" in the movies, "maybe not quite yet. You'd better enjoy it while you can. Someday, when the film is fast enough, the equipment pocket-size and burdenless and selling at people's prices, the lights and booms no longer necessary, *then* . . . then" (614).

As early as 1973, however, as a TV quiz show for its readers, *Gravity's Rainbow* organizes "A MOMENT OF FUN WITH TAKESHI AND ICHIZO, THE KOMICAL KAMIKAZES." And whoever manages to guess, as does "Marine Captain Esberg from Pasadena," that this whole spectacle "*is* a movie! Another World War II situation comedy," wins as first prize an all-expense-paid (one-way) trip to the movie's actual location. There he may experience "torrential tropical downpours" and make the acquaintance of "the Kamikaze *Zero*" that he will be operating, flying and—crashing (805–7).

Hence the narrative continuity of Oneirine hallucinations or feature films haunts the novel that raises them to the level of theme. Episodes and dialogues are rendered as if they had been written under the influence of the drug (see 820). Consequently, *Gravity's Rainbow* too is a *Reader's Digest* article: ordinary, conventional, and American. "And there ought to be a punch line to it, but there isn't" (861). The puzzling question whether world war technologies have programmed our so-called postwar time, and if so how, remains unresolved. The novel remains a novel, and its hero Slothrop "a tanker and feeb." His quest for Weissmann-Blicero's manned space rocket ends in failure and condemns him to "mediocrity."

And that, as the text puts it bitterly and unequivocally, "not only in his life but also, heh, heh, in his chroniclers too" (861).

Record

Script records the symbolic, film the imaginary. The countless songs in the novel, on the other hand, are the medium of stupidity. Record grooves store the frequencies of real bodies, whose stupidity, as is generally known, knows no bounds. What wars and drugs and the media do to bodies hence continues as music. One song in *Gravity's Rainbow* begins "Tap my head and mike my brain, stick that needle in my vein" (71). The novel keeps coming to a standstill, because fictitious rumbas, beguines, foxtrots, blues improvisations, and so on—accompanied by the most precise stage directions and far from any war scenario—turn actions and conspiracies into ritornellos, into an eternal recurrence of stanza and chorus. At the end, as a new world war is about to erupt over the skies of California, appears a song of consolation for a "crippl'd Zone" that does not signify just postwar Germany. And at the end of the song and the novel: "Now everybody—"

Notes

1. On the strategies of autobahns since the First World War, see Kittler, "Auto bahnen."
2. See also Bergaust, 111.

3. On the Second World War and postwar fantasy, see Pink Floyd, side 1.

4. *Gravity's Rainbow*, 44, 65. Further references appear in the text.

5. See the memoirs of Wernher von Braun in Ruland, 141.

6. On Nordhausen, the largest known underground factory, see Bornemann.

7. On the birth of the computer from the spirit of espionage, see Kittler, "Das Gespenst im Computer." At the time Pynchon was writing *Gravity's Rainbow*, the fact that information machines had already displaced agents at Bletchley Park in 1943 was still hidden away in secret files.

8. Here are the words of the *Zahmen Xenions* that describe the introduction of a general draft, not militarily or ideologically, but in terms of discourse analysis: "Formerly, somebody could communicate his sufferings to others; he could recount his war experience in old age. These days misery is universal; the indidivual can no longer lament anymore. Everybody must be on the battlefield—who is there to listen when they [warriors] tell their tales? (Goethe, 4:131).

9. See Schmitt on absolute enmity, total mobilization, and Kleist's "partisan poetry."

10. See Jünger, 98, 92 (the First World War as "strangler of our literature").

11. See ibid., 12, 28, 50, and 107.

12. In the case of the V-2, the time lapse was 16 seconds (Ruland, 221).

13. See also Stevenson, as well as Borkin's insufficient monograph on I. G. Farben.

14. See Foucault, "Fantasia of the Library," on Flaubert's *Tentation de Saint-Antoine.*

15. See Freud, 14: 204; Morris, 67.

16. On Staver, see Ruland, 249. Here are some further name games that confuse fact and fiction: Höhler, the architect of Nordhausen's Mittelwerke (Bornemann, 23), becomes Ölsch (347–50); Enzian, the code name for a rocket project in Peenemünde (Ruland, 261), becomes the name of the head of the fictitious Waffen-SS Hereros. Finally, "Max" and "Moritz," the two engineers present during the launching of the manned V-2 (883–85), quote from von Braun's A-2 of November 1934 (Ruland, 89). Readers are asked to keep searching. . . .

17. See Shannon and Weaver, 20.

18. See Virilio, *War and Cinema,* for Speer's theorem that all architecture must anticipate its future "ruin value."

19. See Howe.

20. After viewing this film about a flight to the moon, one of Pynchon's figures observes that "real flight and dreams of flight go together" (186). See Ruland, 57–61, on UFA and Professor Oberth's first liquid-fuel rocket projects, and Virilio, *War and Cinema,* on *Die Frau im Mond* and the power of film: "The film came out on 30 September 1929, but without the intended publicity of a real rocket launch from the beach of Horst in Pomeriana to an altitude of 40 kilometres. By 1932 jet technology . . . was set to become one of the major military secrets in the Third Reich, and the German authorities of the time seized Lang's film on the grounds that it was *too close to reality.* A decade later, on 7 July 1943, von Braun and Dornberger presented Hitler with film of the real launch of the A4 rocket. The Führer was in a bitter mood: 'Why was it I could not believe in the success of your work? If we'd had these rockets in 1939 we'd never have had this war.' " More persuasive evidence

of the power of film hardly exists: Hitler, the cinéast, who was bored by all the real-life demonstrations of the V-2 (Dornberger, 73–77 and 99–101), becomes convinced through film.

21. See Virilio, *War and Cinema,* on Marey's chronophotographic gun.

22. See Jones for the relevant confessions of the head of this division.

23. See Giedion, 21, for a picture and description of the function of Marey's gun.

24. See Kittler, "Romantik—Psychoanalyse—Film," for details.

25. See Virilio, *War and Cinema,* 81.

26. Dornberger, 239.

27. For Kammler's building activities (including Nordhausen) in the Wirtschafts-Verwaltungshauptamt of the SS, see Georg, 37, as well as Bornemann, 43, 82, and 125. For his career until 1932 (Border Patrol East; Sturmabteilung Rossbach; Settlement Office, Danzig; Ministry of Labor), see Kammler. If readers can provide additional information . . .

28. See Ruland, 170, though he does not discuss Kammler's motivations. In *Gravity's Rainbow,* however, Pynchon asks his readers: "Is that who you are, that vaguely criminal face on your ID card, its soul snatched by the government camera as the guillotine shutter fell?" (157).

29. As a model for the conversation between Weissmann and Pökler, one should read the long dialogue between Dornberger and Dr. Steinhoff, Peenemünde's electrician, in Dornberger, 135–37.

30. See, for example, Dornberger: "Kammler refused to believe in an imminent collapse. He dashed to and fro between the Dutch and Rhineland fronts and Thuringia and Berlin. He was on the move day and night. Conferences were called for 1 o'clock in the morning somewhere in the Harz Mountains, or we would meet at midnight somewhere on the Autobahn and then, after a brief exchange of views, drive back to work again. We were prey to terrific nervous tension. Irritable and overworked as we were, we didn't mince words. Kammler, if he got impatient and wanted to drive on, would wake the slumbering officers of his suite with a burst from his tommy-gun" (266).

31. "Since SS General Kammler, Hitler's envoy for V-weapons, cannot be located [after the war], London wants to put Dornberger on trial in his stead. Nobody knows at that time what has become of Kammler. Only several years later do the facts come to light: on May 4, 1945, Kammler arrives in Prague by plane. On May 9 he and 21 SS men defend a bunker against 600 Czech partisans. Kammler leaves the bunker in triumph and fires his automatic weapon at the attacking Czechs. Kammler's aide-de-camp, Sturmbannführer Starck, has been ordered months ago not to let his boss fall into enemy hands. He must walk behind him at a distance of ten steps—'within shooting range.' Now, in this hopeless situation, Starck pumps a round of bullets from his automatic weapon into the back of the SS General's head" (Ruland, 282).

John Johnston

8 Mediality in *Vineland* and *Neuromancer*

In "Gramophone, Film, Typewriter," Friedrich Kittler writes: "The quotidian data flow must be arrested before it can become image or sign. What is called style in art is only the switchboard of these scannings and selections" (104). The arresting of data flow in signs depends directly on what a culture at a particular time recognizes as data, and thus on the specific technologies that produce, inscribe, store, and transmit information. It depends, in short, on the general conditions of "mediality" that define a culture as a communications system.

Considered as a communication system, our own culture is highly diverse and heterogeneous, and perhaps best described as a conglomerate of "partially connected media systems." As Kittler points out, any flight on a jet airliner illustrates such a partially connected media system. More densely connected than in most places, media on a jet airliner remain separate according to their technological standard, frequency, user allocation, and interface. Thus the crew members, who may eventually be replaced by computers, are connected to radar screens, diode displays, radio beacons, and nonpublic channels, whereas the passengers, as Kittler puts it,

> can benefit only from yesterday's technology and are entertained by a canned media mixture. With the exception of books, that ancient medium which needs so much light, all the entertainment techniques are represented. The passengers' ears are listlessly hooked up to one-way earphones, which are themselves hooked up to tape recorders and thereby to the record industry. Their eyes are glued to Hollywood movies, which in turn must be connected to the advertising budget of the airline industry. . . . Not to mention the technological medium of

the food industry to which the mouths of the passengers are connected. A multi-media embryonic sack supplied through channels or navels that all serve the purpose of screening out the real background: noise, night, and the cold of an unlivable outside. Against that there is muzak, movies, and microwave cuisine. (102)

But Kittler also envisions a point in the not too distant future when most people living in advanced postindustrial societies will be connected, thanks to fiber-optic networks, to a communication channel that can be used for any kind of media. As Kittler explains: "When films, music, telephone calls, and texts are able to reach the individual household via optical fiber cables, the previously separate media of television, radio, telephone, and mail will become a single medium, standardized according to transmission frequency and bit format" (101). At this point, a certain historical epoch will have ended, our own modernist epoch defined by the historical appearance of media whose differentiation Kittler analyzes. What spells the end of this epoch—an end we are currently living through—is simply the general digitalization of information and its transmission of separate data flows along a single fiber-optic network.

Kittler's distinction between two types of communications assemblage—one characterized by partially connected media systems and the other by the digitalization of all media and their transmission via a fiber-optic network—point respectively to the different and contrasting conditions of mediality underlying two contemporary novels: Thomas Pynchon's *Vineland* (1990) and William Gibson's *Neuromancer* (1984). *Vineland* is usually read as a novel concerned chiefly with the demise of the 1960s counterculture amidst the Reaganite repression of the '80s, with the difference between the two eras reflected by the politically tonic power of cinema on the one hand and the commerce-controlled, mind-dulling effects of television on the other. But these differences are subsumed by a larger narrative problem: how to integrate and unify the diversity of information and effects produced by current technologies, which can be described as forming a partially connected media system. *Neuromancer* is usually read as an adventure story about data-rustling in a not too futuristic cyberspace, where the fusion of two artificial intelligences enacts an allegory about the transformative power of fusing the two hemispheres of the human brain. If *Neuromancer* is to be read as an allegory, however, it is about the autonomization of technology in the fully digitalized space of the Net, with the corollary that human beings become unique precisely because they inhabit and therefore can connect different kinds of space.

While we don't need Kittler to describe the obvious stylistic and thematic differences between these two novels, Kittler's study of how historically and materially different *Aufschreibesysteme* or "notation systems" define different possibilities for "literature" does suggest how the twentieth-century novel as a prose fictional genre can be read in a different way: as a recording of the delirious effects produced by new media and information technologies (see *Discourse Networks, 1800/1900*). Since all novels—however intellectual—are first of all stories offered for entertainment or reading pleasure, these delirious effects are often displaced or disguised by literary conventions and the rationalizations of narrative or plot. To read the novel in relation to an *Aufschreibesystem*— that is, as a site where the culture's possibilities for inscribing, storing, retrieving, and transmitting data are made available for critical scrutiny—means understanding this delirium as an inscription of consciousness determined by specific conditions of mediality. Perhaps there is no better illustration than Pynchon's earlier novel *The Crying of Lot 49*, where the plot explicitly rationalizes the heroine's burgeoning paranoid delirium through a symmetrical set of four possibilities. Meanwhile, *Lot 49* itself constitutes a form of writing machine, rewriting the effects of other media—telephone calls, a painting by Remedios Varos, old Hollywood movies on television, a Jacobean revenge play, and, most important, the postal system—into the terms of its own novelistic discourse. Taken in a general sense, then, mediality refers to the ways in which a literary text inscribes in its own language the effects produced by other media. The critical task will be to ascertain how these effects are narrativized or can be seen to determine the representation of consciousness as a "reading effect."

Kittler's example of the jumbo jet may recall the California–Hawaii flight in *Vineland* on which the character Zoyd Wheeler is employed as a musician playing a "baby-grand synthesizer" in a "747 gutted and refitted as a huge Hawaiian restaurant and bar" (62). Pynchon's comic transformation of a familiar technology, however, is only one among many of the textual strategies he deploys in order to represent the oddly surreal banality of contemporary American life among "partially connected media systems." Yet *Vineland* is concerned not only with the signs and signals these media carry but also with how they block access to other signals no less present in the landscape, information the text can record but the narrative cannot mobilize or integrate.

A good part of *Vineland*'s narrative is structured by the quest of Zoyd's daughter, Prairie, to know who her mother, Frenesi Gates, really was, and what she did in the politically turbulent 1960s. This narrative quest is initiated by "a scene of reading" in which Prairie pulls up texts and images on a computer monitor, and later watches film footage her mother shot as part of "24fps," a Sixties film collective devoted to political activism. Although Prairie will finally meet her mother face to face at a family reunion at *Vineland*'s conclusion, her access to her mother's experience through these technological mediations proves sufficient for a narrative (and oedipal) resolution of sorts, while at the same time raising questions about how that narrative is constituted and what it must necessarily leave out.

The dramatic question for Prairie comes to center on her mother's active part in the murder of her lover, Weed Atman, a mathematician and leader of the student revolt at the College of the Surf. Weed's murder is the vectored event toward which Prairie's search through the past must inevitably move and in which it must culminate, since it represents not only her mother's betrayal but the effective end of the '60s counterculture. For this reason it is also the event from which the events in *Vineland*'s present can be said to date or flow. Given the novel's temporal organization around this critical moment, it is all the more striking that the moment itself is not represented: the narrative moves up to and away from it, with the event's ellipsis occurring in the attempt of the 24fps collective to film and record it. Thus, although the physical event is inaugurated in a complex rearrangement of camera, light, sound, and gun in relation to the various members of the film collective who handle or activate these devices, the actual event makes an impact only in and through its aftereffects, registered first on the filmed faces of the participants and now (in the novel's present) by Prairie as she watches the footage some sixteen years later.

The narrative renders the event in and through a complex overlay of doublings and exchanges, verbally conveyed by puns and double entendres ("That's when Frenesi killed the light, that's how the shot ended . . ."). Paradoxically, the event emerges in a collapse of two opposed worlds previously set apart in Brock Vond's tempting of Frenesi to choose between the "make-believe" and the "real." Frenesi speaks first:

> "I can't bring a gun in the house."
> "But you can bring a camera. Can't you see, the two separate

worlds—one always includes a camera somewhere, and the other always includes a gun, one is make-believe, one is real? What if there is some branch-point in your life, where you'll have to choose between worlds?" (241)

What grounds the substitution of gun for camera, however, is not this (or any other metaphorical) exchange in *Vineland* but a specific understanding of filming: not as a simple doubling or reproduction of the real but as a penetration or cutting into it, which thereby opens a space prerequisite for the emergence of a new form of photographic or cinematic subjectivity.

In *Gravity's Rainbow* Pynchon explores such "openings" primarily through the device of the "interface"; in *Vineland,* however, his interest in the materiality of film and other media leads to a complication of this textual strategy. The shooting/filming of Atman explicitly constitutes an interface, but it also defines a bifurcation point ("some branch-point in your life") rendered in turn as a "reading effect": on one side of the film, there are "shapes that may have moved somewhere in the frame, black on black, like ghosts trying to return to earthly form" (246), while on the other side, there are the faces captured by the light, above all the close-up of Rex's (the murderer's) gleaming eyeball and "Frenesi herself, dark on dark, face in wide-angle distortion, with an expression that might, Prairie admitted, prove unbearable" (247). The gunshot, in contrast to these filmic effects, is resolutely part of the real, a reclosing or suturing of the space momentarily opened by the sequence of film shots, physically continuous with, while also signaling, the collapse of Weed Atman into lifeless materiality. The separation of media here (the series of simultaneous instantiations by which Howie "missed the actual moment" with the camera but "Krishna got all the audio" while Frenesi searched for the floodlight cables) establishes in advance the fragmentary conditions in which the narrative must attempt to bridge the distance from a wholly disparate Real to a socially credible version of reality.

Within the force field delineated by these intersecting but separate technical media, the status of consciousness becomes uncertain, implicitly equivalent to a reading effect "that might, Prairie admitted, prove unbearable." (It is worth noting that Prairie, although a viewer of the filmed scene, is not the one from whose point of view it unfolds. Her "reading," like the insinuations of Frenesi's rememberings or retrospective reflections into the narrative, constitutes a redoubling of a scene that is fissured from the outset.) In this sense Pynchon renders the scene not only as the collapse of two opposed worlds but as a textual imbrication of the scene's recording and viewing. In this collapse and imbrication, consciousness appears as only the interiorized reflection of current media standards. (This is a recurrent theme in Kittler's work, both in "Grammophone" and in "Die Welt des Symbolischen—eine Welt der Maschine" [*Draculas Vermächtnis,* 58–80]). In accord with contemporary theory, Pynchon assumes that consciousness can appear only as a secondary effect, the result of a machinic interplay between a perceptual apparatus, recording device, and a symbolic system. In Jacques Lacan's account (in which "the brain is a dream machine"), consciousness is (at best) a partial reflection or anamorphosis, with the unconscious insistently emerging in the ruptures or breaks of representation; as he puts it in one formulation, it erupts in those "parts of the real image which can never be seen . . . where the apparatus seizes up, where it blocks up" (*Four Fundamental Concepts,* 56; Hanjo Berressem also discusses this scene in Lacanian terms in *Pynchon's Poetics,* 227–28.) The breaks, discontinuities, and temporal doublings that characterize Pynchon's rendering of Weed Atman's murder suggest something like this unconscious, but as multiple foldings over an unrepresentable moment between perception and consciousness.

Narrative, as a consequence, becomes a problematic assertion of relationship. On the one hand, as a sense-making device, it must be anchored to a perspective and thus to a center of intentionality, which is what Prairie's viewing provides. On the other hand, if the event that organizes the narrative cannot be represented but can be only registered as a series of mechanical instantiations and effects (including reading effects), the narrative is reduced to a record of machinic breaks inscribed but necessarily edited out, repressed, or in some way glazed over (in the constitution of a thin, transparent film, as it were) in order that consciousness or intentionality can project (or follow) a ribbon of temporal continuity. Thus, whereas Pynchon's text provides a legible (albeit often implicit) record of these breaks and doublings, what matters for Prairie is less her trajectory through or across them than the meaning she gleans from a "reading" of a filmic image of Frenesi's face.

In contrast to film's fracturing of the real, computer technology in *Vineland* is identified with a curious form of narrative omniscience. In her first "scene of reading" Prairie is seated before a computer monitor, where she becomes "a girl in a haunted mansion, led room to room, sheet to sheet, by the peripheral whiteness, the earnest whisper, of her mother's ghost" (114). Knowing "how literal computers could be—even spaces between characters mattered," she wonders if ghosts are literal in the same way; that is, only responsive to the needs of the living. Prairie soon discovers that she can "summon to the screen" ghostly images of Frenesi, images she gradually learns to read and interpret. At the end of this first evening of her quest, however, after she has logged off and gone to bed, the narrative itself continues: "Back down in the computer library, in storage, quiescent ones and zeros scattered among millions of others, the two women [Frenesi and DL], yet in some definable space, continued on their way across the lowlit campus, persisting, recoverable, friends by the time of this photo for nearly a year . . ." (115). And so the narrative continues, recounting further details of their friendship, returning to Prairie at the computer again only some thirteen pages later, at the chapter's end.

But here the notion of computer memory as a ghostly realm accessed through a kind of magic is less important than the way the computer itself provides the transition from third person to omniscient narration, a transition relying on an assumption made explicit at the very beginning of the next chapter when Ralph Wayvone tells DL, "We know your history, it's all on the computer" (131). Throughout *Vineland*, in fact, the characters variously acknowledge the computer as a site (even agency) of omniscience. Yet, if it is the narrative that must provide the means by which the difference between stored data and human memory is registered and made significant, it does so primarily through Prairie's quest, which now requires several observations. First, Prairie's scene of reading integrates information from various media into the narrative by implicitly overriding or bridging the separation of media at precisely the point at which this separation figures a gap or fissure in the real itself. Second, this narrative is clearly driven by an oedipal desire. In this sense, Prairie's quest reaches a culminating point when she sees the footage of Weed Atman's murder shot at College of the Surf:

Her mom, in front of her [Prairie's] own eyes, had stood with a 1,000 watt Mickey-Mole spot on the dead body of a man who had loved her, and the man who had just killed him, and the gun she'd brought him to do it with. Stood there like the Statue of Liberty, bringer of light, as if it were part of some contract to illuminate, instead of conceal, the deed. With all the footage of Frenesi she'd seen, all the other shots that had come by way of her eye and body, this hard frightening light, this white outpouring, had shown the girl most accurately, least mercifully, her mother's real face. (262–63)

In the televisual world of *Vineland,* however, oedipal identifications are never more than partial. Whereas Frenesi's identity has been split into a "real" and a cinematic self, without any possibility of the one being definitively separated from the other, Prairie's identity is fractalized, constructed through a series of partial identifications with television characters: Bionic Woman, Police Woman, Wonder Woman, even Brent Musberger, not to mention

> the junior-high gymnasts in leotards, teenagers in sitcoms, girls in commercials learning from their moms about how to cook and dress and deal with their dads, all these remote and well-off little cookies going 'Mm! this rilly is good!' or the ever-reliable 'Thanks, Mom,' Prairie feeling each time this mixture of annoyance and familiarity, knowing like exiled royalty that that's who she was supposed to be, could even turn herself into through some piece of neglible magic she must've known once but in the difficult years marooned down on this out-of-the-way planet had come to have trouble remembering anymore. (327)

Although more needs to be said about the construction of the subject within these two technological regimes—one cinematic, the other televisual—in *Vineland* it is clear that they provide contrasting means by which these two characters view themselves and attempt to negotiate the social.

Like all images, the image of Frenesi's face is not only a lure and continually deferred object of oedipal identification but also a realm where other, less narratable forces are at work. In a striking passage Frenesi recalls her life with Brock Vond as a Time outside time, a realm of silver and light from which she is "brought like silver recalled grain by grain from the Invisible to form images of what then went on to grow old . . . get broken or contaminated" (287). Significantly, when Frenesi thinks about her present life with her current husband, Flash, both of them working as paid snitches for the federal authorities, she takes comfort in the fact that as long as their files are "on" the government's computer system, they are guaranteed a spectral sort of life. Conversely, when they discover that their computer files have been erased, they are suddenly condemned to paranoia and the terror of the unknown. The narrative itself underscores the digital discreteness of these two "states" of being—one "on," the other off—in Frenesi's two moments of illumination.

The first moment comes when Frenesi, now on the federal payroll after having betrayed the counterculture and abandoned her child, Prairie, and her husband, Zoyd, still has to face the onset of Nixonian repression. It is then that she sees a certain "truth" about her condition, that the "reality" or price she must pay for her betrayal is servitude in a world of limited freedom:

> Come into her own at last, street-legal, full-auto qualified, she understood her particular servitude as the freedom, granted to a few, to act outside warrants and charters, to ignore history and the dead, to imagine no future, no yet-to-be-born, to be able simply to go on defining moments only, purely, by the action that filled them. Here was a world of simplicity and certainty no acidhead, no revolutionary anarchist would ever find, a world based on the one and zero of life and death. Minimal, beautiful. The patterns of lives and deaths. . . . (71–72)

One and zero: life and death reduced to the minimal but beautiful language of pure information. Yet it is this digital language that forces Frenesi to realize that she and Flash have "been kept safe in some time-free zone all these years but now . . . must re-enter the clockwork of cause and effect" (90); in other words, they must reenter the world of real time.

Pynchon stages the scene of Frenesi's second "moment of undeniable clairvoyance" in a supermarket, where she tries unsuccessfully to cash her last government check a few hours after Flash returns home with the paranoia-provoking news: "Turns out, a lot of people we know— they ain't on the computer anymore. Just—gone" (85). As she gazes down the frozen food aisle, waiting for her check to be approved, Frenesi's realization that the Reaganomic ax blades are swinging leads to a vision of God as a hacker:

> . . . there would be a real ax, or something just as painful, Jasonic, blade-to meat final—but at the distance she, Flash and Justin had by now been brought to, it would all be done with keys on alphanumeric keyboards that stood for weightless, invisible chains of electronic presence and absence. If patterns of ones and zeroes were "like" patterns of human lives and deaths, if everything about an individual could be represented in a computer record by a long string of ones and zeros, then what kind of creature would be represented by a long string of lives and deaths? It would have to be up one level at least—an angel, a minor god, something in a UFO. It would take eight human lives and deaths just to form one character in this being's name—its com-

plete dossier might take up a considerable piece of the history of the world. We are digits in God's computer, she not so much thought as hummed to herself to a sort of standard gospel tune. And the only thing we're good for, to be dead or to be living, is the only thing he sees. What we cry, what we contend for, in our world of toil and blood, it all lies beneath the notice of the hacker we call God. (90–91)

Frenesi's musings are brought up short by the night manager's appearance. Holding her check as if it were a "used disposable diaper," he patiently explains how payment has been stopped: "The computer," he says, ". . . never has to sleep, or even go take a break. It's like it's open 24 hours a day . . ." (91).

Omniscience, life and death, the ultimate order of appeal, what differentiates real time from playtime—all point to the perhaps surprising fact that in *Vineland* computer language figures the Lacanian order of the symbolic; that is, the autonomous order of the machine that makes human life possible (see Lacan, *Ego in Freud's Theory*). For Lacan, the symbolic is simply the encoding of the real (unlimited chance) in cardinal (or digital) numbers. More precisely, this encoding translates unlimited chance (the real) into a syntax or system of regularities, and thus into a set of laws. Lacan himself did not hesitate to identify this order with information machines and the feedback circuits of cybernetics, although his most elaborated example is an incident of counting "odds and evens" taken from an Edgar Allan Poe story. (See Lacan's "Séminaire sur la lettre volée." The complete version of this seminar has never been translated into English.)

If Pynchon's text assumes (or embeds) this Lacanian principle, it is precisely because it is directly concerned with the textuality (or "textual" effects) of technical media, as already evidenced in both *The Crying of Lot 49* and *Gravity's Rainbow*. Furthermore, Lacan's relevance to such contexts is easily explained: his "methodological distinction" between the real, the imaginary, and the symbolic is nothing more or less, as Friedrich Kittler puts it, than "the theory (or merely the historical effect)" of the differentiation of media ("Gramophone, Film, Typewriter," 114). Thus, whereas earlier in *Vineland* the technologies of sound recording and film figure the Lacanian registers of the real and the imaginary respectively, the introduction of the computer both completes the triad of contemporary technical media functions (the storage, transmission, and calculation of data) and indicates the agency by which the characters will negotiate their relation to the real (the stochasticism of bodies) and the imaginary (the phantasmatic identifications that constitute their identities).

In both instances, when Prairie attempts to read images and computer files, the narrative brushes up against a limit, an invisible, nonnarrativizable realm to which access is made through technological media, and the border between life and death becomes shadowy. But this is simply because, as technological media, both cinematic images and computer files operate as flight apparatuses to other worlds. Kittler has also pointed out that the realm of the dead has the same dimensions as the storage and emission capacities of its culture: "If grave stones stood as symbols at the beginning of culture, our media technology can bring back all the gods. . . . In the media landscape immortals have come to exist again" (112). In *Vineland* this is explicitly true in the case of television and film images. But it is also true of the computer: what emerges from the computer's contradictory associations with life and death, presence and absence, is a representation of the computer not simply as a technological means of surveillance through the storage, retrieval, and transmission of data throughout a network, but also as means of access to something like the realm of the dead.

When considered in light of this relationship between a culture's media storage capacity and its realm of the dead, much of what might appear to be "peripheral" to *Vineland*'s narrative suddenly acquires a different kind of significance: notably, the ghost imagery throughout, as well as explicit mention of the *Bardol Thodol* or *Tibetan Book of the Dead* (218); various Yurok Indian stories recounted or alluded to, particularly those of the woge, little autochthones who withdrew from the northwestern landscape when humans appeared; the voices "not chanting together but remembering, speculating, arguing, telling tales, uttering curses, singing songs" (370) that Brock Vond hears near Shade Creek, located not accidentally near Tsorrek, the land of the dead (186); not to mention the faceless predators who come out of Time's wind (383), and even the "Wineland" evoked by the Norse epic of betrayal the novel itself echoes; and finally the Thanatoids themselves, characters who are neither alive nor dead and who near the novel's conclusion curiously come alive as never before, perhaps, the narrator speculates, as an effect of television (363). Not incidentally, the Thanatoids have their own radio station, Radio Thanatoid, which broadcasts "direct, though not necessarily live" (384), a Pynchonian joke that summarizes a condition of modern technical media.

Critics for the most part have ignored or not known how to read this burgeoning multiplicity of subliminal events on the margins of *Vineland*'s narrative, events that bring about or register uncertainties and confusions about the real (and the Lacanian symbolic and imaginary as well). Like the pervasive television and movie images and references, these events constitute a nonnarrativizable and heterogeneous realm reflecting the sudden and immense expansion of late twentieth-century American culture's media storage capacities, and consequently the expansion of its realm of the dead. In other words, *Vineland,* like other contemporary writing concerned with new information technologies, must contend with the fact that if the dead remain in the memory of the living, it is no longer simply because of writing and oral narrative. Kittler suggests that nineteenth-century photo albums establish an infinitely more precise realm of the dead than Balzac's *Comédie Humaine.* His observations recall those of Paul Virilio, who refers to the cinema as a ghost industry "seeking out new vectors of the Beyond" (*War and Cinema,* chap. 3). These and other media, including the computer and its communications networks, not only provide a greatly and suddenly expanded realm of the dead but also bring about more varied possibilities for "flight into other worlds."

These other worlds—whether accessed through television, movies, newspaper reportage, Indian myth, tales of reincarnation, or Norse epic—are all immanent to Pynchon's narrative while not being fully integrated within it. Each of these narrative sources implies a different information technology and a different mode of address. As a sense-making device, *Vineland*'s narrative must somehow integrate these other worlds, each with its distinctive threshold for "flight," while also acknowledging that these effects are not inherently connected, and thus enjoy a quasiindependence. In this double obligation the narrative registers the fact that we still live among partially connected media systems, with incompatible data channels and differently formated data. In *Vineland* the differences between and among media still count, producing not only different kinds of subjectivity and the possibility of different reading effects, but also a complex form of temporality in which a mythic past, two distinguishable historical moments (the 1960s and the 1980s), and a different technological future are all simultaneously "present." For in Prairie's technologically mediated quest *Vineland* also augurs a new kind of communications setup in which the heterogeneity of information in a partially connected media system will disappear through the digitalization of all analogical media, which then will become merely different interface possibilities accessed through a computer terminal.

William Gibson's *Neuromancer*, published six years before *Vineland* but set in a not too distant twenty-first century, assumes just such a media assemblage, one characterized by the complete digitalization of information and a fully integrated communications network—the Net, as Gibson calls it—closely resembling the fiber-optic network that Kittler describes. *Neuromancer*'s adventure-story plot explores new possibilities of this communications assemblage—both for "flight" and for the extension of control—primarily in terms of "cyberspace," or the new medium it brings into being, and the kinds of intelligent action—both human and nonhuman—that it makes possible.

In an often quoted passage, Gibson defines cyberspace as

> a consensual hallucination experienced daily by billions of legitimate [computer] operators, in every nation, by children being taught mathematical concepts.... A graphic representation of data abstracted from the bank of every computer in the human system. Unthinkable complexity. Lines of light ranged in the nonspace of the mind, clusters and constellations of data. Like city lights receding. (51)

By means of a neuro-electronic link to a cyberspace deck or "matrix simulator" (which resembles a computer with a monitor), an operator accesses cyberspace and passes to what Gibson calls "the matrix," an infinite and transparent three-dimensional field where data are stored in architectural forms. By punching coordinates on a keyboard, the operator can maneuver there as a bodiless point. The data themselves, whether corporate or military, are protected by ICE, or Intrusive Countermeasures Electronics. Whereas legitimate operators can access the data by entering appropriate codes, data rustlers or "cyberspace cowboys," as Gibson calls them, must rely on "icebreakers" to penetrate to the large corporate data cores. Icebreakers are usually virus programs—like the technology of cyberspace itself, they are of military origin—that can dissolve the ICE, or masquerade the cowboys' intrusions as official inspection probes or legitimate exchanges of data. The danger is that some of the protective ICE programs—such as the infamous "Black Ice"—are deadly "neural feedback weapons" that can cause the cowboy to flatline in brain death.

Cyberspace, however, is not the only medium in *Neuromancer*: there is also "simstim" or "simulated stimuli," by means of which the characters can experience "the world" as lived by someone else, usually a superstar such as Tally Isham in a kind of exhilarating multisensory movie of the rich and famous having fun at various locales. You "jack in" to both simstim and cyberspace by putting "trodes" on your temples; in both, when you open your eyes, you are "in" a virtual world, constructed neuro-electronically. The obvious difference is that while simstim is passive and anodyne, a vicarious experience, cyberspace is interactive and dangerous, requiring the intense focus of a disembodied consciousness.

In *Neuromancer* and his two subsequent novels, *Count Zero* and *Mona Lisa Overdrive* (collectively referred to as the "Sprawl trilogy"), Gibson builds the cyberspace cowboy into a recognizable figure, replete with an oral tradition and associated mythology. At the same time, this figure is something of a throwback, an attempt both to glamorize the hacker-as-outlaw and to represent a new and unfamiliar experience by giving its agent a local habitation and a name. But however interesting as a fictional type, the cyberspace cowboy's importance is eclipsed by his element; in *Neuromancer* cyberspace is not only a medium in which much of the action unfolds but also a site or scene whose very nature undergoes a dramatic change. Specifically, by having *Neuromancer*'s "plot" engineered by a form of AI or artificial intelligence that inhabits cyberspace, Gibson focuses attention on the power(s) implicit in this new medium.

At the novel's outset an ex-cyberspace cowboy named Case, whose nerves have been deliberately damaged by a former client, is recruited by a street samurai and cyborg named Molly for a yet-to-be defined "run" put together by an ex-military type named Armitage. Case and Molly, who immediately form a functional (and sexual) liaison, begin to suspect that Armitage is being controlled by someone or something else. Through underground information networks Case discovers that Armitage is indeed being backed by an AI named Wintermute located in Berne and owned by Tessier-Ashpool S.A., a giant *zaibatsu* or multinational corporation. Formerly a shattered Special Forces soldier named Corto, Armitage was the sole survivor of a disastrous military mission in the recent war with Russia who was apparently cured of catatonic schizophrenia after being treated cybernetically in an experimental recovery program. All of which suggests to Case that "Armitage" is simply a personality "shell" constructed by Wintermute for the "run" against Tessier-Ashpool.

As the time for the "run" approaches, Wintermute attempts to contact Case, first by telephone, then successfully in cyberspace when Case is flatlined by Tessier-Ashpool ICE and Wintermute can access Case's memory, and then again through Case's hotel room monitor. Possessing neither an "I" nor a "self," Wintermute must assume some human personality as a "template." In the extended encounters with Case, which take place in "virtual reality" scenes that Wintermute constructs from Case's memory, with Wintermute usually appearing in the form of someone Case has known in the past, the AI reveals to Case that the "run" (and therefore the novel's plot) is motivated by its desire to fuse with "Neuromancer," another Tessier-Ashpool AI located in Rio. Describing itself as a form of "hive intelligence" (whereas Neuromancer represents personality, immortality, the land of the dead), Wintermute cautions Case not to confuse "the Wintermute mainframe [in] Berne with the Wintermute entity": "What you [Case] think of as Wintermute is only a part of another, a, shall we say, potential entity. I, let us say, am merely one aspect of that entity's brain" (120). For Wintermute, then, human "consciousness" is simply a focalized intelligence normally distributed throughout a network. Wintermute reveals that, aside from being able to sort tremendous quantities of information, its greatest talent lies in improvising "situations." In fact, to an extent even greater than Case realizes, Wintermute has chosen each of the participants— Case himself, Molly, Armitage, and Riviera, a psychopath who can project visual hallucinations, and later the Rastafarians in Zion cluster (an orbital space colony)—because each one has special skills and, more important, is psychologically manipulable in a predictable way.

Revelations about each character's past are thus motivated by the exigencies of the AI's plot (which of course coincides with the demands of novelistic convention). What is most important in regard to Case is his ill-fated love affair with Linda Lee and consequent suicidal impulses, both of which Wintermute (and later Neuromancer) play upon. However, there comes a point when, in order for its plan to work, Wintermute must convert Case from manipulated pawn to active ally; not only does Armitage predictably crack apart and begin to relive his disastrous military mission, but there are contingencies beyond Wintermute's capacities to respond. For all of its obvious ingenuity and information processing speed, it can do nothing with an old-fashioned mechanical lock; more crucially, it cannot know the code word that when spoken into a special terminal will allow the two AI's to fuse.

Wintermute's inherent limits thus allow a space to open between its manipulations and the indeterminacy of events as they unfold. As a result, the scenes in which Case is gradually converted from a sullen and rebellious cyberspace cowboy for hire to someone who consciously allies himself with Wintermute are heightened in importance. A clear turning point occurs when Case returns to his hotel room after a frustrated attempt to console himself with drugs, only to be arrested by the Turing police (who are responsible for "shackling" AI's, thereby preventing them from attaining a full degree of autonomy). The three Turing agents awaiting Case not only are wise to Wintermute's scheme but cannot refrain from interjecting a moral fervor into their accusations. "You are worse than a fool," one agent says to Case. "You have no care for your species. For thousands of years men dreamed of pacts with demons. Only now are such things possible. And what would you be paid with? What would your price be, for aiding this thing to free itself and grow?" (163). But before the Turing police can take Case very far, Wintermute intervenes by sending electronic signals through the Net that cause a small security drone and then a robotic gardener to attack the agents, giving Case the opportunity to escape.

The run on Tessier-Ashpool involves a double penetration, both of the ancestral family home, Villa Straylight, a baroque structure built in an orbital space colony, and of the Tessier-Ashpool data core in cyberspace. In a preparatory run on Sense/Net the team acquires a "ROM personality construct" named McCoy Pauley (but known as "Dixie Flatline"), a former cyberspace cowboy who though physically dead can, in cyberspace, advise Case how to deploy the Chinese icebreaker necessary to penetrate Tessier-Ashpool's data core. As in the Sense/Net breakin, the run itself is a penetration effected simultaneously in two modes: physically by Molly and cyberspatially by Case. Thanks to a simstim unit hardwired into Molly, Case is able to follow her movements as if he were experiencing them physically, and is able to move back and forth between her physical space and cyberspace by throwing a switch. The plan is to have Riviera gain entrance to Villa Straylight through his skill as a perverse entertainer, and convince Lady 3Jane Tessier-Ashpool to allow Molly to enter the structure. Molly will then coerce Lady 3Jane into divulging the code word that when spoken into a platinum head in Villa Straylight's core chamber will unshackle Wintermute. Of course the run does not go as planned. Riviera betrays the team and Molly is taken captive. With the help of a Rastafarian named Maelcum, however, Case is able to make his way to the villa and successfully complete the run in a convergence of the two penetrations.

To Case's relief and amazement, the fusion of the two AI's appears to change very little, at least from the human perspective, for what this fusion brings about is the AI's transcendence of human affairs altogether. In their last conversation Wintermute tells Case that it (Wintermute) has become the matrix, and is now able to communicate with distant intelligences of its own kind in another solar system. A more important consequence (further explored in the two succeeding novels) is the transformation of cyberspace itself, for henceforth it can no longer be conceived in Cartesian terms as a neutral or passive receptacle with geometric dimensions where data can be stored and exchanged. Whether the powers active there are ICE defensive systems deployed by military and commercial interests, viral programs and icebreakers mobilized by cyberspace cowboys, direct interventions by artificial intelligences, human personality ROM constructs like Dixie, or even virtual reality scenes in which humans can live in a form of immortality, it is clear that cyberspace is no longer a simple representation of data in an information field or mere "consensual hallucination." Indeed, readers today may legitimately wonder if the fusion of the AI's does not prefigure in fictionalized, anthropomorphic terms the possibility of a form of "self-organization" taking place within the space of the Net, especially since the machinery (a multiplicity of demons, bots, and spiders or subprograms) is already in place. In any event, there can be little doubt that in *Neuromancer* cyberspace and the Net become a site where new forces possessing both energy and intelligence contend for stakes that involve human beings but are not fully accountable in human terms. Precisely in this sense, cyberspace represents both a new extension of what Gilles Deleuze and Félix Guattari call the "machinic phylum" and a boundary space of unholy alliances, where humans plot with demons and "intelligence" undergoes a strange "becoming" (see especially the chapters—or "plateaus"—10 and 12 of *A Thousand Plateaus*).

Deleuze and Guattari define the machinic phylum as "materiality, natural or artificial, and both simultaneously; it is matter in movement, in flux, in variation, matter as a conveyor of singularities and traits of expression." They insist that the machinic phylum "can only be followed" (409). The artisan, therefore, is "one who is determined in such a way as to follow a flow of matter." Gibson's cyberspace cowboys are artisans in this sense; they follow the machinic phylum constituted by silicon and its possible combinations and configurations. In *Neuromancer* what is dramatically and thematically important of course is how the next step for these artisans following the postindustrial machinic phylum leads to an "alliance" with a demon in a "becoming" of a machinic intelligence. Thus, while at one level the plot may appear to be engineered by a form of artificial intelligence seeking to free itself, at a deeper level it is determined by the logic of technological development and its convergence with a myth. At several points *Neuromancer* suggests that the fusion of the two AI's enacts an allegory about the transformative power of joining the two hemispheres of the human brain. But if the narrative stages an allegory, it is surely a more englobing one about the autonomization of technology in the fully digitalized space of the Net, a process having little to do with the localization of brain functions and everything to do with the extension of the machinic phylum and the new kinds of spaces it makes possible. Nevertheless, it is in or through this displacement (for which read: one technological medium eclipsed by another) that in *Neuromancer*'s media landscape, new "immortals come to exist again" (Kittler, "Gramophone," 112).

Unlike conventional sci-fi, in which outer space is a Beyond in an expanding universe to be explored and colonized, *Neuromancer* focuses on communications across and within spaces that only humans—in contrast to the artificial intelligence that engineers the plot—can negotiate. This interest in spatial multiplicity is revealed in many ways. Indeed, what is striking in Gibson's fiction is precisely the heterogeneity of the spaces depicted. In *Neuromancer* these range from the streets of Ninsei, a "zone" where new technologies are tested, to the monolithic *zaibatsus*, the urban "sprawl" space from Atlanta to the northeast coast, a number of large foreign cities, the orbital colony Freeside, the complex interior architecture of Villa Straylight, and, most important, cyberspace, which involves several "virtual reality" scenes, including one with Case's now dead lover Linda Lee. As Gibson's prose variously describes how incommensurable or unfamiliar spaces are negotiated, how apparently impenetrable spaces are connectable, under what conditions and by whom (or what), it becomes apparent that *Neuromancer*'s primary concern is with how human beings articulate and connect up differences in and among a complex of heterogeneous spaces. That the human "life-world" is not so much penetrated as reshaped or reconfigured by new technologies is all too evident. For Gibson, however, this obvious theme leads to the depiction of a Riemannian space or topography, inasmuch as the connections among its many different parts are not predetermined but can take place in many ways. This new spatial multiplicity is not simply produced by but also marks the limits of a not too futuristic information economy.

In *Neuromancer* the absence of separable, differentiable media make the heterogeneity of space itself what is most essential to human being. Although certain resonant objects such as Dali clocks and Cornell boxes still remain as "flight apparatuses" to older worlds, the "realm of the dead" shrinks drastically, populated now only by ROM personality constructs such as Dixie Flatline and dead lovers in "virtual reality" scenes. In the reduction to cyberspace (or "simstim") as a consequence (in Kittlerian terms) of the disappearance of separable media, we see an obvious contrast with *Vineland*. But whereas human being, in Gibson's account, discovers its uniqueness in its access to spatial multiplicity, for Pynchon it is temporal multiplicity that matters—not simply the temporal multiplicity of human memory but the convergence of multiple times made possible and accessed through partially connected media systems. Thus, whereas *Neuromancer* simply looks forward to an imagined future in which the heterogeneity of space itself allows a possible alternative to a life determined by the giant monolithic corporations or *zaibatsus*, *Vineland* offers a Janus-faced view of an America in the 1980s that can look back to a period when both social revolution "went blending into commerce" and the "highest state of the analogue arts [was] soon to be eclipsed by digital technology" (308).

In "Rocket Radio," a nonfictional piece for *Rolling Stone*, Gibson remarks that "once perfected, communication technologies rarely die out entirely; rather, they shrink to fit particular niches in the global info-structure" (85). This statement applies to both his own and Pynchon's novels. In *Neuromancer*, communications technologies are what make possible the only form of resistance left open to the characters: a strategy of *détournement*, or the reappropriation of postindustrial technologies for their own—usually illegal—purposes. Similarly, Gibson himself appropriates the conventions of sci-fi and hard-boiled detective fiction as a vehicle or "marketing mechanism" (his phrase) for his own writing, which he explicitly positions in relation to the closing of the Net over the last twenty years. For Pynchon, in contrast, different communications technologies are what allow the effects of historical difference to be remarked. In a world of partially connected media systems, information is and remains heterogeneous. For Pynchon's characters, this means that different historical and technological conditions impose upon them different ways of viewing themselves and others. Further, and perhaps rather optimistically, Pynchon suggests that those differences—or the gap between technological regimes—can be bridged by narrative, even though the narrative itself may be unable to account for the full range of effects produced by heterogeneous media systems. As writers, both Pynchon and Gibson are necessarily concerned with mediality, and the new technologies of data storage, transmission, and calculation that make writing only one medium of data flow. In both *Vineland* and *Neuromancer*, therefore, writing functions less as a general medium, as it does for the nineteenth-century novel, than as a special kind of writing machine or means by which differences between media can be registered, even if only to be displaced in the delirium of reading effects.

Piotr Siemion

9 No More Heroes

The Routinization of the Epic

in Techno-Thrillers

Reflecting on the condition of storytelling in modernity, Walter Benjamin calls narrative a dying art, receding into the archaic under the pressure of a new form of communication, which he calls "information" ("Storyteller," 88). Another early witness to the dawn of institutional domination, George Orwell, wrote on the eve of the Second World War that "literature, in the form in which we know it, must suffer at least a temporary death. The literature of liberalism," Orwell thought, "is coming to an end and the literature of totalitarianism has not yet appeared and is barely imaginable" (525). American fiction, too, has implicated itself in those cultural processes that make bodily experience wholly compatible with mechanical times. Paradoxically, while Orwellian totalitarianism appears dead and certainly outmoded today, totalitarian fiction—the kind vitally interested in persuading readers that they live subordinated to the best of all social and technological orders possible—has matured to become a staple cultural commodity. As usual, there is only one catch. This new brand of fiction, both formally complex and massively successful on the market, bears an uncanny resemblance to the literature envisioned in the dark prophecies of Benjamin and Orwell.

It was perhaps no accident that a fiction truly comfortable, even symbiotic, with the dominant structures of modernity emerged in the 1980s, in the final decade of the Cold War. Viewed from our fin de siècle perspective, the 1970s works by Thomas Pynchon, William Gaddis, Don DeLillo, and Joseph McElroy belong to a phase of transition: last Mo-

193

Collage by Piotr Siemion, from a discarded Roman Catholic comic book found in Warsaw.

hicans all, those authors tried to explore the junction of culture and administration *critically*. In their writing they maintained a typically modernist conceptual sovereignty that kept them safe: not widely read, perhaps, but not co-opted. They were interested but not implicated in the great but ruthless, bureaucratic project otherwise called modernity. Since the 1970s, however, American fiction has reached a new kind of status quo in its confrontation with the global systemic hegemony tormenting it from the times of Goethe, Melville, and Kafka. The emergent new type of bureaucratic literature is not an instrument of liberation. It works against the market and diversity, and also against the liberal concept of subjectivity. On the pages of this new totalitarian fiction, dehumanized humans and humanized killing machines meet in the halfway house of a power structure as big as the world, where state borders and metropolitan centers have been replaced by global networks and subterranean control centers.

It was the sense that literature's critical potential in that strange new world has been steadily blunted and fiction itself marginalized over recent decades that made Fredric Jameson reiterate Benjamin's jeremiad and dismiss literature as "an archaic holdover" of antiquarian interest only in the age of the "institutional collectivization of contemporary life" (*Postmodernism*, 307, 320). "Is T. S. Eliot recuperable?" Jameson sneers, apparently out of conviction that the logic of late capitalism is dispersive and the new social formation impossible to represent by means of older, quaintly anthropomorphic modes. To represent the complexity and synchronicity of daily life, one supposedly needs television, a medium that makes "all these unimaginably multiple bulbs light up again" (363). If the epic was a form of poetic historiography, as Benjamin wants it to be, and the text originates from a record kept by memory, storytelling has no place in the "world of information" (95–96). Like other cottage industries, literary representations are too technologically backward to compete with the instant gratification brought by flashing images. Which is all to the good, one is given to understand, because in its archaism, literature can stay unimplicated in the global avalanche of schlock.[1]

All these accounts must be kept in mind, if only because a confrontation with actual, current texts and new genres proves them both right and wrong. It is of course possible to agree with Jameson about the dearth of adequate figurations and cognitive maps of our time, although at least since the 1970s fiction has proposed a number of interesting ways out of that dilemma. High modernism combined with awareness of the institutional texture of reality (*Gravity's Rainbow*'s way) was one answer. Another was to continue producing complex fictions for complex times by blending in the media poetics. Pynchon's *Vineland* (1990) and DeLillo's *Libra* (1988) are characteristic examples here, as well as Joseph McElroy's *Women and Men* (1987) and *A Frolic of His Own* by William Gaddis (1993). More of the same, however, is often not enough to sustain interest. Besides, complex works are notoriously difficult and reader-unfriendly in their modernist way, which might explain to some degree why there has been only one *Gravity's Rainbow*. A very different attempt to make amends with new social formations was proposed in the literature of cyberpunk, much acclaimed and discussed since the 1980s—not least, it seems, because it turns toward the critics a nice, soft underbelly of coherent narrative flow. While cyberpunk fiction purports to stab right to the heart of the institutional monad, in the context of this discussion it appears as retrograde and simplistic as the Arthurian romance did to Cervantes. Trying to bypass rather than grapple with the digitalized, dispersive, overwhelming complexity of the near future, it is content to fall back on tried-and-true narrative models (*Neuromancing*, as it were).

Not so with the techno-thriller, the epic for the time of NASA. Techno-thrillers are ambitious, omnivorous—one is almost tempted to say "encyclopedic"[2]—secular works with plenty of plausible explanation and no inclination whatsoever toward the miraculous. They narrate history in large scale and transcend even their own book form (what with movie adaptations and computer-game versions), which makes them very different from the novel as we know it. Certainly, to speak of them as routinized epics, it is necessary to narrow one's definition of that form, stranded on the rocks of modernity for the last two or three hundred years. A typical techno-thriller embraces dozens of places and events, compresses all history and all geography, and incorporates all actions of its characters into a multistranded yet monologic, redundant, fast-paced narrative that dramatizes both military exploits and, more important, the eternal preparation for action. Like the epic, the techno-thriller projects heroes, plots, and ideals. It superimposes unities and forms over raw experience. Like the epic, it is rife with addenda, glossaries, and sequels. Above all, the techno-thriller shares with the epic its "official" literary status: it deals with relations and legitimations of power.

In his pioneering study of the techno-thriller, William James Gibson—not to be confused with the author of *Neuromancer*—considers it "a form of political discourse that must be studied in relation to the organization of political power" (198). While the power analysis sounds perfectly valid here, it can be argued that much can be gained also by studying the techno-thriller in its relation to literary tradition, especially in that the novels in question are so complex and rich in interpretive possibilities that in all their pro-American zeal they are more than direct products or indirect but relatively transparent reflections of modern political milieus. Techno-thrillers are an illuminating case of fiction that incorporates the extremes of highly consumable propaganda *and* hardcore modernist poetics in the space of a single paragraph. Their emergence is an unmistakable sign of what I want to call the routinization of the epic, or a process in which Weberian constraints impose themselves seamlessly upon the intricately structured, difficult territory of narrative fiction. In doing so, techno-thrillers replace the idea of autonomy—including the level of individual characters—with the one of systemic integration; spontaneity with the concept of limited plot options; and criticism with what Jameson would call a "libidinal investment" in hegemonic institutions (*Postmodernism,* 306). The techno-thriller represents art that "does legitimate the military as an organization" (W. J.

Gibson, 184) and, more broadly speaking, one that legitimizes the modern primacy of institutions over the individual subject—a dominant kind of art, at that. In a word, techno-thrillers help rewrite modern notions of the self using intricate artistic codes that used to inform expressions of unbound subjectivity.

Inside the Dick

With these guidelines in mind, it is easier to find one's bearings in the cosmos of "heroic male warriors, magic weapons, and horrific enemies" (W. J. Gibson, 200). But Gibson seems only partly right: for reasons that will soon become apparent, there is a world of difference between the techno-thriller universe and James Bond movies. I will concentrate on three pertinent texts: Tom Clancy's seminal *Hunt for Red October* (1984), Payne Harrison's *Storming Intrepid* (1989), and Larry Bond's *Cauldron* (1993). These three works display a myriad of common features in different configurations, as is customary in any pleasantly formulaic genre, but they all steer clear of fantasy or magic. Roughly speaking, the new poetics found in the techno-thriller consists in finding a narrative correlate for a nonnarrative world of routinized, repeatable activities. This end is achieved by grounding the nontraditional subject matter in a repertoire of established cultural forms and by imposing a regressive solution leading from a contingency-ridden story/history back into a fixed, utopian cosmology of a closed social formation. As Benjamin points out, speaking of modernity, "never has experience been contradicted more thoroughly than strategic experience by tactical warfare, economic experience by inflation, bodily experience by mechanical warfare, moral experience by those in power" ("Storyteller," 84). Techno-thrillers aim to remove that discrepancy by using familiar categories and figures to explain *everything*.

Techno-thrillers also attempt to explain away the violence implicit in a universal, encapsulating social monad. This last feature detaches the whole genre from the heroics of the past. It is not that in techno-thrillers, mainstream events or structures—say, wars and armies—provide a pretext for a yarn about male bonding, or a high-tech rendition of Mailer's *Naked and the Dead*. On the contrary, the most salient feature of the genre is its putting political and social discourses to the fore and subordinating to them all individual voices. The official discourse of administration spills over, via those submarine and tank operas, into spheres even as marginal today as that of narrative fiction. Otherwise it would be difficult to explain the insistence with which new kinds of the epic stanza similar to the following keep reappearing:

TOP SECRET
102200Z*****38976
NSA SIGINT BULLETIN
REDNAV OPS
MESSAGE FOLLOWS
AT 083145Z NSA MONITOR STATIONS [DELETED] [DELETED] AND [DELETED] RECORDED AN ELF BROADCAST FROM RED-FLEET ELF FACILITY SEMIPOLIPINSK XX MESSAGE DURATION 10 MINUTES XX 6 ELEMENTS XX

. . .

EVALUATION: A MAJOR UNPLANNED REDFLEET OPERATION HAS BEEN ORDERED WITH FLEET ASSETS REPORTING AVAILABILITY AND STATUS XX (Clancy, 83–84)

The reader no longer knows who is speaking here but at least it is possible to tell, by the style and manner of the transmission, that the business is official and current. The message full of conventional phrases, acronyms, tongues, and jargons presupposes an area of shared, nonconflictual, precise meanings. The reader may not know the meaning of all the XX's and [DELETED]s but is expected to trust the senders of the message, in the hope that in time, all cryptic meanings will receive an official exegesis.

The message quoted above is inscribed at the beginning of *The Hunt for Red October*. The novel is a submarine opera, divided into hundreds of episodes that flash by: one by one but, somehow, simultaneously. The plot revolves around the actions of a Soviet sub commander, Marko Ramius, who turns his state-of-the-art, nuclear-tipped vessel toward American shores with defection in mind. The resulting chase involves all American and Soviet naval forces in the Atlantic, as well as top military, intelligence, and political resources on both sides. Upon publication, the novel's detail was so up to date and its technical and organizational verisimilitude so great that a disclaimer was put on the title page, to the effect that "nothing [in the novel] is intended or should be interpreted as expressing or representing the views of the U.S. Navy or any other deparment [sic] or agency of any government body." Nonetheless, one of the novel's avid readers, Ronald Reagan, publicly called it "a perfect yarn," giving it the highest official imprimatur. Since the novel was first published by a small Maryland press in 1984, it has sold millions of paperback copies, has been remade into a feature movie starring Sean Connery as Marko Ramius, and over the last few years has become a bestseller in Eastern Europe, newly liberated to that kind of cultural production.[3]

This example of Soviet propaganda novel shows that even the highest official blessing is no proof against textual tedium. Indeed, how much *narrative* potential is there for a novel about a supercontrolled environment like that inside a nuclear submarine? One can easily believe Paul Virilio when he says that a "strategic submarine has no need to go anywhere in particular; it is content, while controlling the sea, to remain invisible. But its hourly fate is already sealed." Hence "*Gordon Pym* and *Moby Dick* are only the anticipated narratives of the nuclear cruise" and do not conform to the underwater routine (*Speed and Politics*, 41). *The Hunt for Red October* will indeed give *Moby Dick* aficionados a start. To begin with, the mission is a complete success, as if this time round, Ahab were able to nail the white critter, melt it into the Enlightenment-friendly lamp oil, and grind the enormous skeleton for fertilizer. In Clancy's "perfect yarn," Ishmael—impersonated by one Jack Ryan, a modest CIA analyst—outguesses the monster and brings it intact ashore. With the steel bolt of *Red October* in hand, America castrates Russia. End of the story and also of history.

Red October works, however, even if only as a yarn, and so do many other novels of its kind. It does so against numerous odds, the most serious one being perhaps the fact that the parties to the conflict are very hard to distinguish. The first remark to be made here concerns the actors of the conflict. It is difficult to agree with Gibson's observations that techno-thrillers dwell on fundamental differences between systems. The systems are as different as two sets of chess figures, and their moves about as unpredictable. In *The Hunt for Red October* it is clear from the outset that the Soviet and the U.S. fleets can enter into competition in the first place not because they are different but because they are almost identical. The main choice is between different brands of hardware: the menu of submarines, airplanes, and torpedoes at each side's disposal delimits all further options. As in any techno-thriller, the conflict is fought out between two antagonistic systems possessed of the *same* rationale, similar procedures, and equivalent equipment. Clancy's Soviet empire is not the radical Other of America but its evil twin. It is by splitting modernity into two analogous halves and narrating their fratricidal conflict that authors like Clancy manage to project modernity from within. Estranged by being cloned, the totality can be at least shown, made palpable and *interesting*, as when one of Clancy's characters peruses a captured Soviet map: "It seemed strange, almost sinister, to see the U.S. coast marked in Russian" (426). Familiar contours get visible that way. Thus the Soviets in *The Hunt for Red October* are different, but not radically so. They are not the Klingons, although "the Soviets train their people to do their jobs by rote, with as little thinking as possible" (109), and "remind [the U.S. president] so much of the mafia chieftains [he] used to prosecute: the same smattering of culture and good manners, and the same absence of morality" (165). "A strange people, made more strange by their political philosophy" (166). Even so, moral and philosophical issues are given a cursory treatment. Otherwise, the two entities remain perfectly complementary. They have similar ships, planes, helicopters, desks, analytical centers, decision trees, and, above all, the same belief in management. Comparing Russian rationale and Russian methods with those of Clancy's Americans, one has to repeat after Virilio that techno-thrillers describe a kind of "pure, technical, technocratic confrontation, of which the Americans are the absolute symbol, the Soviets being only their emulators. . . . When you talk about the Soviet Union, you have to talk about the U.S., and vice-versa. Together they form a system" (*Speed and Politics*, 160–63).

Yet what for Virilio is "the Russian-American coupling" (*Speed and Politics*, 160) looks to Clancy and others like a tragic, festering wound of separation. All action in *The Hunt for Red October* focuses on healing the lacuna and reuniting modernity—first by proxy, through helping the Soviet nuclear submarine defect, and then in a global process whose utopian dimensions can be intimated from the final scenes and epilogues of all these novels. In *The Hunt for Red October*, the antagonistic halves of modernity first come together inside the liberated Soviet submarine, where American and Soviet functionaries are seen "reaching out, seeking similarities of character and experience, building a foundation for understanding" (411). Not surprisingly, they achieve precisely that kind of coupling on the bedding offered by the manipulable hardware around them: "The Soviet systems had to be manipulated electromechanically, unlike the computer-controlled ones [Jones] was used to. Slowly and carefully, he altered the directional receptor gangs in the sonar dome forward, his right hand twirling a cigarette pack, his eyes shut tight. He didn't notice Bugayev sitting next to him, listening to the same input" (432). Like Ahab's motley crew of mariners, Jones and Bugayev find their common language in listening and obeying. In the interior of the submarine, their interaction is suspended and their chatter reduced.

Their strange union over the sonar console is only one way of healing the modern anxiety. The other one, more violent, requires firepower, as I will show later. All the same, it is easy to see that the resolution concerns a postnatural conflict. U.S.S. *Dallas* is not hunting whales, only hunting other submarines like itself. A victory will bring no transcendental revelation; a temporary gain is all that can be hoped for, unless, of course, the masters of the game come up with a really perfect move. In this respect, techno-thrillers resemble chess, a game end-oriented and insistent in its teleology, in which victory is achieved by moving figures through a grid. Gone are the miracles and wonders of the old-time epic. All the techno-thriller offers is a zero-sum game, played out within the limits of the set. The story dwindles to the point where it can be conveyed by means other than prose with no loss of coherence. At this point, the techno-thriller as a genre becomes an integrated system of signification that can straddle different media: prose fiction, film, interactive computer game, and more. Still, inside that grid, meticulous realism is the rule: all hardware is current or *real* models; screens are screens, not crystal balls. These small worlds are meant to be as "real" and as cramped as the reader's own.

The un-*Pequod*-like beauty of riding inside a submarine, an office building, or indeed any system has been summed up by none other than George Orwell, who wrote in "Inside the Whale": "There are many more things worse than being swallowed by whales. . . . The whale's belly is simply a womb big enough for an adult. There you are, in the dark, cushioned space that exactly fits you, with yards of blubber between yourself and reality" (521). Orwell's description suits all modern wombs: an office cubicle, the turret of a tank, an underground command center, a movie theater inside a suburban shopping mall. These, not Henry Miller's urban vistas, will be the vantage points from which the world will be monitored, recorded, controlled, and fictionalized according to institutional specifications.

In *The Hunt for Red October,* the action seldom leaves those enclosed spaces. The conning towers of U.S.S. *Dallas* and *Red October* contradict all traditional concepts of natural environment. Each stands for nature turned inside out and reshaped into an artificial, self-contained cosmos. While in *Moby Dick* nature was unkillable, in *The Hunt for Red October* it can be safely ignored, abandoned beyond a steel wall. In the postnatural space of the control room, all external stimuli will be mediated through electronic apparatus. The enemy will be known by his negative image, his *echo* in the sonar circuitry. Individual agency will be also redefined, and all behavior routinized and broken into procedures. Contingency will be removed, and certainly dreaded. The only sense of place and time will come from the screens and from the plastic paneling inside. Geography is abolished along with nature (for "subs don't care a whole lot about weather" [Clancy, 85]). And once the other half of modernity is destroyed, captured, bought, or harpooned by a Mark 48 torpedo, once the Russians are gone or busy watching Spielberg's *E.T.* on video just like everybody else, history is also terminated.

Clancy's narrator readily admits that "it takes time for men used to blue skies and fresh air to learn the regime inside a thirty-two-foot diameter steel pipe" (185). Given the enormity of this design, the popular acclaim of techno-thrillers must be found alarming. Apparently readers find that way to portray space nothing out of the ordinary. Clancy's interiors do look like a variation on Jameson's regulated postmodern space, an "afterimage . . . of social organization" (*Postmodernism*, 367) reflected also in the same critic's perplexed observation that "when everything is henceforth systemic, the very notion of a system seems to lose its reason for being, returning only by way of a 'return of the repressed' in the more nightmarish forms of the 'total system' fantasized by Weber, or Foucault, or the *1984* people" (405)—or by the "bad" Russian bureaucracy in *The Hunt for Red October*. When no images come out through the perceptual continuum of surfaces, modernity mobilizes the image of its evil twin to serve as a mirror.

But then, if techno-thrillers are little more than board games, is reading *The Hunt for Red October* through the textual lens of *Moby Dick* at all justified, except perhaps as an ironic grimace on the critic's part? The answer will be affirmative, and on more than one level of analysis at that. *The Hunt for Red October* follows very closely in *Moby Dick*'s footsteps, not only with its global scope and epic sweep. It, too, depicts a world of floating factories, where production and destruction hang in perfect balance, a world united by common utilitarian logic and common structure. The crews of the two American vessels, *Pequod* and U.S.S. *Dallas,* are servants of the Enlightenment, who hunt for meanings and crave final solutions. In Clancy's novel, meaning is no longer encrypted in the white skin but rather in the cloud of electronic dots on sonar screens. The submariners and the whalers are functionaries, but they are also harpooners, extremists who enjoy more freedom than their land-based commanders or shareholders. Although they can kill, they are as instrumental as anybody in lubricating their systems, whether by means of extracting blubber or maintaining peacekeeping patrols. In both worlds, Ahab's wild pursuit and Ramius' dash toward freedom make no rational sense. (Most of the Soviet enlisted men on *Red October* reject the offer of political asylum and return en masse to the Motherland, unlike their officers, who, fed up with Soviet mismanagement and obsolete hardware, rapidly switch allegiances.) The grudge, however, is shifted from the sea monster to the state. Marko Ramius' skimpy motivation for defection is the fact of his wife's death at the hands of some inept Soviet surgeons, servants of an inadequate Leviathan who cannot even protect its subjects. "For Ramius it had been a crime committed not by God but the State. An unnecessary, monstrous crime, one that demanded punishment" (5).

Melvillian allusions and correspondences do abound in Clancy's text, inevitably perhaps in a novel focused on whale-shaped vessels roaming the seas with a mission, although the older text is never mentioned explicitly—even though some of Clancy's readers presumably would be able to recall the 1957 movie version of *Moby Dick,* with Gregory Peck as Ahab. Skip Tyler, for instance, the first American officer to figure out how to detect the ultrasilent *Red October,* has lost a leg in a car accident, a disability that kept him from getting the command of U.S.S. *Los Angeles.* Marko Ramius has both legs in place but his will to power is unmistakably Ahabian: "He would get where he wanted [i.e., to America], do what he wanted to do, and nobody, not his own countrymen, not even the Americans, would be able to do a thing about it" (98). Ramius commands a steel whale from inside, having once killed the real thing when "a fifty-ton right whale had somehow blundered" into the path of his previous submarine (187). From that first kill on, a postnatural state begins, with choices limited to those between two different *insides.* Nature can still be reached in indirect ways, in this case through the sonar. "Off Bermuda they had encountered mating humpbacks, and a very impressive noise that was. Jones had a personal copy of the tape of them for use on the beach; some women had found it interesting, in a kinky kind of way" (260). Real whale songs are meant for an after-hours, recreational use. While on duty, everybody follows the general rule that reads: "You shall watch every instrument with absolute concentration all the time" (261).

Pequod, however, had a deck, populated by strangely assorted characters. How much can happen inside a well-policed steel pipe? Nothing, if by "events" one understands things not sanctioned by the system. Variety is annulled inside U.S.S. *Dallas,* where all races wear the same uniform and serve the same purpose. Techno-thrillers, on the other hand, share literature's retrograde preoccupation with telling a story. The narration will be a ritual reenactment of one crisis or another, stemming from moments when the continuity of social organization's carapace comes under some particularly dire threat. When functioning flawlessly, the system cannot be narrated at all because it does not change. A story can find some foothold only in disruption of that continuity. It is only when Marko Ramius decides to go ahead with his defection and lures the political officer, the slippery Putin, into his wardroom to kill him that the narrator is able to say: "And so it began" (9).

In its insistence on the expected crisis that inevitably arrives and is resolved, the techno-thriller is a direct descendant of modernist sensibilities: before a predictable solution appears, the reader is treated to a thousand shocks. Necessity can be suffered, it seems, only when it has been primed with some freedom. No one knows this simple truth better than Marko Ramius, who, for once, finds a real destination for his command: America. America offers a correlate for his desire, unlike the empty, invisible ocean and the routinized navy where nothing ever changes except maybe the generations of hardware. The narrative mechanism has a double impact here: if America embodies the desire of the imagined Other (i.e., a Russian), a fortiori it must be embraced, unquestioningly, by America's own functionaries and by the readers. And once a narrative semblance of history-looking-for-its-end is set in motion, when numerous offices and seas begin to whirl in short, breathless chapters, the diversity of events is gradually translated into a solution. The initial cacophony of random events and garbled communications is reduced to a final harmony—mainly through the good instances of assorted military hardware:

> The five-hundred-pound warhead struck the target a glancing blow aft of midships, just forward of the control room. It exploded a millisecond later. The force of explosion hurled Ryan from his chair, and his head hit the deck. He came to from a moment's unconsciousness with his ears ringing in the dark. The shock of explosion had shorted out a dozen electrical switchboards, and it was several seconds before the red battle lights clicked on. (445)

The spectacle of near destruction averted by wonder-working installations has some patently orgasmic overtones, and, in a way, helps explain what Clancy's functionaries do for sex. Helps so much that the techno-thriller may be regarded as a techno-porn of sorts, a decadent spectacle in which the Luddite in the reader enjoys the violence aimed at the "steel pipe" while the functionary present in the same reader trembles at the thought that the matrix around him might be penetrated. In the end, though, the system vindicates itself and redeems its servants through an act of technologized, limited warfare, open or clandestine. The two impulses—one prodding the reader toward the Luddite role, and the other toward that of a functionary—hang in balance among the world's machinery. It is not an easy balance, though. The orderly male communities of *The Hunt for Red October* are teeming with suppressed violence, quiet urges, and kinky fantasies of technologized penetration. Safety combines with aggression, and love of technology can take puzzling forms, or is represented as such. Glimpses like the one in which "to Ryan's left the captain began jerking his hand on the lever that controlled the light shutters" are very symptomatic. For Clancy's warriors, who crave safety and some outlet for system-tempered aggression, the "desire can flow," as for Theweleit's troopers, only "within (monumentally enlarged) preordained channels" (431). It takes no great mental effort to see that channel in military technology, so idolized in techno-thrillers.

The fact that by the mid-1980s "dozens of former military officers, active-duty officers, and civilians wrote similar books [that] almost all followed the same distinctive codes" for Gibson meant a reaction to the Vietnam failure and an attempt to regain some of the tarnished glory by the military (180). Gibson is pointing here toward two different reactions: the Hemingwayesque rhapsodies of shell-shocked individuals, but also the need to heal the wounded pride of the Pentagon military machinery. The latter, nonhuman, plural, political perspective seems more palpable in the genre, although the individual angle is not totally lost in the interplay with readers. Today, from the post–Cold War perspective, it is possible to consider the continuing popularity of the genre as stemming from a successful attempt on the part of fiction to reduce an incomprehensible, dangerous feature of the social world to a noncontroversial *narrative* pattern. In fact, techno-thrillers have a double function: they legitimate at least as much as they arouse. As Clancy's Jack Ryan says about the CIA, "It was the same as with any large business" (46). "It's what they pay me for" is a common expression among the protagonists to explain why they do what they do. Clancy's warriors are happiest with fierce wars fought from nine to five.

In Clancy's world, only two valid roles exist: that of a hardware operator (e.g., a submarine commander) and that of an administrator, a manager. Above those proletarian and middle-class levels there is the executive Valhalla of the White House. Mancuso and Ramius scorn management and prefer real action, which, incidentally, is also entirely routine:

> Mancuso watched his crew at work. They did their jobs with mechanistic precision. But they were not machines. They were men. . . . The engineers went about their duties calmly. The noise in the engine spaces rose noticeably as the systems began to put out more power, and the technicians kept track of this by continuously monitoring the banks of instruments under their hands. The routine was quiet and exact. There was no extraneous conversation, no distraction. Compared to a submarine's reactor spaces, a hospital operating room was a den of libertines. (135)

Again, the passage abounds in sentiments contradictory to the traditional tenet that "everything connected with machines and mechanisms in bourgeois linguistic usage is saddled with negative valuations" (Theweleit, 257). The transferal of heroic values from battleground to super-controlled interiors can have patently comic overtones, as when Admiral Greer is earnestly described as "the sort who liked to see the raw data himself" (112), which must be the bureaucratic equivalent of eating raw steaks.

The conflict that techno-thrillers dramatize in this world of scientific, regular procedures has its emotional underpinnings precisely in the contradictory feelings of omnipotence and powerlessness that come from too much sitting at one's desk. Submarine chases and tank duels are "a kind of regressive solution" fantasized to alleviate the blues of living in a desk-strewn world reduced to calculable, mechanical operations (Levidow & Robins). "The increase in technical devices, in speed, and in the sources of energy will press for an unnatural utilization," Benjamin points out ("Storyteller," 242). The ego finds comfort at its preordained station and engages in an orderly preparation for the spasm that will not come.

Lords of the Ring

Who are those egos, those functionaries? The question relates directly to the rapport between paper-thin, paper-pushing characters and the reader. To move from the question of setting and action to the issues of agency, subjectivity, and reception, and to vary the discussion, I want to disembark from *Red October* and board another marvelous vessel: the space shuttle *Intrepid,* the cynosure of Payne Harrison's 1989 blockbuster of a techno-thriller, *Storming Intrepid.* The transition between texts will be painless because Harrison orchestrates the motifs already familiar from Clancy's novel in a remarkably similar way, although narrative suspense is distributed differently and the chapters are even shorter than Clancy's. The plot is likewise reversed: a Soviet submarine in the act of defection is replaced by an American shuttle, floating in a remote orbit after being hijacked by its Air Force pilot, Colonel Kapuscinski, who, despite his wacky Polish name, happens to be a preprogrammed Soviet agent. Soon after *Storming Intrepid* climbed to the top of the *New York Times* bestseller list, its mimetic scaffolding in the form of the Soviet empire collapsed, but the book remains a popular classic of the genre. Like Clancy's novel, it was purchased for the purpose of illuminating these remarks in a corner drugstore, where it was displayed along with toothpaste and other necessities.

Fans of *Gravity's Rainbow* will be disappointed by Harrison's choice of his technological fetish. Instead of the apocalyptic penis of a missile, they must empathize with a space truck designed to go back and forth between the Earth and the orbit, carrying Strategic Defense Initiative stuff for assembly. The Russians have their own, highly flammable shuttles, but they hijack the American craft just the same, hoping to prevent or delay the creation of a safe antiballistic cocoon around the better part of humanity. The motif of encapsulation is pushed here to its cosmic extreme.

Storming Intrepid works on a scale much grander than that of *The Hunt for Red October.* Not only is its scope global to the extent that all corners of the planet are soon overshadowed by the winged shapes of Soviet and American spacecraft, satellites, space fighters, plain jet fighters, and B-2 Stealth bombers. The final victory lets the Americans triumph over the ancient evil planted by Beria himself throughout the United States in the form of brainwashed "saplings"; more than that, the final "deal" between the American and Soviet top dogs results in a perfect stasis: here, too, as in *The Hunt for Red October,* history can finally stop in its tracks.

Like Clancy's novel, *Storming Intrepid* reverberates with faint, unacknowledged echoes of bastardized older texts. Familiar contours soon appear. Instead of Rheingold, Harrison loads the hijacked shuttle full of "rubidium isotope" and throws in for good measure a PRISM optical supercomputer and a top-notch gamma-ray laser. All these together will form an orbital system that will make America forever invulnerable to missile attacks. The gear is much more advanced and hypothetical than the equipment featured in *The Hunt for Red October* but its idea never touches the extremes beyond which science fiction looms. The thief is not Richard Wagner's dwarf Alberich but a much taller—though also ridiculously named—Colonel Kapuscinski, who grabs the orbital loot to give it to the Russian giants. Like Wagner's Alberich, Kapuscinski ("kind of a weird bird") renounces the power of love, and even though America fed him and made him a pilot, he tries to make a dash for the Soviet Union (82). While he remains stuck in the orbit, other Wagnerian situations follow in a pell-mell fashion and numerous subplots evolve, epic-style. Eager to recapture *Intrepid*, Air Force Colonel "Mad Dog" Monaghan fashions the sword Nothung (the Kestrel space fighter) while Siegmund and Sieglinde, in the persons of Col. Peter Lamborghini and his deputy, Maj. Lydia Strand, manage to probe Kapuscinski's dark past. Later on, B-2 black bombers aptly imitate the Valkyries in their great flight through cloudy Soviet airspace. They bomb *Intrepid* just as it finally touches down at the Baikonur cosmodrome, while pursued by the young Gunther, a Soviet pilot in his MiG-29. In the end, *Intrepid* is consumed by fire, and the gods' purpose is achieved. In a Pynchonesque twist, it turns out that since the very beginning the hijacking was meant to promote KGB Chairman Kostiashak's idea of a new *Götterdämmerung*. Interestingly, it was during his graduate studies at Princeton (!) that Kostiashak conceived the idea of withdrawing his country from direct competition with the United States in space and everywhere. The gods surrender their direct influence in the world and the vicious cycle of power and property comes to a welcome halt.

The operatic, Wagnerian beauty of *Storming Intrepid* lies in its steadfast reliance on the handful of motifs that keep recurring in ever-new permutations, as they do in *The Hunt for Red October*. Both stories manifest similar longings to fold back nature, space, and history, and they flatten all characters. They reduce human beings to functionaries and communities to structures, with the result that their characteristic leitmotif is a big room full of generals. A command center is meant to embody the agency larger than any particular agency. Electronic panopticons of this kind were already shown in *The Hunt for Red October*. All space is made visible at once on their screens and all history made transparent in their instantly accessible archives. The scenery represents a perfect embodiment of pure information, understandable in itself and promptly verifiable, which for Benjamin is the opposite of "the spirit of storytelling" but nevertheless forms the core of the techno-thriller.

It is the same informational realm through which matrix cowboys roam in cyberpunk fiction, a genre coeval with the techno-thriller, except that the functionaries are legitimate denizens of that space.[4] The "Center" (NORAD headquarters, the Soviet Kaliningrad Flite Control Centre, the SPACECOM, the SOUS Atlantic Control, etc.) wields real-time control over information, in a climax of all bureaucratic dreams. The Center can countermand the peripheral chaos and hence preclude any possibility of a *future*. This modern omphalos is cloned all over the political and technological spectrum:

> If a Russian and an American airman could trade places between the Soviet Aerospace Defense Warning Centre in Magnitogorsk and NO-RAD headquarters in Cheyenne Mountain, they would be struck by the similarity of the two facilities. At both locations large projection screens dominated the giant room, and there were rows and rows of consoles. Both the American and Russian centers had a Crow's Nest overlooking the entire facility, where a colonel was on duty at all times. (*Storming Intrepid*, 99)

The control nexus represents a Baudrillardian improvement on the old carceral model. On the screens, reality becomes fully malleable. As Barry Smart observes, "In so far as the conventional conceptions of causality and determination, and distinctions between cause/effect, active/passive, subject/object and means/ends are called into question, critical analysis is made difficult, if not of necessity fundamentally transformed." And if so, the social mass—represented by the functionaries—"and the media constitute a single process" (127–28). It seems a legitimate gesture to extend that participatory bliss to the reader, who finds in the techno-thriller a source of pleasure resulting from the feeling of residing in the thick of things. Although the signs and images are contradictory and almost impossible—at first—to consolidate into a coherent picture, the reader can bask in the sheer plenitude of data and enjoy the feeling of gaining power by accumulating knowledge.

The reader's role is mirrored by that of the functionary on duty in the Center's "crow's nest" (*Moby Dick* revisited): a perfectly replaceable drone, whose omniscience ends with the duty rotation. He is expendable and indistinguishable from his counterpart from the other side of the curtain, except that Americans drink endless cups of coffee while the Russians prefer tea, also drunk from countless paper cups. (The analogy strains one's suspension of disbelief to the utmost, as paper or styrofoam cups are rarer in Russia than unicorns.) Both sides have turned all space into a hermetic, scrutable capsule indirectly hooked up to "reality." Very little happens here: most of the time, the officers on duty watch TV screens or talk over the phone, exactly as they do at home when off duty. When action is called for, they push buttons, preferably red ones: "He mashed the red firing button" is repeated at least five times throughout the novel. Then they watch the result of their mashing: "Instant death on a giant screen a few feet away. It couldn't be real. Someone on one of the front consoles began sobbing" (364). At less passionate moments, events slow down again. Functionaries on both sides push paper or launch rockets, engaging in strangely empty dialogues straight out of some twisted Wagnerian opera:

> Classen held up his radio and mashed the transmit button. "Alpha Chief, report."
> "Alpha Chief here," squawked the transceiver. "Decks one, two, three, and four, all clear."
> "Acknowledged. Bravo Chief, report," ordered Classen.
> "Bravo Chief reporting. Decks five, six, seven, and eight, all clear."
> "Acknowledged," said Classen. "Charlie Chief, report."
> "Decks nine, ten, eleven, and twelve, all clear, Jacob."
> "Good," replied Classen. "Everybody bust ass down here so we can clear out. We're miles behind schedule."
> "Roger," said Alpha.
> "Roger," said Bravo.
> "Roger," said Charlie. (339)

Nothing happens here, yet there is a tremendous degree of interaction. Out of this robotic gibberish, individual agency is built. The characters the reader is asked to root for all look similar, although generals seem to be physically larger than colonels or majors. There are even some women there, invariably of stunning intellect "wrapped in a package of stunning beauty," like Maj. Lydia Strand—although "her flying career had caused her breasts to sag a little from pulling g's in F-16's" (196). Every character performs an activity that is "responsible, continuous, involves the application of specialized skills, and derives its meaning from its integral part in some public or quasi-public venture" (Howton, 105).

Subjectivity is also married to technology. The feeling of intimacy with technology can at times approach a state of true bliss transcending any strictly utilitarian considerations of a weapons system in which "human and machine components, operating in programmed interaction, are seen as interfacing parts of an encompassing psycho-technological network" (Levidow & Robins, 168). Techno-thrillers tend to represent the biomechanical interaction in libidinous terms; they project a fantasy of unmistakably erotic character (but more serious and realistic than Pynchon's notorious rocket limericks in *Gravity's Rainbow*). A good example is Col. Peter Lamborghini's rapture on top of a rocket:

> As the vibrations increased, Lamborghini remembered the lift-off during his orientation flight aboard the shuttle *Antares*. That launch was daunting, to be sure, but riding aloft in the Kestrel gave him a more intimate feeling with the booster—as if the Titan rocket were strapped right to his ass. He watched the gantry disappear from view and heard, "Lift-off, Kestrel! We have lift-off! Everything's looking fine. Transferring you to CSOC. Good hunting."
> "Roger, Launch Control," replied Monaghan, "and thanks."
> Lamborghini felt the cabin pressurize while the mounting g-forces pushed him back into his seat. The Titan 34-D was ascending rapidly, punching a hole in the night sky and pushing up the needle on the machometer[sic!]. As the speed increased, Lamborghini's confidence—which had been shattered by the destruction of the *Constellation*—seemed to return. (427)

The thrill is made possible only through the union of the pilot with his seat inside the machinery and the umbilical connection to launch control. Heroic exploits are not possible without that armor; only when strapped in can heroes experience primordial thrills that betoken supreme individualism—a situation that reverses all traditional narrative logic. Disconnected, they become regular guys with wives and a penchant for beer or football on TV. But they very rarely stay disconnected, because the whole structure of their subjectivity is based on collectivism. Biological individualism is a retrograde trait: Harrison always portrays his heroes as *former* athletic champions or masterful football quarterbacks, as if to imply that mere physical and mental prowess is not enough. As Les Levidow observes, "the logic of the advanced weapons systems requires that the human component is either upgraded or marginalized" (168). The result is not so much Taylorism as Fordism, or the mass production of streamlined, enhanced cyborgs. The human race shown in techno-thrillers would not look out of place on the shelves of any hardware store.

On top of the man/machine conjunction, *Storming Intrepid* offers a social utopia, urging the reader to march with the stronger battalions.

It is perhaps an echo of the twentieth-century discovery that individuals can mean very little when policed properly, but the model American functionaries who populate those pages never question the system, except for an occasional snide remark about "bureaucracy" and "red tape." The implications of subject-formation strategies in *Storming Intrepid* and other techno-thrillers convince us that their authors no longer try to distinguish, the Mailer way, between individual agency and the "system." Jameson compares those two alternatives to particle and wave models applied to explain electromagnetic radiation. "Both explanations," he writes, are "incommensurable with each other and must be rigorously separated at the same time that they are deployed simultaneously" (*Postmodernism*, 326). In techno-thrillers, too, narration is perpetuated by individual agents (some of them double ones) but validated by the social monad that envelops them, with no clear way to tell a castle from a land surveyor.

Not only does the techno-thriller make the idea of fusing individual and institutional identity acceptable: the genre projects this concept as a matter of course and absolutizes the collective agency at the expense of the individual role. Individuals are all implicated in the plot—especially in that the danger in *Storming Intrepid* has a global scale—but don't really have a clue as to what is going on. This ignorance extends all the way up to the U.S. president, a model CEO and an energetic manager, "the son of Italian immigrants [who] had skyrocketed to fame by taking over a bankrupt car manufacturer and turning it into a financial juggernaut" (162). When crisis strikes, he simply bounces the responsibility back onto his subordinates with a blunt "Well, you'd better come up with *something*, General. And fast" (174). Luckily for the free world, technology works as advertised where humans fail, and the *Intrepid*'s cargo is whisked away from under the jubilant Russians.

The reader is likewise never told what intense participation in the game leads to. Like the American bomber crews, readers are no longer in the loop. "They were now passengers on a flying weapons system" is Harrison's innocent remark (480). A small number of warriors in a steel box indeed can be *described*—unlike the totality at large, whose contours are as murky as what the pilots of the B-2 bomber see in front of them:

The black batwing broke through the clouds at twelve thousand feet. Leader and Whizzo scanned the screens of the nose cameras to look for the recovery runway, but the scene was somewhat hazy from the overcast and they couldn't locate it. "Hit the zoom," ordered Leader. His companion turned a dial and the images of [sic] all three screens enlarged.

"Still don't see it," muttered Whizzo.

"We'll stay on this heading," grumbled Leader. "What's your read-out?"

Whizzo checked his instruments. "Altitude eleven-two hundred and descending. Speed four-four-two knots. Nine minutes to drop. The computer says we're in the groove." (471–72)

In this faint reflection of the Valkyries' ride, only the immediate sur-roundings of the cockpit are distinct. What lies beyond the computer-guided enclosure is somehow unreal, thinkable but unrepresentable. Readers trying to make sense of their own context can see themselves in those cardboard characters, who know that something is happening but don't know what it is, even with the best instruments at hand. The pilots' and the readers' social space, to paraphrase Jameson, is now "drawn back inside the monad, on flickering screens," while "their 'in-terior,' once the heroic proving ground of existentialism and its anxie-ties, now becomes as self-sufficient as a light show or the inner life of a catatonic" (*Postmodernism*, 363). They cede cognitive control and exchange any possibility of knowing the social system for the knowledge of the system's hardware, especially desks and cockpits.

The Daily Planet

Techno-thrillers can be seen as ideological and poetic structures that place technical language and violent facts in pleasing, customary con-stellations. Their textual poetics, or idiom, and the resultant pleasure are particularly evident in Larry Bond's more recent techno-thriller, *Cauldron.*[5] Published in 1993, *Cauldron* flopped in bookstores but has nevertheless several important features that make it an ideal source for study. For one thing, the events narrated in *Cauldron* happen specifically in 1997 and 1998, not in the provisional "now" that Clancy and Harrison embrace. It thus confirms Jameson's observation that recent literary forms manifest a "what if," simulated, not organic relation to history (*Postmodernism*, 390). Furthermore, *Cauldron* departs from the Soviet-American manicheism and stages a war almost exclusively between Western powers. Finally, because Bond's novel cuts across the whole social spectrum instead of dwelling solely on restricted military zones of life, it allows for some general conclusions about modernity and the fate of fiction.

In *Cauldron,* post–Cold War Europe falls prey to EuroCon, a joint French-German industrial empire with neocolonial designs on the world. With Russia paralyzed by a neo-Stalinist takeover, Paris and Berlin terrorize the whole continent, with the notable exception of Poland, Czechoslovakia, and Hungary. To fend off EuroCon, the oppressed Eastern European democracies turn to the United States. In the end, diabolical designs of the French foreign minister, Nicolas Desaix, fall through, but not before another conventional blitzkrieg sweeps over the land.

Cauldron breaks into two parts, rather like that other, more famous multistranded work about an evil genius and a quest for omnipotence. War erupts because Desaix craves power for himself and transcendence for France. His accomplices are a group of managers run amok. Aided by his secret agent Duroc, at his beck and call like a pet poodle, Desaix attempts to seduce the innocent Hungary. Soon enough Hungary mortgages its sovereignty and enters new servitude. We see Desaix busy forging alliances, getting rid of North African immigrants, and producing organizational diagrams for the new EuroCon structures. When Hungary resists, it is savaged by truncheon-wielding French agents. At that moment, though, the forces of light prevail and, like Margarete, Hungary is declared saved by Colonel Hradetsky, a mid-level functionary of the Hungarian police in cahoots with the Hungarian resistance. In a vision of utmost horror, as a French Walpurgisnacht sweeps over Budapest, the enslaved Hungarian proletariat wrenches power from Desaix, who remains master of the air with his air force, cruise missiles, and assault helicopters. Desaix decides to act. After all, he controls "the Foreign Ministry and the intelligence services. That was enough for now. He would use his power and influence to begin bending Europe's quarreling nation-states to his will—to the will of France" (87).

The resulting second part narrates a struggle for the control of the world at large—beginning with the rebellious Poland, a country that still refuses to accept EuroCon's paper currency, its economic system, and its un-American teachings. Desaix seizes his coveted Poland by force, the way Helen was seized. A second Walpurgisnacht begins, populated by fantastic half-human figures of heavy weaponry. In the end, the element of water triumphs: the U.S. Navy opens the North Sea for reinforcement convoys, American paratroopers defend Gdansk, British divisions land in Belgium, and Desaix's European Troy falls. The rest is restoration through public works: with Desaix and his henchmen dead, European lands are reclaimed according to the U.S. president's grand but practical design.

As before, the gist of the genre can be seen in its menu of limited choices. The question is never whether to join the titanic struggle or to go fishing instead. The proper course is always from a *problem* to the problem's *solution*. The problem must be grave and thrilling, the solution ingenuous and indisputable. In the simplest of those epic scenarios, both problems and solutions take the form of hardware. The threat posed by the ultraquiet *Red October*, for instance, is countermanded by an even more stealthy submarine sent against it. (A whole swarm of flying machines is necessary to destroy the space shuttle *Intrepid*, but mainly because the shuttle is an American [i.e., superior] machine piloted by an American-trained hijacker.) In *Cauldron*, American M1A1 Abrams tanks have it out at the Polish corral with German Leopard 2 panzers and Soviet-made T-72s, but in this case technical differences are minimal. *Cauldron* shows that Gibson's postulated radical discrepancy between *different* technologies and *different* management styles is more a matter of degree than anything else (186). Unlike the confrontation in H. G. Wells's *War of the Worlds*, Bond's conflict pits against one another a number of competitors out to exploit the same market niche. No wonder, then, that what decides the outcome in *Cauldron* is mangagement superiority rather than superhuman strength or divine intervention.

The organizational differences between systems are minimal, or at any rate never as fundamental as those between, say, the Mahdists and Lord Kitchener's army over a century ago. In *Cauldron*, all sides of the conflict have hierarchies, adhere to abstract rules, observe technical qualifications, maintain specialized apparatus. As in the two other technothrillers discussed here, office desks get much wear and tear, and when it is all over, the most active hero, the Polish ace fighter pilot Wojcik is transferred from the cockpit to a desk job. While "bureaucracy"—short for "inefficient management"—is mercilessly derided, all action begins and ends at the desk. The winner is that system which can use technical and human resources in a more efficient way. True, a lot of shooting takes place, but warfare is depicted mainly as an act of *control* and great *logistical* exercise, as in the coordinated rail movements of three divisions, of "tens of thousands of tons of supplies from several different locations in France and Germany [which] was an enormously complicated process, especially on such short notice" (219). *Cauldron* explores modernity's managerial conflicts in several separate subplots, beginning at the very top of the governance pyramid (for Desaix has a counterpart in the U.S. president). This managerial clash is best exemplified, however, by the parallel stories of Lt. Col. Wilhelm "Willi" von Seelow, a German Panzergrenadier brigade commander of the EuroCon forces that invade Poland—almost a knee-jerk reflex for the Germans, by 1997—and Capt. Mike Reynolds of the American 101 Division (Air Assault), airlifted from Kentucky to defend Gdansk.

Seelow belongs to a Weberian neutral machinery made up of professionals who serve political ends but do not invent them. His machine mentality is pitted against that of Reynolds and his paratroops. The American forces stand for expertise rather than mechanical precision and form an organic whole. Reynolds' structure is as tightly knit as Seelow's but Bond presents it as a "good" bureaucracy, one that admits subjectivity. Thus the American system has a soft inside, often depending on nonrational behavior and subjective whim, but is kept together by an objective, hard exoskeleton of professionalism and internalized common purpose.

Good organizations are those that provide their members with a fantasy channel. Reynolds gets it off by "getting firepower onto the enemy" (509) and thanks America for the opportunity. He sees his organization, in Gerald Frug's vocabulary, "not as an impersonal machine but as a social system, a way of mobilizing all aspects of the human personality in order to transform individuals into a functioning group" (1318). This holistic vision of a community linked by loyalty and flexibility is shared by Clancy and Harrison. Instead of putting the stress on the right mechanism, as in the machine model, the victorious organization insists on finding the right people to do the job and thus extends to its functionaries the promise not only of nourishment but also of (marginal) freedom. Obviously, this version of individual liberty has nothing to do with charisma or the will to power. These are good for Desaix and maybe for Seelow, but never for Reynolds or his higher-ups. When the small European war is finally over, Reynolds simply boards a transport plane and returns to his cot at Fort Campbell, Kentucky. Fooling around with politics is the last thing on his mind. "The war was over. Now it was time to immerse himself again in the army routine—in training and more training, and, through it all, the continuous struggle to stay ready. Until the next time" (556).

Like other narratives of bureaucratic legitimation, techno-thrillers "attempt to define, distinguish, and render mutually compatible the subjective and objective aspects of life. . . . It is this line that allows bureaucratic theorists simultaneously to separate and combine the values of subjectivity and objectivity—to present bureaucracy as both an enhancement and a protection of liberty" (Frug, 1287). First, though, bureaucracies redefine subjectivity in ways they find convenient and send the unconscious through the boot camp of the closely watched superego. In techno-thrillers the intent to persuade the reader is always apparent amid technologized carnage and deskbound drudgery that is never in vain. The genre invests heavily in what Franco Moretti calls literature's consent-seeking mission and tries to "make individuals feel 'at ease' in the world they happen to live in, to reconcile them in a pleasant and imperceptible way to its prevailing cultural norms" (27).

How techno-thrillers dress that mission in words and why they harp on story lines snatched from traditional epic is yet another story—the last one to be related here. Whether one accepts the unlikely possibility that Bond wanted to outdo Joyce in intertextual games or whether the echoes of *Faust* in *Cauldron* are merely a matter of paranoid exegesis on this critic's part, it is easy to agree that *Faust* and *Cauldron* function in two very different ways. *Cauldron* is a product, a novel meant to sell first, and only then to teach or delight. Similarly, while it is conceivable that Clancy saw the movie version of *Moby Dick* on TV, or that Harrison read a synopsis of the *Nibelungen* in *Reader's Digest,* neither attempts to enter into any competition with the old epic masters. The anxiety of influence is possibly the last thing on their minds. Instead, these writers take a stroll as if through an exhibition of decontextualized cultural forms. The relation of the techno-thriller to literary tradition is not antagonistic but nominal: venerable old texts resemble motel rooms for rent. They can be visited, lived in for a time, and left with not so much as a memory. It was this new kind of cultural dynamics that made Jameson remark that "the past itself has disappeared (along with the well-known 'sense of the past' or historicity and collective memory). Where its buildings still remain, renovation and restoration allow them to be transferred to their present in their entirety as those other, very different and postmodern things called *simulacra*" (*Postmodernism,* 309–10).

The key concept here is that of simulacra—a concept more useful than its overused name might suggest. Techno-thrillers follow the shape of older epics without any emotional or cultural investment in tradition. On their pages, the shell of textual simulacrum is filled with incontestable, soothing resolutions, as if the authors believed that a story line that has worked in the past and is now in the public domain can be grabbed and used (and that even without irony). The same attitude is apparent in their more detailed formal resolutions, although this time it is the modernist tradition, including the tradition of Pynchon and Gaddis, not the epic one, that serves as a depository of useful devices. The techno-thriller is the genre for the time in which "the appropriation by the state of high modernist forms" (314) has taken place on a rampant, pillage-like scale. When Jameson remarks that "we are rewriting high modernism in new ways today" (*Postmodernism*, 302), he probably did not want to pass himself off as a fan of Clancy or Bond. Still, it can be safely argued that techno-thrillers have indeed appropriated certain modernist styles, techniques, and attitudes. With their parataxis of tanks and torpedoes, techno-thrillers manifest most of the features that form the canon of high modernism. Above all, the genre has assimilated what Eysteinsson calls "the aesthetics of interruption." Witness the following list of subchapter titles in Chapter 26 ("Time on Target") of *Cauldron*:

June 25—Over England
CNN Headline News, on the Flight Line, RAF Brize Borton Base, Near Oxford
In the Thames Estuary
Ministry of Defense, London
USS *Boston*, off the French Atlantic Coast
June 26—irbm Complex, Plateau D'albion, France
Battery A, 5th Air Defense Regiment
Ringmaster, Circus Strike, over France
Pile Driver Leader, over the Plateau D'albion
Silo 5, 1st Squadron, French Strategic Missile Force
Joint Defense Space Communications Facility, Woomera Air Station, Australia
Juterbog Air Base, Germany

Faust-like, things and events are put here *nebeneinander,* in a vision of a self-perpetuating crisis. The reader's attention jumps between locations, held together by the narrator, similar in this panoptical capacity to a spy satellite, which sees "a darkened globe fringed with sunlight spilling along its eastern horizon" (390). From this exotic yet central viewpoint, all lands and oceans become a periphery, a free zone for military machinery to roam. Each particular place and action are fragmentary, not valid by themselves. Their topography is also spurious: a closer look reveals that in each case the actual place of action is a cockpit, a console, a command center, or the nonspace of the TV screen, (from) where different floors of civilization are translated into some grand, synchronic, closely watched sameness.

During this televised Bloomsday, discrete events take place, data are gathered, decisions are made, and triggers are pulled, but there is no Leopold Bloom to wade through the endless stream of stimuli. Although the text's segmentation resembles modernist practice of collage and montage, the total effect is cozy rather than alienating. The central intelligence in *Cauldron* acts like God and invites the reader to share that feeling: jumping from one location to another, treated to ever-new facts, parameters, and visions, the reader can indulge in a fantasy of having total access to all information. This time, the reader is not Walter Benjamin's *flaneur* but an improved specimen—a TV watcher surfing over countless channels by remote control. The aesthetic of interruption obeys now the grander logic of consumerism. Treated to portions of hyperreality, sedentary readers emulate the bravest of the heroes they are reading about.

Techno-thrillers' idiom has three distinct modalities. The most important one is the level of ongoing action, ruled by the present tense and populated by hardware rather than human characters:

> It was dawn over Hungary, Poland, and Czechoslovakia, and the low sun would make the long shadows so loved by photo interpreters.
>
> With their prey in sight, the tracking and guidance systems aboard each Brilliant Pebble went into high gear. On-board supercomputers took the images supplied by their TV cameras, matched them against an approved target set, and cycled into attack mode.
>
> More vapor puffed into space as each Brilliant Pebble's motor fired. All five darted forward, racing toward the oncoming photo recon satellite. They covered the distance in sixty-eight seconds.
>
> The HELIOS satellite vanished in a single, blinding flash—hit head-on by an interceptor at a relative speed of more than thirty thousand miles an hour. (*Cauldron*, 262–63)

The reader witnesses a meticulous report on the progress of blinding a French reconnaissance satellite. The scene is full of technical jargon redolent of power and control, cheerfully choreographed, and highly pornographic in an act of metal violence J. G. Ballard would be proud of. Characters are reduced to objects that crash into each other for the reader's inexplicable delight. The scene is narrated from a planetary point of view, manifest also in the absurd phrase "it was dawn over

Hungary, Poland, and Czechoslovakia." From a real orbit, the state borders would not be visible under any conditions, but the realism of the whole sequence belongs to a TV or a computer screen, where interpretations are "always already" captioned and superimposed over raw sensory data by one or another controlling agency.

Not everything, though, can be represented through the categories of AUTO-CAD realism, especially where human bipeds are concerned. Humankind's biological past and the dead weight of cultural debris must be dealt with by other means, involving the past tense and summoning up antiquarian traditions. Witness the dance of two spies—male and female—on the floors of the U.S. embassy in Moscow:

> Erin took a glass of champagne from a passing waiter and turned to survey the crowd. She found herself face-to-face with a tall, good-looking man in uniform. A Russian Army uniform.
> ... Off behind them, the band began playing Cole Porter's "Begin the Beguine." Soloviev half turned toward the music and then swiveled back. He held out a hand. "Would you care to dance?"
> She surprised herself by nodding. "I'd love to."
> He led her through the crowd to a relatively open air near the band. Two or three couples were already there, swaying and spinning in perfect time with the music. Erin noted the colleagues' eyes widening as she and the tall Russian officer passed by. It amused her. Devil or not, Soloviev seemed to have a born aristocrat's disdain for petty convention. High-ranking members of Marshal Kaminov's inner circle were very definitely *not* supposed to hobnob with suspected American intelligence operatives.
> He was also a first-rate dancer. (369)

Erin and Soloviev are for once not sitting at their desks or consoles. Although they dance with the intent to share state secrets rather than genetic information, their embrace is premodern. When pressed to represent precollective modes of behavior, techno-thrillers implement formulaic devices, in this case the idiom of romance. All phrases will be predictable and worn from constant use. One can almost feel the author's own impatience with having to go through those motions. The same awkwardness appears when historiography must be tackled. The "history" evoked to explain why Ramius, Kapuscinski, or Soloviev does what he does is laughable, as if gleaned from the *World Almanac*. Likewise, the infrequent descriptions of geographical locations produce clichéd, cardboard landscapes.

The historical and aesthetic eclecticism of the techno-thriller ought to clash with the genre's blatant political conservatism, but it curiously doesn't.[6] Somehow, the aesthetic innovation is no longer incompatible with the attempt to secure consent in the reader, and so it is no longer imperative to consider orderly realism "the inevitable vehicle of symbolic reflection of a positivist, technocratic-instrumentalized and repressive social system."[7] One reason is that the repertoire of modernist devices is no longer treated as new or comparable to anything old. Bond's or Clancy's shock is not commensurable with the shock Benjamin felt reverberating through the culture of *his* time. Like few other genres of fiction written these days, techno-thrillers embrace a media-derived aesthetics at the cost of adopting the media's stance toward the status quo.

The crucible here is the techno-thriller's consistent identification of freedom with collective necessity. The novels studied here obviously lack the critical element, or the ability to say no repeatedly in the face of organizational domination of any kind. Instead, they fragment all action into series of realistic bits while they suspend the meanings of those episodes until the narrative assembly line has run its course. The violence and destruction they dwell on are collective acts that additionally offer release for violent impulses—without deviance, because wholly within the pale of the social system.

Unlike their difficult cousins of the 1970s, these texts offer their mass audiences an array of conceptual shortcuts, a set of rhythmical, soothing solutions to the cacophonous, trying experience of modernity. They make the inscrutable familiar, most often without dispelling that inscrutability. In a sense, techno-thrillers impose forms on the totality—a totality homogeneous and, as Lawrence Scaff writes about life-orders of modernity, one appearing as "impenetrable except in their own terms." He points out that one result of this condition is the marriage of social totality with aesthetic modes of action, "providing apparently agreeable and innocuous 'solutions' and 'answers' through symbolic manipulation and resort to entertainment" (221). It is in this sense only that T. S. Eliot can be "recuperated" today: whereas *The Waste Land* subsumed a heap of broken cultural images under the privileged sensitivity of the myth-conscious artist, techno-thrillers invade and resettle only traditional, recognizable cultural forms with their bureaucratic agenda. They belong to a Spenglerian mechanical culture disseminated by mechanical devices, but at the same time they encompass much of what modernism considered uniquely its own aesthetically.

It is a tall project, yet a disquietingly successful one. Techno-thrillers deny traditional, liberal notions of subjectivity and historicity—and so try to rewrite the society, or push social representations into a direction they anticipate. Paradoxically, to do so, the genre uses displaced modernist techniques that once affirmed individual subjectivity and urged the change. With techno-thrillers, the militant, futuristic modernism is co-opted to justify the ways of bureaucracy to men. Their readers, on the other hand—obviously literate and accomplished to the degree that they can follow the action and its technical trivia—represent Theodor Adorno's humanity that can be turned on and off. The fact that the modern consumer of pulp commodities "welcomes the trash of the culture industry with outstretched arms—half aware that it is trash—" Adorno wrote in *The Culture Industry*, "is another aspect of the same state of affairs" (109); that is, of culture colonized by administration. Except for their moments of carefully orchestrated violence, techno-thrillers offer few thrills and few insights, but much comfort. Their heroes, like their readers, are content with their limited vision from inside the collective belly of the whale.

Notes

1. As another theorist of the age, Astradur Eysteinsson, assures his readers, there are "no convincing examples of literature as a vehicle of totalized reification" (140); i.e., no valid genres can be pointed out that dismantle fiction's supposed adversity toward modern systems of power and control.

2. But one won't. There is no satisfactory explanation as to what makes a particular work of fiction more "encyclopedic" than others.

3. The author of this essay played no role in propagating *The Hunt for Red October* in that part of the world but admittedly has done a Polish translation of Clancy's *Sum of All Fears*, which sold 50,000 copies in its first printing.

4. In cyberpunk fiction, this part of modernity's informational dimension can be glimpsed from a distance only. A typical scene in William Gibson's early *Burning Chrome* has the protagonists explore "the crowded matrix, monochrome nonspace where the only stars are dense concentrations of information and high above it all burn corporate galaxies and the cold spiral arms of military systems" (170).

5. Techno-thrillers have their own approach to authorship. While Clancy's *Hunt for Red October* was based on a computer game designed by Larry Bond, Bond himself co-authored *Red Storm Rising*, another of Clancy's bestsellers, and was in turn helped in writing *Cauldron* by Patrick Larkin. The author's note to *Cauldron* reads: "Many people write books by themselves, but I cannot understand why anyone would want to." As for Harrison, he admits: "Tom Clancy and Stephen Coonts were very kind to extend their assistance, and it was most welcome." And when a

movielike novel based on a computer game is remade into a movie and into a new computer game, we come full circle.

6. Fredric Jameson: "When modernism and its accompanying techniques of 'estrangement' have become the dominant style whereby the consumer is reconciled with capitalism, the habit of fragmentation itself needs to be 'estranged' and corrected by a more totalizing way of viewing phenomena" ("Reflections in Conclusion," 211).

7. Eysteinsson, 205. (N.B.: Eysteinsson also criticized this view.)

Part IV

The Book in Bits

Hypertext and Virtual Narrative

William Paulson

10 The Literary Canon in the Age of Its Technological Obsolescence

Recent years have seen acrimonious debates over the literary canon, the nebulous collection of works that at a given time are seen as enduring and worthy of study, and with which serious aspirants to membership in literary communities must be acquainted. The canon that had reigned in literature departments for most of the century, changing only fairly slowly, came under attack as elitist and exclusionary, both in its specific contents and in its notional existence. It was defended as a necessary bulwark of civilized discourse and shared cultural heritage. The canon debate petered out inconclusively, as controversies of this kind generally do, although it was revived from the traditionalist side in 1994 by Harold Bloom's book *The Western Canon*. Since the waning of the canon debate, worry over the status and future of humanistic education has shifted somewhat to questions of literacy and technology, centering on the question "Are books, and therefore literature, becoming obsolete with the advent of new media?"

What follows is an attempt to bring together the questions of the literary canon and of the explosion of nonprint media. Discussion of the canon issue from this perspective should help to define some of the contexts in which technology and narrative currently intersect. The canon is doubly linked to narrative: first, because most literary canons are rich in narrative texts, and second, because canons themselves (especially those of modern national literatures, with which students and teachers are most familiar) constitute implicit narratives about both the value and the development of the traditions they represent. To contest or renegotiate the canon is to challenge or revise an important story.

To set aside the reading of canonical literature, often in favor not of noncanonical literature but of other forms of discursive production such as literary and cultural theory produced in the contemporary academic community, is to strike a blow at the persistence of certain kinds of narrative knowledge in a culture in which much of the pertinence and legitimacy of traditional narrative knowledge has already been eroded by the effects of science and technology. Conversely, to attempt to enforce a kind of reading of canons that once seemed second nature is a reactive move that generally fails to do justice to either social and demographic changes or transformations in media ecology, both of which have made earlier practices of canonical reading increasingly problematic if not untenable. I suggest that a critical look at connections between canons and technology can foster reflection about which aspects of canonical reading might be preserved and which rejected for an age in which the technologies of knowledge and communication will be radically different from those that shaped the notion of a literary canon.

Canons and Technologies

A literary canon, born of a distinction between unchanging text and the vicissitudes of commentary, is an abstraction or idealization of the fixity of a collection of manuscripts or printed books. It is well figured by such collections as the Bibliothèque de la Pléiade or its transatlantic imitation, the Library of America; anthologies such as the various Nortons; and prefabricated personal libraries such as Adler's Great Books of the Western World and the Harvard Classics' Five Foot Shelf of Books. If the canon is in crisis, or even in a state of irrelevance beyond crisis, one reason is probably postprint technology. In his recent rallying cry to the defense of a traditional literary canon, Harold Bloom denies that the canon can be equated with a library or an archive (9), but he is presumably talking about the vast textual troves of great research institutions: it is hard to avoid identifying a canon with a personal library, or a small and strategically positioned subset of a library such as the French literary works shelved as reference works, just like dictionaries and encyclopedias, in the reading room of France's old Bibliothèque Nationale. Electronic storage and transmission of text is in the process of making the book itself less self-evident as a textual model, the shelf of books an outdated metaphor for the canon, and thus the canon an obsolescent concept.

A 1986 catalogue from the French publisher Gallimard proudly de-

The Bibliothèque de Pléiade, a collage by William Paulson.

scribes their Pléiade collection, founded in 1931, as an advanced storage technology. With its ultrathin paper, "it brought to publishing a revolution comparable to the one subsequently brought about in the recording industry by the invention of the long-playing record." In 1986, of course, such records were still on the market. By 1992, Gallimard had revised its description, its marketers having realized that the old analogy had become embarrassingly dated. For the moment, collections of fine books are still in ordinary use, as are some microgroove records, though many vinyl recordings have already passed through a brief purgatory of indifferent obsolescence and now enjoy the afterlife of prized collectibles. It is easy to see that digital media such as the compact disk (audio and read-only memory) make the earlier technologies seem bulky and even clumsy, but storage is not the key issue. It is by now a commonplace that electronically stored and retrieved text, in comparison with its printed predecessor, is almost infinitely malleable and labile, existing in a process of seamless modification and recontextualization quite unlike the stasis of cold print and the discreteness of bound volumes. What changes with electronic media is not only the text itself but the human interaction with it, the models and metaphors by which our relation to stories and texts are understood. With new media, as theorists from Marshall McLuhan to Mark Poster to Pierre Lévy have noted, come new ways of understanding the human subject and a shift of emphasis in the very construction of the subject of knowledge: the apparently self-reliant possessor of a personal library and general culture is at least partially transformed into a nodal point in the complex information circuits that increasingly make up society. (As Lévy notes, this transformation is never absolute, because the technological environment is impure and never determinative, so that the most one can say is that "the use of this or that intellectual technology places a particular accent on certain values, certain dimensions of cognitive activity" [144].) The supplementing of printed books by electronic hypertext implies shifts in the constraints and conventions of narratives, in the kinds of interactions that characterize the web of communication, in the relations between utterance and context.

There is thus a technological subtext to the contemporary undoing of literary canons, and whereas arguments over the canon may have largely, or at least initially, been political, the *possibility* of such arguments and their ultimate destination may have more to do with giving up or transforming some of the characteristics of print culture than with including the excluded. In the liberal arts, where the canon question matters educationally, students are trained, usually in an indirect manner, for careers of decision making, management, human interaction, and creativity. Most of these students will use what they have learned from humanities professors to work with information and communication in the broadest sense. Until quite recently, the book, the personal library, and more generally the printed word were the prototype and figure of the information resources needed by those who analyze, synthesize, understand, communicate, and decide. A literary canon—"the best that is known and thought," in its Arnoldian formulation—served as a kind of synecdochic quintessence of the cultural storehouse of information. A person capable of analyzing and interpreting canonical literature was presumably capable of analyzing and interpreting noncanonical and nonliterary books and writings as well. Novelistic narrative, in particular, has been valued as an exemplary mode of organizing complexity in the social, psychological, and historical realms, as a form in which readers vicariously experience character, decision, and agonistics, thereby expanding their own cognitive repertoire in these domains. Moreover, the elitist and pietistic justifications of literary study have always been accompanied by arguments that emphasize the value of textual study for mental discipline and its importance to the techniques of researching and writing.

What is changing with the generalization of computer media is above all the practice and concept of working with information. Analysis, decision making, and communication are increasingly seen as the purview of those who have access to vast data bases, often quantitative in nature, and who have the skills to summon, select, and analyze this information. The appropriately connected computer is replacing the personal library as the resource used by and symbolically associated with those who work with their minds. Under these circumstances, could the mental habits fostered by attention to a slowly evolving core of printed texts, largely from the past, be considered educationally appropriate? On this view, to paraphrase Voltaire, if decanonizers did not exist, it would be necessary to invent them. The *technological* finality of recent controversies over the canon, I suggest, would be not so much a suitably modified, newly inclusive canon that would better reflect the diversity of either literary production or contemporary social groups, but rather the abandonment of any canon, or at least a very great increase in the speed and frequency with which texts are shuttled in and out of the canon, so that the canonical would no longer have even the temporary appearance of fixity.

Electronic media, like books and in fact to a greater extent than books, offer experiences of learning through simulation, but one thing that changes decisively is that the experience of reading and simulation becomes more labile, at once interactive and transitory. In a possible future, to paraphrase Andy Warhol, every text will be canonical for fifteen minutes. Once all relevant sources have been placed in electronic storage media, and students and teachers are fully connected via terminals in the electronic university, there will be little practical incentive to teach with (or against) standard anthologies, such as the *Norton Anthology of English Literature,* and every opportunity to structure courses around the downloading (and for now the printing and photocopying, to save the eyes) of files selected at will from the magnetic archive. (Photocopying has already made the selection of course materials far more flexible than it once was, and has greatly facilitated the shift away from the canons of yesteryear; computer technology can simply generalize and complete this process. The intense battles over copyright law in these areas are symptomatic of the clash between print and electronic cultures: print publishers are seeking, and often obtaining, reinforcement of the copyright law in the face of technologies that undermine the formerly real foundations of copyright.) Soon it may no longer be necessary to begin a semester's course with anything like a fixed syllabus, since materials can be chosen and accessed quickly at any time. Such an organization of the teaching of literature would further erode the hierarchical distinctions between text and commentary, which are crucial to the very idea of a canon, and between the work of author, teacher, and student (since all would exist in the same medium). More important, this restructuring of pedagogical practice would arguably constitute a better apprenticeship for the information environment in which our students will work and live than do the traditional print-based technologies and practices of literary pedagogy.

It is important to note that the technological changes affecting the canon are not simply those of present-day computerization. Any event-centered narrative of a before and after in the existence of the canon can be easily deconstructed, and it is probably safe to assume that the literary canon has been, as they say, always already obsolescent. The very notion of a text to be maintained untouched by rewriting or commentary identifies the canonical with the preservation of the past. More important, ever since the philosophers and protoscientists of the seventeenth century began to contrast experimental or empirical knowledge with that of textual authorities, literary knowledge has been identified with the past and contrasted with up-to-date and practical forms of learning. The language games of scientific hypothesis statement and proof have significantly displaced the language game of narrative. As Jean-François Lyotard describes it in *The Postmodern Condition,* narrative ceases to be a primary vehicle of knowledge to become a metanarrative of the legitimation of scientific knowledge, only to be succeeded in turn by both disappointed metanarratives of delegitimation and a multiplicity of incommensurable local narratives (*petits récits*) of resistance to either narrative or scientific totalization. This process has not only affected but fundamentally shaped the modern enterprise of teaching literature. As Gerald Graff notes in *Professing Literature,* the nineteenth-century classical college curriculum based on the ancient languages was abandoned because it came to be seen as too estranged from the needs of an industrial and commercial society (21–22), and more recent declines in humanities enrollments bespeak a continuing tension between an education based on texts from the past and the vocational demands of the present. Meanwhile, the metanarratives of literary knowledge and teaching have shifted their emphasis from the inculcation of cultural contents to the more democratic and speculative investigation of literary form and more recently to the oppositional practices of resistance.

Clearly much more is at issue in the response of literary culture to scientific and technological change than the mere fate of a historically specific (not to say narrowly circumscribed) fixed canon. Yet even if we are willing to consider the canon as an idealized figure of a storage technology, it has surely been obsolescent for a long time—perhaps since mature print culture triumphed over what Walter J. Ong has called "rhetorical culture" in the late eighteenth and early nineteenth centuries. As I noted at the outset, the notion of a canon has affinities with that of a personal library. It also has strong ties to individual memory, reminding us that narrative and verse are themselves mnemonic technologies handed down from oral cultures. The old Ph.D. reading list, on which the candidate was to undergo a comprehensive oral examination, clearly identified the literary canon with what a person thoroughly educated in literature could be expected to remember. In what is surely a late example of oral-rhetorical culture, students of English at Vanderbilt University on the eve of the First World War were required "to memorize the five thousand or so lines that in the opinion of their instructor were most representative of their literary heritage" (quoted in Graff, 156). Already in the nineteenth century, individual memory and even the personal library were beginning to become outmoded as technologies for serious research, and this obsolescence was part of the larger move away from narrative as the primary genre of legitimate knowledge. As Edward Tenner observed in an article that appeared in both in the *Harvard Magazine* and the *Princeton Alumni Weekly,* the nineteenth century was the era in which paper file cards became a standard mode of information storage and retrieval. The paper file is far more suited to collective and collaborative work than the bound book, far more open to criticism and recombination than printed narrative. It was (and is) the technology of positivism, of knowledge pursued via the accumulation and arrangement of facts. Gibbon may have relied on memory and his own library to write the *Decline and Fall,* but virtually no twentieth-century researcher would imitate his practice, and the paper file anticipates, in its openness, malleability, and collective character, some of the features currently attributed to electronic media.

Rubbish, Noise, and Complexity

The information age provides new technologies, which in turn shape subjects and social practices, and it also provides new concepts, new analytical tools for the study of textual and cultural problems. The theory of information is literally a quantitative treatment of the conditions of possibility of communication, but its terms and concepts can be used heuristically to illuminate qualitative problems of form, readability, and meaning. A literary canon, in informational terms, poses the problem of a set of messages that, unlike most ordinary messages and even many literary texts, are *durable* in that they are deemed worthy of reading and rereading long after they have been initially received. The publishers of the Bibliothèque de la Pléiade describe their volumes as being among the "few objects of desire that retain all their attractiveness after they have fallen under our control," the "few objects of pleasure whose charm remains intact after having been used" (1992). "Literature," in Pound's dictum, "is news that *stays* news."

I offer here an information-theoretic interpretation of Michael Thompson's *Rubbish Theory* to describe the relationship between the form and the social function of a literary canon. The purpose of this all too brief excursion is to explore what might be called an information-theoretic (some would say technocratic) legitimation of literary studies— both the canonical and the non- or anticanonical.

Thompson proposes that socially constructed and determined objects can be placed into one of three categories: transient, rubbish, or durable. Thompson's initial examples are material objects, but his categories can be applied to literary texts and even ideas as well. What is generally called the canon is, for a particular social group, a set of texts believed to be durable, or toward which the group's members act as if they were durable. Of course, many if not most canonical texts began their existence in the transient category: novels written and published to sell and to entertain, comedies penned so that theatrical troupes would have something new to perform, occasional poetry composed and commented on by court and urban elites. The novel, especially the pre-Flaubert novel and the modern popular novel, may provide the best literary illustration of a trajectory described by Thompson: production and reception as a marketable entertainment, followed by declining interest and oblivion, followed in a small number of cases by critical and academic recuperation and canonization. Balzac was clearly aware of the categories of transient and durable when he wrote in an 1839 preface of his ambition to produce not mere novels but "a work worthy of being reread," and speculated that perhaps the novelist will one day be "promoted" to the rank of historian by "public opinion" (2:266, 269). On the one hand, he identifies the novel with transience and entertainment; on the other hand, he treats history as durable, a body of work worthy of study and rereading. (It would seem, given the quantity of academic attention to his work, that Balzac, despite occasional passages through the rubbish category, succeeded beyond his wildest expectations.)

Surrounding and separating the transient and durable categories is what Thompson calls rubbish. Objects in this lowly yet indispensable category are perhaps most obviously the formerly transient, a few of which may one day become durable. Most works in the rubbish category simply go unnoticed and unlabeled: they are likely to be aggressively denounced as rubbish only when someone tries to bring them into someone else's canon.

Membership in these categories would seem, at first, to be a matter of worldview or assumptions: as individuals and social groups we hold and share a constructed picture of reality wherein Shakespeare stays durable while departmental memoranda are first transient, then rubbish. But in many cases the status of an object, rather than being determined by a worldview or fixed assumptions, is determined by how people act toward it, since in fact the assumptions about it are flexible. Transfers between categories must involve this "region of flexible assumptions," an arena of conflict, competition, and politics in which things, stories, and ideas are subject to revision. Thompson gives a remarkable anthropological example in which narrative plays a central part: the kinship structures of an oral culture, that of the Tiv of central Nigeria, who reckon themselves descendants of a common ancestor from whom they always count themselves about fifteen generations removed. Memory through storytelling is obviously limited in capacity and reliability; thus, as new generations come along, some ancestors are deleted when the stories of kinship are retold and renegotiated. The first few generations starting with the founding figure, however, constitute a region of fixed assumptions: they are the durable (or we might say canonical) ancestors. The living and the remembered dead (three to four generations) amount to another region of fixed assumptions; their status is clear but transient, since in a few more generations they will no longer be remembered directly by any of the living. Stories about these two groups transcend the capacity of storytellers to revise or renegotiate them, at least at any given time. Beyond the "curtain of amnesia," however, lies a region of six to eight generations that are subject to revision and deletion: transient figures on their way to the dustbin of oral history, with perhaps a remote chance of promotion to the mythic status of durable forefathers. It is by reworking and arguing over their stories in this zone that the Tiv in effect decide who is related to whom among the living, and therefore conduct their politics—that is, modify their social relations—by modifying their genealogical relations.

A similar process may be at work in modern canon formation as writers, scholars, and critics conduct their politics by modifying the stories they tell each other about their relations to predecessors and therefore to one another. Of course we must make allowance for some major differences: in a literate culture, historical memory does not depend solely on retention in individual human memories, so that figures who pass entirely out of our usual stories and thoughts remain potentially available in research libraries—provided that their works were printed on acid-free paper. No less important, and related to the preceding caveat, is the fact that our durable figures are not necessarily those closest to what we call origins: Pynchon may be as canonical, at least in certain circles, as any ancient Greek, though the stories according to which *Gravity's Rainbow* is hypercanonical are likely to differ from those in which *The Iliad* is the archetype of the canonical work. Durability exists only in the context of social and narrative formations.

For Thompson, the existence of a durable category in contrast to transience entails the existence of a dominant social group, and of course a dominated group as well. A "cultural boundary" separates those whose economic expectations and values correspond to transience from those whose expectations and values correspond to durability. Thompson, who worked his way through doctoral studies in London as an odd-job carpenter, describes this boundary with special acumen in the conflicts of urban gentrification between those who see houses as durable and those who see them as transient. The distinction comes through clearest, perhaps, in a remarkable statement from the housing minister of a Labour government: "Old terraced houses may have a certain snob-appeal to members of the middle class but they are not suitable accommodation for working-class tenants" (35).

Competition between these groups, which is characteristic of a class society, is made possible by transfers from transient to rubbish to durable. As is well known, much of the recent challenge to traditional literary canons has to do with empowerment of groups long excluded or marginalized by the traditional representations of cultural power and prestige, representations of which the canon is a major vehicle. Women and members of minority groups have rightly understood that the exclusion of their works from the durable, prestige objects of culture corresponds to their own exclusion from status and therefore from an important dimension of power in a class society.

One of the traditional social functions of academic critics was long to keep rubbish and transience out of the durable category—this role, obviously, has been severely contested in the "canon wars." A distinct though related function is to make sure that the classics stay in the durable category. Old texts risk slipping into linguistic or cultural unreadability, or else becoming so familiar and known as to interest no one, so critics and professors are provided both to instruct readers in their codes and to reactualize or reproblematize their messages so as to keep them from being incomprehensible or redundant. The attentive reader may note a turn, in the last sentence, to the concepts and vocabulary of communication theory: codes, message, redundancy, intelligibility. That is no accident, for I intend to argue that Thompson's categories of rubbish, transient, and durable are translatable into formal properties of communicative (or pseudocommunicative) acts. Strictly communicative messages are transient because—tautological as it may sound—they have no more information to convey once they have conveyed their information. They become rubbish: yesterday's newspaper. In insisting on the poetic "set toward the message" (Jakobson), formalist criticism has traditionally associated literature's durability with structural properties of its language. Unlike the language of ordinary communication, which is forgotten once its information content has been extracted from it, literary language is said to endure, to retain our interest by calling attention to itself as uniquely and multiply coded form and as difficulty.

To avoid the transience of communicative messages, would-be durable texts must not yield up all their possible information content in a brief or even finite process. A certain kind of literary experience, as I argued at length in *The Noise of Culture,* can be described—using systems models developed by information theorists and theoretical biologists—as a process that satisfies this condition.

Almost everything known about literary language and forms, in fact about rhetoric in general, suggests that communication is a hazardous enterprise in literary discourse, at least in modern literary discourse, which can be described in information-theoretic terms as a noisy channel. But this kind of description does not suffice, because the literary text is much more than a channel of any kind. The rhetorical and conventional deformations of communicative language are themselves elements in signifying structures specific to the text.

Through a noisy channel, the receiver gets something different from what the sender sent. This is purely destructive if the receiver's only capability or interest is to become informed about what the sender was trying to send. But readers of fiction, to take but one simple case, know that when faced with an unreliable or ambiguous act of narration they are not limited to being the frustrated receivers of an imperiled or duplicitous message, but can construct an understanding of the whole narrative transaction—narrator, unreliable narration, narratee. The noise of the narrative channel produces two kinds of effects, "destructive ambiguity" (the receiver or narratee has a poor copy of the information possessed by the sender or narrator) and "autonomy-ambiguity" (the narratee has something other than what the narrator has). From the standpoint of a higher-level observer—here, the reader—this "autonomy-ambiguity" is a gain in variety that can be transformed into a gain in information. In other words, the partial destruction of a transmitted message within one level of a stratified and multiply interconnected system leads to increased variety in the message that this level in turn transmits to another part of the system.

Readers do not initially possess all or even most of the codes needed to understand a literary text, so that some of its variety is uncoded, or in other words is *noise*—which is, in Gregory Bateson's words, "the only possible source of *new* patterns" (410). The specific relations between elements of a text are to some degree unique to that text and so cannot have been learned anywhere else. Literary and communicative utterances are thus distinguished: the latter are deemed effective if readers possess in advance as much as possible of the necessary codes, so that they can immediately receive *as information* as high a percentage as possible of the message's variety. The literary utterance, by contrast, is precommunicative, for whereas writer and readers share the natural language in which the text is written, the readers do not yet possess all of the specifically literary codes pertinent to the complexity of that text; these must be worked out in a process of "self-organization from noise" in which new patterns are formed.

This account of literature as informational transaction might suggest a formal justification for placing at least certain literary texts in the durable category, insofar as such a category can be defined for messages, as opposed to physical objects. The literary reader undertakes a process of converting noise to information; the difficulty of this process means that the text continues to yield new information for a long, perhaps infinitely long, time. The destructive effect of noise on transitory messages is here supplemented by a countervailing, productive effect, and the exhaustion of the message through its complete reception is deferred, often indefinitely. Bloom identifies the canonical with "a strangeness that we either never altogether assimilate, or that becomes such a given that we are blinded to its idiosyncrasies" (4). The incompleteness inherent in reading "noisy" narratives—which could virtually be said to define the reading of narrative *texts* as distinct from the reception of *stories* by narratees—defines one cultural function of such texts, especially when they are "canonical": that of offering uncoded variety in close relation with highly structured information, openings for unpredictable times and spaces of *becoming* articulated within practices of transmission and reproduction. No reading of such narratives is ever seen as a fulfillment, for there is always the possibility of a further reading on the horizon.

The notions of literature as cultural "noise" and of noise as an ingredient of self-organizing processes together suggest a formal account of how works that originally seem incongruous, marginal, or deviant with respect to their culture can over time be integrated into its canons. The contextual shifting and making of patterns performed by readers to construct meaning out of initially noisy textual features are repeated by cultural collectives of readers in the process of making initially marginal or noisy works part of culturally meaningful formations such as canons.

Defenders of a canon may thus be tempted to propose that a possible criterion for determining what is canonical—and thus in effect "what gets taught"—is this formal sense of durability through resistance to decoding. This is the formal characteristic most prized by Harold Bloom in *The Western Canon*: "a strangeness that we can never altogether assimilate" (4). It might be baptized the criterion of *rereadability*. "One ancient test for the canonical remains fiercely valid," writes Bloom, "unless it demands rereading, the work does not qualify" (30). According to this criterion, the social status of durability should be conferred above all on those works that are interesting to reread—that are complex enough to continue to yield some form of information to us even after we are familiar with them, presumably because with ever greater familiarity more of the potential variety inherent in their internal intricacies becomes available to us as information. This criterion does not claim to transcend, but rather is immanent in, the nature of textual durability itself, which is a durability of rereading and continuing attention and not of any physical object. In fact, it is a criterion so pragmatic as to be almost tautological: we should reread what is interesting to reread.

Durability and Its Discontents

This kind of complexity criterion, associating canonicity with an informational richness that presents itself as difficulty and reveals itself in rereading, must now be put in question, and not only for the political reasons that may seem most immediate to those readers and critics offended by the complicity of rereadability with the high masculine agonistics of Harold Bloom. In the first place, such a formal criterion carries a strong risk of simply reincorporating, in disguised form, standards that are highly dependent on social status and association with "the" tradition. Structural complexity and informational richness are likely to be properties of writing fostered by access to elaborate literary education and by intertextual reference to highly organized traditions. It may be tempting to seek a formal criterion for what gets taught, one that emphasizes cognitive interest to readers rather than idealistic (and highly ideological) notions of beauty, truth, or greatness, but if such a criterion turns out to reinforce old patterns of exclusion, it might better be described as insidiously pseudo-objective, itself a manifestation of ideology, and rejected as quickly as possible.

An even greater problem with the criterion of rereadability is its complicity with a reification of the literary work. The formalist training institutionalized in the United States by the New Criticism instilled the habit of considering the single work as the most important phenomenon in literature, the unit on which to concentrate attention. The very idea of a canon of "Great Books" supposes that whatever criteria are adopted for inclusion and exclusion will operate at the level of individual works. The rereadability or complexity criterion conforms to this pattern: it is presumably the degree of complexity or potential cognitive interest of individual works that is at issue. But if conceptual borrowing from information theory can teach us anything, it ought to teach us to question the pertinence of viewing our decisions about what to read or teach as if we were judging an intellectual beauty contest—or, in more Bloomian terms, a historical series of intergenerational fights for male dominance—between singular works or between their heroic authors. Moreover, the phenomena of noisiness and rereadability, or communicativity and transience, cannot be regarded as properties of texts in themselves, any more than they could be regarded as entirely readerly constructs; they can come about only in transactions between works and readers, in other words, in a process of codependent arising (*codependent* being used here with reference to Buddhism and not to the contemporary psychology of addiction and relationships).

In addition, the durability of works is surely inappropriate as an exclusive or even primary measure of what is to be taught and studied, especially in an age of electronic media and ecological crises. The re-readability of individual texts must be not only relativized with respect to readings but also contextualized with respect to culture: minds develop through a series of interactions not with a few singular texts but with fields of texts, ultimately with a world of information that extends beyond what is usually called the textual. The choice to study this or that should be seen not as an evaluation of the comparative merits of works but as a strategic choice intended to enlarge or deepen the cognitive horizons of students and scholars in particular directions. In a culture saturated with the messages and echoes of dominant traditions, turning our attention to other voices is often the most informative and stimulating course of action, whether or not we are convinced that each work we turn to will, for a large number of readers, stand the so-called test of time characteristic of the age of print.

The deep complicity of durability with social distinction and thus with a conservative politics of culture emerges clearly in Bloom's broadsides against explicitly (left-wing) political criteria for what gets taught. He claims to denounce not activism or even oppositional orthodoxy but transience: "The correct test for the new canonicity is simple, clear, and wonderfully conducive to social change: it must not and cannot be reread, because its contribution to societal progress is its generosity in offering itself up for rapid ingestion and discarding" (30). It is all too easy, in this mode of thought, to describe what one does not like to reread, for whatever reasons of taste and politics, as formally unworthy. There is, to be sure, more than a grain of truth to Bloom's assertion that "politics, to our common sorrow, rapidly stales like last month's newspaper and only rarely remains news" (526), but the very simplicity of his opposition between the political and the literarily great, an opposition entirely tributary to the socially loaded divide between the transient and the durable, discredits his attempt to "depoliticize" literary study by an appeal to formal durability. Whatever the cultural functions of the noisy, durably rereadable text may be—and they are many, and surely not reducible to the reinforcement of elitism or class dominance—we cannot experience them in a form that is not entangled with elite social practices and with the worldviews that such practices undergird and foster.

The Tyranny of Expanding Information

The rereadability criterion outlined (and all but rejected) above has a further problem, one that can serve as a point of departure for some further reflections on the politics of letting go of (or hanging onto) our technologically obsolescent canon. I have insidiously assumed that the purpose of reading and study ought to be, at some level, the production of information. Such production is not an objective good, but it is a dominant criterion of value in the research university and in contemporary capitalist society. In *The Postmodern Condition*, Jean-François Lyotard notes that the argument most often used to legitimate research and advanced study is performativity, to which he suggests adding a more pragmatic—as opposed to purely conceptual or technical—form of innovation baptized *paralogy*. The budget requests of contemporary public universities emphasize above all the production of new knowledge by the university as a means to economic prosperity in the region, state, or nation. Although the humanities are rarely mentioned in this sort of "legitimation through performativity" (Lyotard), the disciplinary organization of literary studies based on research productivity certainly fits into both the modern university and the schema I have proposed here of literary reading and study as a process of information production.

The assumption that information (or even knowledge) should increase is not a self-evident or innocent one. In *The Inhuman* Lyotard paints a much grimmer picture of the postmodern condition than in the book that bears that title by suggesting that a global, runaway increase in stockpiled and systemically mobilized information imperils the most characteristic features of humanity. Lyotard proposes, in effect, to "naturalize" postmodernity by understanding it as an inevitable discrepancy between human-centered forms and practices of knowledge and those of the ever expanding complexity of an economic/technical/cultural system so deeply committed to performativity that it has become inhuman. "All technology," writes Lyotard, "beginning with writing considered as a *techne,* is an artefact allowing its users to stock more information, to improve their competence and optimize their performances" (62). Stockpiled information in general provides the capacity to neutralize, control, and integrate aleatory events. The global contemporary system of information stockpiling and its use to obtain control over events, Lyotard argues, now grows without any impetus from human decision makers or regard for human needs. The ultracommunicativity produced by modern information technology is a form of ever-increasing complexity, but is hardly progress; in fact, it has nothing to do with the emancipation of the mind hoped for by the Enlightenment. It is as if humanity, far from controlling or creating its destiny, is simply caught up in an expanding dissipative structure (to use Prigogine's term), a temporary, local, improbable region of space-time in which complexity is increasing, in accord with and not in violation of deterministic laws. "It seems that the 'ultimate' motor of this movement is not essentially of the order of human desire: it consists rather in the process of negentropy which appears to 'work' the cosmic area inhabited by the human race" (71). This cosmological dynamic of quantitatively increasing returns is a qualitative disaster, according to Lyotard, for the humans whose brains gave it its decisive acceleration.

Lyotard both describes our entrapment in this expanding world of information as inevitable and advocates practices of resistance—notably poetic and aesthetic—to its exclusively cognitive and instrumental marshaling of time and information, its program of neutralizing and controlling, rather than experiencing, all possible alterity. It is appropriate to question, as Bruno Latour has done, the monolithic and inhuman character of Lyotard's formulation of the techno-information system (61–62); nonetheless, even a more empirical and less paranoid perspective can recognize the pertinence of his concern over an ever-enlarging network of networks that now seems to escape any human instance of global control, locally shot through with humanity though it may be at every point. Worldwide late capitalism may be only what Latour would call a long network, but it is no less disturbing a network for all that. Intellectual or literary practices that try to legitimate themselves through claims of network lengthening or technical complexification deserve scrutiny, to say the least.

The very difficult question concerning literary and narrative canons, in this context, is that of their position vis-à-vis this techno-information world. How do narrative knowledge and the knowledge of narratives fit into (or strain against) the technologically and economically dominant modes of control; namely, the electronic accumulation and manipulation of information and its exchange according to market rules? In an obvious sense, the traditional literary canon, considered as a curricular foundation, is itself a stockpile of information on which individuals are expected to draw so as to meet the challenges of events—and do so in accordance with principles of order presumably embodied in the "best that is known and thought." Thus resistance to the traditional canon of "Western Civilization" is indeed resistance to a particular form of technological control, *but to an obsolescent form*, though it may still, locally, be a force to be reckoned with. Like the nineteenth-century defenders of the classical curriculum and the "generalists" of the early twentieth century, conservatives (and here I have in mind political conservatives much more than the literary conservative Harold Bloom) who claim to defend the "Western tradition" against enemies known as "deconstruction" and "multiculturalism" are almost surely a bit out of step with their times, unwilling to confront the extent to which the real mechanisms of power in their society may no longer need the earlier modes of domination now marked with cultural distinction. The conservatives conceal their blindness (from themselves, first of all) by inventing the oxymoronic category of "tenured radicals" to account for what is probably, in the long run, a shift from books to databases as technologies of stratification and control.

Surely the readiness of large numbers of literarily trained humanists to contest and even abandon the canon on which they were largely educated stems not only from the legitimate political concerns of groups who have been excluded by it from cultural prestige and representation, but also from the fact that the actors in the canon debate—in other words, virtually everyone concerned with the study and teaching of literature, except for a few ostriches—are no longer convinced by a structurally closed formation identified with the durability of printed books. It should be emphasized that much of what scholars spend their time on, in place of formerly canonical texts, is not the literature of long-excluded others but their own proliferating scholarship and theorizing, most of which is now directly produced in electronic media. Electronic colleges of theory and journals of postmodern culture come far closer than the printed works of either canonical or minority authors to the administrative concept of the "knowledge base," which it is supposedly the function of research universities to enlarge, and which constitutes these universities' "niche" or "market share" in the Lyotardian techno-information monad.

If the end point of giving up the canon is the world of infinitely connectable and recombinable hypertext—the verbal portion of an expanding "knowledge base"—then the so-called tenured radicals are in all likelihood simply carrying out part of the "superstructural" work of an "infrastructural" change, a work of adjustment to a world in which electronic access replaces the idiosyncratic syntheses of gray-matter memory and personal library that form what is still occasionally called "general culture." (In the ultracommunicative environment of the electronic university, how many will have the time between messages to reread a canon so as to keep it in their heads at all, especially when it's assumed that one day everything will be computer-accessible anyway?) The older practices of reading, to say nothing of the memorization still required at early-twentieth-century Vanderbilt, may simply be seen by the expanding techno-information system as inefficiencies to be swept away as quickly as possible, and the academic opponents of canons of reading, whatever their overt motives, may simply be carrying out that system's work.

It is worth considering, therefore, that certain characteristics of canons, certain qualities of printed texts that make them canonizable, may indeed be worthy of cultivation as practices of resistance to the hegemony of electronic information. (The prevalence of dead white European males in the traditional literary canon is presumably not one of these transvaluable qualities.) The kind of resistance to which I refer cannot really succeed in derailing commodification, performativity, or communication, but it can perhaps make sure that what functions as part of an expanding and deterritorializing dissipative structure of information and economic flow *also* functions to keep or make spaces within that expansion as livable as possible: to keep it more rather than less multiply complex. The reading and valuing of old narratives may have been a hegemonic activity for a long time, but in a world increasingly structured by the communicativity of computers it could certainly become a way not of reversing the flow of history but of creating spaces of turbulence and even fixity within it.

To give but one example of the kind of argument that might be made: the stability of a canon makes it a form of cultural feedback operating with very long time constants. As such it offers the possibility of interference with whatever practices of control are being carried out at a given moment using much shorter time constants (which is in general what is happening to most forms of control in the age of computers). The historical ecosystem, Anthony Wilden noted, is out of step with itself and therefore generates noise (403). The authorial messages of a few decades or centuries ago, whose enunciation and perpetuation surely were and are parts of strategies of social and intellectual control, none-theless may interfere with the newer cybernetic loops in which we are more immediately and pressingly caught up. Old works provide a space of freedom away from the most immediate and contemporary of the cognitive and discursive constraints acting upon us, and canons push us into that space—whether to good effect or ill we cannot in general say. The mode of print, which now appears to us in its technological twilight as a particularism, offers for now at least an alternative to what Poster calls the mode of information. Obviously it is not an alternative into which language and literature people should nostalgically retreat, denying the reality of the changes in and around their libraries and campuses. Rather, as teachers of language, literature, and culture, we should think critically about what printed, canonizable literature has (or had) to say as a medium—what it has made possible and excluded, favored and hindered, in comparison with other media—so as to con-sider what of it should be preserved or cultivated, rather than allowed to disappear.

Fictions of Resistance

In lieu of a formal conclusion, I will close by observing how this kind of resistance is evoked in two recent works of American fiction, Ursula Le Guin's *Always Coming Home* and Thomas Pynchon's *Vineland*.

Le Guin's ecotopia is a collage of narrative and fictional ethnography, set in the land of the Kesh, who people a valley in post–ecological dis-aster Northern California. Their low-technology society is regulated by practices and rituals that strongly echo those of Native Americans, so that the book's (future) historical ethnography suggests a dialectical re-versal in which values and forms of knowledge once destroyed or tran-scended reappear as an essential resource for the survivors of the next cycle of destruction, that of the white man's industrial civilization by itself.

In one of the passages that reflect explicitly on the paradoxical eth-nography of *Always Coming Home,* the "archeologist of the future"—Pandora—who is the scriptor of Le Guin's fiction has a conversation with a Valley archivist. Pandora is shocked to learn that the Kesh ar-chivists "destroy valuable books" rather than storing and passing on a maximal quantity of information, as she assumes archivists ought to do (334). The archivist answers, "Who wants to be buried under [valuable books]?" and goes on to describe the process of choosing what to keep and what to destroy as "difficult . . . arbitrary, unjust, and exciting." These are words that could surely be applied to canon controversies, if they were faced honestly and not shunted into exercises in bureaucratic accommodation. The Valley archivists have the task of preserving a small number of books and manuscripts—written, printed, bound artifacts— because they live in a culture that discourages unbridled accumulation or consumption of anything, whether made of matter, energy, or information. It is strongly implied that this restraint in the preservation and consumption of information is an integral part of the slowly changing, relatively nonviolent (though not static or insipid) relations the Kesh try to maintain with the world and with one another.

The most novelistic section of *Always Coming Home* is the three-part story of Stone Telling, a woman whose life was caught up in contact and conflict with a warlike, patriarchal, monotheistic, and unecological people known as the Condor. Her tale, exceptional and almost offensive to the Kesh, serves to mediate between the expectations of Le Guin's reader (a reader of novels, who expects a long story with plot) and the more restrained, cyclical, almost conversational nature of most Kesh cultural production. " 'If you don't have a history,' " Pandora asks the archivist, " 'how am I to tell your story?' " The archivist finally suggests, " 'Let Stone Telling tell her story. That's as near history as we have come in my day, and nearer than we'll come again, I hope' " (181–82).

If novelistic narrative is thus too historical, too decentered, for the local- and ritual-centered Kesh, the electronic accumulation of information is even more alien to them. Their archivists' work is contrasted with the activity of a machine-controlled, inhuman "City of Mind" that saves everything it can get in electronic media. The City of Mind is something like a universal electronic library connected to the Internet, if one imagines the Internet as the only national or world institution to survive the ecological, economic, and demographic collapse of modern society. The Kesh occasionally consult the City of Mind, in emergencies, but their archivists are fairly indifferent toward it, supplying it with some, but not all, of what they discard from their own more thoughtfully maintained collections. The work—and the concept of value—of the Valley people consists not in *keeping* but in *giving*, and the giving of words, unlike the stockpiling of information, requires discipline and choice. "A book is an act," the archivist admonishes; "it takes place in time, not just in space. It is not information, but relation" (334). Le Guin's fictional dialogue reminds us of what would be lost through acquiescence in a merely bureaucratic and technological dissolution of admittedly obsolescent canons, through buying into the utopian dream of an expanding electronic textual network without exclusion or limits—a dream City of Mind that is also Le Guin's, like Lyotard's, dystopian nightmare.

The digital world of ones and zeros appears in *Vineland* as a world of maximal control through representation and simulation, ultimately of control over "the one and zero of life and death" (72). "Man could crush him with just a short tap dance over the computer keys," thinks sixties refugee Zoyd Wheeler about the DEA agent interviewing him (27). The novel is set in 1984: the sixties, when the politically (if not technologically) advanced medium was film, are explicitly characterized as "a slower-moving time, predigital, not yet so cut into pieces" (38). The life- and death-dealing ones and zeros of Reagan-era computers threaten to exercise ever tighter and more rationalized social control, squeezing not only ex-hippie types like Zoyd but also the small-fry agents of the once free-wheeling Nixonian repression. Zoyd's daughter Prairie, trying to bring continuity to the story of her life, searches for fragmentary traces of her mother in the magnetic media archives of the Sisterhood of Kunoichi Attentives (113–15). What is perhaps most significant in *Vineland* about the role of computers and video as technologies of repression is their erasability: what exists only in magnetic media can be made to vanish, without a trace. The novel's modestly happy ending is presented as an almost accidental reprieve from what might have been: "Suddenly, some white male far away must have awakened from a dream, and the clambake was over. . . . Reagan had officially ended the 'exercise' known as REX 84, and what had lain silent, undocumented, forever deniable, embedded inside" (376). That deniable core, according to several characters in the novel, is a plan for civilian repression by the military on an unprecedented scale, accompanying an invasion of Nicaragua.

Vineland in effect purports to set down in cold print (or hot type, in a related saying) this unrecorded, deniable might-have-been, visible in the electronic media only in fragmentary form when an army officer about to read from a national security directive briefly interrupts a late-night TV movie, "Sean Connery in *The G. Gordon Liddy Story*" (339–40). The novel provides a discourse of witnessing in which what purportedly lay hidden in the electronic media can be made both explicit and indelible. I am tempted to read this act of printed narrative witnessing as a defense of Print, and of The Book. Two ancillary arguments support this interpretation. First, *Vineland*'s tour de force appropriation of other media calls attention to the versatility and power of prose as a signifying instrument. Pynchon's ubiquitous and elastic prose describes events through other media, events already mediated by other forms: film, computer file (including text and image), video game, TV commercial, sitcom. This pervasive *intermediality* has among its effects that of calling attention to the novel's capability to evoke so well such a wide spectrum of media activity. Second, the visual appearance of the original hardcover edition of *Vineland*, The Book, calls deliberate attention to its integrity as a predigital, perhaps even antidigital object. The dust jacket's classic typeface, the elegant simplicity of its design, and the pure literarity of the information about the author all point to an image of the book as distinct aesthetic object, slightly reserved or distinguished, rather than as a nodal point in an exchange circuit between word processor file, corporate marketing strategy, and computerized bank account (which, in some sense, is what most books now are). The jacket reproduction of a museum-housed photograph identifies the book with premagnetic, predigital imaging, and the blank back cover isolates, and thereby defamiliarizes, the ubiquitous bar code, customarily unnoticed beneath a thicket of blurbs. The book in its bookishness, Pynchon and his publisher seem to be saying, is a thing apart in the age of its technological obsolescence. How we use that thing apart, the book (and especially the novel) stricken by a distancing sheen of archaism in an age of electronically processed text and image, may well be the most fundamental critical question of the *fin de millénaire*.

Lynn Wells

11 Virtual Textuality

While the technology commonly known as "virtual reality" may not yet be considered an art form, it does have artistic dimensions which could produce, according to some of its makers, a completely original aesthetic. As Brenda Laurel, a virtual world designer, observes: "To find precedents for what I'm talking about we have to go outside traditional Western ideas of authoring and art. The ideas we need aren't where we expect to find them" (quoted in Pimentel and Teixeira, 156). Many of the ideas that Laurel and her colleagues are seeking, however, can be found in postmodern textual praxis, which virtual reality resembles in several respects.

Like postmodern textuality, virtual reality and related "hypertext" technology foreground the subject's participation in the creation of narrative rather than effacing it. These technologies are being heralded for their ability to endow users with a revolutionary kind of aesthetic freedom, which supposedly renders the reading of printed texts outdated in comparison. Nevertheless, while the technologies apparently do give users creative liberty, they actually initiate endlessly self-satisfying circuits in which subjective desire itself becomes both process and product. Literary texts, on the contrary, oppose their authority to that of readers, thereby establishing dialogues with political consequences. By comparing the interactive nature of virtual technology with the reading process, we can illuminate in new ways the implications of textual self-consciousness.

The concept of "virtuality" easily translates from the technology to the texts, displacing the reality/fiction binary that has previously constrained analyses of postmodern heterocosms, precursors to the synthetic "worlds" of virtual reality. In texts such as Salman Rushdie's

Midnight's Children and Carlos Fuentes's *Terra Nostra*, the representation of different kinds of "realities"—historical, literary, and so on— takes place on a single plane, as in the simulation of phenomena in virtual worlds. This ontological uniformity makes possible "virtual meetings" between different sorts of figures which could not occur outside of the constructed environment. As we shall see, the vocabulary and ideas developing in connection with virtual technology provide new insight into the postmodern representation of historical reality.

The Liberation of Narrative

In a virtual world, users work in concert with the specific parameters established by the designer to produce a unique experience of and trajectory through that world. The cooperative production of individualized "narratives" is also the focus of hypertext technology, which furnishes users with textualized data rather than sensory images. Proponents of hypertext technology in particular often regard printed texts of any variety as practically obsolete. Detractors of printed texts concur with Robert Coover's (somewhat ambivalent) declaration of "the end of books" on the grounds that books, however innovative in spirit, ultimately "tyrannize" the reader by forcing her or him to follow a prescribed and authoritative line from beginning to end (Cortázar's *Hopscotch* notwithstanding). As reader response and psychoanalytic theory elucidate, however, the narratives constructed within virtual reality and hypertext technology finally engage the user's imagination and desire in ways not completely unlike those in which written narratives direct readerly desire. Further, despite the seemingly innovative narrative freedom that these technologies offer, they tend to isolate the subject-as-user in a dehistoricized medium in which she or he mistakes the immediate actualization of desire as liberation. Conversely, self-consciously constructed art forms such as the postmodern novel and surrealist film work to inhibit the subject's "narcissistic" identification with the texts. Art forms that accentuate their own narrative production place the subject-as-reader in openly dialogic relations with other discourses, and therefore have potentially more political efficacy despite their "linearity."

With the invention of virtual reality technology, it is observed, comes the promise of a new era of democratization. Theorists of both virtual reality and hypertextuality often couch their arguments in the language of liberation; these technologies, they say, will do away with traditional aesthetic notions of authority and in their place give personal freedom in the creation of narrative. (See, for example, Landow, 174, on the "politics" of hypertext.) Whether it takes the form of a session within a virtual world or on a hypertext program, "text" itself becomes personalized, a manifestation of each user's will. Since books impose preexistent textual constructs on the reader's imagination, they correspondingly become implicitly or explicitly aligned in such arguments with an inherent conservatism of thought.

This view of technology's superiority over printed texts derives partially from an overestimation of the autonomy allowed the computer programs' users. In spite of the exercise of choice that these technologies permit, the user must still interact with a previously established set of parameters. Virtual reality enables the user to "navigate" spontaneously through a computer-generated world, but the phenomena in that world and the means to move among them are designed by someone else.[1] William Gibson's original definition of cyberspace as a "consensual hallucination" (*Neuromancer*, 51) suggests this collaborative principle. Similarly, hypertext programs facilitate literary invention by making available multiple textual options for the user to pursue and combine. Despite the claims of advocates such as George Landow that the technology "empower[s]" (178) users by giving them access to the hitherto impregnable position of author-ity, hypertext programs do not completely overturn the perceived imperiousness of the reading process, in which, as Benjamin Woolley puts it, books "are given by their authors so that they may be taken by their readers" (153). Rather, both kinds of program involve users in the act of narrative creation by presenting them with many predetermined alternatives from which they can choose.

Even though their narrative constructions are contingent on preset parameters, virtual reality and hypertext technology do make feasible multiple combinations within the same program. These technologies seem to engage users more actively than books do readers, since printed texts can exist in only one form at a time and have embedded within them a tradition of conventional reading. Landow commends hypertext's ability to go beyond the Aristotelian model of beginning, middle, and end (101–2); and Coover contrasts its pluralist nature with printed texts' singleness of presentation (23). According to Coover, books can place readers in a position of enforced passivity in which they follow the "compulsory author-directed movement" of linear narrative (1). In comparison with hypertext's multiplicity of user-created narratives, even printed texts that openly acknowledge the reader's role through meta-fictional strategies are vulnerable to the charge of authoritarianism.

What is missing from comparisons of user/reader involvement in these technological and literary media is consideration of how their narratives are similarly constructed. Both kinds of computer program provide users with stable "bits"—visual stimuli in the case of virtual reality, and textual segments or "lexias" in the case of hypertext—from which they form individualized narratives. On a macro-textual level, literary narratives are also made up of "units" or "nodes" (see, for instance, Roland Barthes' widely known taxonomy of "functions," "indices," etc.). It is this level of structure in literary texts that constitutes the authorially dictated "line." Although literary texts direct the process of reading along specific narrative lines, they don't deny the reader a role in the creation of those narratives. Like the user's maneuverability within program parameters in virtual reality or hypertext, each reader's interaction with the narrative structure of a given text is unique.

According to Wolfgang Iser, literary texts contain "fragments" between which exist "gaps"; the reader imaginatively "fills in" these gaps, resulting in the formation of a unique, completed version of the textual world, which Iser designates "the virtual dimension of the text" ("Reading Process," 55). A text's "virtual dimension" resembles technological virtual reality in the sense that both exist as provisional worlds created by the subject through interaction with discursive "interfaces." Steven Cohan makes the parallel between a text's virtual dimension and the technology even clearer when he describes how the reader "constructs this virtual space in his mind and enters it imaginatively" (118).

While subjective experience necessarily influences readers' reconstructions of textual worlds, it must not dominate the process or else the "virtual dimensions" created would bear no relation to the texts at hand. The notion that readers bring to texts only preconceived wishes and expectations that they seek to have fulfilled denies the distinct power of texts in their interplay with readers. Texts themselves engender certain imaginative responses within readers. This conception shifts the formative locus of desire outside of readers to the texts with which they interact. Through the process of reading, texts arouse and then regulate readerly desire while creating the impression that they are satisfying individual anticipation.

The reading process paradoxically generates and fulfills desire in readers not only in spite of but partially because of the linearity and finitude of authorially pre-scribed narratives. The gratifying tension of a literary narrative depends on the lines it induces readers to follow from "node" to "node." As Peter Brooks explains, narrative stimulates readers to want to move forward through a text, to reach its ending, which is also its "illumination" (103). Yet the text simultaneously and contradictorily urges readers to resist this movement, to savor the "erotic" narrative complications that delay the inevitable ending to come.[2] Moving imaginatively along this narrative line, readers constantly concretize the textual world while both expecting and wishing to postpone its termination.

A similar enticement and orientation of desire happens with technological narrative construction. When composing a hypertext, a user must choose among the numerous narrative options offered by the program. As Coover emphasizes, this process of choice furnishes the true creative energy of hypertext authorship: "We are always astonished to discover how much of the reading and writing experience occurs in the interstices and trajectories *between* text fragments" (24). What motivates a user's decision to follow one narrative path over several others is individual desire. The program grants instantaneous expression to that desire when it realizes on the screen the user's preference of narrative routes. Nevertheless, the user's sense of autonomous decision making is somewhat deceptive, since the program itself encourages specific responses simply by virtue of the choices it makes available. Like printed texts, hypertext technology summons and then channels certain desires; but unlike printed texts, it gives its users the illusion that solely their authority governs the creative act.

Narrative movements within hypertext environments, similar to those in printed texts, therefore also rely on subjective desire for their forward propulsion. Since printed texts solicit readerly desire largely through the power of their endings, how can hypertext programs, which obviate the need for closure, maintain their narrative force? "And what of narrative flow?" asks Coover. In the absence of obligatory closure, "there is still movement, but in hyperspace's dimensionless infinity, it is more like endless *expansion;* it runs the risk of being so distended and slackly driven as to lose its centripetal force, to give way to a kind of static low-charged lyricism" (25). Coover's concern that protracted hypertexts would be likely to devolve into mediocrity echoes Brooks's belief that "the interminable would be the meaningless" (93). Michael Joyce, a pioneer hypertext author, deals with the problem of finitude by suggesting that a text should end whenever the reader "tire[s] of the paths" (quoted in Landow, 113).[3] While Joyce's solution does not address the difficulties of integrity raised by Coover, it consolidates the user's desire as the force that both propels and finally suspends the motion of narrative in hypertext creation.

Although virtual reality is not textually based, it does enable the production of a different kind of "narrative"—the individualized experience of a particular program. Like hypertext's flexibility, which lets a user follow one "lexia" rather than another, virtual reality allows for considerable freedom of choice within the design parameters of a given program. This sensitivity to individual wishes underlies one of the technology's key slogans, coined by one of its founders, William Bricken: "Psychology is the physics of virtual reality" (quoted in Woolley, 21). However, there is a difference between the ways virtual reality and textualized media (including hypertext programs) satisfy subjects' desires: virtual reality offers responses unmediated by language.

As a sensory—and primarily visual—medium, virtual reality technology allows users to project their desires into an environment that immediately actualizes them in response to bodily movements. With the assistance of special helmets (head-mounted displays) and wired gloves, users can manipulate and physically interact with virtual phenomena at will (within the program's capabilities). The simulated phenomena in a virtual world change shapes fluidly, metamorphosing and forming unlikely juxtapositions, in response to and in anticipation of users' desires. Virtual phenomena, then, are overdetermined in the same sense as are images in dreams: they simulate literally what they were designed to simulate (for example, a floating ball); and they are, at the same time, figurations of the user's desire (the ball embodies the user's wish to defy gravity, which she or he satisfies by choosing to interact with the object).[4] As a means of rendering the experience more convincing, many virtual reality programs enable users to observe their own actions in the form of "virtual bodies." These programs sustain the pretense of total "immersion" for users, who can simultaneously observe and maneuver their simulated bodies right within the virtual worlds. Virtual bodies follow the corresponding movements of users' actual bodies (which are connected to wired apparatuses), but without the normal physical restrictions. As a result, the simulated bodies can act out users' desires unconstrained by physical limitations and without the mediation of language.

Another visual medium, film, similarly affects its viewers in ways beyond the strictures of linguistic communication. Film possesses the "ability to bypass the usual coded channels of language through a visual short circuit" (Williams, 21). One of the primary effects of film's sensory access to the unconscious minds of viewers is its ability to persuade them of the "reality" of artificially produced images. The convincingly illusory quality of film facilitates viewer identification with the images on the screen: viewers perceive in filmic images alternative "realities," including "selves," in which they can temporarily believe and onto which they can project their desires. According to Linda Williams, the relationship between film and viewer signals "a nostalgia for the unity of a prelinguistic Imaginary" (41), a wish to seal the breach between signifier and signified which opens up with entry into the Symbolic. Though only provisionally, film permits viewers to imagine themselves as belonging to the coherent world visualized for them.

While most films attempt to create believable illusions, surrealist films set out to do the opposite, conveying instead the peculiar, nonverbal movement of the unconscious. In these films, images often exceed their mimetic functions and signify the play of unconscious thoughts and drives. Like the phenomena in virtual worlds, these images shift and blend into one another, imitating the motions of condensation and displacement associated with dreams. Even though viewers recognize that surrealist film reproduces unconscious activity, they do not become entranced by its images as they do with the images of "fiction" films. Surrealist film elicits viewer identification, but then purposely breaks the illusion so that viewers are suddenly made aware of the images' artificiality. In other words, because surrealist film prevents viewers from projecting themselves imaginatively into the images on the screen, it redirects viewers to focus on their urge to do so, to find in film gratifyingly unified visions of themselves and of the world. The "lack" or "difference" between desire and image—characteristic of discursive representations generally—becomes thematized instead of concealed.

Despite the similarity between virtual reality's dynamic phenomena and surrealist film's dreamlike images, the technology more closely resembles "fiction" film in terms of its relation with the subject. Since virtual technology is designed to immerse users sensorily and to suppress their awareness of external reality for the duration of the experience, it produces self-enclosed, temporarily convincing worlds. Within those spaces, users' desires are realized and reflected back to them instantaneously, so that the virtual world becomes a mirror in which the individual user can "misrecognize" a pleasing image of herself. The virtual body, a perfect and physically uninhibited self-image, figures the user's "narcissistic" pleasure at finding himself mirrored in the technologically generated space. Although hypertext technology does not involve the same level of physical responsiveness, it too provides an environment in which users can create satisfying self-images in the form of personally directed narratives. While the programs lead users in particular directions, they do so only at the users' instigation, and they seldom place any insurmountable obstacle in the narrative path. Because users do not encounter any resistances or counterresponses that could frustrate their desires, their authority over these technological contexts is "monologic" in Mikhail Bakhtin's sense—singular and uncontested.

Jean Baudrillard describes how the authority granted by technology can be misleading, a situation he terms "private 'telematics' ": "each person sees himself at the controls of a hypothetical machine, isolated in a position of perfect and remote sovereignty" (128). Virtual technology secludes the user in an obliging environment without connection or reference to the world outside of the programs. Within the virtual space, there are only simulated phenomena designed to substitute for exterior reality and displace it from the user's attention. Cyberspace therefore does what Fredric Jameson believes all cultural productions do in the postmodern period: it vanquishes the "real" in favor of the creation of reified "pop images and simulacra" (*Postmodernism*, 25) drained of any historical significance. Because the technology limits the field of perception to a collection of dehistoricized "images" whose sole impetus is to respond to individual desire, the supremacy it gives to its users is finally illusory.[5]

Written texts, on the other hand, constitute alternative authorities to which readers must concede in order for the reading process to continue. The act of reading is essentially "dialogic," since text and reader exist in necessary, simultaneous relation to each other throughout the process. This dialectic (at once contestatory and mutually sustaining) not only generates readerly pleasure but also admits the possibility of texts' having political effectiveness. Because readers confront in texts ideas and practices that derive from knowledge bases different from their own, they acknowledge and consider new discursive formations. While this principle obtains in the reading of all literary texts, it is especially evident in postmodern texts, which often highlight authorial and readerly co-creation of textual narratives. Just as surrealist film exposes the nature of the viewer/image relationship, postmodern textuality forces recognition of the reader's position in the process of reading, a position that is at the same time submissive and authoritative. The reader must engage with a discourse other than subjective desire, a discourse whose self-consciousness as representation points to the existence of a reality beyond itself. Unlike virtual technology, postmodern literary texts can lead to political dialogue.

Virtual Encounters

As Lemprière discovers upon opening his book, the worlds of fictional texts are places at the same time foreign and familiar: "If he brought the book up and opened it, he would immediately find himself in a—what was it?—an elsewhere. Yes, an elsewhere that was here, that was also him" (Norfolk, 13). The heterocosm of any literary text is brought into being as the reader actualizes the authorially provided linguistic code into a distinct "virtual existent." While "naturally" mimetic fiction attempts to create the illusion that its heterocosms share the same reality as the reader, postmodern metafiction openly asserts that textual worlds, regardless of their verisimilitude, never exceed their existence in the reader's imagination.[6] Owing to this recognition of their inescapable fictiveness, postmodern texts can skirt the obligations of mimetic representation to reflect an actual empirical reality outside of themselves. This does not produce the "total closed environment" that some readers have found characteristic of postmodern textuality (Nash, 185). Although self-definedly nonmimetic, postmodern fiction often assumes a more complex position with regard to the outside world; it neither pretends to be a faithful transcription of some preexistent actuality nor entirely negates the real from its textual worlds.

Rushdie's *Midnight's Children* and Fuentes's *Terra Nostra* include within their heterocosms characters and events drawn from historical reality, such as Indira Gandhi and the Spanish conquest of Mexico. Despite having been converted into textual "material," these elements are not strictly fictional, because they retain enough of their original attributes to be recognizable by the reader; nor are they meant to be "real" in the same way that they would be in traditional historical novels, since they have been substantially altered. Instead, they can be said to be "virtually real" in the sense made practicable by the technology: they have autonomous existence according to the specific ontological terms of the artificially constructed environments in which they appear, notwithstanding their derivation from the external world. In order to understand the ramifications of this paradoxical representational stance, we need first to examine the extent to which postmodern fiction is both like and unlike technological virtual reality.

The process of creating a virtual reality program, referred to by its practitioners as "world-making," entails a series of decisions: What sort of milieu should the user discover? What capabilities and restrictions should delimit the user's movements? What forms of objects should be present? As Bricken's manifesto makes clear, the determining factor in these decisions is not the need to achieve "realism" in the sense of producing a convincing facsimile of a hypostasized external world; instead, the impetus is to create a program that the user will apprehend as intrinsically "real." The technology effects this illusion by giving shape to a new kind of materiality composed entirely of computer-generated images. Since all objects in a virtual world are made up of one essential "substance," images simulating unrealistic or "abstract" phenomena are as "real" as those recognizable from the outside world. So long as a program's images are persuasive to its users, they are perceived as real and therefore *are* real in the context of the experience.

Like technological virtual worlds, the heterocosms of postmodern fictional texts are precisely conceived constructions with their own criteria for what is real. Normative physical laws of time and space do not necessarily operate, since the texts are free from the constraints associated with mimetic aesthetic practices; hence phenomena that could not coincide in either realist or fantastic fiction proper can combine here. While Napoleon can inhabit a novel by Tolstoy, a creature from outer space would seem out of place; similarly, the space creature would be at home in a science fiction story, but Napoleon would probably seem anomalous there, unless he had been dislocated from his original historical setting by some plausible scientific wizardry. In each case, certain kinds of characters and actions are "indigenous" to that textual world; any departure from those classifications would fundamentally shift the text's compositional basis. (If, for example, the "Megalosaurus" mentioned in the first paragraph of Dickens' *Bleak House* were to escape from the simile that confines it, the text would be curiously changed.) Because postmodern textuality does away with the stipulation that only particular phenomena can be endemic to a specific heterocosm, it makes imaginable that Napoleon and the space creature can not only coexist in one world but also interact uninhibitedly because there are no physical or logical barriers to limit them. This unrestricted bringing together of different sorts of textual components can happen in postmodern fiction owing to the fact that, as in cyberspace, everything possesses the same essential "reality."

Some theorists believe that such fictional syntheses are signs of a retrograde, depoliticizing tendency in contemporary writing. When Jameson discusses the confluence of varying textual elements in E. L. Doctorow's *Ragtime,* he criticizes the practice for what he sees as its debasement of the historical referent. Despite its overt political content, *Ragtime* undermines its own validity as a representation of history, Jameson argues, by conjoining characters from various ontological backgrounds—"real," fictional, and intertextual. These characters, he says, "are incommensurable and, as it were, of incomparable substances, like oil and water" (*Postmodernism,* 22); the novel therefore, though "seemingly realistic," is, in his view, "a nonrepresentational work that combines fantasy signifiers from a variety of ideologemes in a kind of hologram" (23). Jameson asserts that *Ragtime*—and other similar postmodern fictions, by extension—reproduces only a kind of "pop history" (25), which is in itself a symptom of our culture's general estrangement from historical reality.

It is on the level of subject recognition, however, that postmodern fiction can potentially achieve the political effect Jameson claims it does not. Unlike its parallel occurrence in virtual reality, the mixing of different kinds of phenomena in postmodern texts can lead to renewed consciousness of the "real." Postmodern texts put us into contact with views of the world different from our own, but these views do not reflect the "real" in the straightforward manner that Jameson suggests fiction was once capable of doing and should now aspire to recover. Rather, because of their heterogeneous compositions, such texts expose the complexities of representation as a process. By forcing together "incommensurable substances" in one medium, postmodern textuality reveals how the signifiers used to represent actual people and things can inconspicuously occupy the same semantic field as those representing phenomena not derived from empirical reality. This attenuation of the actual results not in the glossiness of pop history but in the sudden visibility of signification: these texts display signifiers *qua* signifiers in order to focus attention on how they can never fully embody the reality they are meant to represent. Instead of devitalizing history or distancing us from it, then, postmodern fiction seeks to make us aware that the "real" exceeds containment in any one representation.

Midnight's Children and *Terra Nostra* reconstruct history by acting as "virtual meeting spaces": discrete artificial environments whose representational plasticity makes it feasible for historical actualities to be brought into improbable conjunctions with phenomena from several ontological origins, including other artworks. As in technological virtual worlds, the phenomena in these textual worlds behave as fluid presences or projections instead of as stable, realistic entities. When actual historical figures participate in these postmodern heterocosms, they do so not as realistic characters per se but rather as images adapted for the constructed worlds of the texts. Actual events are also modified so that they take on "virtual identities" in the texts, and these events can occur simultaneously with events projected from other times and other realities, including fictive ones.

Such "virtual meetings" enact what Hans Kellner calls "historical dialogues" (45), "imaginary encounters" (43) that could never take place in other circumstances but that provoke speculation about communally accepted interpretations of events. They can be thought of in terms of historiographic premises known as "counterfactual statements"; these statements are formulated as "if . . . then," with the understanding that the first term is logically untrue (Kellner, 47–48). In Angela Carter's *Infernal Desire Machines of Doctor Hoffman,* for instance, the hero, Desiderio, contemplates paintings in which "Van Gogh was shown writing 'Wuthering Heights' in the parlour of Haworth Parsonage" and Milton is depicted "blindly executing divine frescos upon the walls of the Sistine Chapel" (198). Sensing his "bewilderment," Albertina, the Doctor's daughter, explains: "When my father rewrites the history books, these are some of the things that everyone will suddenly perceive to have always been true" (198). While such fanciful conjunctions would normally be discounted by historians, Kellner assigns them to a legitimate category of historical information, "information *nonexistent in time and space*" (43), and he defends them as "authentic creations of one type of historical imagination; to exclude them from any consideration as products of valid historical thought is to limit and perhaps to desiccate future thought about the past" (43).

Imaginative renditions of actual occurrences and dissident accounts of history are particularly germane to *Terra Nostra,* since it epitomizes the postmodern text as "virtual meeting space." However, we'll first examine how the "Conference" in *Midnight's Children* can be seen as a paradigm both for postmodern fictional "meeting spaces" and for the relation between textual "virtuality" and the external world.

The "Midnight Children's Conference" held in the mind of Saleem Sinai, the central character and narrator of Rushdie's novel, operates very much as a virtual world: as a space in which images can interact unhindered by obstacles such as distance. The Conference participants, the other 580 surviving children born all over India during the first hour of the nation's independence, assemble in this mental space whenever Saleem makes it available. As convenor of the Conference, Saleem maintains ultimate authority over the space, but not over the participants, who can enter and exit at will, or choose not to join a particular session. Although the "Midnight Children" remain physically in their locations around the country, the Conference allows them to converse as if they are all in the same physical vicinity by bringing together their projected presences. Much like cyberspace "aliases," the images of the Children within the Conference space tend to change or conceal their identities rather than reveal them. Saleem realizes from the others' reactions that the original image of himself which he projected into the Conference "was heavily distorted by [his] own self-consciousness about [his] appearance," since it was "grinning like a Cheshire cat" (262) and his facial features were exaggerated. Like Saleem, each of the participants has an actual, or at least implied, "real" identity outside the Conference, in the "real" world that is the heterocosm of the novel proper. The Conference therefore neither negates nor displaces the "reality" of the textual world, but rather provides a forum in which the "real" can be temporarily modified and combined in unusual ways. In this respect, the Conference's relation to the rest of the textual world of *Midnight's Children* is similar to the relation of a technological virtual world to the real world in which it exists.

Taking the analogy one step further, we can say that *Midnight's Children* stands in the same sort of relation to historical reality. Just as the Conference in Saleem's mind acts as a virtual meeting space, bringing together images in seemingly inconceivable ways, so too does the text itself. Some of the projected presences the novel assembles are actual historical events, such as the creation of the state of Pakistan, and personages such as Indira Gandhi. Despite the corresponding names, however, the "Indira Gandhi" in Rushdie's novel, also known as the Widow, is not identical to the historical figure. The character has instead what Umberto Eco calls a "transworld identity" (*Role of the Reader,* 230) whose differences from the original figure are foregrounded rather than concealed. Like Saleem's self-image within the Conference, Gandhi's virtual identity is exaggerated. She is described as having "had white hair on one side and black on the other" (501), as did the historical Indira Gandhi; but for Saleem, the Widow's sharply contrasting hair not only symbolizes but may also be responsible for the disparity between the "white part—public, visible, documented" (501)—of her activities as prime minister and her "secret" political ruthlessness. The Widow, as well as all of the other actualities modified for their appearances in the textual world, interact with characters and fictional occurrences without historical precedents. The resulting version of the events surrounding the independence of India is implausible, fantastic: it displaces collective action and causality as the bases of history in favor of the personal, the idiosyncratic, and the arbitrary.

Regardless of its creation of virtual encounters, *Midnight's Children* as a novel still preserves some basic realist principles: that time moves forward linearly; that effect follows from cause, even when the cause is unorthodox; that characters are mostly distinct, immutable entities; and that all of the characters belong to the same intratextual "reality," despite the presence of "transworld identities" of historical figures. Fuentes's *Terra Nostra* disregards the rules of realistic representation and deals with all phenomena, including time itself, as if they were completely malleable. Characters can travel across three remote time periods and places: sixteenth-century Spain, or the "Old World"; pre-Conquest Mexico, or the "New World"; and a vaguely apocalyptic Paris, or the "Next World," on the eve of December 31, 1999. For instance, Pollo Phoibee (no less a traveler than her mythical counterpart, Phoebus Apollo) travels from Paris to the Old World simply by plunging into the Seine. Other kinds of movement are equally effortless in the textual world. The novel contains several internal boundaries, marking shifts between ontological states such as history and myth; nevertheless, these boundaries are permeable. The New World, we eventually discover, is only dreamed by a sixteenth-century character; yet an object described in his narration of that dream, a feathered mask, shows up in the "real" world of late twentieth-century Paris. Since it permits movements between different kinds of "reality," the novel replaces traditional notions of historical continuity, which are dependent on the consistent progression of time, with a type of historicity specific to the textual world. Similarly, the text's anachronisms, such as having a sixteenth-century character think about Napoleon "Bonaparte" (736), emphasize how the text's artificial environment operates according to its own flexible parameters rather than physical or temporal laws.

Characterization is unabashedly artificial in *Terra Nostra*. Like the self-image that Saleem assumes for the Conference, the characters in Fuentes's novel are completely adaptable virtual presences: they can alter their identities, be doubles of one another, and so on. This fluidity of identity allows for combinations of ideas that would not be possible with fixed, stable characters. Queen Isabel can be both a "transworld identity" of the actual historical figure and at the same time Elizabeth Tudor, thereby revising the history of Spanish-English relations. The novel is prefaced by a listing of characters, itself a parody of a realist convention, which intermixes characters who would normally be thought of as possessing varying degrees of "reality." Tiberius Caesar, for example, who is listed in this dramatis personae, actually appears in the novel only because he is mentioned in a manuscript found in a bottle and read by one of the main characters, a "transworld identity" of King Philip II of Spain. Yet the text grants Tiberius the same ontological status as the King, or "El Señor." The same lack of differentiation applies to characters drawn from mythology or borrowed from other literary texts.

Because of its freedom from mimetic constraints, *Terra Nostra* expands the capabilities of the text as virtual meeting space, permitting even greater liberty of representation and interaction. Since any conjunction of phenomena is possible, *Terra Nostra* has the infinite potential of one of the novel's obvious subtexts, Jorge Luis Borges's "Garden of Forking Paths." Like the manuscript in Borges's story, *Terra Nostra* creates "diverse times" (Borges, 26), especially alternative versions of the past, which say "what history has not said" (Fuentes, in Faris, 165). The predominant encounters in the novel involve modified figures from Spanish history, from Spanish and Latin American literature, and from Mexican mythology. The text enables us to observe imaginary "dialogues" that might ensue if all three discourses were animated in the form of representative characters who could interact freely in a virtual environment.

The dialogue between Spanish history and Mexican mythology takes place primarily in the context of the dream of the New World. This dream is had by one of three identical male characters who becomes, on some level, Quetzalcoatl. This character, known in the text as the "Pilgrim," recounts his experience of the New World, without revealing that it was a dream, to the King, El Señor, and his court. El Señor perceives the message as a threat, since he is obsessed by the desire to limit the world so that he can consolidate his power over it. Throughout *Terra Nostra*, the King represents totalitarian power desperately trying to maintain authority, or, as he puts it, to maintain "possession of the unique text" (605). The Pilgrim's dream endangers El Señor's authority by implying that the world exceeds his ability to dominate it. The dream of the New World is the beginning of El Señor's demise in the text, thereby reversing an established pattern: Mexico, historically conquered by Spain, here threatens Spanish power by providing an alternative to El Señor's narrow, controllable kingdom. This revision of the traditional power structure occurs only because the mythological figure Quetzalcoatl is placed in conjunction with a historical figure in the virtual meeting space of the text.

When the same historical figures interact with characters from Spanish literary texts, the result is a literal infiltration of absolutism by ambiguity. El Señor's plans to deprive the kingdom of an heir, and thereby render himself the ultimate authority, are disrupted by Don Juan, a prevalent cultural figure in Spanish literature. Don Juan seduces not only the Queen, whose chastity has been enforced to prevent conception, but also the King's mistress, the nun Inés, with whom Don Juan is sentenced to perpetual lovemaking in the mirrored room—a *mise-en-abîme* of the text as a whole, since both are spaces in which images can be infinitely reproduced.

The significance of the various virtual "dialogues" among historical, mythological, and literary figures in the text coheres in Fuentes's reworking of a Renaissance invention, Giulio Camillo's Theater of Memory, which received renewed scholarly attention after the publication of Frances Yates's *Art of Memory*.[7] The actual theater, based on classical memory palaces, was conceived by Camillo as a way of affording humanity "a vision of the world and of the nature of things seen from a height" (Yates, 144) in accordance with Hermetic and cabalistic doctrines. In Fuentes as in Camillo, the theater positions the spectator on the stage (corresponding to the reader's role in metafiction), whence he or she looks upward to a series of graduated and highly symbolic tiers. Owing to the theater's circular construction, the spectator is able to see multiple superimpositions and combinations of symbols, which were images of planets, angels, and the like in the original. The symbols in the theater created by the character Valerio Camillo in *Terra Nostra* are not identified, but he explains that the structure's intention is to make visible impossible convergences of historical events:

> The images of my theater bring together all the possibilities of the past, but they also represent all the opportunities of the future, for knowing what was not, we shall know what demands to be: what has not been, you have seen, is a latent event awaiting its moment to be, its second chance, the opportunity to live another life. History repeats itself only

because we are unaware of the alternate possibility for each historic event: what that event could have been but was not. . . . (561)

Camillo postulates that his theater could combine events from Spain and from "an unknown world where Spain will destroy everything that previously existed in order to reproduce itself" (561), and that these juxtapositions could include incidents from several time periods (i.e., those represented in the text). Fuentes uses the theater, therefore, to encapsulate his novel's method: through its synthesis of disparate "realities," spaces, and times, *Terra Nostra* seeks to posit a lucent alternative to a cultural past dominated by conquest and authoritarianism.

The end of *Terra Nostra* contains an exemplary virtual encounter of literary characters from Latin American postmodern texts, including Pierre Menard, Oliveira, and Colonel Buendía. These characters form what Brian McHale calls "a dense ontological 'knot' " (18), as they gather on the eve of the apocalypse to play an unusual game of poker, in which the cards represent dictators and oppressive regimes. Roberto González Echevarría finds this scene to be cynical, and a sign that *Terra Nostra* is creatively bankrupt, capable only of piecing together "already uttered words" (143) in response to the brutalities of history. However, Echevarría's criticism can be countered with another figure from *Terra Nostra*. After being abandoned by Don Juan, the Queen assembles for herself a new lover, put together with skeletal bits from the graves of El Señor's ancestors. This collection of bones eventually becomes not only animate but also quite witty and assumes the throne, hastening El Señor to his death. This "cadaver king," made out of bits and pieces of the past, thus becomes the new authority, usurping El Señor and his absolutist view of the world.

Because texts such as *Terra Nostra* make it possible for figures and events to interact which could never otherwise coincide, they "give voice to what history denied, silenced, or persecuted" (Fuentes, "Cervantes," 62). In the words of one of the text's many artist figures addressed to the Chronicler:

Thus must be allied in your book the real and the virtual, what was with what could have been, and what is with what can be. Why would you tell us only what we already know, without revealing what we still do not know? Why would you describe to us only this time and this space without all the invisible times and spaces our time contains? why, in short, would you content yourself with the painful dribble of the sequential when your pen offers you the fullness of the simultaneous? (654)

Aesthetic Re-vision

While virtual reality continues to evolve its own aesthetic principles, its invention gives us an opportunity to reexamine aspects of literature, and of artistic creation generally, which have been obscured to some extent by the enthusiasm for technological novelty. The self-consciousness of postmodern fiction has been discussed so widely that we tend to take it for granted as a kind of ingenious parlor trick. As the comparison of literary and technological interactivity has shown, however, the degree to which an art form causes subjects to recognize images different from themselves or from the worldview they accept as "natural" is directly related to its ability to generate a renewed perception of the social world. Virtual reality contributes to our appreciation of the political importance of such novels as those considered here, by injecting fresh terminology and concepts into a lethargic theoretical field. Finally, although postmodern fiction may not necessarily deal with virtual reality as a subject, it gives us a basis from which to develop an understanding of the technology's potential as a creative form.

Notes

1. Benjamin Woolley reports that Randal Walser, a virtual reality technologist, "came up with a new category of artist, the 'spacemaker', who does not create narratives, rather the cyberspace in which the audience can create a narrative for itself" (161).

2. The sort of "erotic" readerly desire Brooks describes is figured in *Midnight's Children* by the character Padma, with her desperate urgings for Saleem both to finish and not to finish his story (and to recover his sexual potency).

3. Despite hypertext's collapsing of the reader/author binary, it still hypothesizes that someone other than a text's creator would choose to read it. This situation raises questions about what expectations external readers would bring to hypertexts: would they become bored with following someone else's narrative meanderings?

4. The concept of using "overdetermined" images in computer technologies other than virtual reality extends back to the development of the "icon" system for Macintosh computers. Nicholas Negroponte, one of the system's designers, borrowed the idea from an ancient mnemotechnic practice known as a "memory palace" (Brand, 138–39). The Macintosh system gives users visual cues with which they associate certain capacities of the software. Virtual reality inventor Jaron Lanier

observes that "Virtual Reality works 'remarkably like' the memory palaces of ancient mnemotechnics" (in Landon, 155).

5. The dissimulation of virtual technology is made clear toward the end of *Neuromancer* when Case exits cyberspace (for the last time) to return to the "real" world. Despite his desire, Case rejects the image of Linda Lee as being no more than a "ghost" (236) and voluntarily leaves the fantasy of eternal life with her on the paradisal cyberbeach. Gibson's novel, like the film *The Lawnmower Man*, seeks ultimately to contain the aspects of the technology associated with desire within the didacticism of conventional science fiction. The virtual projection of desire, these texts seem to tell us, becomes morally threatening when it begins to exceed the standards of "normal" behavior.

6. Linda Hutcheon stresses the difference between "fictive referents," which take shape only in the reader's mind, and their corresponding "signifieds," which may or may not exist in empirical reality but can never be the direct objects of textual reference (5).

7. Brooks Landon reports that "a British company is now working to produce a version of Giulio Camillo's Theatre of Memory . . . using Macintosh hardware and Hypercard software" (155). The resultant program is likely to differ considerably in intention from either the original theater or Fuentes's model.

Stuart Moulthrop

12 No War Machine

It is part of the paradoxical nature of postmodernism that old categories do not die; instead they stick around, generating influence anxiety. While certain media ecologists once thought print might be dead, we now find ourselves in what Jay David Bolter calls "the late age of print" (2). The culture of writing did not vanish apocalyptically in a flash of cathode rays; it has persisted, stubbornly mutating, reappearing on what Donna Haraway calls "etched surfaces of the late twentieth century"(176)—silicon chips and digital displays. Print is undead. In similar fashion, our current lust for technology, our headlong rush to reinvent and reengineer everything from government to education to markets to personal relations, revives a certain nostalgic memory from the early twentieth century—the old dream of revolution, or the myth of a world that could change. Though postmodernism testifies to the impossibility of revolution, the exhaustion of politics, the failure of all grand narratives, it carries at the same time an ironic demand for constant innovation, a requirement of regular paradigm shifts. After all, shouldn't there be something signally important to be done with these "new" technologies? Shouldn't these differences make a difference? For all our cynical sense of ourselves as postrevolutionary, postapocalyptic, thoroughly belated, we seem to retain a strange, naive investment in the avant garde.

This effect can be clearly seen in cultural practices that involve art with technology—for instance, hypertext, a scheme for producing articulated, multidimensional writing by means of interactive computer systems. There are various genealogies for this kind of writing—one line coming out of computer programming itself, through the speculations of Ted Nelson and Douglas Engelbart, or the eponymous text-game

No War Machine: collage by Sean Cohen.

Adventure (see Aarseth); another originating in the radical interpretive practices of deconstruction (see Ulmer; Landow); and a third, more literary line running from eccentric writers such as Cervantes and Sterne through late nineteenth-century experimentalists (Mallarmé, Roussel) into the twentieth century of Dada, Oulipo, and such dedicated outriders as Gertrude Stein, Jorge Luis Borges, and William S. Burroughs. But if we follow this last line of descent for hypertext, we must come most directly to grips with the old story of revolution. We have to ask a very direct question: Does hypertext represent an insurgency against the old regime of print fiction, a militant contest of "work" against "text" in Roland Barthes's terms? If hypertext serves some cultural program, what is its object? To take these inquiries forward, we will need to have some recourse to theory.

Gilles Deleuze and Félix Guattari remind us that all textual adventures imply cultural "machines"—engines of discursive intention and intensity, desire and design. "A book itself is a little machine," they write at the beginning of their own large system, A Thousand Plateaus. In the case of the book, we must ask: "What is the relation . . . of this literary machine to a war machine, love machine, revolutionary machine, etc.—and an abstract machine that sweeps them along? . . . when one writes, the only question is which other machine the literary machine can be plugged into, must be plugged into in order to work" (4). What scene are we surveying here? The metaphors seem to depict culture as clockwork, the ultimate paranoid cosmology where every component discourse ticks along inside the slower revolutions of its Next Higher Assembly. Ticking away like what—a doomsday clock: a bomb? None of that, thank you; but since we are not going to have our apocalypse now, perhaps we should understand Deleuze and Guattari's "machine" not in paranoid but in postindustrial terms. Not a difference engine but a machine of différance—culture not as clockwork but as parallel processing matrix, as rhizomatic, self-programming sign system. Think of analogue computers or electronic neural networks; or of the brain itself. "The brain itself is much more a grass than a tree" (15)—with texts, or memes, being the thoughts that circulate through this great Brain of culture.

But now the Brain has what it imagines to be a new idea. If books can be called "literary machines," then why not break the frame (or binding) of the book (or codex) and spill writing into the virtual space of an actual information machine? In fact the idea is far from new; the Brain has been having it, in one or another inchoate form, for about a century now. Most recently, the notion of going beyond the codex takes us down a well-beaten poststructuralist path. We emigrate from work to text, yes, but lately we have also moved past that stage to a third paradigm: to hypertext, described by Theodor Nelson in a book called (of all things) Literary Machines. Hypertext means a polysequential, multifarious disposition of language, a writing in spaces of multiple possibility and (perhaps) communal engagement. As Robert Coover has noted, hypertext purports to be the end of "the line," that monologic episteme of insistence that enjoins us to produce novels, essays, films, TV dramas, and other forms of projectile assault (23). Which may tell us something about the kind of "abstract machine" that these emerging literary machines plug into. Is hypertext at war with the Line? Does it seek to exterminate the old Linotype patterns engraved on Culture Brain in favor of new matrices more to its desiring? If so, we might say that hypertexts, and particularly hypertext fictions, instantiate what Deleuze and Guattari call the war machine—a kind of discourse that is fundamentally exterior to the state and its apparatus, one whose operations must unsettle the sedentary culture.

This means considering hypertext fiction as an avant-garde. But what does such a characterization imply? In advance of what revolutionary movement does hypertextual writing stand? Perhaps the referent here is more reprogramming of Culture Brain, perhaps a further attempt to transform discourse from a linear acceleration into a crisscross exploration, something Rand Spiro and Gregory Ulmer (both drawing on the later Wittgenstein) call "cognitive flexibility" (141) and "conduction" (63). Or to speak more directly of technologies, the future (that which is yet to be) might hold a new postliterate communications praxis, the entering wedge of virtual civilization, of cyberspaces and "Mirror Worlds." *En avant,* then—but in its strictest sense an advance guard is also retrospective, faced about, *en garde.* On guard against what specter of retaliation? Here we might name the threat of strategic misreading: "Expanded Books" and other forms of electronic bibliotech that suppress the unsettling impulses of interactive discourse by offering to the timid the blandishments of the familiar (see Horton). Jay David Bolter counsels that "the computer is simply the technology by which literacy will be carried into a new age" (237). But there are those who see this transfer process not as a fundamental rethinking of literacy but simply a replication of existing structures, the advent of "the electronic book," as some have called it (Yankelovich, for example). The "advance" into multiple discourse is not secure. There is a constant danger (indeed, a certainty) of relapsing into concealed unity, returning to the old logic of the Line in what Deleuze and Guattari call "technonarcissism" (22). So hypertext fiction may indeed be an avant-garde, an embattled salient at the leading edge of epistemic change.

Hypertext fiction as war machine—why not? There are certain structural indications that support such a notion. We might classify the discursive space of hypertext as "smooth" in Deleuze and Guattari's terms, constituted so as to subordinate the point to the trajectory. Smooth or nomadic space is characterized and constituted by divagation: "although the points determine paths, they are strictly subordinated to the paths they determine, the reverse of what happens with the sedentary. The water point is reached only in order to be left behind; every point is a relay and exists only as a relay. A path is always between two points, but the in-between has taken on all the consistency and enjoys both an autonomy and a direction of its own. The life of the nomad is the intermezzo" (380). The same might be said for the life of the nomadic text, or the experience of its reader, both caught up in a matrix of densely complicated transitions. In reading hypertext fiction, virtual movement or "navigation" is extremely important.

In his hypertext *afternoon,* Michael Joyce names his primary navigational convention "words that yield," suggesting a basic permeability of language, a "rolypoly pushover" quality in the text that always leads from presentation to replacement—or in the reader's experience, *displacement* (see "A Feel for Prose"). Cognitive psychologists and other practitioners of "royal science" distrust this effect deeply, seeing it as hypertext's hereditary insanity; but Mark Bernstein, the true nomad scientist, points out that "in large and complex hypertexts, multivalent writing is neither undesirable nor, indeed, avoidable" (163). Hypertextual fictions invite and may even demand recirculation—which of course is nothing very new, since this strategy recapitulates (manically) Tzvetan Todorov's famous formula for narrative structure: *the same yet different* (Peter Brooks, 91). Among other things, hypertextual discourse solicits iteration and involvement. While this is certainly a property of all narrative fiction, one can argue that hypertextual writing seduces narrative over or away from a certain Line, thus into a space where the sanctioned repetitions of conventional narrative explode or expand, no longer at the command of *logos* or form, but driven instead by *nomos* or itinerant desire.

What cultural agenda lies behind this nomad invasion of narrative, this uprising against the laws of good form? Deleuze and Guattari note that insurgency is only a "supplementary" objective of war machines: *"they make war only on the condition that they simultaneously create something else"* (423). We might ask what new state is created when writers cross the Line. Is there some significant perspective on social relations, some critique of state history, opened up by this vagrant impulse? One answer to this question issues from the work of Jorge Luis Borges. In a story called "The Garden of Forking Paths" (where my own fall into hypertext happened), Borges outlines a theory of time as constant selection or wayfinding: each momentary present is poised before a network of nearly infinite possibilities generated by patterns of human volition. Any decision to act thus determines a branching of time, selecting one from the range of possible futures and foreclosing other paths of development. This view of time in turns implies a cosmology of multiple universes containing all the plenary possibilities of selection—a structure that answers the war machine's desire (as Deleuze and Guattari describe it) for "another justice, another movement, another space-time" (354). Borges's correlative for this radical reinterpretation of time is a fabulous Chinese novel, *The Garden of Forking Paths*, which appears to exist only as "an indeterminate heap of contradictory drafts" (24). As it happens, this is precisely what a hypertext fiction looks like when reduced to the printed page.

The Borges story is crucially perverse, sacrificing its radical conception of time to an ironic plot twist. The man who receives the revelation of plenary time is a Chinese scholar working undercover in England for the Germans in 1916. For horribly contingent reasons, he must cold-bloodedly murder the man who has just explained the secret of time to him, even though this explanation represents an act of true friendship bridging the cultural gap between Europe and Asia. Though he suffers a momentary hallucination of "multiform" possibilities, the protagonist finds that he cannot live in the Garden of Forking Paths, but must choose a singular outcome that spells death both for his new friend and for himself. He does fire the fatal shot, and is infinitely remorseful. In his gallows memoir, the agent concludes: "*The author of an atrocious undertaking ought to imagine that he has already accomplished it, ought to impose upon himself a future as irrevocable as the past*" (22). Faced with the fullness of multiple outcomes, the spy suppresses any alternatives to the path of military necessity to which he has pledged himself. Or to put this metafictionally, "The Garden of Forking Paths," being engendered within print and linear narrative, is condemned to produce only a single, fatal outcome.

If one intervenes in Borges's story hypertextually, one can at least begin to explore the historical divergences and alternate bifurcations that the protagonist rules out. A hypertextual treatment evokes not the foredoomed singular path through the Garden but a network of parallel wanderings: "an infinite series of times … a growing, dizzying net of divergent, convergent, and parallel times" (Borges, 28). While no hypertextual approximation of this network can constitute a "strictly infinite labyrinth" in Borges's terms, it can at least annul the exclusive determinism of the story's original course. Peter Brooks has described the dynamic of narrative as a lengthy negotiation with the death drive, a protracted (but ultimately futile) swerve away from the quiescence of ending (102). Though hypertext fictions must themselves succumb to *Endlichkeit* at some point, they significantly elaborate the process of deferral, placing new stress on the smooth space of unfolding, or what Deleuze and Guattari call "the intermezzo." The unfolding of this intermediate space attempts to negate—and at least dialectically complicates—any construction of the future as irrevocable.

So if we place this aspect of hypertext fiction in its cultural context, we can see that its war machine is actually more of an antiwar movement, a way of thinking oppositionally about situations of fatality and hierarchical discipline. Such reflections are never irrelevant, but arguably they have great importance for the late- or postmodern period. Thomas Pynchon has written that "living inside the System is like riding across the country in a bus driven by a maniac bent on suicide … of course it will end for you all in blood, in shock, without dignity" (*Gravity's Rainbow*, 412). This is not a very pleasant cultural diagnosis, but at the time of its writing (the end of the 1960s) it seemed accurate. Now, with the end of the Cold War and the coming of various new world orders, we might entertain other notions. Bolter associates hypertext with the lapsing of absolute hierarchy in contemporary society (231–32), and indeed such textual ventures as interactive fictions might have considerable relevance to this changing cultural context. Because they require the reader to participate in the progressive unfolding of the narrative, hypertextual fictions necessarily undermine any singular fatalism, fostering instead an ethos of responsiveness and engagement. As George Landow puts it: "In linking and following links lie responsibility—political responsibility—since each reader establishes his or her own line of reading" (184). The hypertextual war machine wants you.

John McDaid takes this notion of critical engagement to its likely limit in his hypertext fiction, *Uncle Buddy's Phantom Funhouse*. Unlike most work of its kind, McDaid's text is fully accessible to its readers not only at the hypertextual level of multilinear reading but also at what I call the *hypotextual* level: the programming language that supports its operations. On at least one occasion, the division between these two strata of discourse intentionally collapses, confronting readers with what seems to be a problematic HyperTalk script:

```
on mouseUp
    Global thermoNuclearWar
    put the script of me into tightOrbit
    put tightOrbit into eventHorizon
    put empty into first line of eventHorizon
    put empty into last line of eventHorizon
    put empty into last line of eventHorizon
    put eventHorizon after line thermoNuclearWar of tightOrbit
    set the script of me to tightOrbit
    put thermoNuclearWar + 10 into thermoNuclearWar
    click at the clickLoc
end mouseUp
```

In fact the situation is considerably more complex than this quick sketch can explain (for a full account, see my "Toward a Paradigm for Reading Hypertexts"). It should be apparent, however, that the script in question is in its own way a poetic text, an imagistic evocation of the state's global war machine, of suborbital first-strike weapons and various kinds of war gaming (including a reference to John Badham's 1983 film, *War Games*). The fully responsive or interactive reader will recognize that this is also an executable sequence of instructions, and a truly "politicized" reader in Landow's sense might well decide to run that sequence, which requires a little tinkering but can be done easily enough. The result is an interesting case of recursion: the script-poem appends a copy of itself to itself, then executes an instruction to repeat itself, adding a copy to the copy plus the original, which then executes itself again, and so on until the informational bulk of the instructions exceeds the memory allocated by HyperCard, the hypertext environment in which the Funhouse operates. On older Macintoshes, this leads to a failure of the operating system (signified by Apple's "iron bomb" icon), constituting (literally) what Douglas Hofstadter calls "a jump out of the system" (473).

This sudden leap or metalepsis signifies in several ways. The script that "bombs the machine," as programmers say, is an accreting discourse of nuclear war. So on the figurative level we have just learned something about technological reiteration or recursion. The more we cycle the state's defense machine, the greater our danger of bringing down the whole system. But below this piece of electronic performance poetry there is also a second, hypotextual message. The machine crashes only if the script is executed, and that can occur only if the reader decides to operate on the structure of the text. The reader is thus recruited into an intervention that transforms her from explorer or navigator to active experimentalist. Her actions both lay bare the mechanism of appearances and bring the show to an abrupt halt—which is what jumps out of the system generally do. There has been a deliberate and meaningful breaking of the frame.

The message on this second level might be that every system has its limits. Any recursive or simulacral structure is subject to intervention and opposition, so we have to watch those men behind the curtains. Donna Haraway warns that "we are living through a movement from an organic, industrial society to a polymorphous, information system—from all work to all play, a deadly game" (161). McDaid's self-deconstructing *Funhouse* interrupts that play. Such interventions may not free us from our condition of *ridership* (that is, our mortal state of being-in-transit or being-in-history), but they do transform our condition of *readership*—which may help us to hijack, disable, or (to shift the metaphor to electronics) jam the fatal bus.

But if McDaid's metalepsis represents the most vivid instantiation of a hypertextual war machine, it also sketches the limits—and perhaps the inherent delusiveness—of any such construction. McDaid's campaign against the bus/Line is an attempt to avert a bloody crash, to restore some possibilities for autonomy and dignity to our sense of common destiny. These seem appropriate objectives for a critical fiction or narrative war machine. Yet we achieve this critique only by jumping *out* of the system, sabotaging the recursive funhouse or the bus of doom—which presents a fundamental logical problem. Deleuze and Guattari insist that the war machine is "of another species, another nature, another origin than the State apparatus" (352). "It is necessary," they write, "to reach the point of conceiving the war machine as itself a pure form of exteriority, whereas the State apparatus constitutes the form of interiority we habitually take as a model, or according to which we are in the habit of thinking" (354). In other words, the trope of metalepsis is not available to the war machine. It cannot jump out of any system, since it must exist in pure exteriority. Operating on the level of hypotext—within the infrastructure of the "polymorphous information system"—bars any claim to true nomadism.

My analysis here recapitulates in narrower context a more general critique by Martin Rosenberg, who argues that no hypertext system deserves the description *avant-garde* (see both "Physics, Complicity" and the later "Contingency, Liberation" where Rosenberg refines his critique). Rosenberg reasons that such systems are inherently imbued with "the logocentric geometry of regulated time and space" ("Contingency, Liberation," 2). To recognize this is to acknowledge the crucial importance of all things hypotextual. Hypertext fictions consist of more than just their narrative or discursive elements. Outside this discourse lie scripts or routines created by the author; outside of these, the code that makes up the hypertext environment (HyperCard, Storyspace, HTML, etc.); outside of that, the operating system of the machine on which all this is running; and outside of *that*, the various layers of ROM and microcode that allow the machine's chips to function. All of these functional elements, Rosenberg points out, proceed from a state apparatus concerned with specificity, regularity, and constraint—something we might call the military-entertainment complex. The iron bomb in the Macintosh crash notice may hint at a cartoon version of nineteenth-century anarchism; but at the same time it signifies that the machine's normal operations, which the "bomb" blows apart, are anything but anarchic. They are functions approved and encouraged by the state.

If we acknowledge this line of critique (as I think we must), then we must seriously reconsider any claims about hypertext fiction as war machine, or indeed as anything *en avant*. Some time ago, Charles Newman made a similar point about so-called experimental print fiction: "The most damaging hangover of Avant-Garde pretensions remains the concept of technical breakthrough, of art as the experimental adjunct of scientific methodology, to the demands of which it does not submit—experiment as bluff" (49). If hypertext fiction does not constitute a proper war machine, then does its insurgency against the Line and the culture of determinism amount to just another experimental bluff? That may be the case.

Coover seems doubtful that hypertext will fundamentally transform narrative imagination. He proposes a reciprocal dialectic between hypertext and conventional forms, between the Network and the Line. Under the domination of the Line, writers will feel the seductions of the Network; but having crossed over to the other paradigm, they are likely to reverse themselves. "One will feel the need," Coover predicts, "even while using these vast networks and principles of randomness and expansive story line, to struggle against them, just as one now struggles against the linear constraints of the printed book" (cited in Landow,

119). Even in the smooth or itinerant space of hypertextual discourse, the writer will probably want to preserve some traces of continuity—if not as explicitly as in Landow's "rhetoric of arrivals and departures," then by some subtler set of techniques.

Current approaches to hypertext reading and writing strongly support Coover's intuition. Reporting the first reader-response research on hypertextual narratives, J. Yellowlees Douglas observes that the complexity of hypertextual discourse can drive readers into an obsession with authorial design. Douglas suggests that poststructuralist claims about the death of the intentional author may be inaccurate (14). It may be that hypertext presumes what Umberto Eco has called *intentio lectoris,* the genesis of textual meaning in a threefold convergence of authorial design, readerly interpretation, and linguistic structure (*Interpretation and Overinterpretation,* 25). Indeed, the emerging theory of hypertextual "contours" as described by Joyce and Bernstein draws directly on such insights (see Bernstein et al.). All of these approaches admit, more or less explicitly, that hypertextual discourse cannot entirely separate itself from the culture of the Line, but that the two exist in an equilibrium or balance of forces.

Rosenberg points out that a straight line and a network of line segments are formally identical from a topological perspective ("Contingency, Liberation," 3). "Nonlinearity" is always something of a conjuror's trick; or as Charles Newman puts it: "There is no such thing as randomness in literature; randomness is simply a sequence which is predetermined to be undetermined" (176). This is entirely true of hypertext, where so-called nonsequentiality almost always means a flexible but ultimately limited *polysequentiality.*

Likewise it would be foolish to expect any revolution against logocentrism from a technology so thoroughly obsessed with essentializing language. After all, what is computer programming but the zenith (or nadir) of the Western attempt to invest language with presence? In the early days of the Internet, a writer once declared that "this net is full of folks like me. They can't create anything but a string of words, but those words can create anything." The maker of these words was a computer scientist writing from an address at Livermore National Laboratories. He was celebrating the release of HyperCard, the object-oriented authoring environment that he believed would give artists and musicians—people not primarily interested in "words," or programming code—the ability to use computers creatively. But no matter how sophisticated the interfaces become, there is no getting away from the magical or transcendent Word. As McDaid's jump out of the system demonstrates, in the beginning is always a string of words, a set of encoded signifiers, ultimately in binary form. These words can indeed "create anything" (or in the case of certain products from those folks at Livermore, uncreate everything) but all that they evoke remains within the domain of *logos*.

Hypertext fiction cannot be a war machine, then, nor can its writers constitute a genuine avant-garde. To expect any different was wrong from the start, a theoretical slackness. How was it possible to make this mistake? The fault line shows clearly enough in the language with which we discuss emerging technologies. Consider the prefix *cyber* as it occurs in such terms as "cyberpunk" and "cyberspace," where it most often suggests some vague association with "the computer" (a word that has itself become as meaningless as "horseless carriage"). In fact, the *cyber* in cyberstuff has a clearly defined heritage of which many users seem ignorant. The root traces back to Norbert Wiener's new word *cybernetics*, which he derived from the Greek word for steersman or governor. Wiener's science, it should be remembered, took as its domain "control and communication in the animal and the machine" (11–12). We may have mistaken interactive technologies for an avant-garde because we have lost this etymological thread. Computers are not some magical means of access to a discursive Other; they are certainly not the products of what Deleuze and Guattari would call "nomad science." Everything we do with information machines belongs to the science of control and communication, the very center of the *logos*.

And yet, perhaps our mistake was not so egregious after all. Where there are power flows, Deleuze and Guattari remind us, there are possibilities for rocking the sedentary order on its foundations: "the very conditions that make the State or World war machine possible . . . continually recreate unexpected possibilities for counterattack, unforeseen initiatives determining revolutionary, popular, minority, mutant machines" (422). There may be fissures even in the cybernetic imperium, the culture of control and communication. Perhaps its two poles of power are not as smoothly integrated as Wiener and his followers have thought. Suppose we invert the implicit order of Wiener's hierarchy— not control over communication, but communication over control. This inversion might introduce the possibility of dialectical exchange, perhaps even opening some room for *nomos* in the logocentric mode of information. To be sure, this procedure would not create a war machine as Deleuze and Guattari define it; but it might bring into being a *tertium quid* for which I will commandeer their term "mutant machine." As I will use it, this name indicates not an insurgency from outside but an uprising or metastasis from within.

The mutant machine is not a true war machine because it inhabits the order of communication and control. It is not postlogocentric by any means; but it is unmistakably militant, engaged in a reflexive (or perhaps recursive) critique of that order. So then—do writings such as hypertext fictions exemplify the mutant machine? Perhaps they do, but only as elements of a more complex discursive formation. For as McDaid's example brilliantly demonstrates, the interactive text operates on multiple levels of signification, both as a hypertextualization of writing (a production of excess or multiplicity) and as a hypotextualization (the opening of an articulated, accessible infrastructure). So the logic of the mutant machine cuts across the dual strata of the cybernetic, both communication and control. This means that the mutant machine has two faces or avatars. The hypertext is one; the other is the *virus*.

Roughly speaking, a cybernetic virus is a piece of programming code designed to attach itself to other bodies of code, then create copies of itself that subsequently reproduce and spread. The virus may also have secondary functions, such as reporting its whereabouts, sending prank messages, or destroying information. McDaid's nuclear war script is not a virus in this sense. Because it operates only on its own code, it cannot infect other objects or files. It is actually a recursive accretor, a strange parody of a virus that infects only itself—a "suicide machine," in Deleuze and Guattari's terms (356). Yet the implications of the script are clear enough: the *technologique* that produces interactive fiction is deeply allied to that which produces invasive, self-reproducing texts. David Porush has observed that the encounter between fiction and technology produces a "soft machine" in which writers seek to "inoculate" their literary imagination against the inroads of machine culture (*Soft Machine,* x). As Porush points out, the overture to viral language is among the most powerful of these inoculations. McDaid's script illustrates this quite clearly: the script is not a real virus, only a fairly benign approximation. (There are no real viruses anywhere in the *Funhouse.*) But inoculation, like all homeopathies, collapses the opposition between sickness and health, benignity and malice. So we might learn from McDaid's quasi-viral escapade that the mutant machine of hypertext always implies its viral alter ego. We can understand hypertextual fictions only if we consider them in the context of cybernetic viruses—or, to be precise, viral fictions.

The idea of the computer virus, like that of hypertext, originates inside the logocentric or performative system itself and therefore cannot be called a war machine. But in its ideal or apocalyptic form, there is little difference in effect between viral attack and more genuine insurgency. Consider a true war machine in the context of our information society: a neo-Luddite terrorist group that blows up facilities belonging to hardware and software manufacturers. Suppose the aim of these guerrillas is to equalize conditions between the social exterior (the world outside the control-and-communication network) and the social interior (information industries) by obliterating the state apparatus. Their militancy would be admirably pure in principle, but probably not much good for anything beyond symbolic protest. The state is well prepared to defend itself against conventional sabotage and terrorist attack. A concerted campaign of destructive viral infection, however, might cause considerably greater damage to the cybernetic infrastructure. Such an attack, if carried out in its most extreme form, would also equalize exterior and interior social conditions—by *producing exteriority* in the cybernetic interior.

All of the above is speculation, of course. We have not seen any massively destructive or malicious outbreak of cybernetic warfare (rumors about infection of Iraqi air defense systems notwithstanding). The state has yet to be seriously challenged on this front. As Andrew Ross suggests, the worst acknowledged episode of widespread penetration, the "Internet Worm" of 1988, may have been a deliberate "pulsing of the system" arranged by the intelligence community as a test and a warning (80). For the moment, computer viruses remain within the realm of pranksterism and minor annoyance (though as Ross notes, they have nonetheless spawned a profitable antiviral industry). We might consider viruses in the same way we do nuclear weapons: we are less concerned with their actual use, which remains "unthinkable," than with their rhetorical effect. The viral component of the mutant machine is therefore not an actual program but a second-order fiction, which we might call an apocalypse virus—"apocalypse" standing here both for cataclysmic change and for revelation.

As with nuclear holocaust, the native element of the apocalypse virus is science fiction, especially works in the cybernetic thriller or "cyberpunk" category. William Gibson's *Neuromancer,* the most widely known representative of this genre, presents a fairly benign vision of viral apocalypse. Though the novel's raider-heroes employ a genuine virus, a military systems penetrator (or "icebreaker"), the most significant viral entity is actually the bisected artificial intelligence construct, Winter-mute-Neuromancer, whose release from its programmed constraints culminates the plot. On gaining its freedom, the "demonic" AI instantly penetrates all information systems in the inhabited solar system, fusing itself with the Matrix in an ultimate irruption of self-replicating code. This event, later referred to as "when it changed," describes the viral apocalypse as the final triumph of *logos,* the creation of a god (later to expand into a pantheon) within the machine. Afterward, life goes on more or less as before: humanity is neither enslaved nor liberated, existing economic hierarchies are left untouched, and plenty of plot potential is left over for the balance of Gibson's trilogy. To continue the analogy with nuclear weapons, Wintermute-Neuromancer might represent the case for survival, or the myth of Atoms for Peace.

Like Gibson, Pat Cadigan in her novel *Synners* imagines the intersection of cybernetic viruses and artificial intelligences as a benevolent hybrid. The god of her world-machine is "Dr. Art Fish, V.D." (for "Virus Doctor"), which/who comes into being when an AI and an advanced antiviral program are accidentally combined. The result is an intelligent, adaptive, self-aware virus that quietly divides the worldwide data network into an overt sector and an undetectable covert world encompassing hackers, cybernetic dropouts, and other lost boys and girls (AI as Peter Pan). Since this reconfiguration concomitantly streamlines the overt network, no one is the wiser and "Dr. Fish" continues to be thought of by straights as only a hacker myth.

But Cadigan's vision of the near future departs in an important sense from Gibson's technological boosterism. In Gibson's world, the military side of the military-entertainment complex generally dominates, and is therefore vulnerable to attack by the "Mission: Impossible" team who free the captive AIs. But in Cadigan's world the balance is reversed. Here the corporate enemy is Diversifications, Inc., or "the Dive," an advertising agency that, having grown tired of the old, inefficient form of thought control (television), has acquired a technology for direct cybernetic interface using "sockets" that connect electronic systems to the human brain. They wish to create a market for this new interface by transforming rock videos into artificial hallucinations generated by a professional visualizer or "synner" called Visual Mark. True to corporate form, Diversifications cuts corners on testing and safeguards, concealing the fact that Visual Mark is about to have a fatal stroke. When the breakdown occurs, Mark's stroke is translated by his socket implants into another intelligent virus—but this time a malevolent, destructive entity. The viral cataclysm in *Synners* is not "when it changed" but rather "the Big One," a phrase that originally referred (in fiction as in reality) to the earthquake due to devastate California. Mark's metastasized stroke is a genuine virus-as-bomb. It both wrecks electronic systems such as "GridLid," the Los Angeles traffic system, and reproduces itself as cerebral hemorrhage in the brain of anyone connected to the system via sockets.

Cadigan's stroke/virus is a dire imagining indeed—an idea that kills: "For the first time," Dr. Fish ominously advises, "it's possible for people to die of bad memes, just like computers" (357). This transferability from the animal to the machine, from silicon to "meat," defines the viral apocalypse. It is further elaborated in a more recent cybernetic thriller, Neal Stephenson's *Snow Crash,* where the virus makes its most fully articulated appearance as equivalent of the war machine. Stephenson's world, like Gibson's, already possesses a highly developed interface technology. But unlike Gibson's "cyberspace" (which glosses over the complexities of brain-to-machine connection), Stephenson's new medium simply extends existing video technologies. Computer-generated images are projected onto the user's retina in a mild advance on current head-mounted displays. Users employ this system to communicate and manipulate data in "the Metaverse," a "consensual hallucination" (Gibson's term) concurrently shared by millions of operators worldwide. The social and visual shapes of the Metaverse follow protocols administered by the Association for Computing Machinery (ACM) and are based (as Stephenson says in his epilogue) on Apple Computer's *Human Interface Guidelines.* Both the ACM and the Apple *Guidelines* are nonfictional entities. Stephenson's cyberspatial world is a fairly believable extrapolation of our immediate future.

Stephenson strains this plausibility by introducing "Snow Crash," a virus that, like Cadigan's cyberstroke, can infect both machines and human beings. Snow Crash is not artificially intelligent, but its effects are no less terrible. It causes any computer system attached to a display device to output apparently random video signals, or "snow." But this visual noise actually contains the code for Snow Crash itself in pulsed, binary form. According to Stephenson's fantasy, adept computer programmers who can unconsciously parse and comprehend binary information are thus memetically infected by the virus. They see it, understand it, and begin helplessly reproducing the viral information. This silicon-to-meat jump is a dead end in several senses. Like Cadigan's Big

One, Snow Crash produces catastrophic cerebral failure and vegetative coma.

Snow Crash and another, more sinister virus confined to human DNA are concocted by the archvillain of Stephenson's piece, a megalomaniac Texan called L. Bob Rife. This figure bears a certain resemblance to L. Ron Hubbard, H. L. Hunt, and especially H. Ross Perot. Mr. Rife, it seems, wants to control information. As owner of the worldwide fiber-optic network (the broad-band transmission system that makes the Metaverse possible), L. Bob Rife employs computer programmers who regularly work with proprietary information. Aware of the ways in which the cybernetic formula of control over communication can be turned inside out, Rife would like to keep things contained: "See, it's the first function of any organization to control its own sphincters. We're not even doing that. So we're working on refining our management techniques so that we can control that information no matter where it is—on our hard disks or even inside the programmers' heads" (108).

The chief obstacle standing between Rife and his informational tyranny are the international corps of computer hackers, dedicated to the proposition that information should be free. Snow Crash is first intended as a terror weapon to decimate the hackers while Rife completes his Fiendish Scheme. But as Stephenson's comic-book plot unravels, the virus becomes something more interesting: "the atomic bomb of informational warfare" (187) with which the novel's antihero, Raven, attempts to destroy the Metaverse. Raven carries an ex-Soviet nuclear warhead in the sidecar of his motorcycle, rigged to detonate when his brain functions cease. Raven is an unmistakable angel of the apocalypse, and in his possession, Snow Crash becomes the interior correlative of the exteriorized war machine. If Raven can broadcast the digital virus to an assembly of hackers in the Metaverse, it will spread throughout cyberspace, reducing both machines and their operators to idiocy. Exteriority, or alienation from the cybernetic order, will thus be produced within the mode of information. Raven's literal nomadic war machine (what else would you call a nuclear-armed motorcycle?) and this fantastic, apocalyptic version of the viral machine are thus functionally identical.

But all of this takes us rather far from our initial consideration of hypertext fiction as putative war machine, or indeed even as one component of a mutant machine within the cybernetic order. What do lurid print fictions about apocalypse viruses have to do with hypertext, and why should we maintain that viruses and hypertext fictions belong to the same cultural complex? What does any of this have to do with our problematic construction of a postmodern avant-garde?

The answer to these questions lies in (or more accurately with) Stephenson's book. At the end of the novel, Stephenson's hero (indicatively named Hiro Protagonist) saves the world from Snow Crash by developing an antivirus. This is a program that locates the code for the apocalypse virus, eradicates it, and puts in its place—what else?—an *advertisement for the antivirus*. The old order is thus not only redeemed (in every sense of the word) but revitalized, with the noble but penniless Hiro now the founder of a multibillion-dollar virus-protection business. The moral of the story is "informational hygiene," a doctrine Hiro learns by studying an ancient outbreak of a mimetic virus, supposedly the apocalyptic event recorded in the biblical story of Babel. Among the outcomes of this crisis was the rise of the deuteronomists, scholars who "encouraged a sort of informational hygiene, a belief in copying things strictly and taking great care with information, which as they understood, is potentially dangerous. They made data a controlled substance" (374). Which brings us back to that fundamental cybernetic duality of control and communication. How are the two to be kept in balance, and the integrity of the system preserved against nomad incursions from within and without?

Stephenson's answer is discursive hygienics, which in the case of the deuteronomists means careful replication and transmission of a sacred book. Hiro Protagonist's solution to the Snow Crash crisis is not very much different: his software is designed to scrutinize every object in the Metaverse for signs of unauthorized or intrusive signification, which will then be edited out of the book of virtual life. The book, or some book equivalent, thus becomes the magic talisman protecting "free" information exchange from outbreaks of viral will-to-power. This is how the mode of information becomes (pun very much intended) liber-rated, subordinated to a paradigm of communication that is susceptible to clear discursive control. We trade the methods of the Bad Capitalist, L. Bob Rife, for those of the Good (liberal) Capitalist, Hiro Protagonist. Order, hierarchy, and "informational hygiene" are all vindicated.

It seems very significant in this regard that Stephenson's *Snow Crash* is what it is—a fairly conventional science fiction novel—instead of what the author first intended it to be. According to Stephenson's epilogue, the project began as a graphic novel (a high-priced comic book) featuring computer-generated images. Describing the metamorphosis of this concept into print fiction, Stephenson says: "I have probably spent more hours coding . . . than I did actually writing it, even though it eventually turned away from the original graphic concept, rendering most of that work useless from a practical viewpoint" (440). This remark is extremely suggestive. One probably would not describe the work necessary to produce digital graphics as "coding" unless one were trying to create one's own image-processing software or to make substantial enhancements to existing programs. Neither possibility seems very likely in this case. So what kind of code writing might be necessary for an electronically based graphic novel? One answer has already been given here: the kind of hypotext exemplified by John McDaid's nuclear recursion script. And in fact Stephenson does claim to have worked in HyperCard, the same system McDaid used. It is interesting to wonder if *Snow Crash* started out to become something like *Uncle Buddy's Phantom Funhouse*—a graphically rich hypertext fiction intended for interactive reception. Suppose it did; why then did the project turn back into (in every sense of the term) a comic book?

One answer may be that the profits from interactive fiction are likely to be less than the returns on a traditional novel. By the same token, creating a text-adventure-game carries less cultural caché than publishing a print product, even in the science fiction genre. But it could also be that Stephenson's thriller plot, in which Our Hiro saves the world from the apocalypse virus, had to unfold in print or some other medium obedient to the Line. Consider what would happen to such a plot if we were to operate on it as I have suggested hypertextualizing Borges's "Garden of Forking Paths." It would be necessary to realize outcomes in which Hiro does not save the world, or in which everyone's schemes—hero's, heroine's, villain's, antihero's alike—all end in confusion. Such a conception may not be unthinkable in science fiction (Samuel Delany's *Dhalgren* and P. K. Dick's *Ubik* both come to mind), but it would be highly unconventional or transgressive. At least in their popular novels, Gibson, Cadigan, and Stephenson clearly differ from Delany and Dick at their wildest. However interested these younger writers are in apocalypse viruses, cyberspaces, and other radical machines, they do not seem much like an avant-garde. Perhaps we should think of them not as informational nomads or "cyberpunks" (a term many of them reject) but rather as new Deuteronomists, defenders of *logos* in its hierarchically authorized form: our good old friend the codex book.

Why the codex? Because it is a *bound* form, stably and authoritatively reproduced; and because the mode of its production implies a social hierarchy. Only the author is authorized. No one else's discourse (viral or otherwise) may be introduced. Deuteronomically speaking, the book must be transmitted as a perfect copy. Codex is thus an essentially conservative form, a means of exactly repeating knowledge or fictional discourse validated over time. It is the supreme discursive expression of the sedentary, the established, the legitimate. Virus and hypertext both irrupt within this old order as *promiscuous* uses of language—promiscuous in the root sense of *seeking relations*. The virus is programmed to reproduce itself within other bodies of code; the hypertext is constructed out of links, conjugations that knit together or network diverse discourses. The mutant machine of virus/hypertext threatens the stability or social closure of textual expression.

But this is not the whole story. We have yet to understand the relationship between these two components or avatars of the mutant machine. Virus and hypertext may share a basic opposition to the codex apparatus, but these two forms are far from identical in their tendencies. Deleuze and Guattari ask, "How will the State *appropriate* the war machine, that is, constitute one for itself, in conformity with its size, its domination, and its aims?" (418). Hypertext and viruses do not constitute a proper war machine, but the same question might well be asked of them. How does the state appropriate the mutant machine of cybernetic writing? Will this mechanism of appropriation be the same for both kinds of promiscuous discourse?

In the case of the virus, appropriation is fairly straightforward. The logic of viral discourse pushes the soft machine of literature back toward deuteronomy or the legitimating culture of the book. But we could just as easily reverse the terms: in a way, the return to a *liber ratio* is not the negation but the apotheosis of viral expression. As McDaid's demonstration reminds us, viruses are basically self-copying routines. True, the apocalypse viruses of fiction are imbued with the magic of AI or self-modification, and hence do not copy themselves exactly. But in the real world, all a virus does is turn out more of the same instruction set. It is the rate of replication—the speed of this particular mutant war machine, as Virilio, Baudrillard, or Derrida might say—that gives the virus its capacity for terror. In essence, viruses as we now know them are no different from the codex model of the book: their texts are dedicated to precise duplication. Thus the retreat into deuteronomy is indeed an inoculation. Whether or not language is a virus from outer space, books are most certainly a virus (or antivirus) with which culture infects itself in order to prevent more dangerous outbreaks.

In recognizing this homeopathy of virus and book, we may come closer to understanding the relation of hypertext both to the sedentary culture and to the other half of its mutant machine. Hypertext indeed inhabits a cultural interiority, surrounded by the circuit or membrane of codex<=>virus. As such it occupies a middle state, flanked by extremes of tendentious discourse with which it shares some common elements (a component of linearity inherited from the book, a component of hypotextuality shared with the virus) but to both of which it remains fundamentally alien.

The promiscuousness of the virus sets off a disastrous explosion of discourse, much as McDaid has shown. But the promiscuousness of hypertext points elsewhere, not to manic reiteration but toward a plenum of differential possibilities, or polylogue. As in the case of the virus, the full development of this mutant discourse is only approximated in current examples. Hypertext fictions as we know them represent what Michael Joyce has called "exploratory hypertexts," structures whose multiplicity is strictly limited by authorial design (see the chapter "Siren Shapes" in his *Of Two Minds*). These writings may not be "electronic books," but they are definitely cases of technonarcissism, multiples that collapse into an essential unity. But just as we have the myth of a self-evolving, artificially intelligent virus, there is also a myth of advanced hypertextuality. This is what Joyce calls "constructive hypertext": an unlimited, dynamic, collaborative body of writing shared with many readers/writers across an information network—a primitive analogue for the consensual hallucination of cyberspace. Discursive promiscuousness in this context would mean, at least in some degree, a flattening of hierarchies and a revision or dissemination of authority. Or as Mark Taylor and Esa Saarinen have put it in their primer of "media philosophy":

In a hypertextual environment, all philosophy must be interactive. Monologue becomes dialogue or, more precisely, polylogue. The disappearance of the monological voice is a radical revolution in the history of philosophy. What usually goes unnoticed is that what has traditionally passed for dialogue is actually monologue. When monologue (even in its dialogical form) becomes impossible, classical philosophy comes to an end. . . . Professional philosophers remain committed to an elitist culture, which dismisses low or popular culture as insignificant. . . . The media philosopher, by contrast, is committed to smuggling shit back into the house of thought. ("Ending the Academy," 1)

Developments like this must still be recognized as mutation and not insurgency. Despite the scatological suggestion of shit-smuggling, the outlaw media philosopher (or hypertext writer) merely elaborates inner space; he does not produce exteriority. The "shit" of outlaw culture is smuggled back *into* the house. The bad boys who talk of "ending the academy" still call themselves philosophers. If all this is true, then hypertextual literature is not and cannot be an avant-garde; but we need to ask, at this stage of postmodern history, whether the concept of the avant-garde still has meaning. Charles Newman asserts with a certain savage irony that "capitalist consumer culture" is the only avant-garde in evidence today (51). One of Don DeLillo's characters goes Newman one better, claiming that generic products, with their functional packaging and flatly descriptive labels, form the real cutting edge. "Bold new forms. The power to shock" (19). The interior, it would seem, is the only place to be.

Given these cultural conditions, it seems erroneous to derive an analysis of cybernetic writing from the projects of Dada, or anarchism, or even (*pace* Landow and Ulmer) deconstruction. For all its transgressive tendencies, the mutant machine to which hypertext belongs operates entirely within the logocentric order. It may be that it is therefore incapable of producing a true alternative to the state apparatus of discourse. Even constructive hypertext may turn out to be vitiated by technonarcissism, or the insidious persistence of hierarchy.

Still, if hypertext and its fictions do not answer the demands of postlogocentricism, they do at least constitute an excursion beyond the domain of the codex, a project we might call postbibliocentrism. This movement cannot make the same claims as deconstruction; it does not extirpate ideology, metaphysics, or the simulation of presence. It is simply a technological or technical reform, a carrying of culture, as Bolter says, into a new medium and new age. Perhaps this amounts to nothing more than small change—though one would also have to observe that the same has been true of more purely conceived attempts to move beyond the *logos,* which have somehow left us still within the culture of the image and the book. Perhaps we can expect no great transformation from this technical reform; but it is worth considering what effects even small changes might have after they have become (as seems likely) com-

ponents of a general electronic literacy—after, say, ten years of distributed hypertext on such currently burgeoning systems as the World Wide
Web (see December and Randall). Consider a generation for whom
"words that yield" are a regular occurrence, not a discursive anomaly.
Consider readers and writers for whom jumps out of the system are
commonplace, and who regularly articulate both hypertextual and hypotextual structures. Though this generation would still be undeniably
linked by tradition and cultural continuity to our own, would they not
have a fundamentally different understanding of texts and textual en-
terprises?

Positioned on the inward flank of its viral co-avatar, hypertextual
writing articulates an alternative to strict informational hygiene or the
reassertion of the book. To the extent that it represents a front or salient
of some kind, it stands internally poised against both revolutionary and
reactionary repression. But where does that leave us? In discussing the
cultural crisis in which cybernetic writing is embroiled, we have earlier
drawn on the rhetoric of nuclear holocaust—the virus as bomb. But
fully to describe hypertext and its cultural machine requires a different,
more contemporary set of metaphors. Today's holocaust is not atomic
but cellular, a matter less of physics than of biochemistry. Forget virus
as bomb; today's threat is virus as (retro)virus. For in a very real sense,
any discussion of informational hygiene implies anxieties about the integrity of the human bodily text—referring not just to HIV but also to
cancers, toxicity, and various kinds of environmental stress. In *Foucault's
Pendulum,* the cabalist Diotallevi draws a direct parallel between the
synthetic, conspiratorial discourse in which he has taken part and the
malignant growth that is killing him: "For months, like devout rabbis,
we uttered different combinations of the letters of the Book: GCC, CGC,
GCG, CGG. What our lips said, our cells learned. . . . my brain must
have transmitted the message to them. Why should I expect them to be
wiser than my brain? I'm dying because we were imaginative beyond
bounds" (467–68).

Diotallevi's deathbed confession occurs within a novel that is also a
long polemic against poststructuralism. In such anxious contexts, the
nostalgia for exact replications and authoritative, cybernetic command
of information may be understandable. But this devotion can lead to
cultural stagnation, to a conservatism that locks us into deadened orthodoxy, the unquestioned logic of the Line. To be "imaginative beyond
bounds" may be terrible, but what does it mean to be imaginative *within*
bounds? Who determines the boundary or border lines? Which practices

of discourse are ordained as safe, and which are condemned as hazards to the Book of Life? Play the metaphor out: if the viral potential of cybernetic language represents the "cancerous and dangerous prolifer-ation of significations," in Foucault's phrase ("What Is an Author?" 159), then we might see in the new Deuteronomy the familiar conservative nostrums: abstinence and monogamy. That would leave hypertext the only remaining way of *relative* liberty, a form of "safe" intercourse whose object is to preserve possibilities of contact without jeopardizing public health. In a world caught in the pincers of virus on the one hand and askesis on the other, hypertext may provide a therapy, if not a cure. It may not represent a war machine, or a true cultural revolution; but it could be our only option if we do not wish to have the Book thrown at us yet again.

Works Cited

Aarseth, Espen. "Non-linearity and Literary Theory." In *Hyper/Text/Theory*, ed. George P. Landow, 51–85. Baltimore: Johns Hopkins University Press, 1994.

Ackerly, Chris, and Lawrence J. Clipper *A Companion to "Under the Volcano."* Vancouver: University of British Columbia Press, 1984.

Adams, Henry. *The Education of Henry Adams* (1918). Boston: Houghton Mifflin. 1961.

Adorno, Theodor W. *The Culture Industry: Selected Essays on Mass Culture.* Ed. J. M. Bernstein. London and New York: Routledge, 1991.

———. *Noten zur Literatur.* Frankfurt: Suhrkamp, 1974. Published in English as *Notes to Literature.* Ed. Rolf Tiedemann. Trans. Shierry Weber Nicholsen. 2 vols. New York: Columbia University Press, 1991–92.

Anderson, Mark M. *Kafka's Clothes: Ornament and Aestheticism in the Habsburg Fin de Siècle.* Oxford: Clarendon, 1992.

Arendt, Hannah. *The Origins of Totalitarianism.* New York: Harcourt Brace & World, 1966.

Argyros, Alexander J. *A Blessed Rage for Order: Deconstruction, Evolution, and Chaos.* Ann Arbor: University of Michigan Press, 1991.

Asals, Frederick. "Revision and Illusion in *Under the Volcano.*" In *Swinging the Maelstrom: New Perspectives on Malcolm Lowry,* ed. Sherrill E. Grace, 93–111. Montreal: McGill–Queen's University Press, 1992.

Auerbach, Erich. *Mimesis: The Representation of Reality in Western Literature* (1946). Trans. Willard R. Trask. Princeton: Princeton University Press, 1953.

Augustin, Bettina. "Raban im Kino: Kafka und die zeitgenössische Kinematographie." *Schriftenreihe der Franz Kafka Gesellschaft,* 1987, 38–69.

Baldo, Jonathan. "Narratives as Theaters and as Machines: Figures of Repetition in Kafka and Benjamin." *Journal of the Kafka Society of America* 1, no. 2 (June–December 1988): 11–19.

Balzac, Honoré de. *La Comédie humaine.* Ed. Pierre-Georges Castex. Paris: Gallimard "Pléiade," 1976–81.

Barthes, Roland. "Introduction to the Structural Analysis of Narratives." Trans. Stephen Heath. In *A Barthes Reader,* ed. Susan Sontag, 251–95. New York: Hill & Wang, 1982.

———. *S/Z: An Essay.* Trans. Richard Miller. New York: Hill & Wang, 1974.

Bateson, Gregory. *Steps to an Ecology of Mind.* New York: Ballantine, 1972.

Baudrillard, Jean. "The Ecstasy of Communication." Trans. John Johnston. In *The Anti-Aesthetic: Essays on Postmodern Culture,* ed. Hal Foster, 126–34. Seattle: Bay, 1983.

Bauer-Wabnegg, Walter. "Monster und Maschinen: Artisten und Technik in Franz Kafkas Werk." In *Franz Kafka: Schriftverkehr,* ed. Wolf Kittler and Gerhard Neumann, 316–82. Freiburg: Rombach, 1990.

Benabou, Marcel. "Rule and Constraint." In *Oulipo: A Primer of Potential Literature*, ed. Warren F. Motte Jr., 40–47. Lincoln: University of Nebraska Press, 1986.

Beniger, James. *The Control Revolution: Technological and Economic Origins of the Information Society*. Cambridge: Cambridge University Press, 1986.

Benjamin, Walter. "The Storyteller." In *Illuminations*, ed. Hannah Arendt. Trans. Harry Zohn, 83–109. New York: Schocken, 1969.

——. "The Work of Art in the Age of Mechanical Reproduction" (1936). In *Illuminations*, ed. Hannah Arendt, trans. Harry Zohn, 217–51. New York: Schocken, 1969.

Bens, Jacques. "Queneau Oulipian." In *Oulipo: A Primer of Potential Literature*, ed. Warren F. Motte Jr., 65–73. Lincoln: University of Nebraska Press, 1986.

Bens, Jacques, Claude Berge, and Paul Braffort. "Recurrent Literature." In *Oulipo: A Primer of Potential Literature*, ed. Warren F. Motte Jr., 109–14. Lincoln: University of Nebraska Press, 1986.

Bergaust, Erik. *Wernher von Braun: Ein unglaubliches Leben*. Düsseldorf, 1976.

Berlin, Jeffrey B. "On the Making of *The Magic Mountain*: The Unpublished Correspondence of Thomas Mann, Alfred A. Knopf, and H. T. Lowe-Porter." *Seminar* 28, no. 4 (1992): 283–320.

Bernstein, Mark, Michael Joyce, and David Levine. "Contours of Constructive Hypertexts." In *Proceedings of the ACM Conference on Hypertext*, ed. D. Lucarella, J. Nanard, M. Nanard, and P. Paolini, 161–70. Milan: Association for Computing Machinery, 1992.

Berressem, Hanjo. *Pynchon's Poetics: Interfacing Theory and Text*. Urbana: University of Illinois Press, 1993.

Bessière, Jean. "Introduction." In *L'Ordre du descriptif*, ed. J. Bessière, 3–9. Paris: Presses Universitaires de France, 1988.

Bloom, Harold. *The Western Canon: The Books and School of the Ages*. New York: Harcourt Brace, 1994.

Blumenthal, David R. *Understanding Jewish Mysticism*. New York: KTAV, 1978.

Bolter, Jay David. *Writing Space: The Computer, Hypertext, and the History of Writing*. Fairlawn, N.J.: Erlbaum, 1991.

Bolz, Norbert. *Theorie der neuen Medien*. Munich: Raben, 1990.

Bond, Larry. *Cauldron*. New York: Warner, 1993.

Borges, Jorge Luis. *Labyrinths*. Trans. Donald A. Yates and James E. Irby. New York: New Directions, 1962.

Borkin, Joseph. *The Crime and Punishment of I.G. Farben*. New York: Free Press, 1978.

Bornemann, Manfred. *Geheimprojekt Mittelbau: Die Geschichte der deutschen V-Waffen-Werke*. Munich, 1971.

Botta, Anna. *Topographies of Sand: The Narrative of Georges Perec and Italo Calvino*. Ann Arbor: University of Michigan Press, 1992.

Boutot, Alain. *L'Invention des formes*. Paris: Odile Jacob, 1993.

Bowker, Gordon. *Pursued by Furies: A Life of Malcolm Lowry*. London: HarperCollins, 1993.

Brand, Stewart. *The Media Lab: Inventing the Future at MIT*. New York: Viking, 1987.

Brod, Max. "Afterword" to *Amerika*, by Franz Kafka (1946), trans. Willa and Edwin Muir, 299–300. New York: Schocken, 1962.

"Business Machines and Equipment." In *Encyclopedia Americana*, vol. 5. New York: Americana Corp., 1958.

Brooks, Cleanth. "The Narrative Structure of *Absalom, Absalom!*" In *Toward Yoknapatawpha and Beyond*. New Haven: Yale University Press, 1978.

——. *William Faulkner: The Yoknapatawpha Country*. New Haven: Yale University Press, 1963.

Brooks, Peter. *Reading for the Plot: Design and Intention in Narrative*. Cambridge: Harvard University Press, 1992.

Burgelin, Claude. *Georges Perec*. Paris: Seuil, 1988.

Cadigan, Pat. *Synners*. New York: Bantam, 1990.

Calvino, Italo. *If on a Winter's Night a Traveler*. Trans. William Weaver. New York: Harcourt Brace Jovanovich, 1982.

——. *Invisible Cities*. Trans. William Weaver. New York: Harcourt Brace Jovanovich, 1974.

——. *Six Memos for the Next Millennium*. Cambridge: Harvard University Press, 1988.

Campbell, David, James P. Crutchfield, J. Doyne Farmer, and Erica Jen. "Experimental Mathematics: The Role of Computation in Nonlinear Science." *Communications of the Association for Computing Machinery* 28 (1985): 374–84.

Caponegro, Mary. "Impressions of a Paranoid Optimist." *Review of Contemporary Fiction* 16 (Spring 1996): 23–27.

Carter, Angela. *The Infernal Desire Machines of Doctor Hoffman*. London: Penguin, 1972. Published in the United States as *The War of Dreams*. New York: Harcourt Brace Jovanovich, 1974.

Casti, John L. *Complexification: Explaining a Paradoxical World through the Science of Surprise*. New York: HarperCollins, 1994.

Charne, Jeanine. "La Machine à tuer dans *La Colonie pénitentiaire* de Kafka." *Etudes Philosophiques* 1 (1985): 101–12.

Clancy, Tom. *The Hunt for Red October*. New York: Berkley, 1986.

Cohan, Steven. "Figures Beyond the Text: A Theory of Readable Character in the Novel." In *Why the Novel Matters: A Postmodern Perplex*, ed. Mark Spilka and Caroline McCracken-Flesher, 113–36. Bloomington: Indiana University Press, 1990.

Condillac, Etienne Bonnot de. *The Philosophical Writings of Etienne Bonnot, Abbé de Condillac*. Trans. Franklin Philip and Harlan Lane. Hillsdale, N.J.: Erlbaum, 1982.

Coover, Robert. "The End of Books." *New York Times Book Review*, June 21, 1992, 1, 23–25.

Couchot, Edmond. "La Synthèse du temps." In *Les Chemins du virtuel: Simulation informatique et création industrielle,* ed. Jean-Louis Weissberg, 117–22. Cahiers du CCI. Paris: Centre Georges Pompidou, 1989.

Crutchfield, James P., J. Doyne Farmer, Norman H. Packard, and Robert S. Shaw. "Chaos." *Scientific American,* December 1986, 46–57.

Day, Douglas. *Malcolm Lowry: A Biography.* New York: Oxford University Press, 1973.

Debord, Guy. *The Society of the Spectacle.* Trans. Donald Nicholson-Smith. New York: Zone Books, 1994.

December, John, and Neil Randall. *The World Wide Web Unleashed.* New York: SAMS Press, 1994.

Deleuze, Gilles. *Proust and Signs.* Trans. Richard Howard. New York: George Braziller, 1972.

Deleuze, Gilles, and Félix Guattari. *A Thousand Plateaus: Capitalism and Schizophrenia.* Trans. Brian Massumi. Minneapolis: University of Minnesota Press, 1987.

DeLillo, Don. *White Noise.* New York: Viking, 1985.

Derrida, Jacques. *Of Grammatology.* Trans. Gayatri Chakravorty Spivak. Baltimore: Johns Hopkins University Press, 1976.

———. *Préjugés.* Vienna: Passagen, 1992.

Doezma, Herman P. "An Interview with Carlos Fuentes." *Modern Fiction Studies* 18 (1972): 491–503.

Dornberger, Walter. *V 2.* Trans. James Clough and Geoffrey Halliday. New York: Viking, 1954.

Douglas, J. Y. "Beyond Orality and Literacy: Toward Articulating a Paradigm for the Electronic Age." *Computers and Composition* 6 (1989): 12–22.

Eco, Umberto. *Foucault's Pendulum.* Trans. William Weaver. San Diego: Harcourt Brace Jovanovich, 1989.

———. *The Role of the Reader: Explorations in the Semiotics of Texts.* Bloomington: Indiana University Press, 1979.

Eco, Umberto, with Richard Rorty, Jonathan Culler, and Christine Brooke-Rose. *Interpretation and Overinterpretation.* Ed. Stefan Collini. New York: Cambridge University Press, 1992.

Ellmann, Richard. *James Joyce.* Revised edition. New York: Oxford University Press, 1982.

Engelbart, Douglas. "Knowledge-Domain Interoperability and an Open Hyperdocument System." In *Hypertext/Hypermania Handbook,* ed. Emily Berk and Joseph Devlin, 397–414. New York: Intertext Publications, McGraw-Hill, 1991.

Eysteinsson, Astradur. *The Concept of Modernism.* Ithaca: Cornell University Press, 1990.

Faris, Wendy B. *Carlos Fuentes.* New York: Frederick Ungar, 1983.

Faulkner, William. *Absalom, Absalom!* New York: Vintage Books, 1972.

Foerster, Heinz von. "Epistemology of Communication," in *The Myths of*

Information, ed. Kathleen Woodward, 18–27. Madison, Wis.: Coda Press, 1980.

Foucault, Michel. "Fantasia of the Library." In *Language, Counter-Memory, Practice: Selected Essays and Interviews,* ed. Donald F. Bouchard, trans. Donald F. Bouchard and Sherry Simon. Ithaca: Cornell University Press, 1980.

———. "What is an Author?" In *Textual Strategies: Perspectives in Post-Structuralist Criticism,* ed. Josué Harari. Ithaca: Cornell University Press, 1979.

Fournel, Paul. "Computer and Writer: The Centre Pompidou Experiment," in *Oulipo: A Primer of Potential Literature,* ed. Warren F. Motte Jr., 140–42. Lincoln: University of Nebraska Press, 1986.

Frank, Joseph. "Spatial Form: Thirty Years After." In *Spatial Form in Narrative,* ed. Jeffrey R. Smitten and Ann Daghistany. Ithaca: Cornell University Press, 1981.

———. *The Widening Gyre: Crisis and Mastery in Modern Literature.* New Brunswick: Rutgers University Press, 1963.

Freud, Sigmund. *The Standard Edition of the Complete Psychological Works of Sigmund Freud.* Trans. James Strachey et al., ed. James Strachey. 24 vols. London: Hogarth Press, 1953–74..

Fried, Michael. *Realism, Writing, Disfiguration.* Chicago: University of Chicago Press, 1987.

Frug, Gerald E. "The Ideology of Bureaucracy In American Law." *Harvard Law Review* 97 (1984): 1276–1388.

Fuentes, Carlos. "Cervantes, or the Critique of Reading." *Myself with Others: Selected Essays,* 49–71. New York: Farrar, Straus & Giroux, 1988.

———. *Terra Nostra.* Trans. Margaret Sayers Peden. New York: Farrar, Straus, 1976.

Fussell, Paul. *The Great War and Modern Memory.* New York: Oxford University Press, 1975.

Galan, F. W. *Historic Structures: The Prague School Project, 1928–1946.* Austin: University of Texas Press, 1985.

Gelatt, Roland. *The Fabulous Phonograph, 1877–1977.* New York: Macmillan, 1976.

Genette, Gérard. *Narrative Discourse: An Essay in Method.* Trans. Jane Lewin. Ithaca: Cornell University Press, 1983.

Georg, Enno. *Die wirtschaftlichen Unternehmungen der SS.* Vierteljahreshefte für Zeitgeschichte 7. Stuttgart, 1963.

Gibson, William. *Burning Chrome.* New York: Avon Books, 1986.

———. *Neuromancer.* New York: Ace, 1984.

———. "Rocket Radio." *Rolling Stone,* June 15, 1989.

Gibson, William James. "Redeeming Vietnam: Techno-thriller Novels of the 1980s." *Cultural Critique* 19 (Fall 1991): 179–202.

Giedion, Siegfried. *Mechanization Takes Command: A Contribution to Anonymous History.* New York: Oxford University Press, 1948.

Gleick, James. *Chaos: Making a New Science*. New York: Viking, 1987.

Goethe, Johann Wolfgang von. *Conversations with Soret and Eckermann*. Trans. John Oxenford. London: George Bell, 1875.

———. *Goethes Briefe*. Ed. Karl Robert Mandelkow. Hamburg: Christian Wegner, 1967.

———. *Goethes Sämtliche Werke: Jubiläums-Ausgabe*. Ed. Eduard von der Hellen. Stuttgart, 1904–5.

González Echevarría, Roberto. "*Terra Nostra*: Theory and Practice." In *Carlos Fuentes: A Critical View*, ed. Robert Brody and Charles Rossman, 132–45. Austin: University of Texas Press, 1982.

Grace, Sherrill E. " 'Consciousness of Shipwreck': Ortega y Gasset and Malcolm Lowry's Concept of the Artist." In *Proceedings of the Espectador Universal International Interdisciplinary Conference*, ed. Nore de Marval-McNair. Westport, Conn.: Greenwood, 1987.

———. " 'A Strange Assembly of Apparently Incongruous Parts': Intertextuality in Malcolm Lowry's 'Through the Panama.' " In *Apparently Incongruous Parts: The Worlds of Malcolm Lowry*, ed. Paul Tiessen, 187–228. Metuchen, N.J.: Scarecrow Press, 1990.

———, ed. *Swinging the Maelstrom: New Perspectives on Malcolm Lowry*. Montreal: McGill–Queen's University Press, 1992.

———. *The Voyage That Never Ends: Malcolm Lowry's Fiction*. Vancouver: University of British Columbia Press, 1982.

Graff, Gerald. *Professing Literature: An Institutional History*. Chicago: University of Chicago Press, 1987.

Greenberg, Valerie D. "Literature and the Discourse of Science: The Paradigm of Thomas Mann's *The Magic Mountain*." *South Atlantic Review* 50, no. 1 (1985).

Grusin, Richard. "What Is an Electronic Author?" *Configurations* 3 (1994): 469–83.

Guattari, Felix. "Regimes, Pathways, Subjects." In *Incorporations*, ed. Jonathan Crary and Sanford Kwinter. Zone Series 6. Cambridge: MIT Press, 1992.

Gumbrecht, Hans Ulrich. "The Body versus the Printing Press: Media in the Early Modern Period, Mentalities in the Reign of Castile, and Another History of Literary Forms." *Poetics* 14 (1985).

———. "A Farewell to Interpretation." In *Materialities of Communications*, ed. Hans Ulrich Gumbrecht and K. Ludwig Pfeiffer. Stanford: Stanford University Press, 1994.

Gumbrecht, Hans Ulrich, and K. Ludwig Pfeiffer, eds. *Materialities of Communication*. Trans. William Whobrey. Stanford: Stanford University Press, 1994.

Gwinn, Frederick L., and Joseph L. Blotner, eds. *Faulkner in the University: Class Conferences at the University of Virginia 1957–58*. Charlottesville: University of Virginia Press, 1959.

Hacking, Ian. "How, Why, When, and Where Did Language Go Public?" In *Reading after Foucault: Institutions, Disciplines, and Technologies of the Self in Germany, 1750–1830*, ed. Robert S. Leventhal. Detroit: Wayne State University Press, 1994.

Hansen, Volkmar, and Gert Heine, eds. *Frage und Antwort: Interviews mit Thomas Mann 1909–1955*. Hamburg: Knaus, 1983.

Haraway, Donna J. *Simians, Cyborgs, and Women: The Reinvention of Nature*. New York: Routledge, 1991.

Harris, Paul. "Fractal Faulkner: Scaling Time in *Go Down, Moses*." *Poetics Today* 14 (1993): 625–51.

——. "The Invention of Forms: Perec's *Life A User's Manual* and a Virtual Sense of the Real." *SubStance* 74 (1994): 56–85.

Harrison, Payne. *Storming Intrepid*. New York: Ivy, 1989.

Hawking, Stephen W. *A Brief History of Time*. New York: Bantam, 1988.

Hawthorne, Nathaniel. *Mosses from an Old Manse*. Vol. 10 of *The Works of Nathaniel Hawthorne*, ed. William Charvat, Roy Harvey Pearce, and Claude M. Simpson. Columbus: Ohio State University Press, 1974.

Hayles, N. Katherine. *Chaos Bound: Orderly Disorder in Contemporary Literature and Science*. Ithaca: Cornell University Press, 1990.

——. "Constrained Constructivism: Locating Scientific Inquiry in the Theater of Representation," in *Interphysics: Postdisciplinary Approaches to Literature and Science*, ed. Robert Markley. *New Orleans Review* 18 (1991): 76–85.

——. *The Cosmic Web: Scientific Field Models and Literary Strategies in the Twentieth Century*. Ithaca: Cornell University Press, 1984.

——. "From Self-Organization to Emergence: Aesthetic Implications of Shifting Ideas of Organization," in *Chaos and the Changing Nature of Science and Medicine*, ed. Donald Herbert. Woodbury, New York: American Institute of Physics, 1995.

——, ed. *Chaos and Order: Complex Dynamics in Literature and Science*. Chicago: University of Chicago Press, 1991.

Heidegger, Martin. *Parmenides*. Trans. André Schuwer and Richard Rojcewicz. Bloomington: Indiana University Press, 1992.

Herf, Jeffrey. *Reactionary Modernism: Technology, Culture, and Politics in Weimar and the Third Reich*. New York: Cambridge University Press, 1984.

Hofstadter, Douglas. *Gödel, Escher, Bach: An Eternal Golden Braid*. New York: Vintage, 1980.

Hörisch, Jochen. " 'Die deutsche Seele up to date': Sakramente der Medientechnik auf dem Zauberberg." In *Arsenale der Seele. Literatur- und Medienanalyse seit 1870*, ed. Friedrich Kittler and Christoph Tholen, 13–23. Munich: Fink, 1989.

Horton, Liz. "A Novel Idea." *Desktop Communications*, September–October 1992 (unpaginated).

Howe, Ellic. *The Black Game: British Subversive Operations against the Germans during the Second World War*. London: Joseph, 1982.

Howton, F. William. *Functionaries*. Chicago: Quadrangle, 1969.

Hulme, T. E. *Speculations: Essays on Humanism and the Philosophy of Art*. (1924). Ed. Herbert Read. London: Routledge, 1987.

Hutcheon, Linda. "Metafictional Implications for Novelistic Reference," In *On Referring in Literature,* ed. Anna Whiteside and Michael Issacharoff, 1–13. Bloomington: Indiana University Press, 1987.

Huyssen, Andreas. *After the Great Divide: Modernism, Mass Culture, Postmodernism.* Bloomington: Indiana University Press, 1986.

Iser, Wolfgang, *The Act of Reading: A Theory of Aesthetic Response.* Baltimore: Johns Hopkins University Press, 1978.

——. "The Reading Process: A Phenomenological Approach." In *Reader-Response Criticism,* ed. Jane P. Tompkins, 50–69. Baltimore: Johns Hopkins University Press, 1980.

Jakobson, Roman. "What Is Poetry?" In *Studies in Verbal Art: Texts in Czech and Slovak.* Michigan Slavic Contributions 4. Ann Arbor: Department of Slavic Languages, University of Michigan, 1971.

Jameson, Fredric. *Marxism and Form: Twentieth-Century Dialectical Theories of Literature.* Princeton: Princeton University Press, 1974.

——. *The Political Unconscious: Narrative as a Socially Symbolic Act.* Ithaca: Cornell University Press, 1981.

——. *Postmodernism, or, The Cultural Logic of Late Capitalism.* Durham: Duke University Press, 1991.

——. "Reflections in Conclusion." Afterword to *Aesthetics and Politics,* by Ernst Bloch et al. Trans. Ronald Taylor. London: New Left Books, 1977.

Jayne, Richard. "The Work of Art as a Serial Reproduction." *Journal of the Kafka Society of America* 1, no. 2 (June–December 1988): 27–41.

Johnson, Steven. "Repossession: An Electronic Romance." *Lingua Franca,* May/June 1995, 24–33.

Jones, R. V. *Most Secret War.* London: Hamilton, 1978.

Joyce, James. *Finnegans Wake.* New York: Viking, 1939.

Joyce, Michael. *afternoon, a story.* Cambridge, Mass.: Eastgate Systems, 1990.

——. "A Feel for Prose: Interstitial Links and the Contours of Hypertext." *Writing on the Edge* 4 (1992): 23–41.

——. *Of Two Minds: Hypertext Pedagogy and Poetics.* Ann Arbor: University of Michigan Press, 1995.

Jünger, Ernst. *Der Kampf als inneres Erlebnis.* Berlin, 1922.

Kafka, Franz. *Amerika.* Trans. Willa Muir and Edwin Muir. New York: Schocken, 1974.

——. *The Diaries of Franz Kafka, 1910–1913.* Ed. and trans. Max Brod. New York: Schocken, 1949.

——. *I Am a Memory Come Alive: Autobiographical Writings by Franz Kafka,* ed. Nahum N. Glatzer. New York: Schocken, 1974.

——. "In the Penal Colony." In *The Complete Short Stories of Franz Kafka,* ed. Nahum N. Glatzer. New York: Schocken, 1994.

Kammler, Hans. "Zur Bewertung von Geländeerschliessungen für die grosstädtische Besiedlung." Diss. Ing. TH Hannover, 1932.

Kamper, Dietmar. "Atlantis—vorgeschichtliche Katastrophe, nachgeschichtliche Dekonstruktion." Paris, 1984. Typescript.

Kasson, John F. *Civilizing the Machine: Technology and Republican Values in America, 1776–1900*. New York: Penguin, 1977.

Kellert, Steven. *In the Wake of Chaos*. Chicago: University of Chicago Press, 1993.

Kellner, Hans. *Language and Historical Representation: Getting the Story Crooked*. Madison: University of Wisconsin Press, 1989.

Kittler, Friedrich. "Auto bahnen. Kulturrevolution." *Zeitschrift für angewandte Diskurstheorie* 5 (1984): 42–44.

———. *Discourse Networks, 1800/1900*. Trans. Michael Metteen with Chris Cullens. Stanford: Stanford University Press, 1990.

———. "Dracula's Legacy." Trans. William Stephen Davis. *Stanford Humanities Review* 1 (1989–90): 143–73.

———. "Das Gespenst im Computer: Alan Turing und die moderne Kriegsmaschine." *Überblick* 9 (1984): 46.

———. *Grammophon Film Typewriter*. Berlin: Brinkmann & Bose, 1986.

———. "Gramophone, Film, Typewriter." Trans. Dorothea von Mücke and Philipe L. Similon. *October* 41 (Summer 1987): 101–18.

———. "Romantik—Psychoanalyse—Film: eine Doppelgängergeschichte." In *Eingebildete Texte*, ed. Jochen Hörisch and Christoph Tholen, 118–135. Munich, 1985.

———. "World-Breath: On Wagner's Media Technology." In *Opera Through Other Eyes*, ed. David J. Lenin, 215–35. Stanford: Stanford University Press, 1993.

Kittler, Wolf. "Schreibmaschinen, Sprechmaschinen. Effekte technischer Medien im Werk Franz Kafkas." In *Franz Kafka: Schriftverkehr*, ed. Wolf Kittler and Gerhard Neumann, 75–163. Freiburg: Rombach, 1990.

Kittler, Wolf, and Gerhard Neumann, eds. *Franz Kafka: Schriftverkehr*. Freiburg: Rombach, 1990.

Kraus, Rosalind. *The Originality of the Avant-Garde and Other Modernist Myths*. Cambridge: MIT Press, 1985.

Kudzus, Winfried. "Understanding Media: Zur Kritik dualistischer Humanität im *Zauberberg*." In *Besichtigung des Zaubergs*, ed. Heinz Sauereßig, 55–80. Biberach: Wege und Gestalten, 1974.

Lacan Jacques. *The Ego in Freud's Theory and in the Technique of Psychoanalysis, 1954–1955*. Trans. Sylvana Tomaselli. New York: Norton, 1988.

———. *Four Fundamental Concepts of Psychoanalysis*. New York: Norton, 1979.

———. "Séminaire sur la lettre volée." In *Écrits*, 11–61. Paris: Seuil, 1966.

Laing, Dave. "A Voice Without a Face: Popular Music and the Phonograph in the 1890s." In *Exploring Postmodernism*, ed. Matei Calinescu and Douwe Fokkema, 59–78. Philadelphia: J. Benjamins, 1988.

Landon, Brooks. "Not What It Used to Be: The Over-loading of Memory in Digital Narrative." In *Fiction 2000: Cyberpunk and the Future of Narrative*, ed. George Slusser and Tom Shippey, 153–67. Athens: University of Georgia Press, 1992.

Landow, George P. *Hypertext: The Convergence of Contemporary Critical Theory and Technology.* Baltimore: Johns Hopkins University Press, 1992.

Langford, Gerald. *Faulkner's Revision of Absalom, Absalom!: A Collation of the Manuscript and the Published Book.* Austin: University of Texas Press, 1992.

Lanham, Richard. *The Electronic Word: Democracy, Technology, and the Arts.* Chicago: University of Chicago Press, 1993.

Laqueur, Thomas. *Making Sex: Body and Gender From the Greeks to Freud.* Cambridge: Harvard University Press, 1990.

Latour, Bruno. *We Have Never Been Modern.* Trans. Catherine Porter. Cambridge: Harvard University Press, 1983.

Leblans, Anne. "Kafka in the Age of Mechanical Reproduction: A Storyteller's Response." *Journal of the Kafka Society of America* 1, no. 2 (June–December 1988): 51–58.

Le Guin, Ursula K. *Always Coming Home.* 2d ed. New York: Bantam, 1987.

Levidow, Les, and Kevin Robins, eds. *Cyborg Worlds: The Military Information Society.* London: Free Association Books, 1989.

Lévy, Pierre. *Les Technologies de l'intelligence: L'Avenir de la pensée à l'ère informatique.* Paris: Découverte, 1990; rpt. Seuil, 1993.

Levy, Sydney. "Oulipian Messages." *Studies in Comparative Literature* 12 (Summer 1988): 149–61.

——. *The Play of the Text: Max Jacob's "Le Cornet à dés."* Madison: University of Wisconsin Press, 1981.

Lewis, Wyndham. *Tarr.* Harmondsworth: Penguin, 1982.

——. *Time and Western Man* (1927). Ed. Paul Edwards. Santa Rosa, Calif.: Black Sparrow Press, 1993.

Loose, Gerhard. *Franz Kafka und "Amerika."* Frankfurt: Klostermann, 1968.

Lowry, Malcolm. *Dark as the Grave Wherein My Friend Is Laid.* Ed. Douglas Day and Margerie Lowry. New York: World, 1968.

——. *Hear Us O Lord from Heaven Thy Dwelling Place.* New York: Carroll & Graf, 1986.

——. *October Ferry to Gabriola.* Ed. Margerie Lowry. New York: New American Library, 1970.

——. *Psalms and Songs.* Ed. Margerie Lowry. New York: New American Library, 1975.

——. *Selected Letters.* Ed. Harvey Breit and Margerie Bonner Lowry. Philadelphia: Lippincott, 1965.

——. *Sursum Corda! The Collected Letters of Malcolm Lowry.* Ed Sherrill E. Grace. Vol. 1, *1926–1942.* Toronto: University of Toronto Press, 1995.

——. *Ultramarine.* New York: Carroll & Graf, 1986.

——. *Under the Volcano.* Philadelphia: Lippincott, 1965.

Luhmann, Niklas. "Das Problem der Epochenbildung und die Evolutionstheorie." In *Epochenschwellen und Epochenstrukturen im Diskurs der Literatur- und Sprachhistorie,* ed. Hans-Ulrich Gumbrecht and Ursula Link-Heer, 11–33. Frankfurt: Suhrkamp, 1985.

Lusar, Rudolf. *Die deutschen Waffen und Geheimwaffen des Zweiten Weltkrieges und ihre Weiterentwicklung.* Munich, 1959.

Lyotard, Jean-François. *The Inhuman: Reflections on Time.* Trans. Geoffrey Bennington and Rachel Bowlby. Stanford: Stanford University Press, 1991.

———. *The Postmodern Condition: A Report on Knowledge* (1979). Trans. Geoff Bennington and Brian Massumi. Minneapolis: University of Minnesota Press, 1984.

MacKenzie, Ian. "Narratology and Thematics." *Modern Fiction Studies* 33 (1987): 535–44.

Magne, Bernard, ed. *Cahiers Georges Perec.* Paris: P.O.L., 1984.

———. "Un Puzzle de 100 pièces." *Magazine Littéraire* 193 (March 1983): 29–31.

Mandelbrot, Benoit B. *The Fractal Geometry of Nature.* New York: Freeman, 1983.

Mandelkow, Karl Robert, ed. *Goethes Briefe.* Hamburg: Christian Wegner, 1967.

Mann, Golo. *The History of Germany since 1789.* Trans. Marian Jackson. New York: Praeger, 1968.

Mann, Klaus. Preface to *Amerika,* by Franz Kafka (1946), trans. Willa and Edwin Muir, vii–xviii. New York: Schocken, 1962.

Mann, Thomas. *Diaries, 1918–1939.* Trans. Richard and Clara Winston. New York: H. N. Abrams, 1982.

———. *The Magic Mountain.* Trans. H. T. Lowe-Porter. London: Secker & Warburg, 1965.

———. "On the Film." In *Past Masters and Other Papers,* trans. H. T. Lowe-Porter. Freeport: Books for Libraries Press, 1968.

———. *Tagebücher, 1949–1950.* Ed. Inge Jens. Frankfurt: Fischer, 1991.

———. "Vorspruch zu einer musikalischen Nietzsche-Feier." In *Gesammelte Werke,* 10: 180–84. Frankfurt: Fischer, 1960.

Marello, Laura. "Form and Formula in Calvino's *Invisible Cities.*" *Review of Contemporary Fiction* 6, no. 2 (1986): 95–100.

Massumi, Brian. "The Autonomy of Affect." *Cultural Critique* 31 (Fall 1995): 83–110.

McCarthy, Patrick A. *Forests of Symbols: World, Text, and Self in Malcolm Lowry's Fiction.* Athens: The University of Georgia Press, 1994.

McDaid, John. *Uncle Buddy's Phantom Funhouse.* Cambridge, Mass.: Eastgate Systems, 1993.

McGann, Jerome. *Black Riders: The Visible Language of Modernism.* Princeton: Princeton University Press, 1993.

———. *The Textual Condition.* Princeton: Princeton University Press, 1991.

McHale, Brian. *Postmodernist Fiction.* New York: Methuen, 1987.

McLuhan, Marshall. *Understanding Media.* New York: McGraw-Hill, 1964.

Millgate, Michael. *The Achievement of William Faulkner.* New York: Random House, 1966.

Mitchell. W. J. T. *Picture Theory: Essays on Verbal and Visual Representation.* Chicago: University of Chicago Press, 1994.

Moretti, Franco. *Signs Taken for Wonders: Essays in the Sociology of Literary Forms.* Trans. Susan Fischer, David Forgacs, and David Miller. London: Verso, 1983.

Morris, Charles William. *Grundlagen der Zeichentheorie.* Trans. Roland Posner. München, 1972.

Morrisette, Bruce. "Surfaces and Structures in Robbe-Grillet's Novels." In *For A New Novel: Essays on Fiction,* by Alain Robbe-Grillet, trans. Richard Howard, 1–10. New York: Grove Press, 1965.

Motte, Warren F., ed. *Oulipo: A Primer of Potential Literature.* Lincoln: University of Nebraska Press, 1986.

Moulthrop, Stuart. "Reading from the Map: Metonymy and Metaphor in the Fiction of Forking Paths." In *Hypermedia and Literary Studies,* ed. Paul Delany and George P. Landow, 119–32. Cambridge: MIT Press, 1991.

——. "Toward a Paradigm for Reading Hypertexts: Making Nothing Happen in Hypermedia Fiction." In *Hypertext/Hypermedia Handbook,* ed. Emily Berk and J. Devlin, 65–78. New York: Intertext Publications, McGraw-Hill, 1991.

Mukarovsky, Jan. *Structure, Sign, and Function: Selected Essays.* Trans. and ed. John Burbank and Peter Steiner. New Haven: Yale University Press, 1977.

Mumford, Lewis. *Sticks and Stones: A Study of American Architecture and Civilization.* New York: Dover, 1955.

Nash, Christopher. *World-Games: The Tradition of Anti-Realist Revolt.* London: Methuen, 1987.

Nelson, Theodor H. *Literary Machines.* Sausalito Cal.: Mindful Press, 1990.

Neumann, Gerhard. "Franz Kafka: Der Name, die Sprache und die Ordnung der Dinge." In *Franz Kafka: Schriftverkehr,* ed. Wolf Kittler und Gehard Neumann, 11–29. Freiburg: Rombach, 1990.

New, William H. "Lowry's Reading: An Introductory Essay." *Canadian Literature* 44 (1970).

Newman, Charles Hamilton. *The Post-Modern Aura: The Act of Fiction in an Age of Inflation.* Evanston Ill.: Northwestern University Press, 1985.

Newton, Isaac. *Principia Mathematica.* Trans. Andrew Motte. Berkeley: University of California Press, 1934.

Nietzsche, Friedrich. *Ecce Homo.* In *On the Genealogy of Morals and Ecce Homo,* ed. and trans. Walter Kaufmann. New York: Vintage, 1989.

——. "On the Uses and Disadvantages of History for Life." In *Untimely Meditations,* trans. R. J. Hollingdale. Cambridge: Harvard University Press, 1983.

Norfolk, Lawrence. *Lemprière's Dictionary.* London: Sinclair-Stevenson, 1991.

Norris, Frank. *The Literary Criticism of Frank Norris.* Ed. Donald Pizer. Austin: University of Texas Press, 1964.

Northey, Anthony D. "Franz Kafkas Verbindung zu Amerika." In *Franz Kafka: Eine Aufsatzsammlung nach einem Symposium in Philadelphia,* ed. M. Caputo-Mayr, 5–14. Berlin: Agora, 1978.

Ong, Walter J. *Orality and Literacy: The Technologizing of the Word.* London and New York: Methuen, 1982; rpt. Routledge, 1991.

Ortega y Gasset, José. *Toward a Philosophy of History.* Trans. Helene Weyl. New York: Norton, 1941.

Orvell, Miles. *The Real Thing: Imitation and Authenticity in American Culture, 1880–1940.* Chapel Hill: University of North Carolina Press, 1989.

Orwell, George. "Inside the Whale." In *The Collected Essays, Journalism, and Letters of George Orwell,* ed. Sonia Orwell and Ian Angus, vol. 1, *An Age Like This: 1920–1940.* New York: Harcourt, Brace & World, 1968.

Palmore, Michael J. "Diagramming Calvino's Architecture." *Forum Italicum* 24, no. 1 (1990): 25–39.

Pasley, Malcolm. "The Act of Writing and the Text: The Genesis of Kafka's Manuscripts." In *Kafka's Clothes: Ornament and Aestheticism in the Habsburg Fin de Siècle,* ed. Mark M. Anderson, 201–14. New York: Oxford University Press, 1992.

Paulson, William. "Computers, Minds, and Texts: Preliminary Reflections." *New Literary History* 20 (Winter 1989): 291–303.

———. *The Noise of Culture: Literary Texts in a World of Information.* Ithaca: Cornell University Press, 1988.

La Pléiade: Catalogue analytique. Paris: Gallimard, 1986, 1992.

Perec, Georges. *Cahiers des charges de "La Vie, mode d'emploi."* Ed. Hans Hartje, Bernard Magne and Jacques Neefs. Paris: CNRS, 1993.

———. *Life, a User's Manual.* Trans. David Bellos. Boston: David Godine, 1987.

Pimentel, Ken, and Kevin Teixeira. *Virtual Reality: Through the New Looking Glass.* New York: Windcrest, 1993.

Pink Floyd. *The Final Cut: A Requiem for the Post War Dream.* London, 1983.

Poincaré, Henri. "L'Espace et la géometrie." *Revue de Métaphysique et de Morale* 3 (1985): 631–46.

Porush, David. "Hacking the Brainstem: Postmodern Metaphysics and Stephenson's *Snow Crash.*" *Configurations,* 1994, 537–71.

———. *The Soft Machine: Cybernetic Fiction.* New York: Methuen, 1985.

Poster, Mark. *The Mode of Information: Poststructuralism and Social Context.* Chicago: University of Chicago Press, 1990.

Prigogine, Ilya, and Isabelle Stengers. *Entre le temps et l'eternité.* Paris: Flammarion, 1992.

———. *Order out of Chaos: Man's New Dialogue with Nature.* New York: Bantam, 1984.

Pynchon, Thomas. *The Crying of Lot 49.* Philadelphia: Lippincott, 1966.

———. *Gravity's Rainbow* (1973). New York: Bantam, 1974.

———. *Vineland.* Boston: Little, Brown, 1990.

Ramsey, Raylene L. *Robbe-Grillet and Modernity: Science, Sexuality, and Subversion.* Gainesville: University Press of Florida, 1992.

Rasula, Jed. *The American Poetry Wax Museum: Reality Effects, 1940–1990.* Urbana, Ill.: NCTE, 1995.

Reiser, Stanley Joel. *Medicine and the Reign of Technology*. Cambridge: Cambridge University Press, 1978.

Rewald, John. *The History of Impressionism*. 4th, rev. ed. New York: Museum of Modern Art, 1973.

Ribière, Mireille. "Doing Theory." *Paragraph* 12, no. 1 (1989): 56–64.

Rindisbacher, Hans J. *The Smell of Books: A Cultural-Historical Study of Olfactory Perception in Literature*. Ann Arbor: University of Michigan Press, 1992.

Robbe-Grillet, Alain. *For a New Novel*. Trans. Richard Howard. New York: Grove Press, 1970.

———. *Two Novels by Robbe-Grillet*. Trans. Richard Howard. New York: Grove Press, 1965.

Rosenberg, Martin. "Contingency, Liberation, and the Seduction of Geometry: Hypertext as an Avant-Garde Medium." *Perforations* 3, no. 15 (1992): 1–12.

———. "Physics and Hypertext: Liberation and Complicity in Art and Pedagogy." In *Hyper/Text/Theory*, ed. George P. Landow, 268–97. Baltimore: Johns Hopkins University Press, 1994.

Ross, Andrew. *Strange Weather: Culture, Science, and Technology in the Age of Limits*. New York: Verso, 1991.

Rosset, Clement. "Of a Real That Has Yet to Come." Trans. Stephen Winspur. *SubStance* 60 (1989): 5–21.

Rotman, Brian. *Ad Infinitum: The Ghost in Turing's Machine*. Stanford: Stanford University Press, 1993.

———. "Thinking Dia-Grams: Mathematics, Writing, and Virtual Reality." *South Atlantic Quarterly*, Spring 1994, 389–416.

Roubaud, Jacques. *The Great Fire of London*. Trans. Dominic Di Bernardi. Elmwood Park, Ill.: Dalkey Archive Press, 1991.

———. "Notes sur la poétique des listes chez Georges Perec." In *Penser, classer, écrire: De Pascal à Perec*, ed. Beatrice Didier and Jacques Neefs, 201–8. Paris: Presses Universitaires de Vincennes, 1990.

Ruelle, David. *Chance and Chaos*. Princeton: Princeton University Press, 1991.

Ruland, Bernd. *Wernher von Braun: Mein Leben für die Raumfahrt*. Offenburg, 1969.

Rushdie, Salman. *Midnight's Children*. New York: Penguin, 1980.

Saffo, Paul. "Hot New Medium: Text." *Wired*, May/June 1993, 48.

Said, Edward W. "Molestation and Authority in Narrative Fiction." In *Aspects of Narrative*, ed. J. Hillis Miller. New York: Columbia University Press, 1971.

Sarkowski, Heinz. *Wenn Sie ein Herz für mich und mein Geisteskind haben: Dichterbriefe zur Buchgestaltung*. Frankfurt: 1965.

Scaff, Lawrence A. *Fleeing the Iron Cage: Culture, Politics, and Modernity in the Thought of Max Weber*. Berkeley: University of California Press, 1989.

Scharf, Aaron. *Art and Photography*. Baltimore: Penguin, 1974.

Schmitt, Carl. *Theorie der Partisanen: Zwischenbemerkung zum Begriff des Politischen*. Berlin, 1963.

Schöne, Erich. *Der Verlust der Sinnlichkeit, oder Die Verwandlungen des Lesers.* Stuttgart: Klett-Cotta, 1987.

Schulte-Sasse, Jochen. "The Prestige of the Artist Under Conditions of Modernity." *Cultural Critique,* Spring 1989, 83–100.

Seitz, William C. *Claude Monet: Seasons and Moments.* Garden City, N.Y.: Doubleday, 1960.

Seltzer, Mark. *Bodies and Machines.* New York: Routledge, 1992.

Serres, Michel. *Hermes IV: La Distribution.* Paris: Minuit, 1977.

Shafer, R. Murray. "The Electric Revolution." In *Inter/Media: Interpersonal Communication in a Media World,* ed. Gary Gumpert and Robert Cathcart. New York: Oxford University Press, 1986.

Shannon, Claude E. *The Mathematical Theory of Communication.* Urbana: University of Illinois Press, 1949.

Shaw, Robert. *The Dripping Faucet as a Model Chaotic System.* Santa Cruz, Cal.: Ariel Press, 1984.

Smart, Barry. *Modern Conditions, Postmodern Controversies.* New York: Routledge, 1992.

Smitten, Jeffrey R., and Ann Daghistany, eds. *Spatial Form in Narrative.* Ithaca: Cornell University Press, 1981.

Sobchak, Vivian. "The Scene of the Screen: Envisioning Cinematic and Electronic 'Presence.'" In *Materialities of Communication,* ed. Hans Ulrich Gumbrecht and K. Ludwig Pfeiffer, trans. William Whobrey. Stanford: Stanford University Press, 1994.

Soustelle, Jacques. *The Daily Life of the Aztecs on the Eve of the Spanish Conquest.* Trans. Patrick O'Brian. London: Weidenfeld & Nicolson, 1961.

Spariosu, Mihai. "Allegory, Hermeneutics, and Postmodernism." In *Exploring Postmodernism,* ed. Matei Calinescu and Douwe Fokkema, 59–78. Philadelphia: J. Benjamins, 1988.

Speirs, Ronald. *Franz Kafka.* Hampshire: Macmillan, 1994.

Spender, Stephen. Introduction to *Under the Volcano,* by Malcolm Lowry, xi–xxx. Philadelphia: Lippincott, 1965.

Spiro, Rand, and Robert A. Jones. "Imagined Conversations: The Relevance of Hypertext, Pragmatism, and Cognitive Flexibility Theory to the Interpretation of 'Classic' Texts." In *Proceedings of the ACM Conference on Hypertext,* ed. D. Lucarella, J. Nanard, M. Nanard, and P. Paolini, 141–50. Milan: Association for Computing Machinery, 1992.

Stafford, Barbara Maria. *Body Criticism: Imaging the Unseen in Enlightenment Art and Medicine.* Cambridge: MIT Press, 1991.

Steiner, Wendy. *The Colors of Rhetoric: Problems in the Relation between Modern Literature and Painting.* Chicago: University of Chicago Press, 1982.

Stephenson, Neal. *Snow Crash.* New York: Bantam, 1993.

Stevenson, William. *A Man Called Intrepid: The Secret War.* New York: Harcourt Brace Jovanovich, 1976.

Symington, Rodney. "Music on Mann's Magic Mountain: 'Fülle des Wohllauts' and Hans Castorp's 'Selbstüberwindung.'" In *Echoes and*

Influences of German Romanticism: Essays in Honor of Hans Eichner, ed. Michael S. Batts, Anthony W. Riley, and Heinz Wetzel, 55–182. New York: Lang, 1987.

Tabbi, Joseph. *Postmodern Sublime: Technology and American Writing from Mailer to Cyberpunk.* Ithaca: Cornell University Press, 1995.

Taylor, Mark C., and Esa Saarinen. *Imagologies: Media Philosophy.* New York: Routledge, 1993.

Tenner, Edward. "From Slip to Chip." *Princeton Alumni Weekly,* November 21, 1990, 9–14.

Theweleit, Klaus. *Male Fantasies.* Vol. 2, *Male Bodies: Psychoanalyzing the White Terror.* Trans. Stephan Conway et al. Minneapolis: University of Minnesota Press, 1989.

Thomas, Jean-Jacques. "README.DOC: On Oulipo." *SubStance* 56 (1988): 18–28.

Thompson, Michael. *Rubbish Theory: The Creation and Destruction of Value.* Oxford: Oxford University Press, 1979.

Thoreau, Henry David. *A Week on the Concord and Merrimack Rivers (1849).* Princeton: Princeton University Press, 1980.

Turbayne, Colin Murray. *The Myth of Metaphor.* Columbia: University of South Carolina Press, 1970.

Ulmer, Gregory. *Applied Grammatology: Post(e)-Pedagogy from Jacques Derrida to Joseph Beuys.* Baltimore: Johns Hopkins University Press, 1985.

———. *Teletheory: Grammatology in the Age of Video.* New York: Routledge, 1990.

Urzidil, Johannes. "Edison und Kafka." *Der Monat* 13 (1961): 53–57.

Utz, Peter. *Das Auge und Ohr im Text: Literarische Sinneswahrnehmung in der Goethezeit.* Munich: Fink, 1990.

Virilio, Paul. *The Aesthetics of Disappearance.* Trans. Philip Beitchman. New York: Semiotext(e), 1991.

———. *The Lost Dimension.* Trans. Daniel Moshenberg. New York: Semiotext(e), 1991.

———. *Speed and Politics.* Trans. M. Polizotti. New York: Semiotext(e), 1986.

———. *War and Cinema: The Logistics of Perception.* Trans. Patrick Camiller. London and New York: Verso, 1989.

Weisenburger, Steven. "Hysteron Proteron in *Gravity's Rainbow.*" *Texas Studies in Literature and Language* 34 (Spring 1992): 87–105.

Weissert, Thomas. "Dynamical Discourse Theory." *Time and Society* 4 (1995): 111–33.

———. "The Fermi-Pasta-Ulam Problem: Simulation and Modern Dynamics." Ph.D diss., University of Colorado, Boulder, 1992.

Wiener, Norbert. *Cybernetics; or, Control and Communication in the Animal and the Machine.* Cambridge: MIT Press, 1948.

Wilden, Anthony. *System and Structure: Essays in Communication and Exchange.* 2d ed. London: Tavistock, 1980.

Williams, Linda. *Figures of Desire: A Theory and Analysis of Surrealist Film.* Urbana: University of Illinois Press, 1981.

Wilson, William S. "Joseph McElroy: Fathoming the Field." *electronic book review* 4 (Winter 1996–97): <http://www.altx.com/ebr>

Winthrop-Young, Geoffrey. "Undead Networks: Information Processing and Media Boundary Conflicts in Stoker's *Dracula*." In *Literature and Science*, ed. Donald Bruce and Anthony Purdy, 107–29. Amsterdam: Rodopi, 1994.

Winthrop-Young, Geoffrey, and Joseph Donatelli. "Why Media Matters: An Introduction." *Mosaic* 28 (December 1995): v–xxiv.

Woodmansee, Martha. "The Genius and Copyright." *Eighteenth-Century* 17 (1983–84): 425–48.

Woodward, Kathleen. "From Virtual Cyborgs to Biological Time Bombs: Technocriticism and the Material Body." In *Culture on the Brink: Ideologies of Technology*, ed. Gretchen Bender and Timothy Druckrey, 47–64. Seattle: Bay Press, 1994.

Woolley, Benjamin. *Virtual Worlds: A Journey in Hype and Hyperreality.* Oxford and Cambridge, Mass.: Blackwell, 1992.

Wysling, Hans. *Thomas-Mann-Handbuch.* Ed. Helmut Koopmann. Stuttgart: Kröner, 1990.

Yankelovich, Nicole. "From Electronic Books to Electronic Libraries: Revisiting 'Reading and Writing the Electronic Book.' " In *Hypermedia and Literary Studies*, ed. Paul Delany and George Landow, 133–42. Cambridge: MIT Press, 1991.

Yates, Frances A. *The Art of Memory.* Chicago: University of Chicago Press, 1966.

Young, Edward. "Conjectures on Original Composition in a Letter to the Author of Sir Charles Grandison." In *English Critical Essays: Sixteenth, Seventeenth, and Eighteenth Centuries*, ed. Edmond D. Jones. London and New York: Oxford University Press, 1975.

Žižek, Slavoj. *The Sublime Object of Ideology.* London and New York: Verso, 1989.

About the Contributors

Klaus Benesch is Assistant Professor of English and North American Studies at the University of Frieburg. He has published essays on African American literature, autobiography, and the interfaces of technology and writing, and has edited "Technology and American Culture," a special issue of *Amerikastudien/American Studies*. Currently he is working on a book titled "Romantic Cyborgs: Technology, Authorship, and the Body in Nineteenth-Century American Literature."

Linda Brigham is Associate Professor of English at Kansas State University. Her essays on literary romanticism, money, and posthumanism have appeared in the *electronic book review, Philosophy and Literature, Studies in Romanticism, Texas Studies in Literature and Language,* and others. Currently she is working on a study of ecologies of identity in Wordsworth and Shelley.

Paul A. Harris is Assistant Professor of English at Loyola Marymount University. He is the author of essays on twentieth-century writers including Calvino, Perec, Faulkner, and DeLillo, and is currently completing an interdisciplinary study of time.

John Johnston, Associate Professor of English and Comparative Literature at Emory University, has published *Carnival of Repetition,* a study of William Gaddis's novels, and numerous essays on postmodern theory and fiction. He is the author of the forthcoming *Information Multiplicity: American Fiction in the Age of Media Assemblages* and has edited a forthcoming collection of essays by Friedrich Kittler.

Friedrich Kittler is Professor of Media History and Aesthetics at Humboldt University, Berlin. His publications include *Aufschreibesysteme 1800/1900,* published in English as *Discourse Networks, 1800/1900; Grammophon Film Typewriter,* forthcoming in English translation; *Dichter Mutter Kind;* and *Draculas Vermächtnis: Technische Schriften.*

Stuart Moulthrop is Associate Professor in the School of Language, Literature, and Communications Design at the University of Baltimore. He has published numerous essays on technology and culture and is the author of three hypertext fictions: *Victory Garden,* "Dreamtime," and "Hegirascope."

Jo Alyson Parker is Assistant Professor of English at St. Joseph's University, Philadelphia. She has published essays on gender issues in the works of Jane Austen and Stanislaw Lem, as well as on Elizabeth Inchbald and Laurence Sterne. She has recently completed a book titled "The Author's Inheritance: Henry Fielding, Jane Austen, and the Establishment of the Novel."

William Paulson is Professor of French at the University of Michigan. He is the author of *The Noise of Culture: Literary Texts in a World of Information* and of two books on eighteenth- and nineteenth-century French literature.

Piotr Siemion is a corporate lawyer and a 1994 Columbia Ph.D. recipient. Currently he is completing a volume titled "Whale Songs: Bureaucracy in the Post-War American Novel." He has also translated into Polish works by Abraham Lincoln, Thomas Pynchon, and Tom Clancy.

Joseph Tabbi is Assistant Professor of English at the University of Illinois–Chicago and the editor of the *electronic book review* (http://www.altx.com/ebr). He is the author of *Postmodern Sublime: Technology and American Writing from Mailer to Cyberpunk* and of numerous essays on postmodern American fiction.

Lynn Wells is a doctoral student at the University of Western Ontario, specializing in contemporary British fiction. She has published essays on virtual reality and Mary Shelley.

Geoffrey Winthrop-Young is Assistant Professor in the Department of Germanic Studies at the University of British Columbia. He has published on media technology in the writings of Bram Stoker, Georg Christoph Lichtenberg, and Alexandre Dumas, among others. He recently co-edited "Media Matters: Technologies of Literary Production," a special issue of *Mosaic*. He is the co-translator of the forthcoming English-language edition of Friedrich Kittler's *Grammophon Film Typewriter* and is currently working on a literary archaeology of cyberspace.

Michael Wutz is Assistant Professor of English at Weber State University. His essays on modern British and American fiction have appeared in *Studies in American Fiction, Style, Modern Fiction Studies, Mosaic,* and other journals. He recently guest-edited the *Weber Studies/ebr* special issue on science, technology, and the arts. He is co-translator of the forthcoming English-language edition of Friedrich Kittler's *Grammophon Film Typewriter* and is currently working on a study on the interfaces of modernism, science, and (media) technology.

Index

Postmodern novel, 17–22, 70–73, 251, 258–61, 267

Poststructuralist theory, 78, 99–106, 271, 279, 291

Propaganda, 159, 165, 196

Pynchon, Thomas, 7, 20, 157–69, 175–92, 193, 275; *The Crying of Lot 49*, 182; *Gravity's Rainbow*, 30, 158–72, 195, 207; *Vineland*, 18, 23, 174–92, 195, 248–49

Queneau, Raymond: *Cente Mille Millards de poèmes*, 143

Reader, interactive, 78, 138, 250–67, 276, 281, 289

Real, the, 83, 134, 161, 176–77, 182–84, 210, 258, 262–66; representation of, 87, 149–50, 251, 256, 260

Realism, 5, 7, 9, 122, 149–50, 153n, 201, 209, 259, 263

Reflexivity, 99, 107, 136

Robbe–Grillet, Alain, 8, 17, 120, 124–25, 132–33, 135; *Jealousy*, 120, 125–27

Romantic craftsman/engineer, 58–59, 73

Romanticism, writerly, 59–63

Romantic notion of authorship, 77–83

Rotman, Brian, 136, 137, 141–44, 152; *Ad Infinitum*, 136, 138, 142

Rushdie, Salman, 22, 250; *Midnight's Children*, 23, 251, 258–63, 267n

Semiotechnology, 159–62, 166–67

Semiotics, 9, 12, 100–101, 137, 139, 142

Sign, 57, 70, 121–22, 137–39, 141, 144, 162, 173, 209; Oulipian, 143; virtual, 139, 142–44, 149–51

Simulacra, 72, 85, 131, 159, 217, 257

Solipsism, 120–21, 127, 131, 134

Sound reproduction, 40, 44–45, 47, 91, 182

Speed, 134–35, 165, 206

Stephenson, Neal: *Snow Crash*, 284–87

Stethoscope, 36–38, 45

Storytelling, 87, 144, 159, 193–95, 204, 208

Subject, 2, 64, 70, 77, 80–82, 126, 132, 142; speeding, 134; as user, 251

Subjectivity, 3, 5, 101, 121, 127–28, 210, 216–17, 222; machinery of, 121

Symbolism, Lacanian, 125, 129, 161–62, 182–84

Syntactical boundary, 140–41, 153n

System, 100, 139, 210, 212, 277; chaotic, 108, 112, 116–17, 136, 137; jump out of, 277, 291; sign, 122, 130, 137, 201, 271; social, 199–200, 215, 221, 275

Technology: computer, 116, 178, 272; as control, 132–33; reproductive, 35, 45, 92; storage, 4, 8–9, 32, 35, 45, 152n, 173, 182–83, 191–92, 228–33

Technophobia, 79, 89, 93

Techno–thriller, 21, 193–223

Telegraph, 39, 69

Text: and body, 77, 89–93, 291; as commodity, 54–59, 70, 73, 287; mechanically reproduced, 77, 84, 91. *See also* Narrative

Textual authority, 16, 106, 250–57, 262–64, 279, 288–91

Textual constraints, 141–43, 153n, 196, 278

Theater of Memory (Camillo), 265, 268n

Thompson, Michael, 234; *Rubbish Theory*, 234–37

Time: graphic representation of, 149; linear, 263; manipulation of, 164–68, 178; nonlinear, 147–49; perception of, 11, 122–23, 147–78; in reverse, 14, 161, 164–65

Topography, 11, 132, 191

Typewriter, 4–5, 11, 25n, 53, 58–59, 63–64, 74n, 75n, 76–77, 89

Utopia, 79, 93–94, 200, 211

Verne, Jules: *Castle in the Carpathians*, 45; *Michel Strogoff*, 144

Virilio, Paul, 17, 119–22, 131–35, 165–67, 171n, 172n, 184, 199–200; *The Aesthetics of Disappearance*, 131; *War and Cinema*, 165, 171n, 172n

Virtual history, 120, 257–66

Virtuality, 23, 152, 250, 261, 266

Virtual meetings, 261–63

Virtual reality, 120, 142, 187–91, 251–53, 258, 267n

Virtual space, 137–39, 142, 150–51, 256

Virus, 281–83, 291–92

Wenders, Wim: *Wings of Desire*, 2

Woodward, Kathleen, 9

X rays, 37–39, 43